The Bible Speaks Today

Series editors: Alec Motyer (OT)
John Stott (NT)
Derek Tidball (Bible Themes)

The Message of
Salvation

By God's grace, for God's glory

The Bible Speaks Today: Bible Themes series

The Message of Salvation

By God's grace, for God's glory

Philip Graham Ryken

Minister of Tenth Presbyterian Church
Philadelphia, Pennsylvania

Inter-Varsity Press

INTER-VARSITY PRESS
Norton Street, Nottingham NG7 3HR, England
Email: ivp@ivpbooks.com
Website: www.ivpbooks.com

First published 2001
Reprinted 2003, 2006, 2008, 2009

British Library Cataloguing in Publication Data
A catalogue record for this book is available from the British Library.

ISBN 978–0–85111–897–0

Set in Garamond
Typeset in Great Britain
Printed and bound in Great Britain by 4edge Limited

Inter-Varsity Press publishes Christian books that are true to the Bible and that communicate the gospel, develop discipleship and stregthen the church for its mission in the world.

Inter-Varsity Press is closely linked with the Universities and Colleges Christian Fellowship, a student movement connecting Christian Unions in universities and colleges throughout Great Britain, and a member movement of the International Fellowship of Evangelical Students. Website: www.uccf.org.uk.

Contents

Part 4: Saved for God's glory

BST The Bible Speaks Today

GENERAL PREFACE

THE BIBLE SPEAKS TODAY describes three series of expositions, based on the books of the Old and New Testaments, and on Bible themes that run through the whole of Scripture. Each series is characterized by a threefold ideal:

- to expound the biblical text with accuracy
- to relate it to contemporary life, and
- to be readable.

These books are, therefore, not 'commentaries', for the commentary seeks rather to elucidate the text than to apply it, and tends to be a work rather of reference than of literature. Nor, on the other hand, do they contain the kinds of 'sermons' that attempt to be contemporary and readable without taking Scripture seriously enough. The contributors to *The Bible Speaks Today* series are all united in their convictions that God still speaks through what he has spoken, and that nothing is more necessary for the life, health and growth of Christians than that they should hear what the Spirit is saying to them through his ancient – yet ever modern – Word.

ALEC MOTYER
JOHN STOTT
DEREK TIDBALL
Series editors

Author's preface

This book is about the best news the world has ever heard – the message of salvation. Put in theological terms, the volume's topic is 'soteriology', from the Greek words *sōtēria* and *logos*, meaning 'the word of salvation'. The Bible itself *is* the word of salvation, the gracious message that glorifies God by persuading sinners to believe in Jesus Christ. A book such as this by necessity has to be selective. In what follows, therefore, I have tried to communicate God's saving message from throughout Holy Scripture, using representative stories, sermons, letters and poems to explain the Bible's own doctrine of salvation.

I am profoundly grateful to Derek Tidball of the London Bible College, as well as to Colin Duriez of Inter-Varsity Press, for the opportunity to contribute to a series of books that has done so much to enhance my own understanding of the Bible. Their welcome invitation prompted me to preach a series of sermons on the message of salvation to my own congregation. As always, I thank God for the prayer and encouragement my preaching received from my friends at the Tenth Presbyterian Church in Philadelphia.

I am equally thankful for the assistance rendered by the editorial team at IVP, and also by many brothers in Christian ministry. James Boice, Adam Brice, Ligon Duncan, Richard Phillips and Leland Ryken helped to shape the original outline; Richard Gaffin, Randall Grossman, Michael Horton, Jonathan Rockey, Stephen Taylor and Timothy Trumper read and commented on all or part of the original manuscript. Each helped to improve my work in significant ways (although perhaps not as much as they hoped, in some cases!).

This book is dedicated to my wife Lisa – my lover, my friend – and to the God who 'saved us, not because of righteous things we had done, but because of his mercy ... poured out on us generously through Jesus Christ' (Titus 3:5–6).

November 2000   PHILIP GRAHAM RYKEN
                                                             Center City, Philadelphia

Chief abbreviations

ASV	The American Standard Version (1901)
AV	The Authorized (King James) Version of the Bible (1611)
BECNT	Baker Exegetical Commentary on the New Testament
BST	The Bible Speaks Today
CTJ	*Calvin Theological Journal*
EBC	*The Expositor's Bible Commentary*
ICC	International Critical Commentary
JBL	*Journal of Biblical Literature*
LCC	Library of Christian Classics
NEB	The New English Bible (NT, 1961, second edition 1970; OT, 1970)
NICNT	New International Commentary on the New Testament
NIV	New International Version of the Bible (1973, 1978, 1984)
TDNT	*Theological Dictionary of the New Testament*, ed. by G. Kittell and G. Friedrich, translated by G. W. Bromiley, 10 vols. (Grand Rapids: Eerdmans, 1964–76)
TNTC	Tyndale New Testament Commentaries
TOTC	Tyndale Old Testament Commentaries
WBC	Word Biblical Commentary

Bibliography

Alexander, Eric J., 'The basis of Christian salvation', in *Faithful Witness*, ed. by James McLeish (Downers Grove, IL: IVP, 1985).

Allen, Roland, *The Spontaneous Expansion of the Church and the Causes which Hinder it* (Grand Rapids: Eerdmans, 1962).

Ames, William, *The Marrow of Theology*, trans. and ed. by John Dykstra Eusden (1627; Durham, NC: Labyrinth, 1983).

Augustine, *Christian Doctrine*, ed. by Philip Schaff, Nicene and Post-Nicene Fathers, First Series (1887; repr. Peabody, MA: Hendrickson, 1995).

Bannerman, James, *The Church of Christ: A Treatise on the Nature, Powers, Ordinances, Discipline and Government of the Christian Church*, 2 vols. (1869; repr. Edinburgh: Banner of Truth, 1974).

Barnhouse, Donald Grey, *The Invisible War: The Panorama of the Continuing Conflict between Good and Evil* (Grand Rapids: Zondervan, 1965).

Berkhof, Louis, *Systematic Theology*, 4th ed. (Grand Rapids: Eerdmans, 1941).

Berkouwer, G. C., *Faith and Justification* (Grand Rapids: Eerdmans, 1954).

Blocher, Henri, *In the Beginning: The Opening Chapters of Genesis*, trans. by David G. Preston (Leicester and Downers Grove, IL: IVP, 1984).

Bloesch, Donald G., *Essentials of Evangelical Theology*, vol. 1: *God, Authority and Salvation* (San Francisco: Harper & Row, 1978).

Bock, Darrell L., *Luke*, 2 vols., BECNT (Grand Rapids: Baker, 1996).

Boice, James Montgomery, *Ephesians: An Expositional Commentary* (Grand Rapids: Zondervan, 1988).

—— *The Gospel of John* (Grand Rapids: Zondervan, 1985).

—— *Romans*, 4 vols. (Grand Rapids: Baker, 1991).

Bonhoeffer, Dietrich, *The Cost of Discipleship* (New York: Macmillan, 1963).

Boston, Thomas, *The Complete Works of the Late Rev. Thomas Boston of Ettrick*, 12 vols. (1853; repr. Wheaton, IL: Richard Owen Roberts, 1980).

—— *Human Nature in its Fourfold State* (1720; Edinburgh: Banner of Truth, 1964).

Boyd, Gregory A., *God of the Possible: A Biblical Introduction to the Open View of God* (Grand Rapids: Baker, 2000).

Brown, John, *An Exposition of the Epistle of Paul the Apostle to the Galatians* (1853; repr. Evansville, IN: Sovereign Grace, 1957).

Bruce, F. F., *Romans*, TNTC (London: Tyndale Press, 1963).

Brunner, Emil, *The Mediator*, trans. by Olive Wyon (1927; repr. London: Lutterworth, 1947).

Buchanan, James, *The Doctrine of Justification* (1867; repr. Grand Rapids: Baker, 1955).

Bushnell, Horace, *God in Christ* (1849; repr. New York: AMS Press, 1972).

Calvin, John, *Institutes of the Christian Religion*, ed. by John T. McNeill, trans. by Ford Lewis Battles, 2 vols., LCC 20–21 (1536–59; Philadelphia: Westminster, 1960).

—— *Tracts and Treatises in Defense of the Reformed Faith*, trans. by Henry Beveridge (Grand Rapids: Eerdmans, 1958).

Carson, D. A., *The Gospel according to John* (Leicester and Downers Grove, IL: IVP, 1991).

—— 'Matthew', in *EBC* 8 (Grand Rapids: Zondervan, 1984).

Chrysostom, John, *Homilies on the Epistles of Paul to the Corinthians*, 14 vols., ed. by Philip Schaff, Nicene and Post-Nicene Fathers of the Christian Church, First Series (1889; repr. Peabody, MA: Hendrickson, 1984).

Clowney, Edmund P., 'The biblical doctrine of justification by faith', in *Right with God: Justification in the Bible and the World*, ed. by D. A. Carson (London: World Evangelical Fellowship, 1992).

—— *The Message of 1 Peter: The Way of the Cross*, BST (Leicester and Downers Grove, IL: IVP, 1988).

Coleman Robert E., *The Master Plan of Evangelism*, rev. ed. (Grand Rapids: Revell, 1993).

Cranmer, Thomas, *First Book of Homilies* (1547; repr. London: SPCK, 1914).

Davis, C. Trueman, 'The crucifixion of Jesus: The passion of Christ from a medical point of view', *Arizona Medicine* (March 1965).

Demarest, Bruce, *The Cross and Salvation* (Wheaton, IL: Crossway, 1997).

Edwards, Jonathan, *The Freedom of the Will* (1754; New Haven, CT: Yale, 1957).

—— *The Works of Jonathan Edwards*, 2 vols. (Edinburgh: Banner of Truth, 1974).

Edwards, W. D., W. J. Gabel and F. E. Hosmer, 'On the physical death of Jesus Christ', *Journal of the American Medical Association*, 255.11 (March 1986).

Ferguson, Sinclair, *The Christian Life: A Doctrinal Introduction* (Edinburgh: Banner of Truth, 1989).

Gaffin (Jr), Richard B., *The Centrality of the Resurrection* (Grand Rapids: Baker, 1978).

Geldenhuys, Norval, *The Gospel of Luke*, NICNT (Grand Rapids: Eerdmans, 1951).

Girardeau, J. L., *Discussions of Theological Questions* (Richmond, VA: Presbyterian Committee of Publication, 1905).

Green, Joel B., *The Gospel of Luke* (Grand Rapids: Eerdmans, 1997).

Habermas, Gary R., *The Historical Jesus: Ancient Evidence for the Life of Christ* (Joplin, MO: College Press, 1996).

Helm, Paul, *The Last Things: Death, Judgement, Heaven, Hell* (Edinburgh: Banner of Truth, 1989).

Hodge, Charles, *A Commentary on the First Epistle to the Corinthians* (1857; London: Banner of Truth, 1964).

—— *A Commentary on the Second Epistle to the Corinthians* (1859; London: Banner of Truth, 1959).

Hoekema, Anthony A., *Saved by Grace* (Grand Rapids: Eerdmans, 1989).

Hooker, Richard, *The Works of Richard Hooker*, ed. by John Keble, 3rd ed. (Oxford: Oxford University Press, 1845).

Hughes, Philip Edgcumbe, *Paul's Second Epistle to the Corinthians* (Grand Rapids: Eerdmans, 1962).

—— *The True Image: The Origin and Destiny of Man in Christ* (Grand Rapids: Eerdmans, and Leicester: IVP, 1989).

Johnson, Phillip E., *Reason in the Balance: The Case Against Naturalism in Science, Law and Education* (Downers Grove, IL: IVP, 1995).

Josephus, Flavius, *The Antiquities of the Jews* and *The Wars of the Jews*, in *The Works of Josephus*, trans. by William Whiston (Peabody, MA: Hendrickson, 1987).

Kähler, Martin, *The So-Called Historical Jesus and the Historic Biblical Christ* (Philadelphia: Fortress, 1964).

Kidner, Derek, *Genesis*, TOTC (London and Downers Grove, IL: IVP, 1967).

Kuyper, Abraham, *Christianity and the Class Struggle*, trans. by Dirk Jellema (Grand Rapids: Piet Hein, 1950).

Lewis, C. S., *The Problem of Pain* (London: Geoffrey Bles, 1940).

Lightfoot, J. B., and J. R. Harmer (trans.), *The Apostolic Fathers*, ed. by M. W. Holmes, 2nd ed. (Grand Rapids: Baker, and Leicester: Apollos, 1989).

Lightfoot, Neil R., *Lessons from the Parables* (Grand Rapids: Baker, 1965).

Lincoln, Andrew T., *Ephesians*, WBC (Dallas, TX: Word, 1990).

Lloyd-Jones, D. Martyn, *God's Way of Reconciliation: An Exposition of Ephesians 2* (Grand Rapids: Baker, 1972).

Lüdemann, Gerd, *What Really Happened to Jesus: A Historical Approach to the Resurrection*, trans. by John Bowden (Louisville, KY: Westminster/John Knox, 1995).

Luther, Martin, *The Bondage of the Will* (1525; Grand Rapids: Eerdmans, 1931).

—— *Letters of Spiritual Counsel*, ed. and trans. by Theodore S. Tappert, LCC 18 (London: SCM, 1955).

——*Luther's Works*, ed. by Jaroslav Pelikan and H. T. Lehmann, 55 vols. (Philadelphia: Fortress, 1955–76).

—— *The Works of Martin Luther* (Philadelphia: Muhlenberg, 1943).

Lyall, Francis, 'Roman law in the writings of Paul – Adoption', *JBL* (December 1969).

McGrath, Alister E., *Bridge-Building: Effective Christian Apologetics* (Leicester: IVP, 1992) = *Intellectuals Don't Need God and Other Modern Myths* (Grand Rapids: Zondervan, 1993).

—— *Luther's Theology of the Cross* (Oxford: Blackwell, 1990).

—— *The Making of Modern German Christology 1750–1990* , 2nd ed. (Leicester: Apollos, and Grand Rapids: Zondervan, 1994).

Machen, J. Gresham, *What is Faith?* (1925; repr. Edinburgh: Banner of Truth, 1991).

Macleod, Donald: *A Faith to Live By: Studies in Christian Doctrine* (Fearn, Ross-shire: Mentor, 1998).

Manson, T. W., *The Gospel of Luke*, Moffatt New Testament Commentary (1930).

Marshall, I. Howard, and David Peterson (eds.), *Witness to the Gospel: The Theology of Acts* (Grand Rapids: Eerdmans, 1998).

Martin, Walter R., *Essential Christianity: A Handbook of Basic Christian Doctrines* (Grand Rapids: Zondervan, 1962).

Martyr, Justin, *The First Apology of Justin, the Martyr*, in *Early Christian Fathers*, ed. by Cyril C. Richardson (New York: Macmillan, 1970).

Morison, Frank, *Who Moved the Stone?* 2nd ed. (London: Faber, 1944; Grand Rapids: Zondervan, 1958).

Morris, Leon, *The Apostolic Preaching of the Cross*, 3rd ed. (London: Tyndale Press, and Grand Rapids: Eerdmans, 1965).

—— *The Gospel according to Matthew* (Grand Rapids: Eerdmans, and Leicester: IVP, 1992).

Motyer, J. Alec, *The Prophecy of Isaiah* (Leicester and Downers Grove, IL: IVP, 1993).

Murray, John, *Collected Writings*, 4 vols. (Edinburgh: Banner of Truth, 1977).

—— *The Epistle to the Romans*, 2 vols. (Grand Rapids: Eerdmans, 1959).

—— *The Imputation of Adam's Sin* (Phillipsburg, NJ: Presbyterian & Reformed, 1959).

—— *Redemption: Accomplished and Applied* (Grand Rapids: Eerdmans, 1955).

13

Nash, Ronald (ed.), *Liberation Theology* (Milford, MI: Mott, 1984).

Old, Hughes Oliphant, *The Reading and Preaching of the Scriptures in the Worship of the Christian Church*, 7 vols. (Grand Rapids: Eerdmans, 1998–).

Packer, J. I., *Concise Theology: A Guide to Historic Christian Beliefs* (Wheaton, IL: Tyndale House, and Leicester: IVP, 1993).

—— *Evangelism and the Sovereignty of God* (London: IVF and Downers Grove, IL: IVP, 1961).

—— *Knowing God* (London: Hodder & Stoughton, and Downers Grove, IL: IVP, 1973).

Perkins, William, *A Commentary on Galatians*, ed. by Gerald T. Sheppard (1617; repr. New York: Pilgrim, 1989).

Pinnock, Charles H., *A Wideness in God's Mercy: The Finality of Jesus Christ in a World of Religions* (Grand Rapids: Zondervan, 1992).

Piper, John, *Let the Nations Be Glad! The Supremacy of God in Missions* (Grand Rapids: Baker, 1993; Leicester: IVP, 1994).

Plummer, A., *The Gospel according to Saint Luke*, 5th ed., ICC (Edinburgh: T. & T. Clark, 1922).

Reardon, Bernard M. G., *Religious Thought in the Reformation* (London: Longman, 1981).

Ryken, Philip Graham, *Is Jesus the Only Way?* (Wheaton, IL: Crossway, 1999).

Ryle, J. C., *Holiness* (Cambridge: James Clarke, 1952).

Schaeffer, Francis A., *The Complete Works of Francis A. Schaeffer*, 2nd ed., 5 vols. (Wheaton, IL: Crossway, 1982).

Schaff, Philip (ed.), *The Creeds of Christendom*, vol. 2: *The Greek and Latin Creeds*, 6th ed. (1931; repr. Grand Rapids: Baker, 1993).

Scougal, Henry, *The Life of God in the Soul of Man* (1677; Fearn, Ross-shire: Christian Focus, 1996).

Smeaton, George, *Christ's Doctrine of the Atonement* (1870; repr. Edinburgh: Banner of Truth, 1991).

Sproul, R. C., *Faith Alone: The Evangelical Doctrine of Justification* (Grand Rapids: Baker, 1995).

Stott, J. R. W., *Basic Christianity*, 2nd ed. (London and Downers Grove, IL: IVP, 1971).

—— *The Cross of Christ* (Leicester and Downers Grove, IL: IVP, 1986).

—— *Men Made New: An Exposition of Romans 5–8* (Leicester and Downers Grove, IL: IVP, 1966; Grand Rapids: Baker, 1984).

—— *The Message of Acts*, BST (Leicester: IVP, 1990) = *The Spirit, the Church, and the World* (Downers Grove, IL: IVP, 1990).

—— *The Message of Ephesians*, BST (Leicester and Downers Grove, IL: IVP, 1979).

Strobel, Lee, *The Case for Christ: A Journalist's Personal Investigation of the Evidence for Jesus* (Grand Rapids: Zondervan, 1998).

Vincent, Thomas, *The True Christian's Love to the Unseen Christ* (repr.

Morgan, PA: Soli Deo Gloria, 1993).

Warfield, Benjamin B., *Biblical and Theological Studies*, ed. by Samuel Craig (Philadelphia: Presbyterian & Reformed, 1952).

—— *The Person and Work of Christ* (Philadelphia: Presbyterian & Reformed, 1950).

White, John, *The Fight* (Downers Grove, IL: IVP, 1976; Leicester: IVP, 1977).

Witherington III, Ben, 'Salvation and health in Christian antiquity: The soteriology of Luke-Acts in its first-century setting', in Marshall and Peterson (eds.), *Witness to the Gospel*.

Witsius, Herman, *The Economy of the Covenants Between God and Man: Comprehending a Complete Body of Divinity*, 2 vols. (1882; repr. Phillipsburg, NJ: Presbyterian & Reformed, 1990).

—— *Sacred Dissertations on the Apostles' Creed*, 2 vols. (1923; repr. Escondido, CA: Den Dulk, 1993).

Wuest, Kenneth S., *Wuest's Word Studies from the Greek New Testament* (Grand Rapids: Eerdmans, 1966).

PART 1: SAVED FROM SIN
'Christ Jesus came into the world to save sinners'
(1 Timothy 1:15)

1. Why we need to be saved
Creation and fall: Genesis 2:15 – 3:6

Humanity has a problem. There are signs of it all over the world. In North Africa women and children are sold into slavery. In Europe ethnic tensions produce warfare and attempted genocide. In the Middle East terrorist acts are committed in the name of religion. In Asia thousands of little girls are forced into prostitution. In North America there are guns and drugs on the city streets. All around the world, people suffer from the greed of the rich, the violence of the strong, and the cruelty of the proud.

Things are not getting any better. If anything, they are getting worse, for the twentieth century was the bloodiest in human history. One intellectual rightly described it as 'the worst century our planet has yet endured – spectacular advancements in science and technology obscured by evil pure and unadorned'.[1] The new millennium can only promise more of the same: more people, more greed, more lust and more violence. There is no doubt about it: humanity has a problem. Or perhaps we should say, humanity *is* the problem.

This book is about God's answer to the problem of humanity. It contains the message of salvation – salvation from sin and death through the crucifixion and resurrection of Jesus Christ. Its argument is that the only hope for our troubled race is for Jesus to save us from sin, by grace, through faith, for the glory of God.

What are human beings for?

To understand God's answer to humanity's problem, it is necessary to understand the problem as clearly as possible. Why do we need to be saved? What do we need to be saved from? Why can't we save ourselves? These questions need to be answered. Yet there is another question that must come first: What are human beings for, anyway? It is only when

[1] Robert Novak, 1990 speech at the Notre Dame Club of Chicago, quoted in Calvin M. Johansson, *Discipling Music Ministry: Twenty-first Century Directions* (Peabody, MA: Hendrickson, 1992), p. 7.

we know our purpose that we can recognize our problem and begin to seek an answer.

Some people say that human beings are made for pleasure. This was the approach taken by the ancient Epicureans, with their popular slogan, 'Eat, drink, and be merry, for tomorrow we die.' According to the *hedonist*, a person is little more than a player, and we should live for all the physical, sexual and aesthetic pleasure we can get. Others say that a person is not a player, but a worker. This is the view of the *communist*, who expresses the value of a human being in economic terms. Our purpose is to be productive. This is also the view of the *capitalist*, although for the capitalist, a person is a consumer as well as a worker. People work for a living, but they live to shop.

Then there is the view of the *pantheist*, who believes that human beings are part of universal being. In one form or another, this is the worldview of Hinduism and Buddhism, and of the many New Age philosophies inspired by Eastern religion. There is no Creator, only the creation, and human beings have no separate existence apart from that creation. Our purpose is to be absorbed into the cosmic ocean, to become part of one indivisible force.

By contrast, the *Islamist* (or Muslim) takes that cosmic force and divides it in two. Since nothing happens without direct divine action, Allah is the source of evil as well as good. He is even the source of human sin, for Allah himself leads people astray. According to this fatalistic determinism, a human being is at the whim of God's arbitrary will.

Many others say that human beings are not *for* anything in particular; we are merely the product of meaningless chance. This is the view of the *naturalist*, and it is often tied to the philosophy of evolution. According to one evolutionary scientist, 'Man is the result of a purposeless and natural process that did not have him in mind.'[2] Thus our biology is our destiny, and we do not have souls, only bodies. A human being is merely another kind of animal, a trousered ape. Professor Marvin Minsky has put it even more crassly: a man is 'just a machine made out of meat'.[3]

If we really are machines made out of meat, the *existentialist* doubts whether our existence even matters. Human life starts with nothing, ends with nothing, and means nothing in between. If one asks what human beings are for, the postmodern existentialist says we are for nothing at all. The *humanist* holds humanity in much higher regard, believing in the inherent power and goodness of human beings. The humanist seeks to help people reach their potential in art, music,

---

[2] George Gaylord Simpson, quoted in Johnson, *Reason in the Balance*, pp. 12–13.
[3] Marvin Minsky, Massachusetts Institute of Technology, quoted in *Christianity Today* (7 December 1998), p. 34.

technology, and the life of the mind. According to the famous dictum of the Greek philosophers, popularized during the Renaissance, 'Man is the measure of all things.'

Those views about what human beings are for have been greatly simplified, of course, but they are roughly the options in the world today. Is a human being a player or a worker? A beast or a machine? Nothing or everything? What is a person meant to be, and what is a person to become?

In the beginning

The best place to learn what human beings are really for is the Bible, especially its first several chapters. Martin Luther (1483–1546), the father of the Protestant Reformation in Europe, described the early part of Genesis as 'certainly the foundation of the whole of Scripture'.[4] More than that, it is the foundation for understanding God, the world and humanity, and thus for understanding the message of salvation.

In the beginning we learn that God created the heavens and the earth (Gen. 1:1). There is a Creator as well as a creation, and thus we have already ruled out pantheism, which denies any distinction between creature and Creator. The climax of this creation comes on the sixth day, when God said, 'Let us make man' (1:26). This rules out naturalism. Human beings are not the random result of meaningless chance; we are the crown of creation, the best product of intelligent design. Although we come from the dust of the ground, God himself breathed life into us to make us living beings, body and soul (2:7).

God not only made us, but he also made us in his image. This fact must be of crucial importance because it is mentioned three times in the space of two verses:

> Then God said, 'Let us make man in our image, in our likeness, and let them rule over the fish of the sea and the birds of the air, over the livestock, over all the earth, and over all the creatures that move along the ground.'

> So God created man
>   in his own image,
> in the image of God
>   he created him;
> male and female
>   he created them (1:26–27).

An image is something made after a model. Like a newly minted coin,

---

[4] Martin Luther, quoted in Blocher, *In the Beginning*, p. 16.

an image is fashioned according to the pattern of an original. Therefore, to be made in the divine image is to be made like God. But in what respect?

One way to define the image of God is to notice what the biblical account of creation reveals about God, and then to look for the same attributes in humanity. The creation shows that God is creative, making all things out of nothing. It shows that he loves beauty, reason and order, and that he makes aesthetic judgments. It reveals that God is able to speak, to command and to rule. The creation even shows that God has the capacity for relationship. 'Let us make man in our image' (1:26), he says, with the phrase 'let us' implying that there are relationships within the Godhead. Then God proceeds to embrace others in his fellowship by making people to love and to cherish. These are all attributes that human beings share in common with God. We have the creativity to make things, and the aesthetic sensitivity to judge their beauty. We are reasonable creatures who can think, speak and rule. We are male and female, and thus have the capacity for loving relationships with God and one another.

A different way to define the image of God is according to God's moral and spiritual qualities. This method of definition was popularized by Luther and the other Reformers. These men took their clue from the New Testament, which speaks of 'being renewed in knowledge in the image of [our] Creator'[5] and 'created to be like God in true righteousness and holiness'.[6] To be like God is to be holy and righteous. Thus the relationship between God and the creatures who bear his image is a religious relationship based on moral and spiritual qualities. However we define it, the divine image constitutes the uniqueness of humanity. God has made us like himself, and we are dependent upon him for the very pattern of our existence.

Made for God's glory

The divine image gives us an important clue about what human beings are made for. Who we are is a reflection of who God is. We did not make and cannot define ourselves. Thus the meaning of our existence comes from God. We do not exist by ourselves, we exist in relationship to him; we do not live for ourselves, we live for him. What is a human being for? A human being is made for the glory of God. We have no purpose or significance apart from him.

The history of creation reveals that God made us to serve him in every area of life.

First, we are to glorify God in our *work*. No sooner had God decided to make human beings in his image, than he decided to give us

---

[5] Col. 3:10.   [6] Eph. 4:24.

work to do: 'Then God said, "Let us make man in our image, in our likeness, and let them rule over the fish of the sea and the birds of the air, over the livestock, over all the earth, and over all the creatures that move along the ground"' (Gen. 1:26).

Work is part of the divine image, for God himself is a worker: 'By the seventh day God had finished the work he had been doing; so on the seventh day he rested from all his work' (2:2). Our Creator is described both as a potter who formed the man out of clay (2:7) and as a farmer who 'planted a garden in the east, in Eden' (2:8), making 'all kinds of trees grow out of the ground – trees that were pleasing to the eye and good for food' (2:9). Our work has dignity because we are made in the image of a working God.

Work was not the result of the fall, but part of God's original plan for humanity. Adam and Eve did not lounge around picnicking all day. They had work to do! God told them to subdue the earth, to 'rule over the fish of the sea and the birds of the air and over every living creature that moves on the ground' (1:28). Theologians call this command 'the creation mandate'. It means that human beings were designated to represent God's rule on this earth. Adam began to carry out the creation mandate by giving names to all the birds and the beasts (2:19–20a). Naming is an act of authority. By naming the animals, the man was exercising his dominion over the creatures. He also had some gardening to do. God put Adam in the garden *to work it and take care of it* (2:15). This is why he needed a *helper* who was *suitable* (2:18): he had so much work to do! Adam and Eve were the caretakers of Eden and the keepers of the Paradise Zoo, for God commanded them to govern and to nurture all the plants and animals he had made.

In the beginning, work was not a curse, but a calling. Adam and Eve did not collapse in the grass at the end of the day, too tired to move another muscle. Nor did they count the days until their next holiday. Their labour was not a labour. They loved their jobs because they worked for the glory of God. When John Milton (1608–74) wrote *Paradise Lost*, his epic poem about the creation and fall of humanity, he depicted Adam and Eve happily and busily at work in the Garden of Eden. Milton's Adam says to Milton's Eve:

> Man hath his daily work of body or mind
> Appointed, which declares his dignity,
> And the regard of Heaven on all his ways.[7]

Work has always been a necessary and pleasurable part of what it means to be a human being made in God's image, and living for God's glory.

[7] John Milton, *Paradise Lost* (1667; New York: Holt, Rinehart and Winston, 1951), Book IV, lines 618–620.

Secondly, human beings are to glorify God with their *rest*. A person is more than a worker. The problem with communism – and with capitalism, as it is usually practised – is that it reduces humanity to a workforce. But human beings are players as well as workers.

God made us to follow a pattern of labour and leisure. This is another part of what it means to be made in God's image: 'By the seventh day God had finished the work he had been doing; so on the seventh day he rested from all his work. And God blessed the seventh day and made it holy, because on it he rested from all the work of creating that he had done' (Gen. 2:2–3). Six days of labour followed by one day of leisure – this is the rhythm of work and rest God established for the creatures he made in his image. Although our play is often pleasurable, we do not play simply for our own pleasure. We play in relationship to God, following his example and reflecting his glory.

Thirdly, we are to glorify God in our *relationships* as men and women. Our identity as males and females is a gift from God that reflects the personality of his triune being:

> So God created man
> in his own image,
> in the image of God
> he created him;
> male and female
> he created them (1:27).

This is a statement of the absolute equality of men and women. Male and female, we are all created in God's image. Whatever is true about the image of God in man is true about the image of God in woman, and vice versa.

The equality of man and woman is emphasized by the way God made the woman: *The LORD God caused the man to fall into a deep sleep; and while he was sleeping, he took one of the man's ribs and closed up the place with flesh. Then the LORD God made a woman from the rib he had taken out of the man* (2:21–22). The female is made of the same stuff as the male. Indeed, this seems to be the first thing Adam noticed about his new companion. As he joyfully burst into the world's first love song, he said, *'This is now bone of my bones and flesh of my flesh'* (2:23a).

Men and women were made for one another. Although we are equal, we are not identical. Male *and* female, we are created in God's image (1:27). Perhaps there is a faint echo here of the doctrine of the Trinity. The one true God exists in three persons – Father, Son and Holy Spirit – so that there is diversity within the unity of the Godhead. In the same way, there is diversity within the unity of humanity. The fact that we are created in two genders shows that we are made to correspond to one another. The woman was the man's counterpart. While Adam could tell right away that Eve was made like him, he could also tell that she was different: *'She shall be called "woman", for she was taken out of man'* (2:23b).

The unity and the complementarity between Adam and Eve were beautifully expressed in their sexual relationship: *For this reason a man will leave his father and mother and be united to his wife, and they will become one flesh* (2:24). Sexual intercourse is a union; it expresses the intimate spiritual oneness of a man and a woman. At the same time, the consummation of their love depends on the physical differences between them. Thus their sexual relationship expresses both their unity and their complementarity. The hedonist uses sexuality for his or her own pleasure. The naturalist reduces it to a biological urge. But the man and the woman were made to enjoy sex for the glory of God. The first thing God said to Adam and Eve was, 'Be fruitful and increase in number; fill the earth' (1:28). From the very beginning, marriage was for the glory of God. Even the sexual relationship between the man and the woman belonged to God, for procreation was part of his plan for blessing the world.

What we learn from creation is that the various activities of human life were never intended to be ends in themselves. We were made to work, but not to become enslaved by it. We were made to play, but not simply for our own pleasure. We were made to have relationships – even to get married and to share sexual intimacy – but not to gratify ourselves. The humanist and the existentialist are both wrong: human beings are not the measure of all things; neither is their existence meaningless. They receive their measure and their meaning from God, who says that they are those 'whom I created for my glory, whom I formed and made'.[8]

Human beings were made for many things, but we have only one primary purpose, and that is to live for God. The most familiar statement of this principle is still the best. It comes from the first question and answer in the *Westminster Shorter Catechism*: 'What is the chief end of man?' 'Man's chief end is to glorify God, and to enjoy him for ever.' If you want to know what human beings are for, the answer is that in every area of life – in our work, our play, our relationships, our families – our purpose is to glorify God. 'So whether you eat or drink or whatever you do, do it all for the glory of God'.[9]

The covenant of life

The only way to glorify God perfectly is to obey him absolutely. To see if the first man and the first woman would do this, God gave them a test. He had given them 'every seed-bearing plant on the face of the

[8] Is. 43:7.   [9] 1 Cor. 10:31.

whole earth and every tree that has fruit with seed in it' for food (Gen. 1:29). There was one restriction, however: *And the LORD God commanded the man, 'You are free to eat from any tree in the garden; but you must not eat from the tree of the knowledge of good and evil, for when you eat of it you will surely die'* (2:16–17).

There was a tree that gave life in the garden, but standing next to it was a tree that threatened death. One tree represented God's blessing and the other represented God's curse. The Bible does not refer to this arrangement as a covenant, but it amounts to much the same thing, for a covenant is a binding relationship in which God promises to bless his people for obedience and threatens to curse them for disobedience. The relationship God initiated with Adam is sometimes called the covenant of nature, the covenant of life, or even the covenant of works. It had many of the features of a biblical covenant, which may explain why in these verses God is given his covenantal name, Yahweh. The covenant that God established in the garden had two parties: God and the man. There was a promise implied: a life of continual happiness in God's beautiful garden, signified by the tree of life. There was a condition stipulated: perfect obedience, summarized in the solitary command not to eat the forbidden fruit. There was a curse threatened: death for disobedience. In short, Adam lived in covenant with God, standing as representative for the entire human race.[10] If he obeyed God perfectly, he and all his posterity would live for ever; if he disobeyed, they would die.

In and of itself, eating or not eating a piece of fruit is a matter of complete indifference. The only reason it was wrong to eat this particular fruit was because God said it was wrong. To some this law may seem arbitrary, especially since it carried the death penalty. But remember that God is the sovereign Creator, and therefore has the right to demand whatever obedience he pleases. Furthermore, the tree of the knowledge of good and evil was the perfect test of human fidelity. The only thing it demanded from Adam and Eve was the only thing that mattered: pure obedience to the revealed will of God. J. I. Packer describes Adam's situation as follows:

> God set the first man in a state of happiness and promised to continue this to him and his posterity after him if he showed fidelity by a course of perfect positive obedience and specifically by not eating from a tree described as the tree of the knowledge of good and evil. It would seem that the tree bore this name because the issue was whether Adam would let God tell him what was good and bad for him or would seek to decide that for himself, in disregard of what God had said. By eating from this tree Adam would, in effect, be

---

[10] See Rom. 5:15–19.

claiming that he could know and decide what was good and evil for him without any reference to God.[11]

The tree of the knowledge of good and evil thus forced Adam to decide whether he would live for God's glory or his own.

Adam was free to choose. The biblical text is quite specific on this point, for God said, *'You are free to eat ... but you must not eat ...'* (2:16). Human freedom finds its place within God's sovereignty, of course, but God created human beings with responsibility for their liberty. The learned Augustine (354–430) used the phrase *posse non peccare*, 'to be able not to sin', to describe the state of our first parents. Milton said they were 'able to stand, but free to fall'. This is because Adam and Eve were positively righteous. This is what made the terms of the covenant of life so favourable. Like everything else God made, our first parents were created good. However, they would remain good only if they passed their probation by choosing to live for the glory of God.

What would have happened if Adam and Eve had kept God's covenant by never eating the forbidden fruit? They would have lived for ever, remaining holy and happy in their fellowship with God. They would have fulfilled their creation mandate, filling and subduing the earth with the help of their godly offspring. Augustine and many other theologians have also speculated that after a time their probation would have ended, and the human race would have attained an even more glorious destiny. The time of testing was never intended to last for ever. Eventually, humanity would have passed into a perfectly blissful state of immortal obedience already enjoyed by God's holy angels, who are unable to sin (in Augustine's phrase, *non posse peccare*).

The first temptation

Perhaps it is unwise to speculate what would have happened if Adam and Eve had never sinned. But one thing is certain: humanity never would have needed to be saved. Nor would we have needed the message of salvation. We would have needed God's sustaining grace, but not his saving grace. The sad reality, of course, is that we do need saving grace because our first parents sinned, plunging the human race into loss and ruin. The Bible does not say how long Adam and Eve remained holy and happy, but it gives the impression that their innocence was short-lived. It takes only a page or two to describe their perfection, and a few verses to tell how they lost it, but the whole of the rest of the Bible to explain how to get it back.

The chapter on humanity's innocence closes with the end of

[11] Packer, *Concise Theology*, p. 80.

Genesis 2, where we read, *The man and his wife were both naked* (2:25). Their nakedness was a sign of innocence and intimacy. They had nothing to hide, either from God or from one another. Sinners that we are, this is so hard for us to comprehend – people living, working and playing in the nude – that the Bible proceeds to add this explanation: *and they felt no shame.*

As we remember our first parents naked in the garden, we sense how vulnerable they were, for next we read that *the serpent was more crafty than any of the wild animals the LORD God had made* (3:1a). Already we sense the danger. There is an Enemy in the Garden. How he got there is another story,[12] but the Bible clearly identifies him as 'that ancient serpent called the devil, or Satan, who leads the whole world astray'.[13]

Humanity's temptation to sin came from the serpent. He began his shrewd attack by questioning the covenant. First he called God's command into question: *He said to the woman, 'Did God really say, "You must not eat from any tree in the garden?"'* (3:1b). The serpent was the world's first Bible critic, casting doubt on God's perfect Word and subjecting it to the suspicion of human judgment. Satan deliberately misquoted and misrepresented what God said. Far from forbidding the man and woman to eat, God had said nearly the opposite, inviting them freely to eat from every tree in the garden (2:16) – with only one exception. The serpent thus turned a positive invitation into a negative prohibition, as if God somehow begrudged Eve the fruits of Eden. He was challenging God's goodness, insinuating that the Creator was overly strict and absurdly stingy. In his brilliant study of these verses, Henri Blocher comments that Satan 'presents the ban as a monstrous deprivation. It is not so much God's word on which he casts doubt as his *goodness*. Of the God who is generosity itself he sketches a portrait of miserliness. He projects the false perspective of a rivalry between God and man; he suggests that man will be the less free as God will be the more sovereign, and vice versa.'[14] To put this another way, Satan presented the forbidden fruit as a violation of humanity's sovereignty, an infringement of the woman's right to choose. For God to prohibit one thing was to prohibit everything.

To her credit, the woman was quick to tell the serpent all this. She said, *'We may eat fruit from the trees in the garden, but God did say, "You must not eat fruit from the tree that is in the middle of the garden, and you must not touch it, or you will die"'* (3:2–3). Eve is often criticized for her paraphrase, putting the words 'and you must not touch it' into God's mouth. Still, there was some wisdom in not touching the fruit, and in any case, she had not yet sinned by eating it. Her real mistake was trying to reason with the devil.

---

[12] See Ezek. 28:12–17; Is. 14:12–15; Luke 10:18.   [13] Rev. 12:9a; cf. 20:2.
[14] Blocher, *In the Beginning*, p. 139.

Satan's response was devilishly clever: *'You will not surely die,'* the *serpent said to the woman. For God knows that when you eat of it your eyes will be opened, and you will be like God, knowing good and evil* (3:4–5). Having challenged God's goodness, Satan now contradicted God's truthfulness. It was the most dangerous of lies – an outright lie mixed with a half-truth. *'You will not surely die'* – that was a diabolical lie, as the rest of human history has shown. What Satan was really doing was looking for a loophole in the covenant. He was rejecting its terms, specifically the threat of mortality. Thus Satan was the first to deny the reality of divine judgment, and what great evil has come into the world because of it!

The rest of what Satan said was half-true: *'Your eyes will be opened.'* True enough, for only moments later their eyes *were* opened (3:7a). What Satan did not tell them, however, was that their eyes would be opened to behold their own shame. *'You will be like God,'* he said, *'knowing good and evil.'* In a way, that was true as well, for eating from the tree did bring firsthand knowledge of evil (3:22). But Adam and Eve were *already* like God, for they were made in his very image. Furthermore, they already possessed knowledge of the good. They had fellowship with a good Creator, serving him in his good creation. There was nothing new they could learn about goodness – except how costly it is to lose.

Sin enters the world

Eve had everything to lose from the forbidden fruit, and nothing to gain worth gaining; nevertheless, she stood there gazing at the tree of the knowledge of good and evil. She was tempted in every way: *The woman saw that the fruit of the tree was good for food and pleasing to the eye, and also desirable for gaining wisdom* (3:6a). The fruit had a physical appeal; it was tempting to the taste. It had an aesthetic appeal; it was beautiful to behold. It had an intellectual appeal, for it held the promise of outwitting God to gain forbidden knowledge. In the end, Eve gave in to temptation. She sinned, and so did Adam. The deadly deed is described in the most matter-of-fact way: *She took some and ate it. She also gave some to her husband, who was with her, and he ate it* (3:6b). In those few words are contained the sum of human misery.

It is crucial to understand that this event took place in human history. There was a man Adam, who took a piece of fruit from the woman Eve, put it in his mouth, bit it with his teeth, and swallowed it down his throat. Much of the language in early Genesis is artistic, even figurative, but it is not mythical. The story of the creation and the fall is not a fable. It is presented as history, and it is treated as history everywhere else in the Bible. For example, Adam is included in the biblical genealogies.[15] And when the New Testament explains what Jesus Christ has done – in history – for our salvation, it is based on what Adam did – in history – to make our salvation necessary.[16] The Bible is the only book in the world that identifies the beginning of evil in the world by showing its origin in a genuinely historical event.

The mention of the origin of evil brings us to another important truth: God is not the author of sin. This is one of the ways Christianity differs from Islam, which calls God evil as well as good. To be sure, God allowed Adam to sin. For reasons known only to himself, he permitted humanity's fall from innocence. But the inexplicable, inexcusable choice to transgress came from the man's free volition, and the one who enticed him to sin was not God, but the devil. To see this is to understand that God is not the origin of evil; on the contrary, he is utterly opposed to it. Henri Blocher offers an eloquent summary of the biblical posture towards evil:

> Nowhere else is evil denounced with such a tireless zeal, intransigence, horror and indignation. It is the disorder that finds no justification, the enemy and the work of the enemy ... Since elsewhere evil is inherent in the original being of reality and is part of the very definition of humanity, then elsewhere it must be excusable because it belongs to fate, and as such it must be invincible. There can therefore be no voice raised in protest against it. The myths and the philosophies that spring from them inevitably stifle the innate sense of the intolerable nature of evil, whether it is the evil one commits or the evil one suffers. But the Bible can stand as accuser and can awaken this sense, because it knows that evil was not there in the beginning, but arises from a subsequent, historical use of human freedom.[17]

There are many ways to describe the evil of the first sin. Emil Brunner calls it 'the rent which cuts through the whole of existence'.[18] It was clearly a transgression, the overstepping of a boundary. It was an act of defiance, a rebellious assault on the sovereign rights of a loving Creator. It was a perversion, the misuse of God's good creation. It was also a disobedience, a violation of the express command of God. It was the breaking of a covenant, the life-covenant between God and Adam. It was, as it is so often called, a 'fall' from standing upright before God.[19]

There are also many ways to define that first sin. Augustine argued that the root of Eve's sin was pride. The Puritans said it was actually a

---

[15] Gen. 5; Luke 3, etc.   [16] See Rom. 5:15, 17; 1. Cor. 15:21–22.
[17] Blocher, *In the Beginning*, p. 167.
[18] Emil Brunner, quoted in Bloesch, *Essentials of Evangelical Theology*, vol. 1, p. 88.
[19] Eccles. 7:29.

violation of all (or nearly all) ten of God's commandments. Taking the forbidden fruit obviously involved coveting and theft. Eating the fruit was also a way having of another god, worshipping the idol of self. The act was based on a lie about God's character, and therefore involved both swearing false witness and taking God's name in vain. It resulted in death for all humanity, and therefore it was a kind of murder, and so forth. More recently, Derek Kidner has emphasized the folly of Eve's selfishness: 'Eve listened to a creature instead of the Creator, followed her impressions against her instructions, and made self-fulfilment her goal.'[20]

There is truth in all these ways of describing and defining the sin of our first parents. But their sin was also this: an attempt to rob God of his glory. Eve was not content to reflect God's glory, she wanted to grab the glory for herself. She wanted to become God rather than to glorify God. This is our problem as well. The problem with human beings is our desire to take God's place, to live for our own glory rather than for *his* glory. At the heart of our sin is the perverse desire to live for self rather than to live for God, which is why we need to be saved. We are sinners who will not, cannot, glorify God until he saves us.

What must we do to be saved?

There are many lessons to be learned from the story of humanity's creation in the garden and fall into sin. First, we should remember our purpose, the meaning of our existence. What is a human being made for? A human being is created by God's power, in God's image, for God's glory. Therefore, we are made to glorify God in our work, our play, our relationships, and everything else we do.

Second, we should lament what we have lost. The story of the first sin and the loss of paradise is a disaster of cosmic consequence. We can hardly think of this tragedy without feeling deep sadness for what has become of the human race. Think of the perfect happiness of Adam and Eve as they were created. Then think of all the misery and suffering that has come from their sin.

When the Scottish Presbyterian Thomas Boston (1676–1732) preached his famous sermons on 'The Fourfold State of Man', he began by preaching on the state of innocence. As he came to the end of his sermons on paradise, he exhorted his congregation to lament what had been lost by comparing humanity to a beautiful palace, now ruined:

Here was a stately building; man carved like a fair palace, but now lying in ashes: let us stand and look on the ruins, and drop a tear ... Happy wast thou, O man! who was like unto thee? no pain nor

[20] Kidner, *Genesis*, p. 68.

sickness could affect thee, no death could approach thee, no sigh was heard from thee, till these bitter fruits were plucked from the forbidden tree. Heaven shone upon thee, and earth smiled ... But how low is he now laid, who was created for dominion, and made lord of the world! 'The crown is fallen from our head: woe unto us that we have sinned' ... Alas! how are we fallen! how are we plunged into a gulf of misery! ... Let us then lie down in the dust ...'[21]

There is at least one saving grace, however. Now we know what our problem is, and now that we know, we can look for the answer. The problem with humanity is sin, plain and simple. Whenever human beings become convinced of their lost and sinful condition – recognizing that they live for their own glory rather than seeking the glory of God – they cry out, 'What must we do to be saved?'[22]

The rest of this book provides the biblical answer to that question. But the answer is no secret. The message of salvation is that there is nothing you can do to be saved. The only thing that can save you is what God has done through the death and resurrection of Jesus Christ. God saves everyone who trusts in Jesus for salvation from sin, by grace, through faith, and all to the glory of God.

[21] Boston, *Human Nature in its Fourfold State*, p. 24.
[22] Cf. Acts 16:30.

2. What we need to be saved from
Sin and judgment: Genesis 3:7–24

The reason we need to be saved is that we have fallen into sin. From the moment Adam and Eve first tasted the forbidden fruit, we have sought to secure our own glory rather than to serve God for his glory. Human beings are not basically good; we are essentially sinful. Therefore, if we are to be saved at all, we must be saved from sin.

The message of salvation is God's answer to the sinfulness of our sin. If that is true, then sin helps to make sense of salvation. Indeed, the doctrine of sin shows what kind of salvation is required. The great Anglican Bishop J. C. Ryle (1816–1900) wrote:

> The plain truth is that a right knowledge of sin lies at the root of all saving Christianity. Without it such doctrines as justification, conversion, sanctification, are 'words and names' which convey no meaning to the mind. The first thing, therefore, that God does when he makes anyone a new creature in Christ, is to send light into his heart, and show him that he is a guilty sinner.[1]

All have sinned

Even before they could wipe the juice from their chins, Adam and Eve knew that they were guilty sinners. As soon as they ate from the tree of the knowledge of good and evil, *the eyes of both of them were opened, and they realised they were naked* (Gen. 3:7a). It may have been the most anticlimactic moment in human history. Satan had promised Eve that she would be 'like God, knowing good and evil' (3:5). So what did she know? Well, she knew she wasn't wearing any clothes, but that was hardly the intellectual advancement she had been promised!

Adam and Eve had always been naked, of course, but before this they had never felt any shame (see 2:25). They were 'shame-less', in the best sense of the word, for they were unembarrassed by either their bodies or their souls. They had nothing to hide from one another and their

---

[1] Ryle, *Holiness*, p. 1.

consciences were clear in the sight of God. But sin changed all of that. As soon as our first parents sinned, they felt exposed, psychologically as well as physically. They were embarrassed by their fatal act of defiant rebellion. Now they *were* ashamed of their bodies, ill at ease with their nakedness. And they were equally ashamed of their souls, unwilling to be known for who they were.

The shame of our first parents provides a clue to the first consequence of sin. Sin has the psychological effect of wounding the conscience, but the shameful way it makes a person feel exposes an even deeper problem. The first result of sin is that it makes human beings guilty in the sight of God. Sin places us under real divine condemnation. The subjective feeling of shame is produced by the objective condition of moral guilt. Deep down, sinners are always ashamed of their sins, for shame is burned into the human conscience. God later asked Adam, *'Who told you that you were naked?'* (3:11). The answer, of course, was that no-one told him he was naked. No-one needed to! Adam could see that he was naked because his own conscience accused him for the guilt of his sin.

Theologians distinguish between two different kinds of guilt, which come from two different kinds of sin. First there is the guilt of original sin, *Sin* in the upper case. 'Original sin' refers to the guilt every person shares for the sin of Adam. Philip Edgcumbe Hughes explains it well:

> The doctrine of original sin postulates that the first sin of the first man, Adam, which was the occasion of the fall, is in a certain sense the sin of all mankind, and that accordingly human nature is infected by the corruption of that sin and the human race as a whole bears its guilt.[2]

As discussed in chapter 1, God established a binding relationship of promise and threat that required Adam to obey him perfectly. In this covenant Adam represented all his descendants. He was not simply a private person; he was the head of the entire human race. Every human being who ever lived was 'in Adam', not only biologically, but also spiritually. When Adam sinned, therefore, he did not sin for himself alone. The first sin of the first man was universal as well as personal. Adam's fall was our fall, the fall of humanity into sin.

The spiritual relationship between Adam and his children is implicit in the story of creation and the fall, but becomes increasingly explicit throughout the Bible. In the book of Genesis, all of Adam's children turn out to be sinners in their own right. Why was this? Was it bad genes? Bad parenting? A bad environment? To one degree or another, all these factors may have been involved. There is a hereditary

---

[2] Hughes, *The True Image*, p. 125.

connection between Adam and all his descendants, and he did set a poor example for his children. It is crucial to understand, however, that Adam's children were not sinners simply because they sinned. Rather, they sinned because they were sinners. They came into the world *as* sinners, and what made them sinners was the guilt they inherited from their father Adam.

We could deduce the doctrine of original sin from Adam's role as representative of the human race. But the solidarity of our guilt is more fully explained in the book of Romans, where the apostle Paul states that 'sin entered the world through one man, and death through sin, and in this way death came to all men, because all sinned'.[3] We sinned in Adam, or, according to the old Puritan couplet, 'In Adam's fall, we sinned all.' We do not come into the world morally neutral, which was the error of the notorious heretic Pelagius (c. 383–410). On the contrary, we are so implicated in Adam's sin that we are all born in sin and misery, objects of God's wrath by nature.[4]

To use the proper theological term, God 'imputed' the guilt of Adam's sin to every member of the human race.[5] In other words, God holds us morally responsible for what Adam did, reckoning his sin to be our sin, and condemning us for it. This is not unjust. Adam was ideally suited to serve as our representative, and he was given every opportunity to succeed. He faced only one temptation, and he faced it as an unfallen man. The temptation itself was a mere trifle: in the whole orchard of paradise, only a single tree was forbidden. Adam had the further incentive of knowing that his actions would affect his entire race. Given the choice between being represented by such a man, in such a situation, or being considered on the basis of one's own merits, who would not choose to be judged in Adam? Far from being unjust, this arrangement ultimately proved to be a gift of God's grace. This is because the principle of our representation in Adam established the pattern for salvation in Christ: 'If, by the trespass of the one man, death reigned through that one man, how much more will those who receive God's abundant provision of grace and of the gift of righteousness reign in life through the one man, Jesus Christ'.[6] In his perfect life, atoning death and glorious resurrection, Jesus represented his people. It was only by standing in their place that he was able to save them. Thus, in the end, being judged on someone else's merits turns out to be the only hope of salvation.

It is often pointed out that the fall of Adam and Eve is not simply a story about what *happened*, but also a story about what *happens*. The pattern of temptation, sin and shame that we witness in the Garden of

---

[3] Rom. 5:12.   [4] Eph. 2:3.
[5] The doctrine of imputation is ably defended in Murray, *The Imputation of Adam's Sin*.
[6] Rom. 5:17.

Eden is repeated every time a human being disobeys God. This is no accident, and what accounts for it is the doctrine of original sin. There is a relationship between the sin of our first parents and our own sin. Our sin is rooted in their sin. Their corruption has become our corruption. Thus the universal sinfulness of humanity comes from our fallen human nature, which has been transmitted to us by the first sin of the first man.

This brings us to a second kind of sin, and also to a second kind of guilt, the guilt of actual *sins*. Actual sins are sins in the lower case. The term 'actual sin' refers not to the universal contagion of sinful humanity, but to the specific misdeeds human beings commit every day. Because we are sinners, we actually sin. If original sin is the root, actual sins are the fruit. Our sinful nature produces individual acts of sin. Even if we never committed any actual sins, we would still be guilty by virtue of the original sin we inherit from Adam. In the words of one scholar, our 'whole being is now marred by a deep-rooted perversity'.[7] But the fact is, of course, that we add to our guilt by committing innumerable sins of our own.

The proper theological term to describe the sinfulness of humanity is *total depravity*. This does not mean that we are as sinful as we can possibly be. By the grace of God, there is still a great deal of good in us, which makes our lost condition all the more tragic. As the French philosopher Blaise Pascal (1623–62) observed somewhere in his writings, 'the greatness of man is evident even in his wretchedness'. God's image is not broken entirely, said Augustine, but our 'right-eousness and true holiness were lost by sinning, through which that image became defaced and tarnished'.[8] Like a face in a carnival mirror, God's reflection in human beings is distorted and disfigured. Total depravity means that every part of every human person is tainted by sin. Sin affects our minds, so that we are unable to think God's thoughts after him. It affects our hearts, so that we set our affections on unholy desires. It affects our feelings, so that we are in emotional turmoil. It affects our wills, so that we will not choose the good. Our whole nature is corrupted by sin. In the way we think, feel and act, we are sinners through and through. As a result of the depravity of our nature, we commit a great many actual sins, all of which add up to a tremendous load of guilt. Our actual sins compound the debt we owe to God for our original sin in Adam, and thus we are doubly guilty in the sight of God.

One of the best indications of our guilt is our shame. We are ashamed of our bodies and our souls, which ought to remind us that the problem with the world is also the problem with us: we are guilty

[7] Bloesch, *Essentials of Evangelical Theology*, vol. 1, p. 89.
[8] Augustine, quoted in Hughes, *The True Image*, p. 65.

sinners. If we are to be saved, therefore, something must be done about our guilty shame. Adam and Eve sensed this immediately. As soon as they realized they were naked, *they sewed fig leaves together and made coverings for themselves* (3:7b). This temporary fix was the world's first cover-up! It was also the world's first attempt at salvation by works. Like all cover-ups – and all attempts to achieve salvation by human effort – it was doomed to fail. Summer foliage is hardly suitable to cover our bodies, let alone the sin of our souls.

We cannot dress up for God, spiritually speaking, but God does have a plan for covering our guilt with his grace. There is more than a hint of what this plan will involve already in Genesis 3. After God finished pronouncing various curses for sin, he *made garments of skin for Adam and his wife and clothed them* (3:21). Clothing our first parents was a way of showing that things could never be the same, that fallen human beings cannot go back to naked innocence. But the clothes were also a sign of God's grace. They showed that God can do something for us that we cannot do for ourselves, and that is to cover up our guilt and shame.

It is not insignificant that an animal had to die as a result of the first sin. Covering the shame of Adam and Eve required a blood sacrifice, which is part of the message of salvation. Sin – both original and actual – brings guilt that must be paid for through a propitiation, a sacrifice of atonement. Only then can we stand righteous before God; in other words, only then can we be justified. Once it has removed our guilt, salvation proceeds to make us righteous, even glorious in God's sight. Thus the message of salvation is about such doctrines as propitiation, justification, sanctification and glorification.

Alienated from God

The first result of sin is guilt – not merely the subjective feeling of shame, but also the objective condition of real moral blameworthiness. The second result is alienation from God:

Then the man and his wife heard the sound of the LORD God as he was walking in the garden in the cool of the day, and they hid from the LORD God among the trees of the garden. But the LORD God called to the man, 'Where are you?'

He answered, 'I heard you in the garden, and I was afraid because I was naked; so I hid' (3:8–10).

These verses afford a glimpse of the wonderful intimacy Adam and Eve enjoyed with God before they sinned. Apparently, it was God's usual custom (perhaps in the form of the pre-incarnate Christ) to walk through the garden during the cool hours of the day. Since God was their close friend, Adam and Eve undoubtedly ran to meet him, eager to converse with him about the day's events. Imagine what it must have been like to walk and talk with God, and thus to enjoy uninhibited communion with the Creator!

It was different once Adam and Eve had sinned, however, for sin demands separation from God. Sinners know instinctively that God is too holy to look upon their sin. This explains why our first parents waited miserably for his approach, dreading the sound of his footfall in Eden. When they heard him coming, they ran into the woods to hide. Literally, they hid from his 'face'.

Though they could run, they could not hide, for no-one can escape God. He is omniscient; he knows all things. He is omnipresent; he sees all things. Therefore, when God asked the man where he was, it was not for his own information. God already knew exactly where our parents were, and why. His question was more like the summons to a judicial proceeding. He was calling Adam and Eve to account, inviting them to approach the bench where he would examine the evidence against them and render his verdict.

God's question (*'Where are you?'*) was designed to expose the un-happy consequence of sin. It forced Adam to admit his alienation: *'I heard you in the garden, and I was afraid because I was naked; so I hid'* (3:10). Here was another new emotion. Sin had already produced shame, the shame that comes from guilt. Now it produced fear, the fear of entering God's presence. This fear was the proof of Adam's sin. God said, *'Who told you that you were naked? Have you eaten from the tree from which I commanded you not to eat?'* (3:11). God knew that only one thing could account for Adam's fear, and that was disobedience. If Adam was ashamed and afraid it was because he had eaten from the unlawful tree. His fear and shame were symptomatic of the disease of guilty sin.

Adam's first instinct was to blame God for all his troubles, and this, too, was a sign of his alienation. Did Adam eat the forbidden fruit? Well, sure, but it was really God's fault: *'The woman you put here with me – she gave me some fruit from the tree, and I ate it'* (3:12). Thus the man excused himself and accused God for his own evil, as human beings have done ever since.

Sin causes alienation from God. Human beings were created to know God and to live with him in a personal relationship of loving trust. As he discovered, to his utter dismay, Adam had forfeited this glorious privilege. We ourselves are sensible that transgression brings alienation every time we sin. Our fellowship with God is hindered, and so we keep our distance, afraid to meet him face to face. Since we are sinners by nature, this is our natural condition. As the Bible reminds us, 'You were alienated from God and were enemies in your minds because of your evil behaviour.'[9] If we are to be saved, therefore, we must be

---

[9] Col. 1:21.

reconciled to God. The breach in our friendship must be repaired. Our communion must be restored. Therefore, the message of salvation must be a message of reconciliation.

Estranged from humanity

The alienation sin brings is horizontal as well as vertical. We are alienated, not only from God, but also from one another, which is a third consequence of sin. Having rebelled against God, we now find ourselves estranged from one another.

The breach between Adam and Eve became obvious the moment they sinned. They felt the need to protect themselves, not only from the gaze of God, but also from the unbearable scrutiny of other human beings. Not long afterwards, Adam launched his first assault on his estranged wife. When God asked if he had eaten from the tree of the knowledge of good and evil, he said, *'The woman you put here with me* – she *gave me some fruit from the tree, and I ate it'* (3:12). How quickly Adam mastered the art of self-defence! What he said was true, strictly speaking, but it was hardly chivalrous. His confession (*and I ate it*) came almost as an afterthought. His real concern was to shift the blame to Eve. This is the way of fallen human beings. We excuse our sin by calling attention to extenuating circumstances. It is always someone else's fault.

Even worse, we seek to dominate one another. This is the meaning of God's subsequent curse against Eve: *'Your desire will be for your husband, and he will rule over you'* (Gen. 3:16b). This verse does not mean, as is sometimes suggested, that the man's spiritual authority in the home and in the church is a result of the fall. Nor does it have anything to do with sex, at least not directly. Rather, it is a prophecy about the battle of the sexes and the struggle for power in all human relationships. The Hebrew word for 'desire' (*tᵉšûqâ*) next appears in Genesis 4:7, where it describes sin's desire to gain mastery over Cain. In much the same way, the woman desires mastery over the man and will manipulate him to get it.

Meanwhile the man rules over the woman, not as a servant leader, but as a harsh taskmaster. The Hebrew word for 'rule' (*māšal*) is a word for military attack, even abuse. The man seeks to take control of the woman; if he has to, he will use force to get it. This is what it means for us to be estranged from one another. Not only are we isolated from one another, but we seek to manipulate and dominate one another emotionally, spiritually and sometimes even physically.

One can only imagine the bitter arguments Adam and Eve must have had during their long, sad years after Eden. 'If only you had never eaten that forbidden fruit!' Eve would say. 'Well, you ate it first!' Adam would retort. In *Paradise Lost*, Milton describes their endless recriminations: 'Thus they in mutual accusation spent / The fruitless hours, but neither self condemning; / And of their vain contest appeared no end.'[10]

Milton was right – there is no end to human conflict. Always sinned against but never sinning, everyone a victim but never a villain, there is discord and disharmony at every level of human relationships. There is estrangement in the home. Wives criticize their husbands and husbands respond in anger. Children disobey their parents, while parents in turn exasperate their children. The elderly are killed off in the name of mercy, while the unborn never see the light of day.

There is estrangement in society, where men and women wage an endless battle of the sexes, usually to the disadvantage of women. There is estrangement in the workplace, where oppression is so woven into the fabric of the global economy that the poor are bound by the cords of injustice. Bosses abuse their power and workers rise up in rebellion. There is estrangement in the church, where each separate group claims to have God on its side. There is estrangement around the globe, often in the form of armed conflict. Nation rises against nation; dictators oppress their own people; terrorists commit random acts of violence; and superpowers provide the weapons that fuel the fires of war.

Little wonder that we ourselves should be called 'man's most intractable problem'.[11] If we are to be saved, we must be saved from ourselves and from all the unspeakable things we do to one another. Therefore, the message of salvation must tell us something more than simply how to get rid of our guilt and be reconciled to God. It must also show us how to love one another, living together in harmony and community – not as aliens and strangers, but as brothers and sisters.

Embattled by the evil one

In many ways, we are our own worst enemies. What we need is for God to save us from ourselves. But we also need to be delivered from an even stronger enemy, and that is the devil. Alienated from God and estranged from one another, we are also embattled by the evil one.

It was the devil who first brought evil into the world, and it was the devil who was first judged for it. When God heard how the serpent had deceived the woman, he said,

'Because you have done this,

> *'Cursed are you above all the livestock*
> *and all the wild animals!*

[10] John Milton, *Paradise Lost* (New York: Holt, Rinehart and Winston, 1951), Book IX, lines 1187–1189.
[11] Hughes, *The True Image*, p. 142.

You will crawl on your belly
and you will eat dust
all the days of your life.
And I will put enmity
between you and the woman,
and between your offspring and hers;
he will crush your head,
and you will strike his heel' (3:14–15).

Notice that God does not dialogue with the devil; he simply passes sentence, condemning Satan for corrupting his creation. This is because God has no plan for the serpent's salvation. His plan is to destroy the devil, and to save his people by doing so. In order to accomplish this purpose, God established a perpetual enmity between the devil and the woman.

For his part, the devil already hated humanity with bitter envy. His plan was to drag human beings into sin and despair, and finally down into the pit of hell. This is still his plan, and to carry it out, Satan uses every means at his disposal. On occasion, he dominates human beings through demonic possession, but that is only the most obvious manifestation of the devil's power. He torments individuals chiefly by tempting them to sin and persuading them that they are powerless to resist his schemes. There are also many ways that Satan and the other fallen angels seek to gain control of the structures of society. Hence the Bible calls them the 'rulers', the 'authorities', the 'powers of this dark world' and the 'spiritual forces of evil in the heavenly realms'.[12] Evil is more than 'man's inhumanity to man'; it is also the result of Satan's devilry against humanity. Behind the great evils of the world – the unjust wars, the unholy regimes, the unspeakable atrocities, the evil empires – there stands an evil one who hates God with unrestrained malevolence.

It is because Satan hates God that human beings must hate Satan. This was God's curse – not that the serpent would hate the woman, for he already hated her – but that the serpent would be hated by the woman. Their enmity would be mutual. Instead of trusting Satan's judgment, and even worshipping him, the woman and her offspring would oppose Satan at every turn.

God promised that, in the end, the woman's offspring would destroy Satan altogether. *'He will crush your head, and you will strike his heel'* (Gen. 3:15b). This is the *protoevangelium*, the first promise of the gospel. It is the very message of salvation. The word 'offspring', or 'seed', is both singular and plural (verse 15a). As a plural, it means that Eve's descendants, the entire human race, will be at war with Satan. As

[12] Eph. 6:12.

a singular, it means that one individual, a single champion (namely, Jesus Christ), will destroy the serpent by crushing his head. This victory will come at great cost, for Satan will strike the Saviour's heel, bruising him with an apparently mortal blow. All of this refers, of course, to the cross where Christ was crucified. Christ was wounded on the cross, but by his death he destroyed the devil.[13]

Sin has brought us under Satan's power, but the message of salvation means death to the devil. One day that old serpent will be totally vanquished. This means that the Bible contains the only really satisfying answer to the problem of evil. Although God has allowed evil to occur, he is still utterly opposed to it and will certainly defeat it in the end. This is part of what it means to be saved, that God will deliver us from the evil one, redeeming us from his power. The message of salvation is a message of redemption.

Paradise lost

Sin has many miserable consequences. It brings shame, guilt, alienation and estrangement. All this, and we have yet to explore the actual penalty for sin, which God pronounced in his curse:

To the woman he said,

> *'I will greatly increase your pains in childbearing;*
> *with pain you will give birth to children.*
> *Your desire will be for your husband,*
> *and he will rule over you.'*

To Adam he said, 'Because you listened to your wife and ate from the tree about which I commanded you, "You must not eat of it,"

> *'Cursed is the ground because of you;*
> *through painful toil you will eat of it*
> *all the days of your life.*
> *It will produce thorns and thistles for you,*
> *and you will eat the plants of the field.*
> *By the sweat of your brow*
> *you will eat your food'* (3:16–19a).

God had commanded the man and the woman to be fruitful, to fill the earth and to subdue it. That creation mandate remained in force. Eve would still give birth; indeed, in the very next verse we read that *Adam named his wife Eve, because she would become the mother of all the living* (3:20). At the same time, Adam would continue to work the ground and to take care of it. Those callings have never been reversed –

---

[13] See Heb. 2:14.

but they have been cursed. What was a blessing remains a blessing, but it also has become a burden.

The woman is cursed in her roles as wife and mother. In part, her curse refers to the physical pains of childbirth, concerning which the Bible means exactly what it says. But the curse refers to much more besides. It refers to childbearing in general, and thus to all the frustrations of womanhood, including not getting married, not having children, and all the heartaches that come with raising and sometimes losing children.

Like the woman, the man is cursed in his calling. He still has to subdue the earth, but now his work becomes toilsome. The ground will yield its fruit only at the cost of sweaty labour, for the creation itself is frustrated by sin.[14] Now, instead of tending a garden, the man has to turn the wilderness into a garden! Having pronounced his curses, God banished Adam from Eden:

And the LORD God said, 'The man has now become like one of us, knowing good and evil. He must not be allowed to reach out his hand and take also from the tree of life and eat, and live for ever.' So the LORD God banished him from the Garden of Eden to work the ground from which he had been taken. After he drove the man out, he placed on the east side of the Garden of Eden cherubim and a flaming sword flashing back and forth to guard the way to the tree of life (3:22–24).

The curse of thorn and thistle is not only for farmers, it is for everyone who lives east of Eden. We all experience the drudgery and stress that come with working on the job. Like the philosopher, we sigh, 'What does a man get for all the toil and anxious striving with which he labours?' (Eccles. 2:22).

The sufferings of Adam and Eve come to poignant expression in Masaccio's famous fresco, 'Expulsion from Paradise'. In the painting, as Adam and Eve are driven away from Eden by a sword-bearing angel, they are engulfed in absolute anguish. Adam is bowed low, covering his face in shame, while Eve's mouth is open in a scream of unbridled woe. Milton's portrait in *Paradise Lost* is equally melancholy:

> They looking back, all th' Eastern side beheld
> Of Paradise, so late their happy seat,
> Wav'd over by that flaming Brand, the Gate
> With dreadful Face throng'd and fiery Arms:
> Some natural tears they drop'd, but wip'd them soon;
> The World was all before them, where to choose
> Their place of rest, and Providence their guide:

---

[14] See Rom. 8:20.

41

> They hand in hand with wand'ring steps and slow,
> Through *Eden* took their solitary way.[15]

This is the reason we are alone in the world. Even at home we are homeless, for we are outcasts from Eden. Having spoiled the garden, we can never go back to our ancestral home. But this is more than a punishment; it is also a sign of God's grace. The fiery angels prevented our first parents from returning to Eden and there eating the tree of life, which presumably would have enabled them to live for ever in a lost and depraved condition. God has a better plan for us. It is the plan of salvation, which takes us not merely back to paradise, but home to glory.

The wages of sin

For the man and the woman, both at home and at work, sin leads to suffering. Their curse encompasses all the frustrations of life. It explains the misery and meaninglessness of our existence. But there is still more. There is also mortality, for the wages of sin, finally, is death.

Death was the penalty God threatened from the beginning: 'When you eat of it you will surely die' (Gen. 2:17). There was something suicidal, therefore, about Adam's sin. What God pronouced against him was the just curse of the covenant:

> *'By the sweat of your brow*
> *you will eat your food*
> *until you return to the ground,*
> *since from it you were taken;*
> *for dust you are*
> *and to dust you will return'* (3:19).

Death comes from disobedience. The dissolution of body and soul is God's punishment for the sin of the first man. Spiritually speaking, Adam was a dead man the moment he ate the forbidden fruit; there was no spiritual life left in him. Adam also began to die physically when he ate from the tree. He became a mortal man, with a body subject to decay and finally death.

We, too, are mortals. Having sinned in Adam, we also die in Adam.[16] We are dead spiritually, dead in our trespasses and sins.[17] One day soon we will die physically. Our inescapable mortality is the irrefutable demonstration that we are sinners who seek our own ungodly glory. Nothing is more ungodlike than death, which strips away every pretension to deity. The futility of our condition is this: that we will end

[15] Milton, *Paradise Lost*, Book XII, lines 641–649.
[16] 1 Cor. 15:21–22.   [17] Eph. 2:1.

up right back where we started. Rather than subduing the earth, we will be subdued by it, for dust we are, and to the dust we will return.

There is another kind of death as well, what the Bible calls 'the second death',[18] or simply hell. God's wrath against sin is absolute. He is utterly opposed to sin and resolutely determined to punish it. Our sins deserve the wrath and curse of God, not only in this life, but also in the life to come. Those who 'die in their sins', as Jesus put it,[19] suffer the torment of eternal separation from God. They will be consigned to perdition, placing themselves beyond the embrace of God's infinite love. Those who stubbornly refuse to receive the message of salvation in Christ will suffer infinite and irreparable loss.

These days people are more likely to believe in heaven than in hell. But to deny the reality of hell is to deny the truth and the justice of God. It is also to misunderstand the message of salvation, for if we are to be saved at all, we must be saved from sin's final, fatal consequence: the second death. The message of salvation, then, must be about the resurrection and the life – the resurrection of the body and the life everlasting.

The promise of salvation

Even this brief survey is enough to confirm that sin is the greatest of all evils. It is the greatest evil because all other evils come from it: guilt, alienation, estrangement, spiritual warfare, suffering, and death. The *Westminster Shorter Catechism* provides this apt summary of the sinfulness of our sin: 'All mankind by their fall lost communion with God, are under his wrath and curse, and so made liable to all the miseries of this life, to death itself, and to the pains of hell for ever' (A. 19).

Many great minds have wondered what is wrong with humanity. The psychologist Erich Fromm, wrestling with his sense of futility over the human condition, wrote, 'While we have created wonderful things we have failed to make ourselves beings for whom this tremendous effort would seem worthwhile ... Ours is a life not of brotherliness, happiness, contentment but of spiritual chaos and bewilderment close to a state of madness.'[20] The insanity of humanity is the inevitable result of sin, with all its miserable consequences. The problem with man, explained Philip Hughes, is that

> There is conflict and disintegration at the very core of his being. He has robbed himself of harmony with his Creator, harmony within himself, and harmony with his fellow human beings. This is the

[18] Rev. 20:14; 21:8.   [19] John 8:24.
[20] Erich Fromm, *Man for Himself: An Inquiry into the Psychology of Ethics* (1947), quoted in Hughes, *The True Image*, p. 136.

source and explanation of all that is wrong with man and the world he inhabits. It is the sickness unto death from which man in his fallenness inescapably suffers.[21]

The best explanation for the tragic condition of our sickness unto death is the biblical doctrine of sin. The world is the way it is, and we are the way we are, because we are sinners.

The sinfulness of our sin shows that salvation is no small matter. We need to be rescued from the guilt of sin in the past, the power of sin in the present, and the punishment of sin in the future. It will take what the Bible calls 'a great salvation'[22] to accomplish all this, and in doing so to solve all the problems sin has brought into the world. It will take a salvation that atones for guilt (propitiation), declaring sinners righteous in the sight of God (justification). It will take a salvation that ends our alienation by restoring friendship with God (reconciliation) and by making us brothers and sisters instead of strangers (adoption). It will take a salvation that destroys the devil, and with him, all evil (redemption). It will take, finally, a salvation that gives us life after death – not only spiritually (which is regeneration), but also physically (resurrection); not only now (sanctification), but for all eternity (glorification).

If that is what it takes to save human beings from the wages of sin, one wonders why there is so little interest in the biblical message of salvation in Christ. Jesus is usually considered nice enough in his own way, but generally irrelevant for the problems of the postmodern world. Most secular people admire Jesus as a good teacher. Muslims call him a prophet. Mormons consider him a son of God. Hindus even recognize his divinity, after a fashion. But what all these opinions about Jesus share is an unwillingness to give him the credit he really deserves. Sadly, many people think that Jesus offers a salvation that no-one really needs.

If the message of salvation in Jesus Christ is considered irrelevant, it must be because people do not understand the extent of the problem he came to solve. A correspondent once asked the apologist Dorothy L. Sayers (1893–1957) to answer two great questions about human existence: 'Why does everything we do go wrong?' and 'What is the meaning of all this suffering?' When Sayers wrote back to her friend, she was able to answer the two questions in only three words: 'The Christian answer to the first is, "Sin", and to the second, "Christ crucified".'[23] The reason everything we do goes wrong is that we are sinners. The meaning of all our suffering, and the only hope for our salvation, is that Christ died on the cross for our sins.

---

[21] Ibid.   [22] Heb. 2:3.

[23] Quoted in Janice Brown, *The Seven Deadly Sins in the Work of Dorothy L. Sayers* (Kent, OH: Kent State University Press, 1998), p. 1.

The message of salvation offers hope that 'God did not appoint us to suffer wrath but to receive salvation through our Lord Jesus Christ'.[24] It promises further that Jesus 'is able to save completely those who come to God through him'.[25] As the Authorized Version expresses it, he is able 'to save them to the uttermost'. This is a way of saying that Jesus will do whatever it takes to save us. He will atone for our guilt and cover all our shame. He will reconcile us to God and restore harmony to human relationships. He will deliver us from the evil one. He will bring an end to all our suffering and grant us the free gift of eternal life. Jesus is the perfect solution to the problem of sin, with all its consequences. Indeed, as we are about to discover, he is the only solution.

[24] 1 Thess. 5:9.   [25] Heb. 7:25a.

3. Why we cannot save ourselves
Inability: Isaiah 59:1–21

'It's just a sinful world, that's all.' A friend wrote these words at the end of a week in which his wife had been stalked by a stranger and a close friend had died after a long, painful illness. 'It's just a sinful world, that's all.' I knew what my friend meant, for during the same week a woman was raped a block from my house, a father in my church walked out on his family, and one of my children was diagnosed with a chronic disease.

It's just a sinful world, that's all. Something has gone badly wrong with the human race. We live in a world of unprecedented techno-logical advance, and of catastrophic moral failure. It is a world of divorce, rape and murder, where people suffer and then they die. On top of everything else, there is our own spiritual unrest. Somewhere deep down, we know that we are not what we ought to be; indeed, that we are not really happy at all.

At the root of all our problems lies the sinfulness of sin. Rather than seeking God's glory, we live for our own glory. Sin is what makes us ashamed, for it renders us guilty in God's sight. Sin is what makes us afraid, for it alienates us from our Creator. Sin is what makes us angry, for it estranges us from one another. Sin is what makes us anxious, for it leads to suffering and finally death. It's just a sinful world, that's all.

Sin and all its consequences

Since we are sinners living in a sinful world, what we need is salvation. So the question becomes: What must we do to be saved from sin, with all its miserable consequences?

The people of Israel found themselves asking this same question in the days of the prophet Isaiah, who said, 'We look for ... salvation, but it is far off from us' (Is. 59:11b, AV). Isaiah was writing some time after the year 700 BC. The prophet could see that his nation was in a state of rapid moral and spiritual decline. Inspired by God's Spirit, he prophesied that God would punish his people for their sins by sending them into exile. Eventually that prophecy came true, for in the first two decades of the sixth century BC, the Israelites were carried off to Babylon.

Isaiah's prophecy looked beyond judgment, however, to salvation. Towards the end of his ministry, Isaiah comforted God's people with the news that they would return from exile and be restored to their land. He promised a king to rule them (40:1–11), a deliverer to rescue them (42:1–4), and a servant to atone for their sins (53:1–12). But as late as chapter 59, God's people were still wondering when – or even if – they would ever be saved. 'We look for ... salvation,' they complained, 'but it is far off from us' (59:11b, AV).

Maybe the problem – so some of them thought – is that God is impotent, that his arm is too short to reach down and save us. Or perhaps God is indifferent, not caring whether we are saved or not. And to this day, these are two of the main reasons many people refuse to glorify God. As they consider all the sin and suffering in the world, they conclude that God is either unable, or unwilling, to do anything about it. Either way – whether he can't do anything about evil, or won't – it is all God's fault. When in doubt, God is to blame.

As Isaiah explained the message of salvation, he began by stating that the problem is not with God at all. The problem is with us:

> Surely the arm of the LORD is not too short to save,
>   nor his ear too dull to hear.
> But your iniquities have separated
>   you from your God;
> your sins have hidden his face from you,
>   so that he will not hear (59:1–2).

God is not impotent: his arm is long enough and strong enough to save. God is not indifferent: his ear is attentive to our cry. The problem is neither divine impotence nor divine indifference, but human iniquity: *Your sins have hidden his face from you, so that he will not hear* (59:2b). Isaiah thus confirms the diagnosis of the human condition we reached in the first two chapters of this book: it is because we are such great sinners that we need such a great salvation.

Isaiah proceeded to describe the misery of Israel's depravity by mentioning the same consequences of sin that we discovered in Genesis 3. First there is guilt: *For your hands are stained with blood, your fingers with guilt* (59:3a). There is blood on our hands! God holds us morally accountable for the things we have done (our sins of commission), as well as for the things we have left undone (our sins of omission). Every sin places a stain on our moral record, a stain it takes a blood sacrifice to remove.

Sadly, our record is covered with such stains. Isaiah understood that we sin every which way we can, using every part of our bodies to transgress God's holy law:

47

> *Your lips have spoken lies,*
> *and your tongue mutters wicked things ...*
> *Their deeds are evil deeds,*
> *and acts of violence are in their hands.*
> *Their feet rush into sin;*
> *they are swift to shed innocent blood.*
> *Their thoughts are evil thoughts;*
> *ruin and destruction mark their ways* (59:3b, 6b–7).

Lips, tongue, hands, feet – there is not one single part of us that is not sinful. This is Isaiah's way of saying that we are totally depraved. Even our minds are depraved, for we think evil thoughts.

As Isaiah considered the totality of human depravity, he concluded that *our sins testify against us* (59:12a). The apostle Paul expanded on this theme in Romans 3:

> There is no-one righteous, not even one ...
> All have turned away,
> they have together become worthless;
> there is no-one who does good,
> not even one.[1]

Then the apostle quoted these verses from Isaiah 59:

> Their feet are swift to shed blood;
> ruin and misery mark their ways,
> and the way of peace they do not know.[2]

We are all sinful, all the way through, and our sin makes us guilty in the sight of God.

Secondly, sin alienates us from God, declared Isaiah. It makes us want to hide from his holiness. It cuts off our communication with him, as the people of Israel discovered. They were praying for God to save them, but still they were not saved. At times it seemed as if God was not even listening. The wall between the holy God and his unholy people was like the separation between heaven and earth: *But your iniquities have separated you from your God* (59:2a). The only other place in the Old Testament where the Hebrew word for separation (*bā̱dal*) appears is in Genesis 1:6, where it describes the permanent separation between the earth and the sky, between the waters beneath and the waters above. Sin introduces the same kind of barrier into our relationship with God, separating heaven from earth.

Isaiah uses several other images to describe our alienation from God.

---

[1] Rom. 3:10b, 12.   [2] Rom. 3:15–17; cf. Is. 59:7–8.

It is like God hiding his 'face' – his seeing, hearing, knowing, personal presence: *Your sins have hidden his face from you, so that he will not hear* (59:2b). To describe it another way, by committing so many actual sins, the people had turned their backs on God:

> *Our offences are ever with us,*
> *and we acknowledge our iniquities:*
> *rebellion and treachery against the LORD,*
> *turning our backs on our God,*
> *fomenting oppression and revolt,*
> *uttering lies our hearts have conceived* (59:12b–13).

Whether God hides his face or we turn our backs, the result is the same: we are alienated from God by our many sins.

We are also estranged from one another, which is a third consequence of sin. Isaiah described a society torn apart by violence, injustice and deception. The people were quick to do one another harm, even to commit murder: *Their feet rush into sin; they are swift to shed innocent blood* (59:7a; cf. 59:3a). There was crime, but there was no justice, for the legal system was corrupt: *No-one calls for justice; no-one pleads his case with integrity. They rely on empty arguments and speak lies* (59:4a). Rather than taking a public stand for righteousness, the people spent their time conspiring to commit sin:

> *they conceive trouble and give birth to evil.*
> *They hatch the eggs of vipers*
> *and spin a spider's web.*
> *Whoever eats their eggs will die,*
> *and when one is broken, an adder is hatched* (59:4b–5).

The reason Isaiah compared the people to venomous serpents and poisonous spiders is that the plans they hatched were so treacherous. This was the end result of their deadly schemes:

> *justice is driven back,*
> *and righteousness stands at a distance;*
> *truth has stumbled in the streets,*
> *honesty cannot enter.*
> *Truth is nowhere to be found,*
> *and whoever shuns evil becomes a prey* (59:14–15).

If the culture Isaiah describes sounds familiar, it is because we also live in violent, unjust and deceptive times.

A fourth consequence of sin – especially all the sins we commit against one another – is suffering. As Isaiah considered the lost and sorry condition of his people, he took up a lament:

> *So justice is far from us,*
> *and righteousness does not reach us.*
> *We look for light, but all is darkness;*
> *for brightness, but we walk in deep shadows.*
> *Like the blind we grope along the wall,*
> *feeling our way like men without eyes.*
> *At midday we stumble as if it were twilight;*
> *among the strong, we are like the dead.*
> *We all growl like bears;*
> *we moan mournfully like doves.*
> *We look for justice, but find none;*
> *for deliverance, but it is far away* (59:9–11).

Suffering has a way of reducing human beings to inarticulate groaning. Whether we growl like bears in our frustration or mourn like doves in our distress, what we are really doing is crying out for salvation.

Though we often try to avoid it, we can never quite forget that all our sufferings will end in death. *We are like the dead*, wrote Isaiah (59:10). And not simply *like* the dead, for as sin brings guilt, alienation, estrangement and suffering, so it leads finally to death. This was Israel's condition in Isaiah's times, as it was Adam and Eve's condition long before, and as it is our condition to this day. Behind it all stands the devil who brought sin into the world, with all its evil consequences.

No-one to save

As God looked at the human race in its fallen condition, what did he think about it all? He was displeased, to say the least. God is displeased whenever we fail to give him the glory he deserves, and thus suffer the ill effects of glorying in ourselves. But what really appalled God was not so much his people's sin as the fact that there was no-one to save them from their sins:

> *The LORD looked and was displeased*
> *that there was no justice.*
> *He saw that there was no-one,*
> *he was appalled that there was*
> *no-one to intervene* (59:15b–16a).

There was no-one to intervene on Israel's behalf, no-one to intercede for her salvation. There was no-one to serve as a mediator, bridging the gap between the holy God and his unholy people. And God was appalled. He had promised salvation, but there was no-one to save. Not that God was surprised by this, of course, because he knows all things. But he was dismayed by it. He has such an intense hatred of sin and such a burning compassion for his people that he is unhappy to see us remain unsaved.

What God saw was that his people were in no condition to save themselves. In the obvious presence of sin, he noted the conspicuous absence of a Saviour. This was true biblically. Though Israel had often been delivered, she had never had a Saviour from sin. None of the mighty men who delivered God's people from danger could save them from sin because they were all sinners themselves. Noah got drunk and naked in his tents.[3] Abraham tried to manufacture the son of promise through a rented bride.[4] Moses struck the rock in proud anger.[5] David was a liar and a murderer, not to mention an adulterer.[6] Elijah got so discouraged that he dropped out of the ministry for a time.[7] Even Isaiah himself, prophet though he was, was a foul-mouthed sinner (6:5).

No mere human being can save humanity from sin. Not only is this true biblically, but it is also true historically. Down through the many centuries, the human race has always tried to improve its condition. In many ways we have succeeded. Agriculturally, we have expanded our capacity to grow food from the earth; artistically, we have created masterpieces of magnificent beauty; medically, we have increased the span of human life; scientifically, we have made great advances in our knowledge of the universe. Morally? Morally, we are as bankrupt as ever. Every human attempt to build utopia has ended in hatred, misery and death.

Unable and unwilling

The one problem we cannot solve for ourselves is sin. Not only is this true biblically and historically, but it is also true logically, and therefore universally. The one who is guilty cannot remove his own guilt. The one who is alienated and estranged cannot reconcile himself to God or to his neighbour. The one who is embattled cannot defeat the devil. The one who suffers cannot ease his pain. And even if we could remove all the other consequences of sin, we cannot make ourselves immortal. Therefore, asking a sinner to save himself is like asking a man to pull himself out of a deep pit, or a prisoner to unlock his own prison cell. Indeed, the Bible suggests it is like asking a corpse to climb out of his own coffin.[8] But as the psalmist was compelled to ask, 'What man can live and not see death, or save himself from the power of the grave?'[9] Hence the apparent futility of our situation.

If it is true that human beings cannot save themselves, it is not for

[3] Gen. 9:20–28. [4] Gen. 16. [5] Num. 20:1–13. [6] 2 Sam. 11 – 12.
[7] 1 Kgs. 19:1–5. [8] See Eph. 2:1. [9] Ps. 89:48.

lack of trying. Some people try to save themselves through religion, by participating in sacred rituals. Isaiah addressed this earlier, in chapter 58, where he told the Israelites not to expect God to rescue them simply because they were fasting. Many people take the same approach today, expecting God to save them because they go to church and receive the sacrament. Others try to save themselves through good works, expecting to merit eternal life by loving their families and giving to charity.

Although these things are good in themselves, they are not good enough for God. As Isaiah will write only a few chapters later, 'all our righteous acts are like filthy rags' (64:6a). The reason our righteous acts cannot save is that none of them answers the real problem of sin. Remember, sin brings guilt, both for original sin and for actual sins, and the only thing that takes guilt away is a perfect blood sacrifice. Therefore, no matter how many good things a person does, they can never make up for even one little sin. If salvation depended on our own merits, then we would never be saved, because we have no merit of our own.

Let's realize, too, that apart from the work of God's Spirit, sinners do not even *want* to be saved. This is another one of the doleful effects of the sinful nature. Earlier we mentioned that there is a connection between Isaiah 59 and Romans 3, where the apostle quotes these verses from the Psalms:

> There is no-one righteous, not even one;
> there is no-one who understands,
> no-one who seeks God.[10]

These verses confirm what we have been saying about the universal depravity of humanity: not one of us is righteous. We all need to be saved because we are all sinners. These verses also explain why we cannot save ourselves. Because we are totally depraved, there is not one part of us that wants to live for God: 'There is no-one who understands'.[11] In other words, sin corrupts the mind, and until God's Spirit changes our minds, we cannot truly understand the message of salvation, let alone accept it. As the Scripture goes on to say, 'The sinful mind is hostile to God. It does not submit to God's law, nor can it do so.'[12]

Isaiah compared our spiritual condition to a blind man trying to feel his way around a building.

> *Like the blind we grope along the wall,*
> *feeling our way like men without eyes.*

---

[10] Rom. 3:10–11; cf. Ps. 14:1–3.   [11] Rom. 3:11a.
[12] Rom. 8:7; cf. 1 Cor. 2:14.

At midday we stumble as if it were twilight;
among the strong, we are like the dead (59:10).

The analogy of spiritual blindness is a good one because the problem a blind person faces is not the absence of light, but the inability to perceive it. In the same way, the fact that we cannot save ourselves is not God's fault, but our own. Our inability is our responsibility, for in his perfect Word God has given us all the light we need to find our way to him. But we are sinners, and therefore our minds are blinded to the pure light of spiritual truth. 'The god of this age has blinded the minds of unbelievers, so that they cannot see the light of the gospel of the glory of Christ'.[13] Our inability comes from our depravity.

Even worse than blindness, however, is the spiritual condition Isaiah describes with the phrase *like men without eyes* (59:10). Alec Motyer comments: 'Blindness is a misfortune which might be corrected, but to have no eyes is, humanly speaking, an irreversible condition, which can only be mended by an act of new creation.'[14] Happily, as we shall discover, a new creation is precisely what God offers through the message of salvation.

Some people are willing to admit their spiritual blindness. Yet even though they acknowledge that they cannot save themselves, they still want to make some small contribution to their salvation. So they say, 'At least I can do this: at least I can choose to follow God.' They believe that salvation depends on their own free choice, as if somehow they can cooperate in their own salvation.

The problem with this view is that human beings are not morally neutral. We come into this world as sinners, and sin not only blinds the mind, but it also binds the will. As Paul put it, in quoting the psalmist, 'No-one seeks God.'[15] Theologians call this condition 'the bondage of the will'.[16] It does not mean that we are unable to make choices. In fact, the Bible sometimes invites us to choose for God: 'Choose for yourselves this day whom you will serve';[17] 'Whoever wishes, let him take the free gift of the water of life.'[18] What the bondage of the will does mean, however, is that our choices are constrained by sin. We are sinners by nature, and thus our natural disposition is to choose sin, in one form or another. Our liberty is enslaved by our depravity. In particular, we cannot choose to believe the message of salvation. The reason we cannot come to God is that we will not. This is what Jesus meant when he said, 'Apart from me you can do nothing',[19] and 'No-one can come to me unless the Father who sent me draws him'.[20] What

[13] 2 Cor. 4:4.
[14] Motyer, *The Prophecy of Isaiah*, p. 487.
[15] Rom. 3:11b.
[16] See Luther, *The Bondage of the Will*, and Edwards, *The Freedom of the Will*.
[17] Josh. 24:15.   [18] Rev. 22:17b.   [19] John 15:5   [20] John 6:44.   .

the Bible says is true: whosoever will may come. But no-one will, which is why God has to make us willing. He does this by breaking sin's stranglehold on the will, and thereby liberating us to come to him. Sinners should not expect God to save them against their will. The first thing God does in salvation is to change the sinner's will, which his Spirit does in regeneration. As the Scripture says, 'Thy people shall be willing in the day of thy power.'[21]

To summarize, there is nothing you can do to save yourself. You are incompetent to contribute to your own salvation. This is the biblical doctrine of total inability, which Louis Berkhof analyses in two propositions:

> (1) that the unrenewed sinner cannot do any act, however insignificant, which *fundamentally* meets with God's approval and answers to the demands of God's holy law; and (2) that he cannot change his fundamental preference for sin and self to love for God, nor even make an approach to such a change. In a word, he is unable to do any spiritual good.[22]

Inability is not a popular doctrine, even in the church. In 1996 the Cambridge Declaration, sponsored by the Alliance of Confessing Evangelicals in the USA, accurately describes the current situation: 'Unwarranted confidence in human ability is a product of fallen human nature. This false confidence now fills the evangelical world – from the self-esteem gospel to the health and wealth gospel, from those who have transformed the gospel into a product to be sold and sinners into consumers who want to buy, to others who treat Christian faith as being true simply because it works.' But the Cambridge Declaration goes on to suggest an alternative, a properly biblical view of human ability: 'We confess that human beings are born spiritually dead and are incapable even of cooperating with regenerating grace.'[23]

As far as your sinful nature is concerned, you are both unable and unwilling to come to God. In the language of the *Westminster Larger Catechism*, you are 'utterly indisposed, disabled, and made opposite to all that is spiritually good' (A. 25). You cannot save yourself from your sins because you are a sinner who cannot, will not come to God. You need God to do something more than help you; you need him to save you!

[21] Ps. 110:3a, AV.

[22] Berkhof, *Systematic Theology*, p. 247.

[23] For a full articulation of this statement, see *Here We Stand! A Call from Confessing Evangelicals*, ed. by James Montgomery Boice and Benjamin E. Sasse (Grand Rapids: Baker, 1996).

The only way

The biblical doctrine of inability helps explain why Christianity is such an exclusive religion. More than anything else, what offends people about the Christian faith is the claim that Jesus is the *only* Saviour. One thinks of the complaint of the self-professed agnostic, Colonel Robert Ingersoll: 'If that religion [Christianity] be true, there is but one Saviour, one inspired book and but one little narrow ... path that leads to heaven.'[24] To the secular mind, anyone who claims to know the absolute truth, not to mention the only salvation, is utterly and hopelessly conceited. In the words of one young man, 'I get real angry at these Christians who tell me that Jesus is the only way to heaven. I mean, what kind of arrogance is that?'[25]

In these postmodern times, so allergic to the very notion of absolute truth, many people prefer to think that all religions are true. An example of such universalism comes from the American film-maker George Lucas (of *Star Wars* fame), who once said: 'I remember when I was 10 years old, I asked my mother, "If there's only one God, why are there so many religions?" I've been pondering that question ever since, and the conclusion I've come to is that all the religions are true.'[26]

Not surprisingly, universalism is beginning to infect the church. The line of reasoning goes something like this: God is love, so he must have a plan for saving everyone. But not everyone is a Christian; therefore, God must save people through other world religions. Even some theologians who identify themselves as evangelicals are promoting Jesus as the One Ultimate Reality who unifies all the diverse religions. According to this view, the spiritual supermarket is full of Buddhists, Hindus, Muslims and many other worshippers who are really 'anonymous Christians'. They are saved by Christ, even though they do not know Christ in a personal way at all.

There are many logical and theological problems with universalism, not the least of which is that different religions offer very different kinds of salvation.[27] But the basic issue is this: What is religion supposed to do? If religion is merely a moral code, or a source of spiritual guidance, then it is easy to see how different religions could be right, each in its own way. But if religion is really about solving the basic problem of humanity, then it needs to explain what the problem is, and how it intends to solve it. For a religion to have any credibility at all, it has to explain what is wrong with human beings, and it has to offer some kind of remedy. By this standard, Christianity is the only credible option. It

[24] Quoted in Martin, *Essential Christianity*, p. 23.
[25] Quoted in Thom S. Rainer, *The Bridger Generation* (Nashville, TN: Broadman & Holman, 1997), p. 30.
[26] Quoted in *Time* (26 April 1999).
[27] For a brief critique of universalism, see Ryken, *Is Jesus the Only Way?*

offers the only true diagnosis of the human condition. Nothing explains what is wrong with our world – and with us – any better than the biblical doctrine of sin. If what we really need is salvation from sin – atonement for our guilt, reconciliation with God, life after death, and all the rest of it – then the only religion even worth considering is one that actually saves.

When we compare the various religions, we discover that Christianity is the only one that gives genuine hope to sinners who have no hope of saving themselves. Judaism and Mormonism are based on keeping the Old Testament law. Buddhism is based on seeking enlightenment. Islam is based on following five pillars of obedience. False Christianity, in all its forms, is based on manipulating the sacraments or performing good works. Authentic Christianity is different from every other alternative. It is not a programme for self-improvement. It is not about getting better educated, or properly medicated. It is not about God 'helping you to help yourself'. It is not about what we do for God at all: it is about what God has done for us in Jesus Christ.

The mortal failure of man-based religion is that we cannot save ourselves. When we see what other religions have to offer, we reach the same conclusion that God reached in the days of Isaiah: *he saw that there was no-one, he was appalled that there was no-one to intervene* (59:16a).

The God who saves

If we are to be saved at all, someone else will have to do the saving. Jesus Christ once tried to explain this basic soteriological principle to his disciples. He told them how hard it is – indeed, how impossible it is – to be saved simply by keeping God's law. His disciples were amazed by this. If a man cannot be saved by doing good, they objected, "'Who then can be saved?" Jesus looked at them and said, "With man this is impossible, but with God all things are possible."[28] This is the message of salvation, that in showing grace to sinners, God makes possible the impossible.

We find this saving message in Isaiah 59. God realized that when it came to salvation, if he wanted it done right, he would have to do it himself:

> *The LORD looked and was displeased*
>   *that there was no justice.*
> *He saw that there was no-one,*
>   *he was appalled that there was no-one to intervene;*

[28] Matt. 19:25–26.

so his own arm worked salvation for him,
  and his righteousness sustained him.
He put on righteousness as his breastplate,
  and the helmet of salvation on his head;
he put on the garments of vengeance
  and wrapped himself in zeal as in a cloak (59:15b–17).

There are several striking features about these verses. One is the repeated use of the third-person pronoun, which emphasizes the role that God plays in our salvation. *He* sees what the problem is, recognizing that we cannot save ourselves. *He* works salvation by the strength of his own might, taking the initiative to save us. *He* arms himself for battle against the forces of the evil one. From beginning to end, salvation is something *he* accomplishes for us. The consistent testimony of Scripture is that 'Salvation ... comes from the LORD'.[29] Or again, 'The LORD is my strength and my song; he has become my salvation.'[30] As Paul reminded Titus, 'when the kindness and love of God our Saviour appeared, he saved us, not because of righteous things we had done, but because of his mercy'.[31] The only thing that can save us is something only God can do – all by himself – through the working of his sovereign grace.

Another striking feature of these verses is that they describe salvation as something for which God has to fight, something that requires heavy armour and fierce vengeance. There are two reasons for this. One is that at the time prophesied in Isaiah's writings, God's people were in exile, dominated by a foreign superpower. What they needed was a military rescue. But these verses are about something more than Israel's return from exile – they are also about salvation from sin. This, too, is something God has to fight for. Since the Garden of Eden, there has been an invisible war between heaven and hell, in which God and the devil fight for the human soul. If God is to win that battle, he must ultimately crush the serpent's head, as he has promised to do.

Isaiah 59 describes one skirmish in God's lengthy spiritual campaign against the devil. The fact that the passage ultimately is about spiritual warfare is confirmed by Ephesians 6, where the apostle Paul describes the armour every Christian must wear to take a stand against the devil. Included in 'the full armour of God', as it is called, are two items Paul retrieves from Isaiah's arsenal: the breastplate of righteousness[32] and the helmet of salvation.[33] The full armour of God is precisely that: the full armour *of God*. The Christian wears second-hand weaponry, hand-me-downs from God's victory over Satan, as first described by the prophet Isaiah. The connection between Isaiah and Ephesians shows that, at its

[29] Ps. 37:39a; Jonah 2:9b. [30] Ps. 118:14; Is. 12:2b. [31] Titus 3:4–5a.
[32] Eph. 6:14; cf. Is. 59:17. [33] Eph. 6:17; cf. Is. 59:17.

deepest level, Isaiah 59 is about spiritual warfare. Isaiah promises divine vengeance:

> *According to what they have done,*
> *   so will he repay*
> *wrath to his enemies*
> *   and retribution to his foes;*
> *he will repay the islands their due* (59:18; cf. 35:4b).

The vengeance Isaiah describes is twofold: God will repay Babylon, first of all, but he will also repay the rest of his enemies, including the evil one.

Despite the fact that God has to fight for our salvation, he does not take up any weapons. This, too, is surprising. What military gear he dons is entirely defensive. God girds himself with the breastplate of righteousness, for example, and the helmet of salvation, wrapped up in a cloak of vengeance. But he carries neither sword nor spear. This is because God is strong enough to win salvation without bearing (or baring!) any arms except his own: *His own arm worked salvation for him* (59:16).[34] This is the familiar Old Testament motif of the Divine Warrior. God is a mighty champion who wins the contest for our salvation with his own bare hands. His arm is not too short after all; even without any weapons, he is fully armed.

The term 'righteousness', which is mentioned twice in these verses, gives a significant clue about what kind of salvation God provides. Righteousness is God's perfect moral rectitude, a rectitude he possesses himself and requires from his creatures. Sinners that we are, righteousness is precisely what we lack, and exactly what we need to be saved. Salvation is a matter of God defending – and granting – his own righteousness. Near the end of Isaiah's prophecy, God identifies the source of salvation in these words: 'It is I, speaking in righteousness, mighty to save' (63:1b). God defends his righteousness by defeating his unrighteous foes and preserving his justice through the cross (propitiation). Salvation is also a matter of God granting his righteousness, which he does by declaring that we are accepted on the basis of Christ's own righteousness (justification). In salvation God gives what he demands: perfect righteousness.

One last feature in Isaiah's saving message deserves our attention. It is the fact that Israel's Saviour is described in personal terms: *The Redeemer will come to Zion* (59:20a). Israel's salvation is located in a specific individual, a Redeemer who will pay the price for salvation. The Redeemer is God, of course, the Holy One of Israel (49:7), apart from whom there is no saviour (43:11; cf. 45:21b). But the closing chapters of Isaiah's prophecy seem to suggest that he is also a man. And what a

---

[34] Cf. Ps. 98:1.

Man! He is the suffering, dying servant who pours out his life unto death for the salvation of God's people (ch. 53).

This mystery is clarified in the New Testament, where we discover that the name of this Redeemer is Jesus Christ, who is both God and man. God offers his one and only salvation through Jesus, his one and only Son. The Bible teaches that 'Salvation is found in no-one else, for there is no other name under heaven given to men by which we must be saved'.[35] The reason Jesus is the only Saviour is that he is the only one who can possibly save us. Only Jesus atoned for guilt by offering a perfect blood sacrifice on the cross. Only Jesus reconciled sinners to God by paying for their sins. Only Jesus grants eternal life by the power of his resurrection. If anyone else could do what Jesus has done to save sinners, perhaps that person could be called the Saviour. But of course no-one else has ever done what Jesus did, or could ever offer the salvation he offers. Therefore we find salvation in Christ alone, not because we are arrogant or intolerant, but because we know that we are sinners in desperate need of a Saviour, and because Jesus is the only Saviour there is.

The glory of salvation

Everything we have been saying about sin and salvation is well summarized by the great New Testament scholar, J. Gresham Machen (1881–1937), who argued that the Bible presents a 'perfectly clear doctrine of the total inability of fallen man and the all-sufficiency of divine grace. Man, according to the Bible, is not merely sick in trespasses and sins; he is not merely in a weakened condition so that he needs divine help: but he is dead in trespasses and sins. He can do absolutely nothing to save himself, and God saves him by the gracious, sovereign act of the new birth. The Bible is a tremendously uncompromising book in this matter of the sin of man and the grace of God.'[36]

The fact that the Bible is so uncompromising about sin and grace should warn us that not everyone will be saved. Although God offers the message of salvation to everyone, not everyone is willing to receive it. Isaiah himself was very clear on this point: 'The Redeemer will come to Zion, to those in Jacob who repent of their sins,' declares the LORD (59:20). The Redeemer is not for everyone, because not everyone will have him. He is only for those who repent, offering God a whole-hearted confession of sin, together with an uncompromising commitment to receive Jesus as Saviour and follow him as Lord. Isaiah had already made confession on behalf of Israel:

> For our offences are many in your sight,
> and our sins testify against us.

[35] Acts 4:12.   [36] Machen, What is Faith?, p. 244.

Our offences are ever with us,
and we acknowledge our iniquities (59:12).

Anyone who wants to be saved must make the same confession, saying, 'My offences are many, O God; I acknowledge all my iniquities.' It only makes sense: if we want to be saved we have to admit that we are lost. Repentance is not a special method for saving ourselves; it is a way of admitting that we cannot save ourselves at all. It is a way of throwing ourselves on the mercy of God and begging the Saviour to save us.

It is only by abandoning ourselves to God's mercy in this way that we will ever fulfil our purpose in life, which is to glorify God. As we have seen, the problem with human beings is that we live for our own glory rather than the glory of God. In salvation, God solves that problem by taking care of our sins entirely on his own. Since salvation is all from God, and takes nothing from us, God reserves all the glory for himself. Knowing that God would work salvation by his own arm, Isaiah could imagine the glorious praise that would redound to his honour: *From the west, men will fear the name of the LORD, and from the rising of the sun, they will revere his glory* (59:19a). This is why God created us in the first place, and why he saves us from our sins – to live for his glory. The reason he accomplishes our salvation all by himself is to keep the glory all to himself.

What is the message of salvation? The message of salvation is that although we cannot save ourselves from our sins, God saves us by the grace he gives in Jesus Christ. At the very end of Isaiah 59, God promises that this saving message will endure for ever: *'my words that I have put in your mouth will not depart from your mouth, or from the mouths of your children, or from the mouths of their descendants from this time on and for ever'* (59:21). This promise was for Isaiah, and also for everyone who repeats his message of salvation from sin, by grace, to the glory of God.

PART 2: SAVED BY GRACE

'For it is by grace you have been saved' (Ephesians 2:8)

4. Chosen in Christ
Election: Ephesians 1:3–14

The first part of this book is about our desperate need of salvation. We need to be saved because, in a word, we are sinners. What we need to be saved from is sin, along with all its miserable consequences, everything from guilt to death. The very fact that we are sinners adds to our predicament, for it prevents us from ever saving ourselves. Therefore, if we are to be saved from sin, we must be saved by grace.

The second part of this book is about the message of salvation by grace. What God does (and has done, and will do) for our salvation is called *grace* because it is the free gift of God's unmerited favour towards sinners. It is called *saving* grace because it meets our critical need for salvation from sin. 'We believe it is through the grace of our Lord Jesus that we are saved.'[1]

The message of salvation by grace is the message of the whole Bible. God's saving grace is anticipated, accomplished or applied, on every page of Holy Scripture. This is why a book such as this on the biblical message of salvation has, of necessity, to be selective, using key passages throughout the Bible which present God's saving message. These passages include various types of biblical literature – stories and poems, histories and parables, Gospels and epistles – organized according to the logic of God's plan of salvation.

The three-personed God

The place to begin is at the very beginning, which is where Ephesians 1 begins. Before you were born – before anyone was born, for that matter – before God made the heavens and the earth, even before the angels first praised their Maker, God was planning to save his people from their sins. We were destined to salvation long ages before the world was ever created.

The plan of salvation required the active engagement of every person of the Trinity: Father, Son and Spirit. In the opening chapter of

[1] Acts 15:11.

Ephesians, the apostle Paul praises first God the Father (Eph. 1:3–6), then God the Son (1:7–12), and finally God the Holy Spirit (1:13–14) for the part each plays in salvation. Salvation is *administered* by the Father, *accomplished* by the Son, and *applied* by the Spirit.

It is sometimes thought that the doctrine of the Trinity is unbiblical, or at least irrelevant. One famous critic was the German philosopher Immanuel Kant (1724–1804), who claimed that 'the doctrine of the Trinity, taken literally, has *no practical relevance at all*, even if we think we understand it; and it is even more clearly irrelevant if we realize that it transcends all our concepts' (emphasis his).[2] It is true that the biblical doctrine of the Trinity is mysterious. It is such a great mystery, in fact, that we may never be able fully to understand it, let alone explain it. One thing we must do, however, is believe in the Trinity, for in his perfect Word God has revealed himself as one God in three persons.

The biblical doctrine of the Trinity can be stated in seven simple propositions:

1. God the Father is God.
2. God the Son is God.
3. God the Holy Spirit is God.
4. The Father is not the Son.
5. The Son is not the Spirit.
6. The Spirit is not the Father.
7. Nevertheless, there is only one God.

This is the doctrine of the Trinity, distilled from Scripture. In his treatise *On Christian Doctrine*, Augustine used somewhat different language to express the same eternal truths:

> The Father and the Son and the Holy Spirit, and each of these by Himself, is God, and at the same time they are all one God ... The Father is not the Son nor the Holy Spirit; the Son is not the Father nor the Holy Spirit; the Holy Spirit is not the Father nor the Son: but the Father is only Father, the Son is only Son, and the Holy Spirit is only Holy Spirit.[3]

The triune God who saves

Ephesians 1 brings those bare propositions to life, for it shows the triune God working out our salvation. God is who he is in his triune being for our salvation. We are chosen by God the Father, in Christ the Son, through God the Holy Spirit. Or, as we have already noted,

---

[2] Immanuel Kant, *The Conflict of the Faculties*, trans. by Mary J. Gregor (New York: Abaris, 1979), p. 65.
[3] Augustine, *Christian Doctrine*, I.5 (2:524).

salvation is administrated by the Father, accomplished by the Son, and applied by the Spirit. To express the same truths in yet another way, the salvation which was *planned* by the Father has been *procured* by the Son, and is now *presented* by the Spirit. Whatever words we use to describe it, the point is that our salvation from sin depends on a gracious cooperation within the Godhead.

Salvation starts with the Father. He is the originator of our salvation:

Praise be to the God and Father of our Lord Jesus Christ, who has blessed us in the heavenly realms with every spiritual blessing in Christ. For he chose us in him before the creation of the world to be holy and blameless in his sight. In love he predestined us to be adopted as his sons through Jesus Christ, in accordance with his pleasure and will – to the praise of his glorious grace, which he has freely given us in the One he loves (Eph. 1:3–6).

The Father deliberately blesses, chooses and predestines his people. He lovingly bestows, reveals and lavishes his grace. This is all part of the eternal plan of the one who *works out everything in conformity with the purpose of his will* (1:11).

The salvation which originated with the Father is located in the Son. The opening verses of Ephesians focus their undistracted attention on the person and work of Jesus Christ, mentioning his person and work no fewer than a dozen times. Everything God does (and has done, and will do) for our salvation, he does *in Christ*:

In him we have redemption through his blood, the forgiveness of sins, in accordance with the riches of God's grace that he lavished on us with all wisdom and understanding. And he made known to us the mystery of his will according to his good pleasure, which he purposed in Christ, to be put into effect when the times will have reached their fulfilment – to bring all things in heaven and on earth together under one head, even Christ. In him we were also chosen, having been predestined according to the plan of him who works out everything in conformity with the purpose of his will, in order that we, who were the first to hope in Christ, might be for the praise of his glory (1:7–12).

By listing so many benefits of salvation, these verses set the agenda for much of the rest of our study of the Bible's saving message: Salvation means *election*, God's choice to save us by his predestinating grace (1:4–5). Salvation means *redemption*, the payment of a price to free us from our bondage to sin. It means *propitiation*, the atoning blood sacrifice that takes away our guilt and secures our forgiveness (1:7). Salvation means *adoption*, the legal act by which God makes us his own sons and daughters (Eph. 1:5). Salvation means *reconciliation*, on a cosmic scale, for in Christ God is unifying everything in the universe (1:10). Christ's reconciling work operates horizontally as well as vertically; it is for the Jews (*we, who were the first to hope in Christ*, 1:12) and also for the Gentiles (*you also were included in Christ*, 1:13). Thus reconciliation ends both our alienation from God and our estrangement from one another. Salvation means, finally, *sanctification* and *glorification*, in which God makes us as morally spotless and as shiningly beautiful as his own dear Son (1:12).

These verses contain virtually the whole message of salvation, which Paul describes as *the mystery of God's will* (1:9). This saving message communicates that all of God's best blessings come through union with Jesus Christ. We are blessed with every spiritual blessing *in Christ* (1:3). Just as we were utterly lost in Adam, through the imputation of his sin, so we are completely saved in Christ, through the gift of his salvation. It is in covenant with Christ that we are predestined, redeemed, forgiven, adopted, reconciled, sanctified and glorified. Christ is not only the beginning and the end of our salvation, he *is* our salvation, for in him we receive everything we need to be saved. The location of our salvation is Jesus Christ.

The salvation that originated with the Father, and is located in the Son, is communicated by the Holy Spirit. Or, as we expressed it earlier, salvation is administered by God the Father, accomplished by God the Son, and applied by God the Spirit:

And you also were included in Christ when you heard the word of truth, the gospel of your salvation. Having believed, you were marked in him with a seal, the promised Holy Spirit, who is a deposit guaranteeing our inheritance until the redemption of those who are God's possession – to the praise of his glory (1:13–14).

Since God's best blessings are spiritual, we can receive them only by his Spirit. First, the Holy Spirit enables us to hear the gospel of truth, which is the message of salvation. Then, he changes us from the inside out, which is regeneration. With regeneration comes the gift of faith, the spiritual ability to believe in the death and resurrection of Jesus Christ. By doing this work in us, the Holy Spirit makes our salvation a present reality. He takes the salvation that the Son accomplished in the past and applies it to us in the present. It is for this reason that the Holy Spirit is called a *seal* (1:13), which in ancient times was the proof of ownership. The sealing work of the Holy Spirit proves that we really do belong to God, and will continue to belong to him for all eternity. Hence the Spirit is also called an advance *deposit* (Eph. 1:14), the purchase of the spiritual transaction God has made with us. The Holy Spirit is a down-payment on eternity, the security of our salvation, now and for ever.

The first half of Ephesians 1 gives a complete overview of the work of God in saving sinners. All the blessings of salvation come from God, in Christ, by the Holy Spirit. Our salvation jointly depends on the electing, predestining work of God the Father; the redeeming, atoning work of God the Son; and the sealing, guaranteeing work of God the Holy Spirit.[4] Anyone who admits the need for salvation can see why the doctrine of the Trinity is so important. Not only is the existence of one God in three persons central to our worship, but it is also crucial for our salvation.

One of the most careful explanations of the doctrine of the Trinity comes from the Athanasian Creed, which was written sometime around AD 400. First the creed states the doctrine:

> There is one Person of the Father: another of the Son: and another of the Holy Ghost. But the Godhead of the Father, of the Son, and of the Holy Ghost, is all one ... The Father eternal: the Son eternal: and the Holy Ghost eternal. And yet they are not three eternals: but one eternal.

That is the doctrine, but the Athanasian Creed then goes on to explain why it matters: 'He therefore that will be saved, must thus think of the Trinity.'[5] The message of salvation by grace depends upon the threefold work of the triune God.

Before the foundation of the world

One of the most amazing things about God's saving work is that it began in eternity past. The emphasis in Ephesians 1 is not so much on the Spirit's *application* of salvation in the present, or even on the Son's *accomplishment* of salvation in the past, but on the Father's *administration* of salvation before the beginning of time. Our salvation was predestined, for we were chosen before the creation of the world (1:4–5). The saving work of Jesus Christ in history thus depends on the saving plan of God from all eternity.

It is becoming increasingly popular for theologians (including some who call themselves evangelicals) to think of God as performing without a script. They say that God is in process. Like the rest of us, he is working things out as he goes along, suffering the vicissitudes of life in this universe and changing his plans to fit the circumstances. There is a creative interchange between earth and heaven which allows human beings to influence God, even to change his mind altogether. God is

---

[4] See Alexander, 'The basis of Christian salvation', p. 30.
[5] 'The Athanasian Creed', in Schaff (ed.), *The Creeds of Christendom*, vol. 2, pp. 66–71.

not sovereign; he is a finite being who does not even know the future, but he is open to the possibilities.[6]

That is not at all the biblical picture of God. It is true, of course, that God is actively at work in human history. He blesses the righteous and curses the wicked. He answers prayers, converts sinners and plants churches. He rules over nature and over nations. But God does all these things strictly according to the plan he established before he created the world. God's participation in history depends on his purpose in eternity. He is working everything out according to his eternal plan, a plan that pre-dates the creation of the universe.

In the first part of this book, we sought to understand the problem of humanity. Now we discover that God knew the solution even before we caused the problem. He developed his plan for salvation before the foundation of the world. Perhaps this helps explain why God permitted humanity to fall into sin. From the beginning, God had planned for us a blessing even greater than mere creation: he had purposed our salvation in his Son.

In one sense, all God's plans were established in eternity. The Bible could hardly be stronger on this point than it is: God *works out everything in conformity with the purpose of his will* (1:11). What is included in God's eternal decree? Everything – everything God has ever done and everything he will ever do. In this verse three different Greek words are used to describe God's plan. One is the word *thelēma*, which simply refers to God's will in general terms. Another is the word *prothesis*, which means God's purpose, especially his foreordained purpose. The third is the word *boulē*, which refers to God's deliberate counsel. Taken together, what these words show is that nothing lies outside the divine intention. God does whatever he does according to his predetermined plan.

If God works out *everything* according to his eternal decree, then his eternal decree must include the plan of salvation. This is specifically what is meant by *predestination* (*In love he predestined us*, 1:4–5). Predestination is one special part of God's cosmic plan. It is his sovereign decision, made in eternity past, regarding the final destiny of individual sinners.

One obvious implication of predestination is that God's grace is God's choice, which is what the Bible means by *election*. Election is God's choice to save particular sinners, selecting them to receive every spiritual blessing in Christ. A fuller definition is contained in the *Westminster Confession of Faith*: 'Those of mankind that are predestinated unto life, God, before the foundation of the world was laid, according to His eternal and immutable purpose, and the secret counsel

---

[6] This view is advocated in Pinnock, *A Wideness in God's Mercy*, and Boyd, *God of the Possible*.

and good pleasure of His will, hath chosen, in Christ, unto everlasting glory, out of His mere free grace and love' (III.v).

We have already seen that we ourselves could never be the origin of our own salvation. We cannot be saved by anything we do because, according to the doctrine of total inability, we are sinners who are unable and unwilling to come to God in faith. Therefore, if we are to be saved, God will have to do the saving. Now we discover that our salvation does not depend on some sudden decision, but upon God's eternal decree. When we make the choice to come to God, it is only because he has already done the choosing. J. I. Packer writes, 'The biblical doctrine of election is that before Creation God selected out of the human race, foreseen as fallen, those whom he would redeem, bring to faith, justify, and glorify in and through Jesus Christ.'[7]

Divine election proves beyond all question or doubt that salvation is by grace alone. Salvation cannot depend on anything we do because we were predestined to it before we ever did anything, even before we existed. The salvation we possess in the present, which gives us certain hope for the future, depends on a decision God made in the eternal past.

Making sure of your election

The doctrine of election naturally causes people to wonder whether they are among the elect or not. Indeed, some people experience high anxiety because they fear that they are *not* among the elect. Their question becomes, How can I know if God has chosen me or not? It is a reasonable question. If salvation depends on election, then it would seem that being sure of my salvation requires being sure of my election.

This question is made all the more urgent by the fact that not everyone will be saved. Theologians sometimes speak of 'double predestination', which means that according to God's decree, some sinners will never repent and thus finally will be lost in their sins. 'Double predestination' is not a biblical term, for the Bible nowhere speaks of anyone being predestined to hell. It reserves the verb 'predestine' (*prohorizō*) for the salvation of sinners unto eternal life. However, even if it is not a biblical term, double predestination expresses a biblical truth: if God has made an advance decision about which people he will save from their sins, he has also made an advance decision about which people he will leave in their sins.[8] The theological term for this is 'reprobation'. It means that when God established his plan of salvation, he decided to pass some sinners by, leaving them to continue in their sins and thus finally to be damned for them. In the words of the apostle Peter, 'They stumble because they disobey the

---

[7] Packer, *Concise Theology*, p. 149.   [8] See Rom. 1:28.

message – which is also what they were destined for.'[9] The apostle Paul described the reprobate as 'the objects of his [God's] wrath'.[10] This prospect is so terrifying that it is little wonder the Bible should command us to 'make [our] calling and election sure'.[11] In other words, Christians are commanded to seek assurance of election.

How can you be sure that you are among God's elect? Here it helps to remember that the elect are chosen *in Christ*. Election in Christ is the only kind of election there is. What God has chosen to do is to unite us to Christ, putting us together with him for our salvation. Therefore, to ask if you are among the elect is really to ask if you are in Christ. If you want to know whether or not God has chosen you, all you need to know is whether or not you are in Christ. You do not need to read God's mind. You do not need to climb up to heaven and peek into the Book of Life. All you need is to know Jesus Christ, who is the location of salvation. Every spiritual blessing God has to offer may be found in him, including election. If you are in Christ, you are among the elect, for the elect are chosen in Christ. John Calvin (1509–64) thus warned that 'if we have been elected in him [Christ], we shall not find assurance of election in ourselves'; rather, Christ 'is the mirror wherein we must, and without self-deception may, contemplate our own election'.[12] The way to make your calling and election sure is to be sure that you are joined to Jesus Christ by faith.

Since election is in Christ, it is usually best understood after one becomes a Christian. In fact, the doctrine of election is sometimes referred to as a 'family secret' (although it is not really a secret to anyone who knows the Bible). While you are still outside God's family, you may not hear about predestination at all; if you do, it hardly seems to make any sense. Once you are in the family, however, it makes the most perfect sense in the world. Indeed, it is the kind of fact that helps to make sense of everything else.

The famous American Bible teacher Donald Grey Barnhouse (1895–1960) often used an illustration to help people make sense of election. He asked them to imagine a cross like the one on which Jesus died, only so large that it had a door in it. Over the door were these words from Revelation: 'Whosoever will may come.'[13] These words represent the free and universal offer of the gospel. By God's grace, the message of salvation is for everyone. Every man, woman and child who will come to the cross is invited to believe in Jesus Christ and enter eternal life.

On the other side of the door a happy surprise awaits the one who believes and enters. For from the inside, anyone glancing back can see

---

[9] 1 Pet. 2:8b; cf. Jude 4.   [10] Rom. 9:22; cf. Eph. 2:3.   [11] 2 Pet. 1:10.
[12] Calvin, *Institutes of the Christian Religion*, III.xxiv.5.
[13] Rev. 22:17.

these words from Ephesians written above the door: 'Chosen in Christ before the foundation of the world' (see 1:4). Election is best understood in hindsight, for it is only after coming to Christ that one can know whether one has been chosen in Christ. Those who make a decision for Christ find that God made a decision for them in eternity past. In the words of an old nineteenth-century hymn, 'I sought the Lord, and afterward I knew / he moved my soul to seek him, seeking me.' Salvation does not come from the sinner's own choice, but from God's sovereign choosing.

A biblical doctrine

The doctrine of election is a difficult doctrine. It is difficult because it shows – in a way almost nothing else can – the sovereignty of God's grace. In other words, it proves that ultimately salvation depends entirely on God, and not on ourselves. Salvation is neither initiated by human choice nor appropriated by human effort; it begins and ends with the sovereign grace of God's electing will. But this inevitably shatters our pride, dashing any last hope of snatching glory for ourselves.

Since we are sinners by nature, and thus desire our own glory, it is only natural that we should resist a doctrine that so thoroughly exalts God and utterly humbles humanity. This may explain why so many objections have been raised to the doctrine of election. Before answering these objections, however, it is important to realize that election is a thoroughly biblical doctrine. Predestination was not invented by Calvin, or by Augustine, or even by Paul; it is the consistent teaching of the Bible.

The first instance of election comes in connection with the first murder. God accepted the sacrifice of Abel, but not the offering of Cain. There has been no end of speculation as to why God accepted the one but not the other. Was it the fact that Abel brought a blood sacrifice, or that he offered the firstfruits of his flock? Perhaps, although these answers assume that salvation is a matter of man's work rather than God's grace. The biblical explanation is a bold statement of God's sovereign choice: 'The LORD looked with favour on Abel … but on Cain … he did not look with favour.'[14] In other words, God accepted Abel's person before he accepted his work, so that Abel's salvation was based on God's sovereign choice.

We find the same electing principle at work throughout the history of the patriarchs. God made Isaac the son of promise, but sent Ishmael out into the wilderness. He loved Jacob, but hated Esau,[15] meaning that he regarded Esau with displeasure and ultimately rejected him. He

---

[14] Gen. 4:4–5.   [15] Mal. 1:2–3; Rom. 9:10–13.

chose Joseph, along with Judah, over the rest of his brothers. Election also explains the exodus. Why did God bring the people of Israel out of Egypt? It was simply because he chose to save them. Hardening Pharaoh's heart and parting the Red Sea were acts of his sovereign will. When the psalmist considered these remarkable historical events, he was moved to say, 'Blessed is the nation whose God is the LORD, the people he chose for his inheritance.'[16]

God not only chose his people, but he also chose their Saviour. The Old Testament promised that a man of God's own choosing would save his people from their sins. Speaking through the prophet Isaiah, God said, 'Here is my servant, whom I uphold, my chosen one in whom I delight'.[17] The name of that servant, of course, turned out to be Jesus Christ. When Jesus came as the chosen Saviour, he in turn chose his disciples. He went to places like the seashore and the tax office and called the men of his choice to follow him. 'You did not choose me,' he later reminded them, 'but I chose you and appointed you to go and bear fruit.'[18] 'No-one knows the Son except the Father, and no-one knows the Father except the Son and those to whom the Son chooses to reveal him'.[19]

The theme of God's electing choice runs right through the Bible. Although it is often identified with Calvin, among others, the doctrine of election is simply plain biblical Christianity. It is not a philosophical speculation, but a biblical revelation. It could not be anything except a revelation, since it deals with the mind of God in eternity. Ephesians 1 teaches us something we could not otherwise know. It gives us privileged information about God's eternal counsel, divulging the divine secret that he has been planning to save us for ever.

In defence of the doctrine

One has to be a Christian to understand the doctrine of election from the inside. This does not mean, however, that all Christians fully accept the doctrine. Indeed, many have serious questions about it. These questions deserve answers, although it is important to recognize from the outset that the Bible does not explain all the mysteries of God's predestinating grace. Somewhat surprisingly, the Bible rarely sets out to defend the doctrine of election. The biblical writers – the apostle Paul is a good example – tend to assume the truth of election rather than to argue for it.

The first and most obvious question about election has to do with God's sovereignty: Isn't predestination actually a form of fatalism? If God's grace is God's choice, then I am only a puppet on a string.

[16] Ps. 33:12.   [17] Is. 42:1; cf. Luke 9:35.   [18] John 15:16.
[19] Matt. 11:27.

Whether he saves me or not, there is nothing I can do about it. Thus divine sovereignty eliminates human responsibility.

Which does the Bible teach – divine sovereignty or human responsibility? The answer is that it teaches both, leaving the paradox unresolved. The Bible denies any autonomy outside God's authority. It always places our responsibility under God's sovereignty. Thus it teaches both that God is absolutely sovereign *and* that we are morally responsible. The same Jesus who said, 'No-one can come to me unless the Father has enabled him,' also said, 'You refuse to come to me to have life.'[20] Even though God's decree is ultimate, our own decisions are meaningful. The choices we make, including our spiritual choices, are real choices. The famous preacher G. Campbell Morgan (1863–1945) was known to ask: 'There are the "whosoever wills" and the "whosoever won'ts" – Which, Sir, are you?' Morgan's question was a way of emphasizing that God holds each person responsible to make a decision for or against Jesus Christ. Election can never become an excuse for failing to exercise faith in Jesus Christ. If you have not yet come to Christ, God holds you responsible for your rebellion. But if you are following Christ, then you really did choose to follow him. But remember that you chose him only because he first chose you, and did so from all eternity.

A second question has to do with God's justice. Both the salvation of the elect and the damnation of the reprobate depend on God's sovereign decree. But how can God save some without saving the others? If he is willing to choose the elect for salvation, it seems unjust for him to reject the reprobate.

The issue of God's justice is not addressed in Ephesians 1, but it is dealt with at length in Romans 9, where Paul puts the question directly: 'Is God unjust? Not at all! For he says to Moses, "I will have mercy on whom I have mercy, and I will have compassion on whom I have compassion." It does not, therefore, depend on man's desire or effort, but on God's mercy.'[21] The key word in Paul's answer is 'mercy'. Election is not a matter of justice, but of mercy. Remember that we are not basically good; we are essentially sinful, and sinners do not deserve to be saved. If salvation were simply a matter of justice, there would be no salvation at all. This principle is captured in the memorable lines from Shakespeare's *The Merchant of Venice*, Act 4 scene 1: 'If justice be thy plea, consider this: that, in the course of justice, none of us should see salvation.' Sinners have no claim upon God. He does not owe us anything; or if he does, it is only punishment for our sins. Therefore, those whom God passes by are condemned by his strict justice. The real mystery of salvation is not that God rejects some, which is perfectly just, but that he chooses any at all, which is sheer mercy.

[20] John 6:65; 5:40.   [21] Rom. 9:14–16.

Another question about election has to do with God's knowledge: Which comes first, election or foreknowledge? Do we choose God because he first chose us, or does God choose us because he knows in advance that we will choose him? Some theologians argue that election is based on foreknowledge. First God foresees our faith, and then he chooses to save us. This interpretation of election appears to find support from the apostle Peter, who wrote 'to God's elect ... who have been chosen according to the foreknowledge of God the Father'.[22] These verses seem to give the impression that God chooses us in eternity *because* he foresees that we will choose him in history.

There are two major problems with basing our election on God's foreknowledge. One problem is linguistic. The biblical term 'foreknowledge' (*prognosis*) means much more than simply to know something in advance; it means to choose beforehand. A better translation would be 'fore-appointment' or 'fore-ordination', for when the Bible says that God 'foreknows' something, it means that he has purposed to bring it to pass.[23]

The other problem with basing election upon foreknowledge is that it asks us to do the impossible; namely, to choose God before he chooses us. If election were simply a matter of God foreseeing our faith, then ultimately our salvation would depend on our own choice. Election would be a matter of post-destination rather than pre-destination. The reality is, however, that left to ourselves we would never choose to come to God in faith. Remember the doctrine of total inability, which we explored in the previous chapter, and recall the words of Jesus Christ: 'No-one can come to me unless the Father has enabled him.'[24] Election cannot depend on anything God anticipates that we will do; it can only depend on his sovereign grace. This is why election is properly described as *unconditional*. Earlier we quoted the first part of the *Westminster Confession of Faith*'s definition of predestination. This is a good place to finish the quotation: 'Those of mankind that are predestinated unto life, God ... hath chosen in Christ, unto everlasting glory, out of his mere free grace and love, without any foresight of faith or good works, or perseverance in either of them, or any other thing in the creature, as conditions, or causes moving him thereunto; and all to the praise of his glorious grace' (III.v). Election is unconditional, for salvation 'does not ... depend on man's desire or effort, but on God's mercy'.[25]

The next question about election is more practical in nature. If salvation depends on God's sovereign election, then what is the purpose of evangelism? What is the point of sharing the message of salvation, if God has already chosen those whom he has elected to save?

---

[22] 1 Pet. 1:1–2; cf. Rom. 8:29–30.   [23] Bruce, *Romans*, p. 176.
[24] John 6:65.   [25] Rom. 9:16.

Part of the answer to this question is contained here in Ephesians 1. Rather than making evangelism unnecessary, election is what makes evangelism effective. It is by hearing the message of salvation that the elect believe the gospel and thus are included in Christ (Eph. 1:13). In addition to choosing some to save, God has also chosen the means by which they will be saved, and that is by evangelism. As J. C. Ryle once put it, preaching is 'the hand of God, who from all eternity has chosen a people in Christ, by which he reaches out and claims them for his own'.[26] Thus we offer salvation to everyone, trusting God to do the saving. Election actually is the best assurance that our evangelism will accomplish God's purpose. We should never say, writes John Stott,

> that the doctrine of election by the sovereign will and mercy of God, mysterious as it is, makes either evangelism or faith unnecessary. The opposite is the case. It is only because of God's gracious will to save that evangelism has any hope of success and faith becomes possible. The preaching of the gospel is the very means that God has appointed by which he delivers from blindness and bondage those whom he chose in Christ before the foundation of the world, sets them free to believe in Jesus, and so causes his will to be done.[27]

Chosen for God's glory

The last question about election has to do with morality. Doesn't election lead to spiritual arrogance, or even worse, to moral indifference? It is sad, but true, that some Christians who hold to the doctrine of election are conceited about their status as God's chosen people. Being numbered among the elect becomes for them a matter of pride. Their attitude is, 'I'm one of the elect, and you're not.' It is also true that some are tempted to presume upon their election. For them, being numbered among the elect becomes an excuse for misbehaving. Their attitude is, 'Since I'm one of the elect, God will save me no matter what I do, so why not go ahead and do whatever I want?'

Wherever the doctrine of election produces arrogance or indifference, we may be sure that it is not properly understood at all, for when it is rightly understood, election is the basis for genuine spiritual humility. God's unconditional election proves our total depravity. It shows that we do not deserve to be saved – indeed, that there is nothing in us worth saving at all. Therefore, if God has chosen to save us, it is only because of his unmerited favour. Once he has saved us, there is

[26] J. C. Ryle, quoted in Alexander, 'The basis of Christian salvation', p. 34.
[27] Stott, *The Message of Ephesians*, p. 48. See also Packer, *Evangelism and the Sovereignty of God*.

nothing left for us to boast about, except for God and his amazing grace.

Rightly understood, election also leads to obedience. How can I turn my back on the God who has loved me from all eternity? Far from making me indifferent to his law, election gives me every incentive to obey his every command. The very reason God chose us was *to be holy and blameless in his sight* (Eph. 1:4a). To put this in theological terms, election is inseparably joined to sanctification, 'for those God foreknew he also predestined to be conformed to the likeness of his Son'.[28] Far from encouraging us to sin, the doctrine of election demands personal holiness, which is the very purpose of our election in the first place. Anyone who claims to have received God's electing grace and yet remains indifferent to the claims of gospel holiness gives evidence of self-deception.

Why have we taken the trouble to defend the doctrine of election? For several reasons. It is a biblical doctrine, for one thing, and the fact that it is biblical is reason enough for its defence. Biblical doctrines need to be defended whenever they come under attack. Another reason for defending election is that it provides the foundation for salvation. If we are to understand God's saving message, we must first understand that it flows from his sovereign grace. But the most important reason for defending election is simply this: it magnifies the glory of God.

The glory of God! This is the beginning as well as the end of our salvation. As we have already seen, the reason God made us in the first place is to glorify him for ever. The glory of God is also the reason our sin is such a disaster. We no longer glorify God because we are too busy seeking our own glory. But God will see to it that ultimately he gets the glory he deserves. Since he is glorified whenever he does for us what we cannot do for ourselves, one of the primary ways he glorifies himself is through the salvation of sinners. We are saved for God's glory, and the glory of salvation begins with God's electing grace.

In reading Ephesians 1 it is almost impossible not to be affected by its mood of joyful exuberance. This passage contains some of the most complex theological concepts in the entire Bible, yet the apostle Paul is not merely teaching; he is also praising God for the glory of his grace. In the Greek original, this whole section of Ephesians, from verse 3 to verse 14, is one long sentence punctuated with praise: *Praise be to the God and Father of our Lord Jesus Christ ... for he chose us in him ... In love he predestined us ... to the praise of his glorious grace ... In him we were also chosen ... in order that we ... might be for the praise of his glory ... You also were included in Christ ... to the praise of his glory.* This torrent of praise contains equal parts theology and doxology. The apostle wants us to do something more than believe the doctrine of

---

[28] Rom. 8:29.

predestination – he wants us to experience the joy that it brings to Christian life and worship. Whether we speak of the origination of election with the Father, the location of election in the Son, or the presentation of election by the Spirit, it is all to the glory of God. If predestination is all to the glory of God, then to object to his electing grace – or even worse, to deny it – is to rob God of his glory. The only way to give God the glory he deserves is to praise him for saving us from sin by the electing grace of his eternal plan.

5. Out of Egypt
Deliverance: Exodus 15:1–21

One of the most remarkable examples of divine election was God's decision to save Israel out of Egypt. At the time of their deliverance, the Israelites were a rather nondescript Middle Eastern people. They were the descendants of shepherds and nomads – Abraham, Isaac and Jacob – men who had accomplished nothing that would commend them to the outside world. They had won no great battles. They had built no large cities. They had produced no beautiful art. They were simply common labourers, slaving away in the desert sun.

The people of Israel had only one thing going for them: they were chosen by God. God had elected to love them and to save them for his glory. His reason for doing so had nothing to do with the Israelites themselves. When the prophet Moses later reflected on Israel's deliverance, he reminded them:

> The LORD did not set his affection on you and choose you because you were more numerous than other peoples, for you were the fewest of all peoples. But it was because the LORD loved you and kept the oath he swore to your forefathers that he brought you out with a mighty hand and redeemed you from the land of slavery, from the power of Pharaoh king of Egypt. Know therefore that the LORD your God is God; he is the faithful God, keeping his covenant of love to a thousand generations of those who love him and keep his commands.[1]

God did not love the Israelites because they were lovable, but because he was loving. He saved them for no other reason than that he chose them to receive the covenant promise of his salvation.

The house of bondage

The exodus from Egypt was one of the great saving events of the Old

[1] Deut. 7:7–9.

Testament. To understand why it was such a great salvation, it helps to realize that under the Pharaohs, Egypt was a brutal and oppressive regime.

The Israelites had first gone down to Egypt during the days of Joseph. There had been a famine in the land, so Jacob and his many sons travelled to Egypt to buy bread. There they settled to raise their families. And raise them they did! Over the next several hundred years, the children of Israel 'were fruitful and multiplied greatly and became exceedingly numerous, so that the land was filled with them' (Exod. 1:7). Eventually, there were so many Israelites that in Pharaoh's mind they posed a threat. He feared what such a large immigrant population might do in the event of political unrest.

Pharaoh's initial strategy for controlling the Israelites was to turn them into slaves. Using whips and chains, he forced them to build great cities in the desert. Yet still they multiplied. They grew so numerous that 'the Egyptians came to dread the Israelites and worked them ruthlessly. They made their lives bitter with hard labour in brick and mortar and with all kinds of work in the fields; in all their hard labour the Egyptians used them ruthlessly' (Exod. 1:12–14). The harder the Israelites worked, however, the stronger they became. When Pharaoh realized that slavery was failing to control the minority population, he turned to infanticide. At first he told the Hebrew midwives to put all their baby boys to death. When they failed to co-operate, he sent out a more general order: 'Every boy that is born you must throw into the Nile' (1:22).

Egypt was a terrible place to live in those days. It was a land of slavery and captivity, torture and murder. The Israelites would have left in a moment, if only they could have done so. But they couldn't. Thus their only recourse was to call upon God for their salvation: 'The Israelites groaned in their slavery and cried out, and their cry for help because of their slavery went up to God. God heard their groaning and he remembered his covenant with Abraham, with Isaac and with Jacob' (2:23b–24). It is the bitter reality of slavery that makes the slave cry for freedom.

God heard the cries of his people, and in his saving mercy he called Moses to lead them out of Egypt. But Pharaoh refused to let them leave. Time and again, Moses went to Pharaoh and said, 'Let my people go!' Time and again, Pharaoh said, 'No!' So God visited the Egyptians with dreadful plagues: blood, frogs, gnats, flies, disease, sores, hail, locusts, darkness and finally death. Yet the worse things got, the more hard-hearted Pharaoh became. He would not let God's people go.

It is little wonder that the Bible calls Egypt 'the house of bondage' (Exod. 20:2, AV). Even to this day, Pharaoh's Egypt stands for everything hateful to God and hurtful to his people. In the biblical message of salvation, it also serves as a symbol for the bondage of sinful humanity. We are bound by sin, for 'the sinful mind is hostile to God. It does not submit to God's law, nor can it do so. Those controlled by the sinful nature cannot please God'.[2] Since we are sinners, we are also bound by Satan, for 'the whole world is under the control of the evil one'.[3] Finally, we are bound to die, for the Bible teaches that sin reigns over humanity through death.[4] Bitter though it is, this bondage is what ultimately leads us to seek salvation in Christ. As Calvin wrote, 'The only way we may enjoy these [saving] benefits of Christ, is to be humbled by a serious realization of our ills, and to seek for Him as hungry men seek their liberator.'[5]

Deliverance!

What people in bondage need is deliverance. And as it turns out, deliverance is the essential meaning of the biblical concept of salvation. The basic Hebrew verb for salvation is *yāša'*, which simply means 'to save' or 'to deliver'. It appears hundreds of times in the Old Testament: 'When I was in great need, he saved me';[6] 'Rescue me and deliver me in your righteousness; turn your ear to me and save me';[7] and so on. The basic Hebrew nouns for salvation (*yᵉšû'â*, *yēša'* and *tᵉšû'â*) are all taken from the verb *yāša'*. They mean 'help', 'deliverance' or 'salvation', and they, too, occur more than one hundred times in the Hebrew Scriptures: 'The LORD is my light and my salvation – whom shall I fear?';[8] 'You are my help and my deliverer; O my God, do not delay';[9] 'In your great love, O God, answer me with your sure salvation'.[10]

Another common Hebrew word for salvation is virtually interchangeable with the ones mentioned above. It is the verb *nāṣal*, which means 'to deliver'. To give but one example, *nāṣal* is used in the refrain of one of the psalms of salvation: 'They cried out to the LORD in their trouble, and he delivered them from their distress.'[11] However, in English Bibles *nāṣal* is often translated by the verb 'to save': 'This poor man called, and the LORD heard him; he saved him out of all his troubles.'[12] These examples show that in the Old Testament salvation and deliverance are virtually synonymous.

There are many stories of deliverance in the Old Testament. Noah and his family were rescued from the great flood. Joseph was lifted out of the pit, and he, in turn, saved his family from starvation. God raised up Judges like Deborah and Samson to deliver the Israelites from their enemies. King David was saved from his enemies on many occasions. Jonah was rescued from the belly of a great fish. Daniel was delivered

---

[2] Rom. 8:7–8.   [3] 1 John 5:19.   [4] Rom. 5:21.
[5] John Calvin, *A Harmony of the Gospels* (Grand Rapids: Eerdmans, 1994), vol. 1, p. 148.
[6] Ps. 116:6b.   [7] Ps. 71:2.   [8] Ps. 27:1.   [9] Ps. 40:17b.
[10] Ps. 69:13b.   [11] Ps. 107:6, 13, 19, 28.   [12] Ps. 34:6.

from the lions' den. Even Israel's return from exile was a kind of deliverance.

But the most daring rescue of all was the exodus from Egypt, which was *the* saving event of the Old Testament, the paradigm of salvation. Throughout the rest of the Hebrew Scriptures, the exodus is considered the supreme example of God's saving grace. The psalmist implored God's people to remember their God as 'the God who saved them, who had done great things in Egypt'.[13] In the days of Hosea, when God was warning his people not to turn their backs on him, he said, 'I am the LORD your God, who brought you out of Egypt'.[14]

It is not surprising that the exodus became synonymous with salvation, for it was a remarkable rescue. Finally Pharaoh decided to let God's people go. So the Israelites – thousands upon thousands of them – gathered up all their belongings and marched out of Egypt. God had Moses lead them down the desert road that led to the Red Sea, where they camped on the edge of the desert. No sooner had the Israelites departed, however, than Pharaoh decided that he had made a major political mistake. 'What have we done?' said his advisers. 'We have let the Israelites go and have lost their services!' (Exod. 14:5b). So Pharaoh readied his troops for battle, climbed into his chariot, chased the Israelites across the desert, and overtook them at their camp by the sea.

From the standpoint of military tactics, the Israelites were extremely vulnerable. On one side, they were hemmed in by the sea. On the other, they could hear the rumble of chariots and the tramping of soldiers on the march. Terrified by what they both saw and heard, they were certain that they were about to meet a fate even worse than slavery. In their desperation they cried out to God and complained against Moses: 'Was it because there were no graves in Egypt that you brought us to the desert to die? What have you done to us by bringing us out of Egypt? Didn't we say to you in Egypt, "Leave us alone; let us serve the Egyptians"? It would have been better for us to serve the Egyptians than to die in the desert!' (Exod. 14:11–12).

The Israelites did not trust God's power to save. Humanly speaking, however, they were making an accurate assessment of their situation, for they were in grave danger. The Egyptians, who boasted the world's strongest army, were determined to destroy as many of the Israelites as necessary and to drag the rest of them back to the house of bondage. Caught between the army and the sea, facing slavery on one side and death on the other, there was nothing they could do to save themselves. Only God could deliver them. Hence their peril is an apt illustration of the human predicament. We are trapped between sin and death, and since we are unable to escape by ourselves, we need God to come and rescue us.

[13] Ps. 106:21.   [14] Hos. 12:19a; cf. Exod. 20:2.

As desperate as the Israelites were, their deliverance was never in any real doubt. This is because – as we have already seen – God had elected them for salvation. Salvation was the first thing God promised Moses when he called him to lead the people. God said, 'I have come down to rescue them from the hand of the Egyptians and to bring them up out of that land' (Exod. 3:8). He reminded Moses of that promise when he told him to camp by the sea: 'I will gain glory for myself through Pharaoh and all his army, and the Egyptians will know that I am the LORD' (14:4; cf. vv. 17–18).

That is exactly what God proceeded to do: to gain glory for himself by saving Israel out of Egypt. The details of this dramatic rescue from impending disaster are vividly and poetically described in Exodus 15, 'The song of Moses and Miriam'. first God parted the waters of the Red Sea:

> *By the blast of your nostrils*
> *the waters piled up.*
> *The surging waters stood firm like a wall;*
> *the deep waters congealed in the heart of the sea* (15:8).

Next the people walked through on dry land, with the Egyptians in hot pursuit:

> *The enemy boasted,*
> *'I will pursue, I will overtake them.*
> *I will divide the spoils;*
> *I will gorge myself on them.*
> *I will draw my sword*
> *and my hand will destroy them'* (15:9).

The repeated use of the first-person singular pronoun 'I' shows Pharaoh's proud ambition. But all his boasting came to nothing, for as he attempted to follow the Israelites on their path through the sea, his chariots got bogged down in the mud. There all Pharaoh's soldiers perished, for the wind changed, the waters turned, and the entire army was gulped down by the sea.

What happened at the Red Sea was only the beginning. In the verses which follow, Moses praises God for finishing the work of his salvation:

> *In your unfailing love you will lead*
> *the people you have redeemed.*
> *In your strength you will guide them*
> *to your holy dwelling.*
> *The nations will hear and tremble;*
> *anguish will grip the people of Philistia.*

> *The chiefs of Edom will be terrified,*
>   *the leaders of Moab will be seized with trembling,*
> *the people of Canaan will melt away;*
>   *terror and dread will fall upon them.*
> *By the power of your arm*
>   *they will be as still as a stone –*
> *until your people pass by, O LORD,*
>   *until the people you bought pass by.*
> *You will bring them in and plant them*
>   *on the mountain of your inheritance—*
> *the place, O LORD, you made for your dwelling,*
>   *the sanctuary, O LORD, your hands established.*
> *The LORD will reign*
>   *for ever and ever* (15:13–18).

These verses are not about coming out of Egypt, but about conquering Canaan. They describe Israel's conquest of Palestine, culminating in the establishment of God's kingdom. By the faithfulness of his covenant love (15:13), God led his people through the wilderness to a new home. There he established his kingdom and lived in his holy temple. One day the promise will be completely fulfilled in God's eternal kingdom, where he *will reign for ever and ever* (15:18).

'The song of Moses and Miriam' shows something important about the pattern of salvation. In its most basic sense, salvation means deliverance from evil. But there is more to well-being than the absence of danger; there is also the presence of peace and plenty. Therefore, salvation is always *to* something as well as *from* something. In the case of the exodus, salvation was from Egypt to the promised land. In the case of salvation in Christ, as we will see throughout this book, salvation is from sin and into glory.

The Lord is my salvation

It is important to understand that the events celebrated in Exodus 15 really happened. The Bible contains many great rescue stories, but they are more than stories.[15] They are actually histories, true stories of God's saving work in time and space. It was not the faith of the Jews that created these stories, therefore, but the work of God in history that gave rise to their faith: 'When the Israelites saw the great power the LORD displayed against the Egyptians, the people feared the LORD and put their trust in him' (Exod. 14:31).

---

[15] The historicity of the exodus is ably defended in James K. Hoffmeier, *Israel in Egypt: The Evidence for the Authenticity of the Exodus Tradition* (Oxford: Oxford University Press, 1996), and John D. Currid, *Ancient Egypt and the Old Testament* (Grand Rapids: Baker, 1997).

Salvation is always a fact, never a fiction. In the case of Israel's emancipation from Egypt, salvation was not only a fact, but it was also a miracle. No merely natural explanation could account for all the details of this amazing rescue. It required the supernatural intervention of Almighty God. Israel's salvation thus teaches at least three important principles about God's saving work. All three are suggested by the theme verse of Moses' hymn: *The LORD is my strength and my song; he has become my salvation* (15:2a).[16]

The first principle is the most general: the Lord is my salvation. From beginning to end, deliverance is divine. What Moses emphasizes throughout his narrative is that it was all God's doing. God personally handled all the arrangements for Israel's salvation. He instructed Moses where to set up camp (14:1–2) and told him how to hold his wooden staff (14:16). He sent his angel to keep the Egyptians away from the Israelites (14:19–20) and held back the sea with a strong east wind (14:21). He trapped the Egyptian chariots in the mire (14:25) and swept them under the waters (14:27). Moses matter-of-factly summarizes all this divine activity by saying, 'That day the LORD saved Israel from the hands of the Egyptians' (14:30a). Later, when it came time to write the lyrics for his song, Moses expressed the same truth in poetic verse:

> *You blew with your breath,*
> *and the sea covered them.*
> *They sank like lead*
> *in the mighty waters* (15:10).

The great truth to be learned from Israel's coming out of Egypt is also the primary message of the Bible: 'Salvation comes from the LORD.'[17] In the first section of this book we discovered that salvation is something that only God can accomplish. Now we are beginning to discover that salvation is something that he actually does accomplish and has accomplished.

Since Israel's salvation required military deliverance, it is not surprising that Moses describes God as a warrior: *The LORD is a warrior; the LORD is his name* (15:3). God's war on Egypt was a 'holy war' in the proper sense of the term. It was not a war in which misguided human beings fought for their own cause, allegedly on God's behalf. Rather, it was a war in which God himself fought the battle, on behalf of his people. In our study of Isaiah 59 (see chapter 3), we noted that the divine warrior goes into battle armed with nothing except his own strength. The same was true of the war he waged against the Egyptians:

---

[16] Cf. Ps. 118:14; Is. 12:2.   [17] Jonah 2:9.

> *Your right hand, O LORD,*
> *was majestic in power.*
> *Your right hand, O LORD,*
> *shattered the enemy.*
> *In the greatness of your majesty*
> *you threw down those who opposed you …*
> *You stretched out your right hand*
> *and the earth swallowed them* (15:6–7, 12).[18]

God saved Israel out of Egypt with his own bare hands.

For ever afterwards, whenever God's people recounted their deliverance from Egypt, the main thing they remembered was the One who did the delivering. As Moses later said, 'We were slaves of Pharaoh in Egypt, but the LORD brought us out of Egypt with a mighty hand.'[19] Or in the words of his father-in-law Jethro, 'Praise be to the LORD, who rescued you from the hand of the Egyptians and of Pharaoh, and who rescued the people from the hand of the Egyptians' (Exod. 18:10). What Moses and Jethro were saying was simply this: the Lord is our salvation.

The Lord is my strength

Not only is the Lord our salvation, but he is also our strength. The way he revealed his mighty strength to Israel was by crushing their enemies. Moses did not hesitate to describe Egypt's defeat in graphic terms. He had watched the Egyptians drown before his own eyes, and thus he was able to describe how God sent them gurgling down to the bottom of the sea:

> *Pharaoh's chariots and his army*
> *he has hurled into the sea.*
> *The best of Pharaoh's officers*
> *are drowned in the Red Sea.*
> *The deep waters have covered them;*
> *they sank to the depths like a stone* (15:4–5).

The description is so vivid that one can practically see the soldiers struggling against the sea. There were no survivors (14:28). Later the Israelites watched the bodies of the Egyptians wash up on the shores of the Red Sea (14:30).

It was an impressive display of God's strength. But some may ask whether it was necessary or even appropriate for God to destroy the Egyptians. In human terms, it was a horrific event, involving the loss of

---

[18] Cf. Deut. 26:8.   [19] Deut. 6:21.

many men, as well as many horses. Yet Moses did more than describe what happened; he also praised God for it!

> *I will sing to the LORD,*
> * for he is highly exalted.*
> *The horse and its rider*
> * he has hurled into the sea.*
> *The LORD is my strength and my song* ... (15:1).

To understand what was so praiseworthy about drowning Pharaoh and all his soldiers, it is important to remember how evil they were. The Egyptians were a brutal, arrogant people who worked the Israelites to death and refused to give God the glory. Therefore, casting the horse and rider into the sea was an act of perfect justice.

Realize also that the conflict between Israel and Egypt was really a spiritual battle, pitting the God of Abraham, Isaac and Jacob against the gods of the Nile.[20] When Moses first asked Pharaoh to let his people go, it was so that they could go out into the wilderness to worship God (see Exod. 3:12; 5:1). The way God persuaded Pharaoh finally to give in was by showing his power over all the gods and goddesses of Egypt. Most of the plagues that were visited on Egypt defeated specific deities. Turning the river into blood showed God's power over Hapi, who personified the Nile; sending the frogs showed God's power over Heqet, who was depicted as a frog; and so forth. By the time God was finished with the Egyptians, he had humbled their gods and goddesses, and thereby fulfilled his promise: 'I will bring judgment on all the gods of Egypt. I am the LORD' (12:12b). It was for this spiritual victory that he was to be praised:

> *Who among the gods is like you, O LORD?*
> [Implied answer: Certainly none of the gods of Egypt!]
> *Who is like you—*
> * majestic in holiness,*
> * awesome in glory,*
> * working wonders?* (15:11).

God is incomparable. His power to save is unique. By working his wonders to bring Israel out of Egypt, he proved that no-one else can match his holy majesty and awesome glory.

Back in chapter 3 we mentioned some of the logical and theological problems connected with believing that all the different religions offer essentially the same salvation. Here we discover a further problem with

---

[20] This theme is developed in Barnhouse, *The Invisible War*, pp. 197–212. See also my *Exodus: Saved for God's Glory* (Wheaton, IL: Crossway, forthcoming).

trying to make biblical Christianity compatible with other religions. The reason it is wrong to worship other gods is that they are not gods at all! The salvation God offers requires the rejection of every false object of worship. Therefore, we cannot be saved by embracing other faiths, but only by excluding them.

Everything that we have been saying so far about God's saving strength has implications for faith in Jesus Christ. As we saw in our study of election (chapter 4), Jesus is the location of our salvation; he is the only one who is able to save us from our sins. That is why the New Testament calls him the Saviour,[21] or 'our Lord and Saviour Jesus Christ'.[22] In fact, 'Saviour' is his very name, for 'Jesus' means 'the Lord is my salvation'.

In many ways, the salvation that Jesus offers is the same kind of salvation that God's people experienced when they came out of Egypt. To begin with, the basic concept of salvation is the same in the New Testament as it was in the Old. Even the terminology is similar. The Greek verb *sōzō* means to rescue or to deliver. The nouns taken from this verb are *sōtēr* and *sōtēria*, meaning 'deliverer' or 'saviour', and 'salvation'. In the New Testament, as in the Old, salvation is a deliverance. In its most general sense salvation in Christ is a rescue. And in order for us to be rescued, it is necessary for Jesus to destroy our enemies, just as God destroyed the Egyptians in the waters of the Red Sea. Salvation is never complete until the enemy is destroyed, for while the enemy lives, it continues to pose a threat to the safety of those who have been saved. But Christ's triumph over our enemies is absolute. When Zechariah (the father of John the Baptist) praised God for sending Jesus, he sang, 'Praise be to the Lord, the God of Israel, because he has come … to rescue us from the hand of our enemies'.[23] Jesus has crushed, is crushing, and will crush all our foes.

Whatever the enemy, Jesus is our strength and our salvation. He saves us from our sins, which is why he came in the first place: 'She will give birth to a son, and you are to give him the name Jesus, because he will save his people from their sins.'[24] Jesus did this through his atoning death on the cross; he 'gave himself for our sins to rescue us from the present evil age'.[25] On at least one occasion, the Bible identifies his saving death as an exodus. On the Mount of Transfiguration, where he appeared to his disciples in all his glory, Jesus spoke with Moses and Elijah about his 'departure'. The Greek word for 'departure' is *exodos*.[26] Jesus understood his crucifixion to be a kind of exodus. The exodus from Egypt was a sign promising the greatest exodus of all: Jesus passing through death's deep waters and landing safe on the far side to save us from sin.

---

[21] Eg. Luke 2:11; John 4:42; Acts 13:23; Titus 3:6; etc.
[22] 2 Pet. 1:11.   [23] Luke 1:68, 74.   [24] Matt. 1:21.   [25] Gal. 1:4.
[26] Luke 9:31.

Sin is not the only enemy from which we are saved, however. Jesus also saves us from sin's bitter consequences. As Peter pleaded on the Day of Pentecost, 'Save yourselves from this corrupt generation.'[27] Jesus also saves us from God's wrath: 'Since we have now been justified by his blood, how much more shall we be saved from God's wrath through him!'[28] One day Jesus will save us from Satan, for the devil's final destiny is to be cast into an eternal, infernal lake of fire.[29] But even now Jesus holds power over our supernatural enemies. This is why the Gospels give so much attention to the casting out of evil spirits. Salvation in Christ involves deliverance from every spiritual attack, including attacks that come from demons and evil people. In the face of all these foes, the Christian's confidence is this: 'The Lord will rescue me from every evil attack and will bring me safely to his heavenly kingdom.'[30]

Jesus Christ is the Saviour who delivers us from sin, wrath and Satan. By virtue of his resurrection, God finally will deliver us from our last enemy, which is death.[31] The apostle Paul asked, 'Who will rescue me from this body of death?' Immediately he gave the answer: 'Thanks be to God – through Jesus Christ our Lord!'[32] The first to be delivered from death was Jesus himself, who was raised from the tomb on the third day. Now God promises to deliver us from death through the risen Christ.

Christians have long recognized the resurrection of Jesus as an exodus, a passing from death into life. This idea is beautifully expressed in a hymn John of Damascus wrote in the eighth century. The first stanza praises God for bringing Israel out of Egypt:

> Come, ye faithful, raise the strain
> of triumphant gladness;
> God hath brought his Israel
> into joy from sadness;
> loosed from Pharaoh's bitter yoke
> Jacob's sons and daughters;
> led them with unmoistened foot
> through the Red Sea waters.

But John of Damascus was using Israel and Egypt as a metaphor for the resurrection of Christ. In the triumphant second stanza, he describes the greatest exodus of all:

> 'Tis the spring of souls today;
> Christ hath burst his prison,
> and from three days' sleep of death,

[27] Acts 2:40b.   [28] Rom. 5:9; cf. 1 Thess. 5:9.   [29] Rev. 20:10.
[30] 2 Tim. 4:18a.   [31] 1 Cor. 15:26.   [32] Rom. 7:24b–25a.

as a sun hath risen;
all the winter of our sins,
    long and dark, is flying
from his light, to whom we give
    laud and praise undying.

The Lord is my song

With this hymn we come to a final truth about God and his salvation. Not only is the Lord my salvation and my strength, but he is also my song. The most obvious feature of Exodus 15 is the one we have saved for last. It contains the lyrics for a chorus:

Then Moses and the Israelites sang this song to the LORD:

> '*I will sing to the* LORD,
>   *for he is highly exalted.*
> *The horse and its rider*
>   *he has hurled into the sea.*
> *The* LORD *is my strength and my song;*
>   *he has become my salvation*' (15:1–2a).

The Israelites sang because they had been saved. '*I will sing to the* LORD.' Why? '*For he is highly exalted … he has become my salvation.*' At the end of chapter 14 we learn that 'when the Israelites saw the great power the LORD displayed against the Egyptians, the people feared the LORD and put their trust in him' (14:31). Having trusted him for their salvation, it was only natural for them to want to sing his praises. Salvation is what puts the song into the believer's heart.

It is significant that 'The song of Moses and Miriam' is the first song in the Bible. There had always been poetry, of course, ever since Adam took one look at Eve and uttered the world's first poetic couplets.[33] There had also been singing before, or at least music. Genesis 4 introduces Jubal, who was 'the father of all who play the harp and flute'.[34] Nevertheless, 'The song of Moses and Miriam' is the very first song to be written down in the Bible.

The reason the people sang was that their exodus gave them something to sing about. Their song provides little, if any, new information about Israel's salvation. The narrative could proceed from Exodus 14:31 to 15:22 without any disturbance in the line of plot. Yet the story would be incomplete without the song. Remember that God saves his people for the purpose of his glory. In order for God to receive the glory he deserves, it is necessary for his people to sing hymns of praise. Thus

---

[33] Gen. 2:23.   [34] Gen. 4:21.

the very reason God saved the Israelites out of Egypt was so that they could stand on the shores of the Red Sea and sing this song. Three times God had promised, 'I will gain glory for myself through Pharaoh and all his army' (14:4, 17–18). That promise was fulfilled; not when the Israelites walked through on dry land, or when the Egyptians were swallowed by the sea – although that was all part of it – but when Moses began to sing. The exodus was meant to be a musical, and not simply a drama.

Salvation always calls for a song. Try to imagine Christianity without music. It is unthinkable, really. When Isaiah heard the promise of the Messiah, he was moved to write:

> I will praise you, O LORD.
>> Although you were angry with me,
> your anger has turned away
>> and you have comforted me.
> Surely God is my salvation;
>> I will trust and not be afraid.
> The LORD, the LORD, is my strength and my song;
>> he has become my salvation.[35]

The reason we are saved is to give glory to God, and what better way to do so than with a song! Johann Sebastian Bach (1685–1750) claimed that 'the aim and final reason ... of all music ... should be none else but the Glory of God'.[36] Since it has the power to touch the heart, music has a unique capacity to increase God's glory by moving us to praise him with our whole being. Calvin was right when he said that 'singing has great power and vigour to move and inflame men's hearts to call upon and praise God with a more vehement and burning zeal'.[37]

Every Christian is a member of the choir, for the song of salvation is for everyone who has been saved. Once Moses had finished singing, the rest of God's people took up the refrain:

Then Miriam the prophetess, Aaron's sister, took a tambourine in her hand, and all the women followed her, with tambourines and dancing. Miriam sang to them:

> *Sing to the LORD,*
>> *for he is highly exalted.*
> *The horse and its rider*
>> *he has hurled into the sea* (15:21).

[35] Is. 12:1–2.
[36] Johann Sebastian Bach, quoted in *Christianity Today* (12 July 1999), p. 61.
[37] John Calvin, quoted in John D. Witvliet, 'The spirituality of the Psalter: Metrical psalms in liturgy and life in Calvin's Geneva', *CTJ* 32.2 (November 1997), pp. 73–297.

In spontaneous, joyful ecstasy, Miriam began dancing on the seashore. With music and singing, all God's women took up the victory dance. Their song began with exactly the same words as the song of Moses. Although it is not recorded in the Bible, in all likelihood they proceeded to sing the entire song. In any case, it was a song for the same salvation, a song for Miriam as well as Moses, for women as well as for men, a song for all God's people to sing with one voice.

The song is for everyone who knows Jesus Christ as Saviour. God has called us out of the Egypt of our sins, saving us from Satan, wrath, death and all the rest of our enemies. Now we have something to sing about. It is time to take up the chorus and shake out the tambourine, to put on dancing shoes and give God the glory. The Lord is our strength and our song, and he has become our salvation.

6. Paid in full
Redemption: Ruth 4:1–22

In its most general sense, salvation means deliverance. The message of salvation is the good news that God has rescued us from sin and death through the crucifixion and resurrection of Jesus Christ. There is more to salvation than deliverance, however, and in this chapter we turn from rescue to redemption.

Rescue and redemption are so closely related that the Bible often brings them together. Our previous study was about Israel's exodus from Egypt. As he celebrated that great escape, Moses first sang, 'The LORD ... has become my salvation';[1] that is to say, 'The Lord is my deliverance.' But towards the end of his song, Moses went on to call Israel's deliverance a redemption: 'In your unfailing love you will lead the people you have redeemed.'[2] Salvation means redemption as well as rescue. The same connection is drawn in the New Testament, with regard to salvation in Christ: 'For he [God] has rescued us from the dominion of darkness and brought us into the kingdom of the Son he loves, in whom we have redemption, the forgiveness of sins.'[3] To be saved in Christ is to be redeemed as well as rescued.

This alerts us to the fact that Christ was doing more than one thing when he died on the cross. From one point of view, the message of salvation is the simplest message in the world. It means being saved from sin, by grace, through faith, to the glory of God. God will save you from sin and all its consequences, by the grace he has shown in Jesus Christ, received through faith in his cross. However, sin is such a messy problem, with so many miserable complications, that it requires a comprehensive solution. No single word or picture is sufficient to capture every dimension of God's salvation. Hence, the biblical message of salvation is about redemption, propitiation, reconciliation and many other saving graces, all of which interpenetrate one another.

---

[1] Exod. 15:2.   [2] Exod. 15:13a.
[3] Col. 1:13–14; cf. Luke 1:68–71.

With him is full redemption

Redemption is one particular kind of deliverance. The word itself comes from the marketplace. It is a commercial term used to describe salvation as a business transaction. In its most basic sense, redemption is the purchase of something that has been lost. It is the securing of a release by the payment of a ransom. Thus there are three parts to any redemption: (1) the property that is lost and needs to be redeemed; (2) the price that must be paid to redeem it; and (3) the person who is able and willing to serve as the redeemer.

There are many different types of redemption in the Old Testament, but in one way or another, they all contain these three elements: the property lost, the price to be paid, and the person to pay it. Consider Israel's redemption from Egypt. The property in need of redemption was God's own people, enslaved in the house of bondage. The only one who was able and willing to redeem them was God himself, who said, 'I am the LORD, and I will bring you out from under the yoke of the Egyptians.'[4] What price did he pay? God said to Moses, 'I will redeem you with … mighty acts of judgment.'[5] In other words, God paid for Israel's redemption by paying back the Egyptians for what they had done. If the events of Passover are any indication, it might even be said that Pharaoh paid for Israel's redemption with the life of his first-born son.[6]

Redemption was part of Israel's history. To give another example, the return from exile in Babylon was later described as a redemption.[7] But redemption was also a significant part of daily life in Israel. The Old Testament law regulated the redemption of animals such as donkeys, sheep and goats.[8] In certain situations there were also provisions for redeeming a person. Although a family's first-born son belonged to the Lord, he could be redeemed by the payment of five silver shekels.[9] Again, if a man's ox gored someone to death his life was forfeit; however, he could redeem himself by paying a ransom price.[10] In each of these cases, what was lost could be regained, provided someone was able and willing to redeem it.

Another form of redemption concerned the manumission of a slave. The most famous example of this procedure comes from the book of Hosea. God wanted to show that he was faithful to his people even when they broke his covenant, so he made his prophet Hosea a living sermon illustration. He told him to go out and marry a prostitute named Gomer, and to remain faithful to her no matter how adulterous she became. To no-one's surprise, Gomer ran off with another man, falling into poverty and eventually slavery. But God sent Hosea to

---

[4] Exod. 6:6a; cf. Ps. 78:42. [5] Exod. 6:6b; cf. Deut. 7:8; 9:26; 2 Sam. 7:23.
[6] Exod. 11. [7] Is. 43:1; 44:22–23. [8] Exod. 13:13.
[9] Num. 18:14–17; cf. Exod. 34:20. [10] Exod. 21:29–32.

redeem her – presumably at the slave market, where he was able to buy her back for the price of 'fifteen shekels of silver and about a homer and a lethek of barley'.[11] Gomer's emancipation was a picture of God's redeeming grace, which goes out to find us and to buy us back when we sell ourselves into sin.

Of all the different types of redemption, perhaps the most common was the redemption of land that had been lost or sold. In the Old Testament, there were two primary ways to redeem such property. One was for the seller himself to buy back his own land.[12] If somehow he returned to prosperity, he could pay the price to regain his real estate. The other way to redeem property was for someone else, usually a close relative, to make the payment. A third way, which seems rarely to have been practised, was to wait for the Year of Jubilee, when all property reverted to its original owner.[13]

As God's people redeemed their livestock, freed their slaves, and ransomed their land, they gained practical experience with redemption. Gradually, they learned to know God as their Redeemer,[14] and to call themselves 'the redeemed of the LORD'.[15] Redemption became the cry of their hearts ('Come near and rescue me; redeem me because of my foes')[16] and the theme of their worship ('Praise the LORD, O my soul … who redeems your life from the pit').[17] They took what they had learned from the world of finance and used it proclaim the message of salvation:

> O Israel, put your hope in the LORD,
>   for with the LORD is unfailing love
>   and with him is full redemption.
> He himself will redeem Israel
>   from all their sins.[18]

The barley-field incident

One of the most beautiful stories of redemption is told in the book of Ruth, which the great German writer Johann Goethe (1749–1832) called 'the loveliest complete work on a small scale'. The story begins in sadness. Through a series of tragic circumstances, a Jewish woman named Naomi and her daughter-in-law Ruth, a foreigner who had sworn allegiance to the God of Israel (Ruth 1:16), found themselves walking from Moab to Bethlehem. They had both lost their husbands. Not only was this a cause for sorrow, but it also left them without food, land or protection. The women were travelling to Bethlehem because it was Naomi's home town. She had been away for more than a decade,

---

[11] Hos. 3:2.   [12] Lev. 25:26–27, 49.   [13] Lev. 25:10, 28.
[14] Is. 49:26.   [15] Ps. 107:2.   [16] Ps. 69:18; cf. 31:5; 44:26; 119:34.
[17] Ps. 103:1a, 4a.   [18] Ps. 130:7–8.

and she had suffered so much during those years that when she strag-
gled back into town, people hardly recognized her (1:19). 'Don't call
me Naomi ["Pleasant"]' she told them. 'Call me Mara ["Bitter"], because the Almighty has made my life very bitter' (1:20).

In those days the people of Israel still followed the biblical pattern
for welfare,[19] or perhaps one should say 'workfare'. The poor, especially
widows, orphans and aliens, were allowed to walk through the fields
and gather whatever grain the harvesters left behind. Ruth qualified on
nearly every count: she was a poor widow and was from Moab. So,
being an enterprising young woman, she said to Naomi, 'Let me go to
the fields and pick up the leftover grain behind anyone in whose eyes I
find favour' (2:2). When Naomi agreed, Ruth went out into the fields
to glean barley behind the harvesters. By this means, God provided her
with daily bread.

Ruth was still in need of redemption, however. She had barely enough
food to live, so she was nearly destitute. She had lost her husband, so she
was still in sorrow. She also faced danger. Ruth was a stranger living in a
strange land during the days of the judges, when 'every man did that
which was right in his own eyes'.[20] Naomi had good reason to fear what
might happen to her while she was out in the fields with the workmen
(2:22). All these difficulties meant that Ruth needed a redeemer. She was
in economic, emotional and social bondage. Since she could not produce
an heir on her own, there was no way she could redeem herself.

Ruth's impoverishment should remind us of our own spiritual
penury. We, too, are in need of a Redeemer. We were made to belong
to God, but we have become slaves to sin. As we have noted before, sin
brings the kind of suffering and alienation Ruth experienced. Even
worse, it brings such intense spiritual bondage that we cannot escape
from it by ourselves; we can be released only by redemption.

Thankfully, the message of salvation promises release from our sins.
The New Testament words for release come from the Greek verb *lyō*,
which means 'to loose' or 'to loosen', to set free by cutting a bond. The
term thus described the loosening of clothes, the unbinding of armour,
the unhitching of animals, and so forth. It was also used for the release
of prisoners, and since prisoners were often loosed from their chains by
the payment of a ransom, the price came to be called a *lytron*. Eventually this led to the development of new words like *lytroō*, which meant
'to release by the payment of a price', and *lytrōsis*, which simply meant
'redemption'.

In the New Testament, the various words for 'redemption' are all
used in connection with the person and work of the Redeemer, Jesus
Christ. Jesus has released us from our slavery to sin: 'All have sinned and
fall short of the glory of God, and are justified freely by his grace

---

[19] Lev. 19:9–10.   [20] Judg. 21:25, AV.

through the redemption that came by Christ Jesus';[21] 'who gave himself for us to redeem us from all wickedness'.[22] Not only has Jesus redeemed us from sin, but he has also redeemed us from all its miserable consequences. He has released us from guilt, for 'in him we have redemption through his blood, the forgiveness of sins'.[23] He has released us from God's wrath, for 'Christ redeemed us from the curse of the law'.[24] One day Jesus will even release us from death. The apostle Paul wrote, 'Where, O death, is your victory? Where, O death, is your sting?'[25] But Paul was quoting the prophet Hosea, and he knew that what Hosea had promised was redemption from death itself:

> I will ransom them from the power of the grave;
> I will redeem them from death.
> Where, O death, are your plagues?
> Where, O grave, is your destruction?[26]

In Jesus Christ we have a Redeemer who provides exactly the kind of redemption we need: release from sin, guilt, wrath and death. The message of salvation is a message of redemption.

Next-of-kin

As we have said, there are three requirements for redemption. One is the property which is lost and needs to be redeemed. Another is someone to serve as the redeemer, and this is where Ruth's story really starts to get interesting.

In the providence of God, it happened that Ruth ended up in the field of the most eligible bachelor in Bethlehem. The man's name was Boaz, and he was everything a young girl could want in a husband. He was godly in his speech, greeting his workers with a blessing and speaking naturally and comfortably with them about spiritual things (2:4, 12). He was obedient to God's Word, allowing the poor to gather the leftover grain from his field (2:8–9a). He was generous with his resources, going beyond the letter of the law to provide Ruth with extra food and water (2:9b, 14–16). He was pure in his conduct, protecting the women in his fields from sexual misconduct (2:9, 22). To top it all off, Boaz was rich. The Bible calls him 'a man of standing' (2:1), which means that he had wealth and power. One can imagine that when the *Bethlehem Times* did its annual feature on the ten most prominent men in the city, Boaz was featured on the cover, with golden sheaves of barley in the background. He seemed like a perfect match for Ruth: his generosity was matched by her industry, his hospitality by her

[21] Rom. 3:23–24.   [22] Titus 2:14a.   [23] Eph. 1:7; cf. Col. 1:14.
[24] Gal. 3:13a; cf. 4:5.   [25] 1 Cor. 15:55.   [26] Hos. 13:14.

loyalty, his charity by her humility.

The most important thing of all, however, was that Boaz was related to Naomi, and therefore qualified to become Ruth's redeemer. This dramatic revelation comes at the end of the second chapter. When Ruth came home from the harvest, she told her mother-in-law that she had worked in the fields of Boaz. "'The LORD bless him!" Naomi said to her daughter-in-law. "He has not stopped showing his kindness to the living and the dead." She added, "That man is our close relative; he is one of our kinsman-redeemers"' (2:20). And she emphasized at the beginning of the next chapter, 'Is not Boaz … a kinsman of ours?' (3:2).

Remember that redemption was always a family matter. The right and responsibility to redeem someone's land fell to a close relative, a man called a *gō'ēl*, or a 'kinsman-redeemer'. When God gave his law through Moses, he stipulated that the redemption of property was to be carried out by the next-of-kin. Thus the impoverished or the imprisoned were to be rescued by members of their own families. If an Israelite was in desperate financial straits, he could sell his field or even sell himself into slavery for a time.[27] But the responsibility for redemption fell to his kinsmen, so that the man's name and property would never leave the family.[28] God intended the ransom to be paid by those who had the greatest personal interest in redemption: the man's own flesh and blood.

The fact that the redeemer was always a kinsman yields an important insight into redemption in Jesus Christ. Like everything else in Scripture, the book of Ruth has to be understood in relation to Christ's person and work. Ruth and Boaz are part of the redemptive history that culminated in his coming. The genealogy at the end of the book shows that their great-grandson was King David (Ruth 4:22), who was a kinsman-redeemer in his own right. David redeemed the Israelites by helping to regain the land of promise. But even David was waiting for a greater Redeemer,[29] a Saviour to redeem all God's people from sin and death. The name of that Redeemer comes at the end of yet another genealogy – the one in the Gospel of Matthew that begins with Abraham, runs through Ruth and David, and ends with Jesus, who is also called Christ.[30]

All of this makes clear that there is a connection between Boaz and Jesus, who is our kinsman-redeemer. The right and responsibility of redemption always rest on the shoulders of a kinsman. Therefore, in order to accomplish our redemption, it was necessary for God the eternal Son to become a man. The price to redeem us from sin had to be paid by a man of flesh and blood, a member of the family of

---

[27] Lev. 25:25–34, 39–55.   [28] Lev. 25:23–24.   [29] Cf. Job 19:25.
[30] Matt. 1:16.

humanity. Our redemption could never be accomplished by an angel, or a beast, or anything else except a perfect human being.

Redemption is one of the primary reasons that God the eternal Son became a man. Theologians call this the doctrine of the incarnation. It simply means that Jesus Christ was both fully God and fully man. He had a human nature as well as a divine nature. In his true deity, he was very God of very God; by his genuine humanity, he was a man among men. This is how the *Westminster Shorter Catechism* defines his incarnation: 'The only Redeemer of God's elect is the Lord Jesus Christ, who, being the eternal Son of God, became man, and so was, and continueth to be, God and man in two distinct natures, and one person, for ever' (A. 21).

The fullest explanation of the relationship between Christ's incarnation and our redemption is provided in the Letter to the Hebrews. First the writer states the fact of the incarnation, that Jesus is our kinsman: 'Both the one who makes men holy [Christ] and those who are made holy [Christians] are of the same family. So Jesus is not ashamed to call them brothers.'[31] Here is a most remarkable truth: Jesus calls us his brothers and sisters because he is made of the same stuff as we are. His reason for becoming God incarnate is to secure our freedom from sin, guilt, death and the devil:

> Since the children have flesh and blood, he too shared in their humanity so that by his death he might destroy him who holds the power of death – that is, the devil – and free those who all their lives were held in slavery by their fear of death ... For this reason he had to be made like his brothers in every way, in order that he might become a merciful and faithful high priest in service to God, and that he might make atonement for the sins of the people.[32]

For Jesus to be our redeemer, it was necessary for him to become our kinsman, to be not just God the Son, but also a son of David. So Jesus was conceived by the Holy Spirit and born of the virgin Mary. By his incarnation he became our blood-brother, the bone of our bone and the flesh of our flesh. Because he was a real human being, he was able to purchase our true redemption. Redemption in Christ is kinsman-redemption.

Paying the full price

The third thing redemption requires is the purchase price. In addition to the property to be redeemed and the person to redeem it, there is also the actual payment to be made. It is at this point in Ruth's romantic

---

[31] Heb. 2:11.   [32] Heb. 2:14–15, 17.

adventure that there is an unexpected complication.

What had happened was this: as Ruth went out day after day to gather barley, Naomi gradually put one and one together and realized that it was time to do a little matchmaking. Since Boaz was eligible to serve as a kinsman-redeemer, the thing to do was for Ruth to get him to marry her. As far as Naomi was concerned, there was no time to lose. Acting quickly and decisively, she gave Ruth the following instructions:

> 'My daughter, should I not try to find a home for you, where you will be well provided for? Is not Boaz, with whose servant girls you have been, a kinsman of ours? Tonight he will be winnowing barley on the threshing-floor. Wash and perfume yourself, and put on your best clothes. Then go down to the threshing-floor, but don't let him know you are there until he has finished eating and drinking. When he lies down, note the place where he is lying. Then go and uncover his feet and lie down. He will tell you what to do' (Ruth 3:1–4).

Everything went according to plan. Ruth bathed, perfumed, dressed and went to the threshing-floor, where she watched Boaz eat and drink, and then she lay down at the far end of the grain pile. Once everyone was asleep, she crept up, uncovered his feet, and lay down beside him. What Ruth was really doing was asking Boaz to marry her and redeem her. Not only was she proposing marriage, but she was also asking Boaz to raise up an heir for Naomi's family, which would include buying back Naomi's property. With her heart pounding, Ruth waited to see what would happen. In the middle of the night, Boaz suddenly awakened, only to discover that there was a woman lying at his feet. When he demanded to know who she was, she said, 'I am your servant Ruth. Spread the corner of your garment over me, since you are a kinsman-redeemer' (3:9). This was according to custom. In those days, if a man was willing to serve as a redeemer, he would signal his intentions by spreading the corner of his blanket over the woman.

Boaz was more than willing to be the kinsman-redeemer, but there was one further complication: he had a rival. There was another man in town who was also eligible to redeem Ruth and Naomi. Boaz explained the situation to Ruth: 'Although it is true that I am near of kin, there is a kinsman-redeemer nearer than I. Stay here for the night, and in the morning if he wants to redeem, good; let him redeem' (3:12–13a). Since this other man was an even closer relative than Boaz, he had the right of first refusal. So the question becomes, Will Ruth get her man, or will another man get her first?

Boaz was not the kind of man to sit around and wait for something to happen (3:13, 18), so when morning came, he went to the city gates to find the nearer kinsman. When Boaz saw him he gave a friendly greeting: *'Come over here, my friend, and sit down'* (4:1). When the man had taken his seat, Boaz casually outlined the facts of the situation: *'Naomi, who has come back from Moab, is selling the piece of land that belonged to our brother Elimelech. I thought I should bring the matter to your attention and suggest that you buy it ... If you will redeem it, do so. But if you will not, tell me, so that I will know. For no-one has the right to do it except you, and I am next in line'* (4:3b–4a).

It must have sounded like a golden opportunity, especially since Boaz wanted to take advantage of it himself. The nearer kinsman would have exclusive rights to a prime piece of real estate. After an initial outlay of capital, the property would be his to manage, and eventually to pass on to his family. So at once he said, *'I will redeem it'* (4:4b). As if to show how eager the man was, the original Hebrew reads, 'I, I will redeem it.' But then Boaz – skilful negotiator that he was – introduced a twist to the deal. He said, *'On the day you buy the land from Naomi and from Ruth the Moabitess, you acquire the dead man's widow, in order to maintain the name of the dead with his property'* (4:5). The point was this: on the day he bought the land, with all its assets, the nearer kinsman would also inherit several liabilities. He would become responsible for the maintenance of Ruth and Naomi. More than that, he would be required to raise up an heir for them.

Boaz wanted to impress the other kinsman with the high cost of redemption. The man may have assumed that the sale of land would come without any financial obligations. Or he may have assumed that he would only have to care for Naomi, a childless widow. In either case, the fields and all they produced would pass into the possession of his own son. But redemption always comes at a price, and in this case, the redeemer would be obligated to marry Ruth, a young woman who was almost certain to bear children. Therefore, the field would never be his to keep; it would always belong to Ruth and to her children. Instead of acquiring more property for himself, the redeemer would have to invest his own capital into someone else's estate. The kinsman had nothing to gain by becoming a redeemer; it was only an opportunity to make a sacrifice.

In the end, it was the high price of redemption that made the nearer kinsman unwilling to be the redeemer. Once he realized that redemption was out of his price range, he forfeited his right to redeem: *'I cannot redeem it because I might endanger my own estate. You redeem it yourself. I cannot do it'* (4:6). Twice the man said, 'I cannot redeem.' The reason he could not was because he would not. He was unwilling to endanger his own estate. When Boaz raised the stakes, the nearer-kinsman formally renounced his right of redemption: *(Now in earlier times in Israel, for the redemption and transfer of property to become final, one party took off his sandal and gave it to the other. This was the method of legalising transactions in Israel.) So the kinsman-redeemer said to Boaz, 'Buy it yourself.' And he removed his sandal* (4:7–8).

The nearer kinsman's refusal to redeem serves to emphasize, by way of contrast, the sacrifice of Boaz. Boaz was both able and willing to redeem. He was *able* to redeem because he was a man of wealth and position (2:1), with fields and servants to spare. But more than that, he was *willing* to redeem. As soon as the nearer kinsman threw down his sandal, Boaz made a public declaration of redemption: *'Today you are witnesses that I have bought from Naomi all the property of Elimelech, Kilion and Mahlon. I have also acquired Ruth the Moabitess, Mahlon's widow, as my wife, in order to maintain the name of the dead with his property, so that his name will not disappear from among his family or from the town records. Today you are witnesses!'* (4:9–10). Boaz was willing to pay the full price of redemption.

The purchase of blood

It is not hard to see that there are many similiarities between the redemption Boaz provided for Ruth and the redemption God has provided in Jesus Christ. In both cases, there was property to be redeemed from its lost and sorry condition. In both cases, there was a person to redeem it, a close relative who was eligible to serve as the kinsman-redeemer. And in both cases, the redeemer was willing personally to underwrite the whole cost of redemption.

It is sometimes suggested that redemption is nothing more than a synonym for salvation, a general word for deliverance. Yet as Leon Morris has amply demonstrated, redemption in the biblical sense always requires the payment of a price.[33] The Bible thus uses the term 'redemption' to emphasize the costliness of our salvation. There was a price Jesus had to pay in order to purchase the souls of God's children back from their bondage to sin, and whenever the New Testament speaks of redemption, it invariably emphasizes how a high a price it was. Consider the great statement Jesus made about his redeeming work: 'For even the Son of Man did not come to be served, but to serve, and to give his life as a ransom for many.'[34] The Greek word translated here as 'ransom' is one of the words for redemption we encountered earlier in this chapter: *lytron*. The price Jesus paid to redeem us was his very life. Quite literally, it took a king's ransom to set us free from sin: the life of Jesus Christ, the King of heaven and earth.

The way Jesus described his saving work is significant: he gave his life as a ransom *for* us. In other words, Jesus died in our place, giving up his life as the substitute for our sins. An event from Israel's history helps to illustrate what Jesus meant. In 54 BC the Roman general Crassus plundered Jerusalem. When he came to the temple, he was confronted

[33] Morris, *The Apostolic Preaching of the Cross*, pp. 11–27.
[34] Mark 10:45; cf. Matt. 20:28; 1 Tim. 2:5–6.

by a priest named Eleazar who was the guardian of the treasury. Rather than surrendering all of Israel's sacred treasures, Eleazar persuaded Crassus to take a single bar of gold worth some ten thousand shekels. In his version of this episode, the first-century Jewish historian Josephus states that the general received the gold from the priest as a *lytron anti panton*, 'a ransom for the whole'.[35] The bar of gold ransomed the other sacred items by serving as a substitute for the entire temple treasury. The Bible uses nearly identical language to explain that God accepted the life of Jesus as a payment on our behalf, a ransom in our place.

Consider the costliness of the redemption Christ accomplished. As costly as it was to redeem Ruth, the price of her redemption is not to be compared with the price of redemption in Jesus Christ. Whereas Boaz endangered his estate, Jesus Christ sacrificed his very body on the cross of Calvary. He 'died as a ransom' to set us free from sin.[36] Whereas Boaz paid in the currency common to his day, Jesus paid with his own life-blood. It was the perfect redemption, the purchase of blood. 'For you know that it was not with perishable things such as silver or gold that you were redeemed from the empty way of life handed down to you from your forefathers, but with the precious blood of Christ, a lamb without blemish or defect.'[37] Or again, the Scripture says that 'we have redemption through his blood'.[38] We will say more about why salvation was such a bloody business in the following chapter. For the moment, it is sufficient to know that the price was, in fact, blood, and that Jesus did, in fact, pay it.

Jesus is the only Redeemer because no-one else would, or even could, pay the full price of our redemption. No other religious faith has ever claimed that the one and only Supreme Deity shed his own blood to save his people. What has Buddha – or Muhammad – ever done to purchase men for God? Yet redemption requires the ultimate sacrifice. Jesus was willing to pay the price because he loves his people. He was able to pay it because he is God the eternal Son, which makes his death of inestimable worth. The psalmist wrote,

> No man can redeem the life of another
> or give to God a ransom for him –
> the ransom for a life is costly,
> no payment is ever enough.[39]

What the psalmist said is true: no mere man can redeem the life of another man. But Jesus is God as well as man, and therefore he was able to 'purchase men for God'.[40]

Theologians have sometimes wondered who it was that Jesus paid

[35] Josephus, *The Antiquities of the Jews*, XIV.107 (p. 372).
[36] Heb. 9:15.   [37] 1 Pet. 1:18–19.   [38] Eph. 1:7.   [39] Ps. 49:7–8.
[40] Rev. 5:9.

for our redemption. Some of the early church fathers assumed that our ransom was paid to Satan, so that in effect redemption was a deal with the devil. 'At the cross,' they said, 'God delivered Christ over to Satan in exchange for the souls the evil one held captive.'[41] The obvious problem with this view is that God does not owe Satan anything. Rather than giving anything up to Satan, redemption is part of God's plan for destroying Satan altogether. The fact is that the Bible never states who, if anyone, received payment for our redemption. If this seems hard to understand, remember that analogies always have their limitations. The Bible is content to mention the high price of our redemption without specifying who received it. If anything, redemption is a price God pays to himself in order to loose us from the bonds of sin. But the point is not so much who received the ransom, as the simple fact that Jesus was willing to pay it.

The grace of God did not come cheap. When the Scriptures say that we 'were bought at a price',[42] it is good for us to remember what a costly price it was and not to set Christ's work at a discount. If ever we are tempted to take salvation in Christ for granted, this can only be because somehow we have forgotten that we were 'bought with his own blood'.[43] The great Princeton theologian Benjamin Breckinridge Warfield (1851–1921) wrote,

> There is no one of the titles of Christ which is more precious to Christian hearts than 'Redeemer' … It gives expression not merely to our sense that we have received salvation from Him, but also to our appreciation of what it cost Him to procure this salvation for us. It is the name specifically of the Christ of the cross. Whenever we pronounce it, the cross is placarded before our eyes and our hearts are filled with loving remembrance not only that Christ has given us salvation, but that he paid a mighty price for it.[44]

The romance of redemption

There is one last thing to be said about redemption: in the Bible redemption is always a romance. Since 'redemption' is the commercial term for 'salvation', it is easy to think of it as little more than a business transaction. But as far as Boaz was concerned, redemption was far more than a rearrangement of his investment portfolio; it was a matter of the heart.

Once Ruth proposed marriage, Boaz behaved like a man suddenly and madly in love. This was because Ruth's kindness touched his heart.

---

[41] Demarest, *The Cross and Salvation*, p. 149.
[42] 1 Cor. 6:20; cf. 7:23.   [43] Acts 20:28.
[44] Warfield, '"Redeemer" and "Redemption"', in *The Person and Work of Christ*, pp. 325–348 (325).

As soon as she asked him to serve as her kinsman-redeemer, he said, 'The LORD bless you, my daughter. This kindness is greater than that which you showed earlier: You have not run after the younger men, whether rich or poor' (3:10). What pleased Boaz was that Ruth did not marry for youth or for money, but only for covenant love.

There is a rare and beautiful painting that captures something of the romance between Ruth and Boaz. It comes from the Wenzel Bible, a fourteenth-century illuminated manuscript in the Austrian National Library. Ruth and Boaz lie under a dark sky, with sheaves of barley bundled all around. They lie, chastely, at either end of a large flowing blanket. They are both dressed in red, as if to show that their two hearts beat as one. In the face of Boaz there is a hint of surprise: who is this woman who lies at his feet? Yet both their faces are serene, for they are at peace with God, and in love with one another. Boaz responded to Ruth's love with the romance of redemption. He did more than provide for her; he married her, and thus they entered into an unbreakable covenant of intimate relationship.

The love that Boaz had for Ruth is made all the more remarkable by the fact that she was a foreigner. The Bible repeatedly draws attention to the fact that she was from Moab (1:3, 22; 2:2, 6, 21; 4:5, 10). What makes this significant is that the Moabites were outside the covenant, and thus explicitly excluded from entering God's tabernacle.[45] But Ruth had sworn her allegiance to the God of Israel. When she decided to accompany Naomi on her return to Bethlehem, she said, 'Where you go I will go, and where you stay I will stay. Your people will be my people and your God my God' (1:16b). When she arrived in Israel, Boaz welcomed her under the protective wings of God's providential care (2:12). Their eventual marriage was one of the first signs that God loves Gentiles as well as Jews. Their multi-ethnic romance thus illustrates reconciliation as well as redemption.

The Bible takes us right up to the threshhold of their honeymoon chamber, where Boaz went to Ruth and the Lord enabled her to conceive (4:13). Then it takes us to the nursery, where their son was born and placed in Naomi's arms (4:16). This is all part of the romance of redemption. Boaz did not simply write a cheque to pay the ransom and then go back to his business. No, when he agreed to be Ruth's redeemer, he undertook marital as well as financial obligations. He went from the courtroom to the living-room to share the rest of his life with her.

It is the same with redemption in Jesus Christ. The fact that Jesus was willing to pay the full ransom price to redeem us from our sins shows how much God loves us. In the words of several hymns quoted by Warfield:

---

[45] Deut. 23:3.

Father of heaven, whose love profound
A ransom for our souls hath found ...

I'd sing the precious blood He spilt
My ransom from the dreadful guilt
Of sin and wrath divine ...

Jesus, all our ransom paid,
All Thy Father's will obeyed,
Hear us, Holy Jesus.[46]

The Bible often compares the relationship between Jesus Christ and his church to the relationship between a loving husband and a faithful wife: 'My lover is mine and I am his.'[47] 'As a bridegroom rejoices over his bride, so will your God rejoice over you.'[48] '"A man will leave his father and mother and be united to his wife, and the two will become one flesh." This is a profound mystery – but I am talking about Christ and the church.'[49] The Bible speaks this way to help us understand how deeply, how tenderly, and how passionately Jesus loves us.

No-one can receive Jesus as Saviour without also loving him as Spouse. To receive the message of salvation is to be married to Christ, to become God's beloved possession.[50] 'You are not your own,' the Scripture says; 'you were bought at a price.'[51] And those who belong to God by redemption must live for him, so the Scripture goes on to say, 'Therefore honour God.'[52] To put it another way, 'Glorify God'. We no longer belong to ourselves; we belong, body and soul, to our Redeemer, and like everything else in salvation, redemption is all for the glory of God.

---

[46] Quoted by Warfield, ibid., p. 332.
[47] Song 2:16a. [48] Is. 62:5. [49] Eph. 5:31–32. [50] Eph. 1:14.
[51] 1 Cor. 6:19b–20a. [52] 1 Cor. 6:20.

7. God, be merciful to me
Expiation and propitiation: Luke 18:9–14

We are beginning to see that there is more than one way to describe the saving grace God gives in Jesus Christ. Salvation means deliverance. It is a rescue from sin's power by God's mighty acts. Salvation means redemption. It is a release from sin's bondage by the payment of a ransom. In this chapter we discover that salvation also means atonement, the removal of sin's penalty by the offering of a sacrifice.

Atonement is not a very popular subject. No doubt this is because it deals with too many things people would rather ignore, like the wrath of God, the punishment of sin, and the old, blood-stained cross. Most unbelievers do not see their need for atonement. 'Why would anyone else have to die for my sins?' they ask. For their part, many Christians do not understand the meaning of the atonement. The notion of a blood sacrifice for sin sounds primitive to them, perhaps even barbaric. Therefore, the cruciality of the cross has all but disappeared from contemporary theology.

It was not always this way. Back in the nineteenth century, in his definitive work on the subject, the great Scottish theologian George Smeaton (1814–89) identified the atonement as 'the central truth of Christianity, and the great theme of Scripture'.[1] Another Scottish divine, John Brown, wrote,

> Let a man preach with the greatest ability and zeal everything in the Bible but the Cross, he shall, as to the great end of preaching, preach in vain ... The doctrine of the atonement ought not to be the sole theme of the Christian ministry, but every doctrine, and every precept, of Christianity should be exhibited in their connection with this great master principle; and the leading object of the preacher should be to keep the mind and the heart of his hearers steadily fixed on Christ Jesus – Christ Jesus crucified.[2]

---

[1] Smeaton, *Christ's Doctrine of the Atonement*, p. 1.
[2] Brown, *An Exposition of the Epistle of Paul the Apostle to the Galatians*, p. 370.

Two sinners at prayer

Jesus himself once told a story to help explain our need for atonement. He told it to a group of people who were quite sure that they needed no such thing: *To some who were confident of their own righteousness and looked down on everyone else, Jesus told this parable* (Luke 18:9). The story, which is often called 'The Pharisee and the publican', concerned two men, two prayers and two destinies.

'*Two men went up to the temple to pray,*' said Jesus, '*one a Pharisee and the other a tax collector*' (Luke 18:10). Already the story contains a surprise, because everyone knows that tax collectors do not go to the temple. If they do, they certainly do not go there to pray. A praying tax collector, or 'publican', is an oxymoron, a contradiction in terms. In the time of Christ, tax collectors were considered the scum of Jewish society, and with good reason. They were in the employ of the oppressive Roman government, and thus they were considered traitors to the Jewish people. They were greedy and dishonest, usually relying on extortion for their profit margin. Not surprisingly, they were barred from serving in public office or giving testimony in a court of law. Make no mistake – the tax collector in Jesus' parable was a crook.

The Pharisee, by contrast, represented everything that was right and good in Jewish society. The historian Josephus described the Pharisees as 'a certain sect of the Jews that appear more religious than others, and seem to interpret the laws more accurately'.[3] They had virtually the best reputation in Israel. It was only natural, therefore, for the Pharisee to go up to the temple to pray. Unlike the tax collector, that was where he belonged.

In some ways, our respect for the Pharisee is increased when we overhear his prayer: '*God, I thank you that I am not like other men – robbers, evildoers, adulterers – or even like this tax collector. I fast twice a week and give a tenth of all I get*' (18:11–12). The Pharisee was a man with few obvious vices and many commendable virtues. He was thankful to God. He did not steal (which, as everyone well knew, tax collectors always did). He did not run with a bad crowd. He was faithful to his wife. In short, the Pharisee kept the whole law of God. Today he would be a renowned seminary professor, a respected elder or a beloved minister.

Furthermore, the Pharisee went well beyond the law in his devotional practice. Not only was he devoted to prayer, but he also fasted twice a week. The law stipulated only one fast a year, on the Day of Atonement,[4] so this man was fasting a hundred times more often than the law required! He also made a point of tithing all his income, setting aside one tenth of everything he received. This, too, was more

---

[3] Josephus, *The Wars of the Jews*, 1.5.2 (p. 551).   [4] Lev. 16:29–31.

than the law required, for the biblical tithe applied only to certain kinds of produce,[5] but not to other forms of income. By tithing everything, the Pharisee proved himself to be an exceptionally devout man. Yet for all his devotion, the Pharisee remained unsaved. None of his pious acts improved his standing with God, because God is never impressed with merely external religion. He does not base his judgment on outward acts of religious devotion, but on the inward disposition of the heart. When the Pharisee's prayers were finished, he went home unjustified, for God knew his heart and declared him 'not righteous' (18:14).

What was wrong with the Pharisee and his prayer? His most obvious problem was pride. Although he began well enough, by addressing God, he spent the rest of his prayer talking about himself. In two short sentences he uses the pronoun 'I' five times. In the words of one commentator, 'He glances at God, but contemplates himself.'[6] In fact, the Pharisee does something even worse than contemplate himself; he actually prays to himself! Notice the way Jesus introduces the man's prayer: *'The Pharisee stood up and prayed about himself'* (18:11a). To translate this sentence more literally, 'The Pharisee stood up and prayed *with* himself', or even '*to* himself'. He was not praying to God at all. For the Pharisee, prayer was a way of reminding himself what a great guy he was!

The Pharisee was so conceited that he refused to admit that he was a sinner. His refusal strikes at the very heart of the message of salvation. As we have seen, the salvation God offers by his grace is only for sinners. Therefore, being saved begins with confessing one's sins. That is why the first section of this book concerned the doctrine of total depravity. The only people who ever truly ask God to save them are people who know that they are guilty sinners. But the Pharisee never saw himself that way. Rather than admitting that he was as depraved as everyone else, he contemptuously thanked God that he was *not* like other men (18:11). Although he could see that there was a problem with humanity, he was too blind to see that he was part of it. To put it bluntly, the Pharisee did not understand the first thing about salvation: his own need to be saved from sin.

Nor did the Pharisee understand that he could be saved only by grace. Instead, he expected to be saved by works. He thought God would accept him on his own merits. After all, he was a good person – better than most, in fact – so he must be good enough for God. Thus the Pharisee was exactly like the people listening to Jesus' story: confident of his own righteousness. He had so much faith in his own ability that he had no need to trust in God. In a word, he was self-

---

[5] Deut. 14:22–23.
[6] Plummer, *The Gospel according to Saint Luke*, quoted in Geldenhuys, *The Gospel of Luke*, p. 452.

righteous. This, too, strikes at the heart of the Bible's saving message. According to the doctrine of total inability, we are sinners who will not and cannot come to God on our own. Only God can save us, and only by his grace.

The sinner before God

Remember that there were two men who went up to the temple – two men who prayed two prayers and met two destinies. Unlike the Pharisee, the tax collector received atonement for his sins. Whereas the Pharisee was counting on his own merits, the 'publican' was begging for God's mercy: *'The tax collector stood at a distance. He would not even look up to heaven, but beat his breast and said, "God, have mercy on me, a sinner"'* (18:13).

There were three parts to the tax collector's prayer: God, the sinner, and the mercy that came between them. His prayer started with God. This is where all prayer should begin, for the first act of prayer is to approach the majestic throne of the Almighty God. Remember that the Pharisee's prayer also began with God, which proves that there is more to prayer than mere words. The first word out of the Pharisee's mouth was 'God', except that he did not really know God at all. The tax collector began his prayer with the same word; the difference was that he had some idea who it was that he was addressing. When the tax collector said 'God', he knew that he was approaching the one true and supreme Deity, who is awesome in his holiness. This is apparent from his posture: the tax collector kept his distance from God, refusing even to look up to heaven. Surely this was because he had a proper fear of God's bright, burning holiness.

An old poem illustrates the difference between the way the Pharisee approached God and the way the publican approached him:

> Two men went to pray; or rather say,
> One went to brag, the other to pray;
> One stands up close, and treads on high,
> Where th' other dare not send his eye.
> One nearer to the altar trod,
> The other to the altar's God.[7]

The poem's last two lines answer the question, Who was closer to God – the Pharisee or the publican? The Pharisee was nearer to the altar, but much farther away from God. He was so full of himself that there was hardly any room for God at all. By contrast, although the publican was far from the altar, he was close to the heart of God, for he came in reverent fear.

[7] Source unknown, quoted in Lightfoot, *Lessons from the Parables*, p. 145.

The reason for the tax collector's fear was that he knew that he was a sinner, which is where his prayer ended. He began with God, but ended with himself, a sinner. To put it more accurately, he ended with himself, *the* sinner, as if he were the only sinner in all the world. The Greek original uses the definite article because, as far as the tax collector was concerned, he was the only sinner that mattered. The problem of humanity was his own problem. Rather than comparing himself to others, the way the Pharisee always did, the publican measured himself against the standard of God's perfect holiness. By that standard, he saw himself for what he was: nothing more and nothing less than a guilty sinner before a holy God.

When it came to confessing his sins, the tax collector's actions spoke as loudly as his words. He stood at a distance. Whereas the Pharisee stood in the temple's inner courts, the publican seems to have stayed in the outer courts, not daring to approach the Most Holy Place. He kept his distance because he sensed that he was separated from God, alienated by his sin. Nor did he dare to look up to heaven. Whereas the Pharisee looked down on everyone else, the publican could only look down to the ground. Ordinarily, people in those days prayed with their eyes raised, but the tax collector could not bring himself to do this because he felt unworthy to seek God's face. He was so weighed down by his guilt that he felt compelled to lower his shameful eyes. All the while, he was beating his breast. This was another sign of his contrition. By standing at a distance, dropping his gaze, and beating his breast, the publican showed that he was a self-confessed sinner.

Unlike the Pharisee, the tax collector *did* know the first thing about salvation: he knew that he was a sinner who deserved nothing except divine wrath. Knowing this was essential, because it prepared him to receive atonement for his sins. As we have already seen, the doctrine of sin helps to make sense of the message of salvation. A superficial awareness of sin results in a superficial understanding of God's saving grace, but those who plumb the depths of their depravity recognize their need of atonement.

When the tax collector calls himself a sinner, we should take him at his word. This parable is so familiar that Christians generally think of the publican as a sympathetic figure. After all, there is something heartwarming about a man bowing down to confess his sins. But the publican was hardly a role model! On the contrary, he was every bit as bad as he said he was, if not worse. As T. W. Manson observed, 'It is a great mistake to regard the publican as a decent sort of fellow, who knew his own limitations and did not pretend to be better than he was ... This publican was a rotter; and he knew it. He asked for God's mercy because mercy was the only thing he dared ask for.'[8]

---

[8] Manson, *The Gospel of Luke*, p. 604.

At the mercy seat

The mention of God's mercy brings us to the most striking feature of the tax collector's prayer. In between God's holiness and his own sinfulness he inserted a prayer for mercy. The Greek verb which is translated 'have mercy' is an unusual one. It is the verb *hilaskomai*, which means 'to propitiate' or 'to expiate' – in other words, 'to atone for sin by means of a blood sacrifice'. But before fully explaining what this means, it is necessary to understand how sacrifices were offered at the temple.

A good place to begin is with the procedure for making atonement given in Leviticus 16. The chapter begins with a warning intended to give the most serious impression of God's holiness:

> The LORD spoke to Moses after the death of the two sons of Aaron who died when they approached the LORD. The LORD said to Moses: 'Tell your brother Aaron not to come whenever he chooses into the Most Holy Place behind the curtain in front of the atonement cover on the ark, or else he will die, because I appear in the cloud over the atonement cover.'[9]

What had happened was this. The sons of Israel's first high priest had sauntered into the tabernacle and offered unholy fire, contrary to God's command. Immediately, they perished; they got burned by God's wrath.[10] God did this to show that he is much too holy to be trifled with. Sin leads to death and brings sinners under judgment. Anyone who comes into God's presence must come in a suitable way, or else be consumed by fire.

Mercifully, God provided a way for sinners to be saved from his wrath. After warning Aaron not to worship any way he pleased, God explained the proper way to come into his holy presence. Once a year, Aaron was to make atonement for the sins of God's people. He was to begin by offering a bull to atone for his own sins, as well as the sins of his household.[11] Then he was to take a perfect male goat and sacrifice it as a sin offering.[12] God said,

> He shall then slaughter the goat for the sin offering for the people and take its blood behind the curtain and do with it as he did with the bull's blood: He shall sprinkle it on the atonement cover and in front of it. In this way he will make atonement for the Most Holy Place because of the uncleanness and rebellion of the Israelites, whatever their sins have been.[13]

---

[9] Lev. 16:1–2.   [10] Lev. 10:1–2.   [11] Lev. 16:6, 11–14.   [12] Lev. 16:9.
[13] Lev. 16:15–16a.

In this manner, the high priest 'made atonement for himself, his household and the whole community of Israel'.[14]

What did all this signify? The goat represented God's sinful people. In a symbolical way, the sins of God's people were transferred to the goat. Ordinarily, before an animal was sacrificed, the sinner would place his hand on the animal's head while he confessed his sins.[15] This was to show that the sinner's guilt was being charged or *imputed* to the animal. Then the animal – in this case a goat – was sacrificed on the altar. This was necessary because once the sins of the people were imputed to the goat, the goat had to die. Remember that God had told Adam that if he sinned he would die.[16] When Adam sinned, God granted him a temporary stay of execution, but the punishment remained in force. Once the goat was made to bear the people's sins, it was the goat that had to suffer sin's punishment. The goat was a substitute dying in the place of sinners. Thus the sacrifice offered on the Day of Atonement was a reminder that the life of every sinner is forfeit to God, that the proper penalty for sin is death.

Once the sacrifice had been offered, the sacrficial blood was the proof that atonement had been made for sin. This is explained in Leviticus 17:11, where God says, 'it is the blood that makes atonement for one's life'. The reason the blood takes away guilt is that it shows that God has already carried out his death penalty against sin. What the priest did with the blood was to sprinkle it on the atonement cover, also called the mercy seat. The mercy seat was the golden lid on the ark of the covenant. It was located in the Most Holy Place of the temple (or the tabernacle), which was the earthly location of the Divine Presence. The mercy seat itself was a place of divine judgment, because the ark contained the law of God, which the people had broken. Sprinkling blood on the mercy seat, therefore, was a way to show that the atoning sacrifice had come between God and his sinful people. Here it should be emphasized that it was impossible for the blood of a mere animal to take away sin;[17] what the animal represented was the sacrifice of the Saviour to come.

When it was placed between God and sinners, there were two things that the sacrificial blood accomplished. They are expressed in two technical theological terms: expiation and propitiation. *Expiation* refers to the covering of sin. It explains what the sacrifice accomplished with respect to sinners and their guilt. Their sin was covered; their transgression was put away; their guilt was removed; their iniquity was pardoned. Expiation is what David had in mind when he wrote, 'Blessed is he whose transgressions are forgiven, whose sins are covered.'[18] Once the blood of the sacrifice had been sprinkled on the

---

[14] Lev. 16:17b.   [15] Lev. 4:3.   [16] Gen. 2:17.   [17] See Heb. 10:4.
[18] Ps. 32:1.

mercy seat, the sinner had made amends. The penalty for sin had been paid and no further guilt remained. In a word, the sins of God's people were expiated.

The second thing that the blood accomplished was *propitiation*. Although propitiation is a difficult word, it is necessary to use because it best describes an essential truth of salvation. Propitiation refers to the turning away of anger. It explains what the atoning sacrifice accomplished with respect to God and his wrath. Wrath is one of the most frequently-mentioned divine attributes in the Bible. It is not a violent emotion or an uncontrollable passion; it is more like righteous indignation. Wrath is God's holy opposition to sin and personal determination to punish it. John Stott has defined it as God's 'steady, unrelenting, unremitting, uncompromising antagonism to evil in all its forms and manifestations'.[19] Since it is right and good for God to hate every evil thing, wrath is one of his divine perfections.

God's anger against sin explains why the high priest never came into God's presence without the blood of a sacrifice.[20] If he came without the blood, he would be destroyed. However, once the sacrifice had died in place of the sinner, no more punishment remained. The priest sprinkled the blood on the mercy seat to show that God's justice was satisfied, his anger pacified. In a word, God's wrath was propitiated. To put it another way, the sacrifice made God propitious, or well-disposed, enabling him to look upon the sinner with favour.

By coming between God and the sinner, the blood sprinkled on the mercy seat was *both* an expiation and a propitiation. Through the atoning sacrifice, the sinner's guilt was expiated and God's wrath was propitiated. With respect to the sinner, the blood was an expiation; it covered the guilt of his sin. With respect to God, the blood was a propitiation; it turned away the justice of his wrath. To bring both ideas together, when the blood of the sacrifice was sprinkled on the mercy seat, the sinner was protected from God's wrath because his sins were covered.

All of this is precisely what the tax collector was praying for when he said, 'God, be merciful to me, the sinner.' There he was, praying in the temple, where atonement was made for sin, through the sacrificial blood sprinkled on the mercy seat. Knowing that he was under God's wrath because of his sin, the only thing he could do was to ask for mercy to come between his guilt and God's wrath. To put it more precisely, he begged for God to be 'mercy-seated' to him, for that is what the Greek verb *hilaskomai* literally means. The tax collector was asking God to atone for his sins, covering his guilt and protecting him from eternal judgment. The order of the publican's prayer is significant because it matches the Old Testament pattern for sacrifice: 'God be

---

[19] Stott, *The Cross of Christ*, p. 173.   [20] Heb. 9:7.

propitiated to me, the sinner.' First comes God, who is perfect in his holiness. Last comes the sinner, who deserves to die for his sins. But in between them comes the blood of the sacrifice that expiates and propitiates, taking away the guilt of the sinner and turning away the wrath of God.

Saved by the blood of the Lamb

The question we should ask is, Where can we find this mercy? Like the tax collector, we are sinners in need of a Saviour. Since God hates sin, we are under his wrath and curse. The only thing that can save us is a perfect sacrifice, for 'without the shedding of blood there is no forgiveness'.[21] But where is the blood, where is the sacrifice, and where is the mercy? We do not keep herds of sheep and goats to offer atonement for our sins. Nor could we, for there is no temple where we could make a sacrifice, no mercy seat where we could sprinkle the blood.

The answer, of course, is that Jesus Christ is the atoning sacrifice for our sins. The great preacher and hymn-writer John Newton (1725–1807) wrote of this in his diary. At the time, Newton was weighed down by guilt. As he lamented his lost and sinful condition he wrote, 'But now I may, I must, I do mention the Atonement. I have sinned, but Christ has died.'[22] Newton understood that God is mercy-seated to the sinner through the crucifixion of Jesus Christ. His death is our substitute; his cross is our mercy seat; and the blood Jesus sprinkled there is both the expiation for our sins and the propitiation of God's wrath.

The New Testament often describes Christ's death on the cross as a sacrifice: 'Christ loved us and gave himself up for us as a fragrant offering and sacrifice to God.'[23] This and many other verses – especially in the book of Hebrews – teach us to understand the work of Christ as the fulfilment of the Old Testament sacrificial system. Like the goat offered on the Day of Atonement, Jesus is the representative for God's covenant people, the substitute who died in our place. He is the most perfect substitute, for he is God the eternal Son, who never committed the least sin.

When we say that Jesus died in our place, we mean that his sacrifice accomplished what the blood on the mercy seat accomplished. His death on the cross was an *expiation*, the removal of our sins. When John the Baptist saw Jesus coming he said, 'Behold the Lamb of God, which taketh away the sin of the world!'[24] John was identifying Jesus as the

[21] Heb. 9:22b.
[22] John Newton, entry for 18 September 1779, quoted in D. Bruce Hindmarsh, *John Newton and the English Evangelical Tradition* (Oxford: OUP, 1996), p. 232.
[23] Eph. 5:2.   [24] John 1:29, AV.

sacrifice for our sins. Like the sacrificial lambs of the Old Testament, Jesus died in our place. Our sins were transferred or imputed to him: 'God made him who had no sin to be sin for us'.[25] 'He himself bore our sins in his body on the tree'.[26] Thus Jesus was bearing our sins on the cross, there to suffer the punishment that his people – and his people only[27] – deserved for their sins: death by the wrath of God. Now our sins are covered. They were punished on the cross, and no further penalty remains: 'Christ was sacrificed once to take away the sins of many people'.[28] 'Christ died for sins once for all, the righteous for the unrighteous, to bring you to God.'[29] In a word, the crucifixion was an expiation. It was the best expiation of all because Jesus atoned for our sin once and for all time: 'He has appeared once for all at the end of the ages to do away with sin by the sacrifice of himself.'[30]

Christ's death on the cross was also a *propitiation*. Propitiation is the act of performing a sacrifice by which God's wrath against sin is averted, which is precisely the kind of sacrifice Jesus offered: a sacrifice to turn away God's wrath. On four different occasions the New Testament describes the death of Christ as a propitiation. The Greek words for this are *hilaskomai*, *hilasmos* and *hilastērion*. The New International Version translates them with the phrase 'make atonement' or 'atoning sacrifice', but the most accurate term is 'propitiate', 'propitiation': 'God presented him [Jesus] as a sacrifice of atonement.'[31] Jesus had to be made like us in every way so 'that he might make atonement for the sins of the people.'[32] 'He is the atoning sacrifice for our sins'.[33] 'This is love: not that we loved God, but that he loved us and sent his Son as an atoning sacrifice for our sins.'[34] When the scripture calls Jesus an 'atoning sacrifice for our sins', it means that he is our propitiation. Not only has his blood covered our sins, but it has also turned away God's wrath against them. Thus Christ's death on the cross has these two great saving effects: it expiates our sin and propitiates God's wrath.

Theories of the atonement?

Some theologians object to this way of understanding Christ's death, and have tried to find some other way to explain it. Some say that the cross has a moral influence on humanity. This view was first popularized by Peter Abelard (1079–1142), who thought that the primary benefit of Christ's sufferings and death was to serve as a good example. By contemplating the horrors of the cross, we are moved to respond to God in love. Thus the efficacy of the crucifixion is subjective rather than objective: it does something *in* us rather than *for* us. Others

[25] 2 Cor. 5:21a; cf. Is. 53:6.   [26] 1 Pet. 2:24.   [27] John 10:15; Eph. 5:25.
[28] Heb. 9:28a.   [29] 1 Pet. 3:18a.   [30] Heb. 9:26.   [31] Rom. 3:25.
[32] Heb. 2:17.   [33] 1 John 2:2.   [34] 1 John 4:10.

deny the need for atonement at all. Human beings are basically good rather than essentially sinful; therefore we have no sin to expiate. Since God is love, he cannot show anger; therefore, God has no wrath to propitiate. This position is held by liberal theologians who locate salvation primarily in Christ's birth rather than in his death. God is reconciled to humanity by his incarnation, not his crucifixion. If the cross has any meaning at all, it is only to show that God is able and willing to suffer with us. 'It is not that the suffering appeases God,' they say, 'but that it expresses God – displays, in open history, the unconquerable love of God's heart.'[35]

Fundamental to these views of the atonement is a resistance to divine justice. In much contemporary theology, there is real hostility to describing salvation in forensic or judicial categories. The Dutch theologian G. C. Berkouwer (1903–96) once tried to explain the recalcitrant modern (and now postmodern) attitude towards 'the substitutionary suffering and death of Jesus Christ'. He wrote: 'Terms common to jurisprudence have been used in connection with Christ's death: satisfaction, sufficiency, payment, purchase, ransom, and punishment. And these terms have made men angry.'[36] There is more to salvation than justice, of course, but since the Saviour is just, his salvation must be just. What the sinner needs is not simply to be inspired by the cross, but to be saved by it – saved from eternal damnation.

One of the theologians who best understood the necessity of the cross was Anselm of Canterbury (c. 1033–1109), who wrote the definitive book on the medieval doctrine of the atonement. The book was called *Cur Deus Homo?*, which means 'Why a God-Man?' Anselm's answer was that God the Son had to become a man in order to atone for sin. He had to be human because humanity had sinned. He also had to be divine. Sin is an offence against the infinite dignity of God's character. Therefore, only the death of an infinite being could vindicate God's wounded honour.

Some theologians object that Anselm's explanation of what Christ was doing on the cross goes beyond the teaching of Scripture. The death of Christ on the cross is a fact, they say, but anything beyond that fact is a theory. Perhaps it is true that Anselm's reasoning was influenced by the medieval understanding of honour. Yet the heart of Anselm's teaching on the atonement was that the cross satisfied God's justice with respect to sin. Is this a mere theory? The fact is that the Bible itself explains what Christ was doing on the cross. It says that his death was a sacrifice. Like the sacrifices of the Old Testament, Jesus was a substitute for sinners, suffering the punishment we deserved for our sins: 'The punishment that brought us peace was upon him ... and the

[35] Bushnell, *God in Christ*, p. 216.
[36] Berkouwer, *Faith and Justification*, p. 90.

LORD has laid on him the iniquity of us all.'[37] Hence, Christ's death may properly be called 'vicarious'. In his death Jesus took the place of others. The atonement is Christ's satisfaction of divine justice, by his sufferings and death in the place of sinners.

The vicarious atonement may also be termed a 'penal substitution' because Jesus suffered God's death penalty against our sin. This is not a theory; it is simply a fact. Donald Macleod comments: 'People speak with horror of "the penal theory of the atonement". But what happened to Christ on the cross? He died! And what is death? It is the penalty for sin! The question of whether Christ endured the penalty for sin is not a question of theory. It is a question of fact. On that cross He was dealt with as sin deserved.'[38]

The reason it matters whether or not Christ's death was a vicarious atonement is that only a penal substitution can establish a solid legal basis for the gift of God's grace. God is mercy-seated to the sinner only if Christ has suffered the full punishment for sin. This is precisely what he has done, and now God is more than propitious: he is as satisfied with his chosen people as he is with his own beloved Son. This was God's plan from the very beginning. We must not think of God as an angry Father who is reluctantly appeased by the death of his sweet Son. Christianity is far removed from such a pagan notion because the initiative for salvation always comes from the Father's loving heart. In the atonement, God propitiates God's own wrath! This great truth is clearly stated in the New Testament teaching about propitiation: 'God presented him [Jesus] as a sacrifice of atonement';[39] God 'loved us and sent his Son as an atoning sacrifice for our sins'.[40]

The atonement, therefore, is not a way of getting something that God does not want to give. Rather, it is God's plan for mercy-seating himself to sinners. From beginning to end, propitiation is all of God. As John Stott writes,

> It is God himself who in holy wrath needs to be propitiated, God himself who in holy love undertook to do the propitiating, and God himself who in the person of his Son died for the propitiation of our sins. Thus God took his own loving initiative to appease his own righteous anger by bearing it his own self in his own Son when he took our place and died for us. There is no crudity here to evoke our ridicule, only the profundity of holy love to evoke our worship.[41]

Out of his great love for lost humanity, God has made atonement, covering our sin and placating his own wrath against it in order that we might be saved.

[37] Is. 53:5b, 6b.
[38] Macleod, *A Faith to Live By*, p. 135.   [39] Rom. 3:25; cf. 8:32.
[40] 1 John 4:10.   [41] Stott, *The Cross of Christ*, p. 175.

Going home justified

This brings us to a very personal question that everyone must answer: Have I received atonement for my sins? To put it in terms of the story Jesus told: Has God been mercy-seated to me, the sinner? Has my guilt been covered, or am I still under the wrath of God? The urgency of these questions is made clear by the parable's conclusion. Two men went to the temple to pray, a Pharisee and a tax collector. There they offered two very different prayers, and as a result, they went home to meet two entirely different destinies.

In the end, the tax collector got what he asked for. His prayers were answered. God was mercy-seated to him. His sins were covered and God's wrath was turned aside. In other words, the tax collector received both the expiation and the propitiation he needed to be saved. Jesus closed his story with these words: *'I tell you that this man* [the publican], *rather than the other* [the Pharisee], *went home justified before God. For everyone who exalts himself will be humbled, and he who humbles himself will be exalted'* (Luke 18:14).

We will have more to say about justification in chapter 13, but suffice it to say that to be justified is to be counted righteous. Justification is the legal declaration that an unrighteous sinner has been made right with God. By this legal declaration, a sinner is acquitted of all charges, spared from all punishment, and considered acceptable to God. Such justification is what the tax collector received. God declared him righteous, vindicating him before the bar of his perfect justice. The tax collector was not justified as the result of anything he had done, because all he had done was to sin. He was justified rather by God's mercy, on the basis of the atoning blood of a perfect sacrifice.

God did not justify the Pharisee, however. Jesus' parable is very specific on this point. The Pharisee was never declared righteous, so he went home unjustified. Even after all his righteous acts, he himself was still unrighteous. In a way, his righteous acts were part of the problem. He was too busy being self-righteous to receive God's righteousness, which only comes as a gift. As long as the Pharisee counted on his works to save him, he could never be declared righteous; he would remain under God's wrath for ever.

The point Jesus was making was that sinners cannot be saved by what sinners do; sinners can be saved only by what *God* has done. In other words, sinners can only be saved by grace. The Pharisee's prayer was all about what he could do for God, which is why all his verbs were active: *'I thank ... I am ... I fast ...* [I] *give'* (18:11–12). What made the tax collector's prayer different was that he was asking God to do something for him. The only verb in his prayer is passive: 'God, be mercy-seated to me.' He understood the message of salvation – that although there is nothing a sinner can do to get right with God, God makes sinners right with himself through his own perfect sacrifice.

Anyone who wants to be saved from sin must go to the mercy seat, there to receive God's grace, which is available for the asking. Earlier we quoted from Romans 3:25: 'God presented him [Jesus] as a sacrifice of atonement.' But the Scripture goes on to say this: 'through faith in his blood'. In other words, the death of Jesus Christ serves as an expiation and a propitiation only for those who trust in his saving work. Atonement always requires faith. It required faith in the Old Testament. When the sinner placed his hand on the head of a lamb to confess his sins, he was exercising his faith, trusting that God would transfer his sins to the sacrifice. Sinners do the same thing at the cross. In one of his many hymns on the atonement, Isaac Watts (1674–1748) imagined himself putting his hand on Jesus' sacred head, the way sinners used to put their hands on the atoning sacrifice, and saying,

> My faith would lay her hand
> On that dear head of thine,
> While like a penitent I stand,
> And there confess my sin.[42]

The message of salvation invites sinners to lay their hands on Jesus, the perfect sacrifice, and to make a full confession of sin, asking God to transfer their guilt to a perfect substitute. Through the blood that Jesus shed on the cross, God is mercy-seated to every sinner who does this.

[42] From 'Not all the blood of beasts'.

8. Together again
Reconciliation: 2 Corinthians 5:14 – 6:2

Christ's death on the cross is often called 'the atonement'. The English word 'atonement' expresses an important truth about salvation – that through Jesus, sinners can be made 'at one' with God.

According to the *Oxford English Dictionary*, the phrase 'at one' was used as early as 1300 to describe two people who had been brought into a state of unity or harmony after a period of disagreement. Though formerly they had been estranged, they were now 'at one accord'. This expression appeared in several early English translations of the Bible. For example, the Geneva Bible, published in 1557, rendered 2 Corinthians 5:20 as follows: 'We praye you in Christes stede, that ye be atone with God.' Eventually, the phrase 'at one' began to be used as a verb. To 'at one', or 'atone', was to 'unite', to 'set or make at one'. New forms of the word began to appear. The 'atonemaker' was a person who made peace between two parties at war. An 'atonement' was 'the action of setting at one, or condition of being set at one, after discord or strife'; it was the 'restoration of friendly relations between persons who have been at variance'. One of the most common uses of the term, of course, was in theology, where atonement meant the 'restoration of friendly relations between God and sinners'.

The closest biblical synonym to the word 'atonement' is the word 'reconciliation'. To be at one with God is to be reconciled to God. This is what the tax collector was asking for at the temple, when he begged God to be 'mercy-seated' to him (Luke 18:13). He was praying that the blood of the sacrifice would take away (expiate) his sin and turn aside (propitiate) God's wrath. If his sacrifice was accepted, then neither his guilt nor God's wrath could prevent him from being at one with God. In a word, God and the sinner would be *reconciled*.

Alienated by sin

Reconciliation is God's solution to our alienation. It is the part of the message of salvation that brings us back together with God. The doctrine of reconciliation is most fully explained at the end of 2 Cor-

118

inthians 5, which teaches that although we are alienated from God by sin, God has reconciled us to himself through Jesus, and has made us messengers of reconciliation to the world. To outline the passage in another way, God is the *author*, Christ is the *agent*, and we are the *ambassadors* of reconciliation.[1]

Near the beginning of this book, we listed some of the miserable consequences of sin: guilt, estrangement, wrath, suffering and death. The message of salvation is that only God can rescue us from these evils, and only through Jesus Christ. As we explore what it means to be saved by grace, we are discovering that Jesus saves us from every last consequence of sin. His redemption frees us from the bondage of our sin; his expiation covers the guilt of our sin; and his propitiation turns away the wrath of our sin. But what about alienation? One of the most painful effects of sin is that it separates us from God. Adam and Eve experienced this in the Garden of Eden. As soon as they sinned, there was a breach in their intimate friendship with God. They could no longer walk with him in the cool of the day; indeed, they felt the overwhelming urge to run and hide. This is because they were alienated from God by their sin. In the end, they had to be banished from the garden altogether.

Human beings have felt the alienation ever since. It explains why we are so lonely in the universe. It explains why our quest to find the meaning of life never ends. If we were living in fellowship with God, we would know that the meaning of life is to enjoy him for ever. But we are so far from God that we cannot find our way back on our own. The American novelist Walker Percy described our situation well when he asked,

Why does man feel so sad in the twentieth century? Why does man feel so bad in the very age when more than any other age he has succeeded in satisfying his needs and making the world over for his own use? We can put people on the moon. We can send rockets into the deepest reaches of space, yet we're no nearer discovering meaning in our world, within its horizons, than we were three thousand years ago.[2]

The Bible teaches that the explanation for our alienation is our transgression. Religious sceptics try to figure out if God is acceptable to them: Does God exist? If he does, why is there so much evil in the world? And so forth. But those are the wrong questions altogether. The real question is not whether God is acceptable to us, but whether we are acceptable to God. The answer, apart from a saving relationship with

[1] Stott, *The Cross of Christ*, pp. 196–201.
[2] Walker Percy, quoted by Andrew Jones in a sermon entitled 'The pleasure principle', preached at St Helen's, Bishopsgate, London, 18 October 1998.

Jesus Christ, is 'No'. The problem of humanity is not that we have something against God, but that he has something against us. The reason we feel empty and alone in the universe is that we are separated from God by our sin.

Sin brings a double alienation: we are hostile to God, and God is hostile to us. Emil Brunner writes: 'Reconciliation presupposes enmity between two parties. To put it still more exactly: reconciliation, real reconciliation, an objective act of reconciliation, presupposes enmity on both sides; that is, that man is the enemy of God and that God is the enemy of man.'[3] From our side, sin itself is an act of war. As the Scripture says, 'Once you were alienated from God and were enemies in your minds because of your evil behaviour.'[4] Since we are hostile to God, he must count our sins against us (2 Cor. 5:19). God is righteous, and can by no means clear the guilty.[5] The sad result, as the great Princeton theologian Charles Hodge (1797–1878) wrote in his commentary on 2 Corinthians, is that 'So long as we are under the wrath and curse of God, due to us for sin, we are aliens and enemies, cut off from his favour and fellowship, which are the life of the soul.'[6]

Alienation: two tests

2 Corinthians 5 suggests two ways to test whether a person is alienated from God. One test is to ask: What am I living for? Those who are alienated from God live for themselves rather than for God. This can be inferred from verse 15: *And he died for all, that those who live should no longer live for themselves but for him who died for them and was raised again.* This verse is about the saving work of Jesus Christ. Those who are reconciled to God live for Christ. But the implication is that if we are living for ourselves, then we are not reconciled to God. So the question becomes, *Who* am I living for? If we spend most of our time complaining about our circumstances, if our chief ambition is financial gain, if we get impatient with the little inconveniences of life, or if we do not have time for the poor and needy, then we are living for ourselves. In one way or another the world revolves around our axis. Very likely, the reason life is not working out the way we hoped is that we are living for ourselves and not for God.

Another way to test whether someone is alienated from God is to ask: What do you think about Jesus? What is your opinion of him? Do you think that he is the Son of God and the Saviour of the world, or do you think he's overrated? Do you value him merely as a wise teacher and a moral example, or do you worship him as Saviour and Lord?

---

[3] Brunner, *The Mediator*, p. 516.
[4] Col. 1:21; cf. Jas. 4:4.   [5] Exod. 34:7, AV.
[6] Hodge, *A Commentary on the Second Epistle to the Corinthians*, p. 142.

A person's opinion of Jesus Christ is one of the best indicators of his or her relationship to God. Notice the contrast Paul draws between the way he used to think about Jesus and the way he thinks about him now: *So from now on we regard no-one from a worldly point of view. Though we once regarded Christ in this way, we do so no longer* (2 Cor. 5:16). Before he came to faith, Paul looked at Christ the way the world looks at him. That is to say, his judgment about Jesus was based on outward appearances. Like most Jews, he was offended by the manner of Christ's death. He knew from his Bible that anyone who died on a tree was under God's curse.[7] Therefore, in Paul's mind, the fact that Jesus was crucified was the proof of his damnation. However, his prejudice against Jesus because of his humiliating death changed when he became a Christian. Then Paul was able to look at things from God's perspective, and to understand that Christ was crucified to suffer the curse against our sin. The point is this: he could not understand what Jesus was all about as long as he remained alienated from God. He had to be reconciled first.

Opinions about Jesus Christ have changed since Paul's day. In these postmodern times it is much more common for people to think that Jesus is irrelevant than to think that he is accursed. Most people believe that Jesus was a historical person. Many consider him a great moral teacher. Others view him as a political revolutionary. But all these opinions about Jesus Christ share one thing in common: they look at him from a merely human point of view. From such a superficial vantage point, Jesus of Nazareth may seem like a common criminal, a venerable sage or a subversive politician, but he will never appear to be the Saviour of the world.

Our estimation of Jesus Christ is the ultimate test of our relationship to God. Anyone who has trouble understanding why people make such a fuss about Jesus is almost certainly alienated from God. Perhaps without even realizing it, such a person is prevented from enjoying a personal friendship with the Creator. As long as we keep assessing Jesus on our own terms, rather than accepting him on his terms, we remain alienated from God.

Reconciled by God

The message of salvation has the answer for our alienation; it is called reconciliation. To reconcile is to make peace between personal enemies. It is to remove enmity between parties that are at war. This is precisely the kind of salvation we need – a salvation that restores our relationship with God. Reconciliation implies that there was once a friendship, the kind of close personal relationship God shared with Adam and Eve in

[7] Deut. 21:22–23.

the garden. It also implies that something has happened to damage or even to destroy that relationship, so that good friends have become mortal enemies. But in reconciliation enemies are turned back into friends, their enmity replaced by amity.

Notice that God is the author of reconciliation. He is the one who does the reconciling. This is stated twice for emphasis: ... *God reconciled us to himself* (2 Cor. 5:18); *God was reconciling the world to himself* (5:19). The grammar of these verses is profound in its theology. The verb is 'reconcile'; the subject of the verb is 'God'; and the object of the verb is 'us', the sinners God is saving in all the world. What this means is that we do not reconcile ourselves to God; God reconciles us to himself. Whenever the verb 'to reconcile' occurs in the New Testament, it is always God who does the reconciling.

What is so remarkable about this is that we were the ones who caused the alienation in the first place. God was not the one who had to cover himself with fig leaves or run away and hide. On the contrary, Adam was the one who sinned, thereby separating himself from God. Like our father Adam, we too have set ourselves against God. Ordinarily, reconciliation is the obligation of the one who caused the alienation in the first place. It is up to the sinner to make amends, not the one who has been sinned against. One would expect, therefore, that it would be incumbent upon us to reconcile ourselves to God. This is the basic premise of paganism, that it is up to human beings to appease the anger of the gods. But Christianity is a religion of grace, and the message of salvation is that God has reconciled us to himself: 'When we were God's enemies, we were reconciled to him through the death of his Son'.[8] God is the wounded party, yet he himself repairs the relationship. John Chrysostom (c. 350–407) proclaimed this truth in a memorable way in his famous sermons on Corinthians: 'Seest thou love surpassing all expression, all conception? Who was the aggrieved one? Himself. Who first sought the reconciliation? Himself.'[9]

God never waits for us to make the first move, but always seizes the initiative in our salvation. As Paul says at the beginning of verse 18, *All this is from God*. This is true in election: God chose us long before we could choose for him. It is true in deliverance: God rescued us when we could not rescue ourselves. It is true in redemption: God paid the ransom we could never purchase. It is true in expiation: God has covered the sins we cannot put away. It is true in propitiation: God has turned aside the wrath we cannot endure. And it is also true in reconciliation: God restores the friendship we cannot repair. Salvation is from God; if there is anything of our very own that we contribute, it is only the sin from which we need to be saved.

[8] Rom. 5:10a.
[9] Chrysostom, *Homilies on the Epistles of Paul to the Corinthians*, 12.333.

The fact that God is the author of reconciliation explains why the verb in verse 20 occurs in the passive voice. The Scripture does not say, 'Reconcile yourselves to God'. but *Be reconciled to God.* It is not our responsibility to make friends with God, but simply to respond to the friendship he offers. Hodge wrote, 'God is the reconciler. Man never makes reconciliation. It is what he experiences or embraces, not what he does. The enmity between God and man, the barrier which separated them, is removed by the act of God.'[10] The only way to be reconciled *to* God is *by* God. Reconciliation is a gift of God's grace that proceeds from him and returns to him.

Reconciled through Christ

How does God do it? How does God reconcile us to himself? The answer is that he reconciles us to himself in and through Jesus Christ. This is implied throughout the passage, and is mentioned twice explicitly: *God ... reconciled us to himself through Christ* (5:18); *God was reconciling the world to himself in Christ* (5:19). Jesus is the location of our reconciliation. Although once we were alienated from God by our sin, God has reconciled us to himself through Jesus. It is as we are united to Christ that we are reconciled to God.

The Bible generally refers to reconciliation in the past tense. There are two examples of this in the verses we are considering: *God* reconciled *us* (5:18); *God* was reconciling *the world* (5:19). Paul also used the past tense in his correspondence with the Colossians: 'Once you were alienated from God and were enemies in your minds because of your evil behaviour. But now he has *reconciled* you by Christ's physical body through death'.[11] The fact that reconciliation is described in the past tense gives a clue that it is based on a real historical event. Jesus reconciled us to God when he died on the cross for our sins. Theologians sometimes call this the 'finished work' of Christ – 'finished' because salvation is something Jesus accomplished in the historical past.

These verses from 2 Corinthians 5 contain nearly everything one needs to know about the finished work of Jesus Christ. His death is first mentioned in verse 14: *We are convinced that one died for all, and therefore all died.* From this we learn that Christ's death was in some sense a substitution. Christ died *for* all. By 'all' the apostle does not mean absolutely all, because in the very next verse he explains that Christ died specifically for those who live for him (5:15). What the apostle means is that Christ died for all his people, from all over the world. Theologians have often made the distinction that although the

---

[10] Hodge, *Second Epistle to the Corinthians*, p. 142.
[11] Col. 1:21–22a.

atonement was *sufficient* for all, it was *efficient* only for the elect. When Christ was crucified, he died for his own people, the ones given to him by his Father's electing love.

What was it about Christ's death that made it a reconciliation? What did his crucifixion do to reconcile us to God? The explanation comes at the end of the chapter: *God made him who had no sin to be sin for us, so that in him we might become the righteousness of God* (5:21). This verse is one of the keys that unlock the biblical message of salvation. From it we learn that Christ's death was not simply a substitution, but also a sacrifice. Like the sacrifices of the Old Testament, Christ's death on the cross atoned for our sins. Remember how sacrifices were made. The first step was for the sinner to find an unblemished animal, usually a lamb or a goat. The animal had to be perfect because the sacrifice could not be defective in any way.[12] The priest would not accept an animal with a broken leg and mangy fur, but only the very best animal from the herd. Once the sinner had chosen his sacrifice, he placed his hand on the animal's head and confessed his sins. This signified that his sins were being transferred to the animal. To use the proper theological term, his guilt was *imputed* to the sacrifice. Then the animal was put to death. It had to be put to death because it was bearing sin, and the penalty for sin is death. Thus the animal died in the sinner's place, and as a result of this sacrifice, the sinner was declared righteous. The penalty for his sins had been paid in full.

All this is called to mind when the Scripture says, *God made him who had no sin to be sin for us, so that in him we might become the righteousness of God* (5:21). The Old Testament sacrifices were intended to teach God's people what kind of sacrifice God required. Ultimately, what God required was the sacrifice Jesus offered on the cross. The sacrifice had to be perfect, so Jesus was perfect, the most perfect sacrifice of all: 'He committed no sin, and no deceit was found in his mouth.'[13] He kept the whole law of God without ever breaking it in thought, word, or deed: 'He appeared so that he might take away our sins. And in him is no sin'.[14] Quite simply, Jesus *had no sin*.[15] Even Pilate could find no basis for a charge against him, and the centurion at the cross said, 'Surely this was a righteous man'.[16]

Since he was without any moral defect, Jesus was eligible to offer himself as a sacrifice. Having no sin of his own, he was able to bear the sin of others. But in order for him to be our substitute, somehow our sin had to be transferred to him. And so it was: *God made him who had no sin to be sin for us.* This is what is meant by imputation: God counting the sinless one as a sinner. He imputed the guilt of our sin to Jesus Christ.

---

[12] Lev. 1:3, etc.   [13] 1 Pet. 2:22.   [14] 1 John 3:5.   [15] Cf. Heb. 4:15.
[16] Luke 23:14, 47.

Once Christ had taken our guilt upon himself, he had to die the death that we deserved to die. The proper punishment for sin is death; therefore, on the cross God executed his death penalty against our sin. This is what it means that Jesus became sin *for* us. It means that when he died a criminal's death he suffered as our sacrificial substitute – he bore our sins, endured God's wrath, and died in our place. To quote from the Scottish theologian James Denney (1856–1917): 'If we all *died*, in that Christ died *for* us, there must be a sense in which that death of His is *ours*; He must be identified with *us* in it: there, on the cross, while we stand and gaze at Him, He is not simply a person doing us a service; He is a person doing us a service *by filling our place and dying our death* (emphasis his).[17]

Now that Christ has died in our place, we have a whole new relationship to God. Since Christ's death counts for us, our sins no longer count against us (5:19). Moreover, God actually counts us righteous. Christ is our representative in God's covenant, and since we are united to him we have become *the righteousness of God* (5:21). God no longer considers us sinners; he considers us righteous. A double imputation has taken place. In the same way that our sin was transferred to Christ, Christ's righteousness has been transferred to us. Christ has taken our place, and we have taken his, with the result that God now reckons us to be as righteous as his own Son. We give Christ our sin; Christ grants us his righteousness; and on this basis we are reconciled to God: 'Christ died for sins once for all, the righteous for the unrighteous, to bring you to God.'[18] Our reconciliation is transacted by way of imputation. John Stott explains this theological connection by saying that 'our sins were imputed to the sinless Christ, in order that we sinners, by being united to him, might receive as a free gift a standing of righteousness before God'.[19]

Theologians sometimes call this double imputation – in which our sin is imputed to Christ, and his righteousness is imputed to us – the 'wonderful exchange'. The term was perhaps first used in *The Epistle to Diognetus*, which was written during the early centuries of the church: 'O the sweet exchange, O the incomprehensible work of God, O the unexpected blessings, that the sinfulness of many should be hidden in one righteous man, while the righteousness of one should justify many sinners!'[20] Martin Luther urged Christians to make this exchange part of their prayers by saying, 'Thou, Lord Jesus, art my righteousness, but I am thy sin. Thou hast taken upon thyself what is mine and hast given to me what is thine. Thou hast taken upon thyself what thou wast not and hast given to me what I was not.'[21] Or consider the words of the

---

[17] Denney, quoted in Hughes, *Paul's Second Epistle to the Corinthians*, p. 194.
[18] 1 Pet. 3:18.   [19] Stott, *The Cross of Christ*, p. 200.
[20] *The Epistle to Diognetus*, in Lightfoot and Harmer, *The Apostolic Fathers*, p. 302.
[21] Luther, *Letters of Spiritual Counsel*, p. 110.

Anglican theologian Richard Hooker (c. 1554–1600): 'We care for no knowledge in the world but this, that man hath sinned and God has suffered; that God hath made himself the sin of men, and that men are made the righteousness of God.'[22]

Once Christ has taken away our sin through his cross, we can be reconciled to God. Sin is what alienated us from God in the first place by erecting a seemingly insurmountable barrier to fellowship with God. But once Christ has exchanged our sin for his righteousness, nothing stands between us, and the breach in our friendship can be repaired. Once we were alienated from God by our sin, but now he has reconciled us to himself through Jesus; 'we ... rejoice in God through our Lord Jesus Christ, through whom we have now received reconciliation.'[23]

The message of reconciliation

The biblical doctrine of reconciliation has many practical implications. It means that we can count on being God's friends for ever. It means that we are at peace with God through Jesus Christ, a peace that will hold firm through all the turbulence of life. It means that we can draw near to God in a relationship of loving trust. We have gained what the Bible calls 'access' to God,[24] especially through prayer.

Reconciliation also means that Christians have a job to do. It is so marvellous to be reconciled to God that we cannot possibly keep this reconciliation to ourselves. For one thing, being restored to friendship with God changes us so dramatically that people are bound to notice. We have a whole new *purpose*. We no longer live for ourselves; we live for Christ (2 Cor. 5:15), which is why we are called Christians. We have a whole new *perspective*. We no longer look at anyone or anything the way the world does (5:16a); we look at everything (especially Jesus himself) the way God does. We are whole new *people*: *If anyone is in Christ, he is a new creation; the old has gone, the new has come!* (5:17). The change that takes place when a sinner comes to Christ is cosmic: God recreates us the way he once created the world – by his Word and his Spirit. Once we become brand new people, with a new purpose and a new perspective, the effects of Christ's reconciling work on the cross should be evident in everything we think, do and say.

The other reason we cannot keep the message of reconciliation to ourselves is that God has made us his messengers. Here we move from the accomplishment of reconciliation to its announcement. In verse 18 our task is called the *ministry* of reconciliation: *God ... reconciled us to*

---

[22] Hooker, 'Sermon on Habakkuk i.4', in *The Works of Richard Hooker*, pp. 483–547 (491).

[23] Rom. 5:11.   [24] Rom. 5:2; Eph. 2:18.

himself through Christ and gave us the ministry of reconciliation. At the end of verse 19 it is called the *message* of reconciliation: *He has committed to us the message of reconciliation*. The point is that once God reconciles sinners to himself, he commissions us to announce his reconciling grace to the world. We are messengers of salvation.

The word the Scripture uses to describe our role as God's messengers is 'ambassador': *We are therefore Christ's ambassadors, as though God were making his appeal through us* (5:20a). This verse refers primarily to the apostles, who were the first official representatives of Jesus Christ. Paul and the other apostles proclaimed the message of reconciliation throughout the ancient world. But this verse also describes the work of Christian ministers, and indeed of all Christians. We are Christ's ambassadors, imploring the whole world to be reconciled to God.

The analogy works on many levels. An ambassador is an official representative from a far country. Just so, as ambassadors for Christ, we represent the kingdom of heaven. A good ambassador embodies the values of his country. Thus Christians are to demonstrate the character of their King. There is a good example of this at the beginning of our passage, where the Scripture says, *Christ's love compels us* (5:14). The apostle Paul was constrained by the love of Christ. As far as he was concerned, God's sending Jesus to reconcile sinners to himself was the most compelling thing he had ever heard. He was so gripped by the love that God had demonstrated through the cross that he wanted to share it with everyone he met. This loving compulsion made Paul the kind of Christian described by Charles Hodge: 'one who recognizes Jesus as the Christ, the Son of the living God, as God manifested in the flesh, loving us and dying for our redemption; and who is so affected by a sense of the love of this incarnate God as to be constrained to make the will of Christ the rule of his obedience, and the glory of Christ the great end for which he lives'.[25] What motivated Paul to become a missionary, a church planter, and an evangelist was the love flowing from the very heart of God. He was so powerfully influenced by that divine affection that he became as loving as his message. The same should be true of every Christian, for we are ambassadors of the kingdom of God's love.

As an official envoy, an ambassador speaks on behalf of his country. Whatever he says, his country says – provided the ambassador follows his orders. The same must be true of every good ambassador for Christ. We must proclaim the saving message which is contained in the Bible, and no other. When we do, we speak on God's behalf, *as though Christ were making his appeal through us* (5:20). Hodge's comments on this verse are worth quoting at length:

An ambassador is at once a messenger and a representative. He does

[25] Hodge, *Second Epistle to the Corinthians*, p. 133.

not speak in his own name. He does not act on his own authority. What he communicates is not his own opinions or demands, but simply what he has been told or commissioned to say. His message derives no part of its importance or trustworthiness from him. At the same time he is more than a mere messenger. He represents his sovereign. He speaks with authority, as accredited to act in the name of his master ... All this is true of ministers. They are messengers. They communicate what they have received, not their own speculations or doctrines. What they announce derives its importance not from them, but from him who sends them. Nevertheless, as they speak in Christ's name and by his authority, as he hath ordained the ministry and calls men by his Spirit into the sacred office, the rejection of their message is the rejection of Christ, and any injury done unto them as ministers is done unto him.[26]

Christ's ambassadors are so closely identified with Christ that their message is his message. This is why ministers who do not teach God's Word faithfully are traitors to his cause. It is also why the best thing a Christian can do to share the message of salvation is to invite a friend to a Bible-teaching church. Ordinarily, sinners are reconciled to God by the preaching of God's Word. It is the minister's announcement of the reconciliation accomplished by Christ that turns God's enemies into God's friends. The message of salvation is a message of reconciliation, and the message *itself* is what reconciles us to God.

A message for everyone

This message is for everyone. Reconciliation has cosmic proportions, for what God is restoring to himself is nothing less than everything: *God was reconciling the world to himself* (5:19). This does not mean that every individual person will be saved, but it does mean that the message of salvation is for all people without exception. And in the process of reconciling all people to himself, God also reconciles them to one another. The reconciliation he brings is horizontal as well as vertical. Even the hostility between Jew and Gentile comes to an end at the cross, for 'now in Christ Jesus you who once were far away [i.e. Gentiles] have been brought near through the blood of Christ ... His purpose was to create in himself one new man out of the two, thus making peace, and in this one body to reconcile both of them [Jews and Gentiles] to God through the cross, by which he put to death their hostility.'[27]

God's reconciling love includes the entire universe within its embrace. The very creation has been alienated from God by human

---

[26] Hodge, ibid., p. 146.   [27] Eph. 2:13, 15b–16.

sin,[28] but God's ultimate purpose is to repair this cosmic dislocation by bringing 'all things in heaven and on earth together under one head, even Christ'.[29] The same God who made the world will reconcile the world to himself through Christ, specifically through his saving work on the cross: 'For God was pleased to have all his fulness dwell in him, and through him to reconcile to himself all things, whether things on earth or things in heaven, by making peace through his blood, shed on the cross.'[30]

For the creatures God has made in his image, this reconciling message comes with real urgency. The message is urgent for Christians. Every Christian is reconciled to God once and for all through faith in Christ, and will remain reconciled to God for ever. However, sin always disturbs the intimacy of the believer's friendship with God. Thus there is a continual need for that friendship with God to be renewed. Christians need to be reconciled to God as often as they sin. If we have been grumbling about our circumstances, pursuing dishonest gain, fooling around with sexual sin, neglecting our families, or failing in our spiritual duties, we must be reconciled to God.

As urgent as the message of reconciliation is for Christians, it is all the more urgent for those who have not yet come to Christ. Christ's ambassadors speak on behalf of the King of heaven to people who are still at war with his kingdom: *We implore you on Christ's behalf: Be reconciled to God* (5:20b). One of the reasons this message comes with such urgency is that it may not come again. 2 Corinthians 6 begins with a solemn warning: *As God's fellow-workers we urge you not to receive God's grace in vain. For he says, 'In the time of my favour I heard you, and in the day of salvation I helped you.' I tell you, now is the time of God's favour, now is the day of salvation* (6:1–2). When he speaks of those who *receive God's grace in vain*, the apostle is referring to people who only seem to be Christians. Although they go to church regularly and often hear the gospel, they refuse to give up their sins, and thus they remain alienated from God.

This is a sober warning. Those who refuse to confess their sins and to be reconciled to God through Jesus have heard the message of reconciliation in vain. And the danger is that they may never hear it again. Now is the time of God's favour for every sinner who trusts in the cross of Christ. Now is the day of salvation for everyone who repents and receives Jesus Christ as Saviour. But the day of salvation will not last for ever. Soon the sun will set on the horizon of eternity, and for those who are not reconciled to God, all will be dark.

---

[28] Rom. 8:18–21.   [29] Eph. 1:10.   [30] Col. 1:19–20.

9. Proof positive
Resurrection: Acts 13:26–49

The message of salvation is that we are saved from sin by the grace of God. Since sin is the greatest of evils, we need the greatest of Saviours. John Calvin wrote that 'the only haven of safety is in the mercy of God, as manifested in Christ, in whom every part of our salvation is complete'. Calvin went on to describe what our great Saviour has done to make our salvation complete:

> As all mankind are, in the sight of God, lost sinners, we hold that Christ is their only righteousness, since, by His obedience, He has wiped off our transgressions, by His sacrifice appeased the divine anger, by His blood washed away our stains, by His cross borne our curse, and by His death made satisfaction for us. We maintain that in this way man is reconciled in Christ to God the Father, by no merit of his own, by no value of works, but by gratuitous mercy.[1]

Calvin's explanation of salvation is a good summary of the major themes we have discussed so far in this book: through his death on the cross as our sacrificial substitute, Jesus Christ has expiated our sins, propitiated the divine wrath, and reconciled us to God. But how do we know that all this is true? How can we be sure that we really are reconciled to God? Is there any proof that God has accepted Christ's death on the cross as the vicarious atonement for our sins? And if there is any proof, what is it?

The message of salvation

There is solid proof that Christ accomplished salvation through his cross, and one of the best places to find it is Acts 13. This passage is especially significant for our purposes because it is the only place where the Bible speaks explicitly of *'the message of salvation'* (13:26).

[1] Calvin, 'Reply to Cardinal Sadolet', quoted in Hughes, *Paul's Second Epistle to the Corinthians*, p. 212.

The man who preached this saving message was the apostle Paul, who was then mid-way through his first missionary journey. Paul and a number of his companions had been commissioned by the church at Antioch to spread the good news about Jesus Christ (13:1–3). Guided by the Holy Spirit, they travelled through Cyprus, and then on to Asia Minor (13:4–5, 13). As they travelled through Pisidia they came to another city, also called Antioch (13:14a), and there they followed their usual strategy for missions. Whenever Paul came to a new city, he went first to the Jews: 'On the Sabbath they entered the synagogue and sat down. After the reading from the Law and the Prophets, the synagogue rulers sent word to them, saying, "Brothers, if you have a message of encouragement for the people, please speak"' (13:14b–15).

Paul had a message all right, but it was more than an encouragement – it was the message of salvation. He stood up, gestured for quiet, and began a brief survey of Jewish history, the story of salvation. What follows in the biblical text is a summary of the saving message Paul undoubtedly proclaimed on many occasions. Since the Jews were God's chosen people, their salvation began with their election: 'The God of the people of Israel chose our fathers' (13:17a). As we learned in chapter 4 of this book, God's grace is always God's choice, and what God had chosen to do was to deliver his people from their bondage in Egypt. So Paul next recounted the history of the exodus: God 'made the people prosper during their stay in Egypt, with mighty power he led them out of that country, he endured their conduct for about forty years in the desert, he overthrew seven nations in Canaan and gave their land to his people as their inheritance' (13:17b–19). God's plan in rescuing his people from slavery was to establish his kingdom, culminating in David, a king after his own heart (13:20b–22).

The purpose of Paul's historical survey was to remind the Jews in Pisidian Antioch that their God was a God who saves. But the past was only prologue. Saving grace was given in the Old Testament to prepare the way for the coming of the Messiah, the Saviour God had always promised, the King who would reign for ever on David's throne.[2] Paul was in the synagogue that day to announce that the Saviour had finally come. What he said next must have caused quite a stir: 'From [David's] descendants God has brought to Israel the Saviour Jesus, as he promised' (13:23). He called Jesus *the* Saviour because he is the one true Saviour of humanity.

The apostle proceeded to explain what Jesus had done to accomplish our salvation. The main thing he had done was to die. Paul reported how it happened:

'Brothers, children of Abraham, and you God-fearing Gentiles, it is to us

[2] 2 Sam. 7:11b–16.

that this message of salvation has been sent. The people of Jerusalem and their rulers did not recognise Jesus, yet in condemning him they fulfilled the words of the prophets that are read every Sabbath. Though they found no proper ground for a death sentence, they asked Pilate to have him executed. When they had carried out all that was written about him, they took him down from the tree and laid him in a tomb' (13:26–29).

These events are familiar to Christians the world over, but they would have been news to the Jews in Pisidian Antioch. Many of them would not have heard of Jesus of Nazareth. They would not have known that he had been prosecuted by Jewish scribes and executed by Roman soldiers. They would not have believed that he had been crucified, dead and buried. Nor would they have understood the most important thing of all, that by his death Jesus had become their promised Saviour.

Twice Paul mentioned that Jesus suffered in precisely the way that he did suffer in order to fulfil the prophecies of the Old Testament. By condemning an innocent man to die, the Jewish leaders had unwittingly fulfilled the *'words of the prophets'* that the Saviour would be despised and rejected – a man of sorrows, acquainted with grief (13:27).[3] Then, by crucifying Jesus without cause, the Roman soldiers *'carried out all that was written'* about the Saviour dying an accursed death (13:29). Paul drew attention to this by calling the cross a *'tree'* (13:29; cf. 5:30; 10:39). According to the law of God, 'anyone who is hung on a tree is under God's curse'.[4] By dying on the accursed tree, Jesus took God's curse against our sin upon himself.[5]

Paul's description of the crucifixion of Christ is a reminder that many Old Testament promises were fulfilled in the Saviour's death. So far we have discussed a number of significant images of salvation: deliverance, redemption, atonement and reconciliation. Each of these aspects of God's saving work was promised in the Old Testament, and each was accomplished through the death of Jesus Christ. The Old Testament promised deliverance, the kind of deliverance that brought Israel out of Egypt. Now God has delivered us through the death of Jesus, 'who gave himself for our sins to rescue us from the present evil age'.[6] The Old Testament promised redemption, the kind of ransom Boaz provided for Ruth. The ransom price was paid by Christ on the cross, 'for ... you were redeemed ... with the precious blood of Christ'.[7] The Old Testament promised atonement, the kind of expiation and propitiation that were accomplished on the day of atonement, so 'God presented him [Jesus] as a sacrifice of atonement, through faith in his blood'.[8] The Old Testament promised reconciliation, a permanent end to the hostilities between God and humanity. Reconciliation, too, was

---

[3] Cf. Is. 53:3–4, 7. [4] Deut. 21:23. [5] Is. 53:5, 12; cf. Gal. 3:13.
[6] Gal. 1:4. [7] 1 Pet. 1:18–19. [8] Rom. 3:25a.

accomplished through the death of Jesus: 'Now [God] has reconciled you by Christ's physical body through death'.[9] The message of salvation keeps bringing us back to the cross. It is by his death that Jesus has rescued us from sin, redeemed us from slavery, covered our guilt, turned aside God's wrath, and made us friends with God.

Yet there is more to salvation than the cross. If all Jesus had done was to die on the cross, we could never be saved. Salvation comes by grace alone in Christ alone, but it does not come through the cross alone. Whenever the New Testament presents the message of salvation, it always preaches the crucifixion *plus* the resurrection. There is a good example of this in the passage in 2 Corinthians 5 that formed the basis for our study of reconciliation: 'And he [Christ] died for all, that those who live should no longer live for themselves but for him who died for them and was raised again.'[10] Or consider Paul's famous statement of the gospel in 1 Corinthians 15: 'By this gospel you are saved ... that Christ died for our sins according to the Scriptures, that he was buried, that he was raised on the third day according to the Scriptures'.[11] In the message of salvation, the cross is inseparably joined to the empty tomb. The heart of the gospel is never the cross alone, but always the cross plus the empty tomb. Jesus saves both by his vicarious crucifixion and by his victorious resurrection.

On the third day

Paul's sermon at Pisidian Antioch presents the resurrection as a historical fact and a biblical fulfilment with a saving function. The sermon is based on a simple fact: *'God raised him* [Jesus] *from the dead'* (Acts 13:30). This statement is made half a dozen times in the book of Acts, in almost identical words (see 2:24; 3:15; 4:10; 5:30; 10:40). But what does the Bible mean, exactly, when it says that God raised Jesus from the dead?

Resurrection does not mean simply that Jesus 'came back to life'. There is more to resurrection that resuscitation. By his supernatural power, God had brought people back to life before. Lazarus is the most famous example, but there were others, in both the Old and the New Testament. In each miracle, a person who was certainly dead was genuinely restored to life. That is not what happened to Jesus, however. His resurrection was unprecedented because he did not simply return to his former physical state, but reached a whole new level of human existence. After spending three days in the tomb, Jesus was raised to receive an immortal body of incorruptible splendour.

Consider the remarkable physical properties of the glorious resurrection body of Jesus Christ. It is *transportable*. After his resurrection,

[9] Col. 1:22a.   [10] 2 Cor. 5:15.   [11] 1 Cor. 15:2–4.

Jesus was capable of travelling vast distances in a single instant, suddenly appearing in the midst of his disciples.[12] His body is *audible* and *tangible*. After the resurrection, Jesus' disciples were able to hear him, and even to touch him.[13] His body is *recognizable*. The first eyewitnesses of the resurrection knew (at least eventually) that they were seeing Jesus. The fact that they saw him with their own eyes shows that his resurrection body is *visible* and *perceptible*. Those who have seen him since he ascended to heaven report that he is beautiful beyond description, dazzling in his radiant glory.[14] Finally, the resurrection body of Jesus Christ is *imperishable*. Jesus is 'alive for ever and ever',[15] and his body will retain its shining luminescence for all eternity, without ever dimming or darkening. This is all part of what the Bible means when it says, *God raised him from the dead.* When God raised Jesus, he did not simply resuscitate him, but gave him a resurrection body that is glorious beyond description.

It is significant that Jesus was raised bodily. Christians have always believed in the resurrection of the body as well as the immortality of the soul. Belief in the bodily resurrection is significant because it places a positive value on physical life. Many religions – like Hinduism, for example, or the New Age movement – value the spiritual more highly than the material. As a result, they consider the human body (and everything associated with it) to be inferior, possibly even immoral. Rather than despising the body, however, Christians have always dignified it. This is part of the biblical doctrine of creation, which teaches that God made everything good, including the bodies of the creatures he made in his own image. It is also part of the message of salvation. God has a plan to redeem our bodies. first he sent his Son to become a man, thus honouring human existence by his incarnation. Then he raised his Son to become immortal, thus glorifying humanity in the resurrection. Christ is 'the firstborn from among the dead',[16] 'the firstfruits of those who have fallen asleep'.[17] In other words, our own future resurrection is included in his resurrection as part of one glorious resurrection harvest.

But is it really true? Did God actually raise Jesus from the dead, or not? The biblical Gospels do not argue for the resurrection; they simply assert it as a plain historical fact. The question is: Can we take their word for it? Can we believe in the resurrection of Jesus Christ as a historical event? There are many people who would say 'No'. Some of them adhere to other religions. Consider this statement from a document formulated by Buddhists in Myanmar near the end of the twentieth century: '[What] the Christians are preaching that Jesus Christ has died on the cross to redeem the sinners of the world with his

---

[12] Matt. 28:9; John 20:19.   [13] John 20:27.   [14] Rev. 1:12–17.
[15] Rev. 1:18.   [16] Col. 1:18.   [17] 1 Cor. 15:20.

holy blood is totally false teaching. The real truth is that Jesus Christ was defeated in his mission works and has paid for his own wrong doings by getting executed and shedding his own blood.'[18] End of story. Yet some of the people who object to the resurrection most strongly are Bible scholars, one of whom, Gerd Lüdemann, reached the appalling conclusion that '*the tomb of Jesus was not empty, but full, and his body did not disappear, but rotted away*' (emphasis his).[19]

These objections demand an answer, because there is no salvation without resurrection. 'If Christ has not been raised,' Paul wrote to the Corinthians, 'our preaching is useless and so is your faith.'[20] Knowing the truth about the resurrection is also important because the most serious historical questions about Jesus of Nazareth concern his being raised from the dead. The facts about his life and death are easy enough to demonstrate. No credible historian seriously doubts that Jesus was born in Bethlehem, raised in Nazareth, and crucified in Jerusalem. These facts have ample attestation outside the Bible and abundant attestation within it.[21] The real historical issue concerns the resurrection: Did Jesus really rise from the dead?

The question is not new. Since the days of the early church, doubts have been cast on the resurrection wherever Christ has been preached. When Paul went to Thessalonica, he went into the local synagogue – as was his custom – 'and on three Sabbath days he reasoned with them from the Scriptures, explaining and proving that the Christ had to suffer and rise from the dead' (Acts 17:2–3a). Later, when he went on to Athens, the philosophers sneered at him for speaking about the resurrection of the dead (17:32). This sceptical attitude has become increasingly prevalent during recent centuries, especially since the European Enlightenment of the eighteenth century. German Bible scholars of the nineteenth century tried to divide the 'Christ of faith', who lives in the heart, from the 'Jesus of history', about whom little can be known for certain.[22] A more recent quest for the so-called 'historical Jesus' has been launched by the highly publicized Jesus Seminar. In each case, what sceptics really object to is the supernaturalism of Christianity. They cannot quite bring themselves to accept the possibility of divine miracles like the resurrection. Their quest is futile because they do not recognize that the Christ of faith *is* the Jesus of history, the Jesus who was raised from the dead on the third day.

[18] Institution of the Buddhist Clergy in Yangon, reported by the Far East Broadcasting Company, and quoted in *Pulse* (3 September 1999), p. 6.

[19] Lüdemann, *What Really Happened to Jesus*, p. 135.

[20] 1 Cor. 15:14.

[21] For a thorough review of the evidence, see Habermas, *The Historical Jesus*.

[22] The history of this idea is traced in McGrath, *The Making of Modern German Christology 1750–1990*. For a relatively recent example of the liberal approach, see Kähler, *The So-Called Historical Jesus and the Historic Biblical Christ*.

Evidence that demands a verdict

What is curious about scholars who object to the resurrection is that they always present their critique as something novel. Each new book claims to be a shocking exposé of error in the biblical history. What is truly surprising, however, is how familiar their arguments always sound. The same tired old criticisms are regurgitated every generation. Only the faces change; the objections remain the same, even though most of the serious questions about the factual nature of the resurrection were answered a century or more ago.

One way to defend the resurrection is to consider the alternatives. Any theory about what happened to Jesus after he died has to answer some serious questions. The theory has to explain the disappearance of Jesus' body. If it was not raised from the dead, then what happened to it? The theory also has to account for the vacant tomb. The fact is that when people arrived at Jesus' tomb on Easter morning, the massive stone was moved and the tomb was empty (or, as we shall see, *almost* empty). Then the theory has to explain why the disciples came to believe in the resurrection. The transformation that took place in their lives was remarkable. One day they were cowering in fear, hiding from the Jews because they were worried that they might be crucified next.[23] Not many days afterwards, with casual disregard for life and limb, they were preaching boldly in the temple, announcing to everyone that Jesus had been raised from the dead (Acts 2ff.). Why the change? And what enabled the first Christians to spread their message about Jesus around the world?

The oldest answer is that someone stole the body. This is the rumour the Jewish leaders tried to spread when the soldiers in charge of guarding the tomb first came and told them that it was empty. In the early hours of the morning an angel had come and scared them half to death,[24] but it would never do for people to hear that an angel had moved the stone:

> When the chief priests had met with the elders and devised a plan, they gave the soldiers a large sum of money, telling them, 'You are to say, "His disciples came during the night and stole him away while we were asleep." If this report gets to the governor, we will satisfy him and keep you out of trouble.' So the soldiers took the money and did as they were instructed. And this story has been widely circulated among the Jews to this very day.[25]

The first thing to note about the soldiers' story is that it concedes one of the central biblical facts about the resurrection, namely, that the

---

[23] John 20:19.   [24] Matt. 28:2–4.   [25] Matt. 28:12–15.

tomb was vacant. When the apostles began to go around Jerusalem preaching the risen Christ, the easiest way to discredit them would have been to display the remains of Jesus. This should have been easy for the Jewish leaders to do. After all, they were the ones who had asked Pilate to place the Roman seal on the tomb. Furthermore, Jesus had been buried in the tomb of Joseph of Arimathea, a member of their own Council. Yet the religious leaders were unable to disprove the apostles by producing Jesus' body. They had to resort to violence and scare tactics instead, because the tomb was empty.

If the Jewish leaders did not confiscate the corpse, then who did? Possibly the disciples. Perhaps the resurrection was a giant hoax perpetrated by Jesus' followers, who stole his body and invented the legend that he had come back to life. Yet this theory meets with several insurmountable difficulties. First, it requires a group of frightened, unarmed civilians to overthrow a band of highly trained and heavily armed Roman soldiers. It should be noted that when Pilate gave the instructions for sealing the tomb, he said, 'Take a guard. Go, make the tomb as secure as you know how.'[26] Next, the stolen-body theory requires the disciples to proclaim something that they knew to be a deliberate falsehood to be the gospel truth, and to do so in the face of persecution, and even death. Yet to a man, the apostles stuck to their story, even when they were executed for preaching the risen Christ. They may have been deceived, but they were not deceivers, for hypocrites do not become martyrs. For all their faults, the biblical disciples did not perpetrate a fraud.

A more recent attempt to deny the resurrection is often called 'the swoon theory'. It suggests that Jesus did not actually die on the cross, but merely fainted. On the cross he passed into a coma, from which he revived while resting in the cool of the tomb. Once he had returned to consciousness and regained his strength, he appeared to the disciples, who believed (wrongly) that he had been raised from the dead.

Like the stolen-body theory, the swoon theory meets with several overwhelming problems. First, there is strong evidence that Jesus did actually die on the cross. The Roman soldiers who executed Jesus carried out crucifixions as a matter of routine and were well able to determine that he was dead. Jesus died so quickly that Pontius Pilate wondered if he really was dead, yet the governor was assured that this was so.[27] Then there is the piercing of his side to consider. When criminals were crucified, it was customary to hasten their deaths by breaking their legs. 'But when they came to Jesus and found that he was already dead, they did not break his legs. Instead, one of the soldiers pierced Jesus' side with a spear, bringing a sudden flow of blood and water.'[28] The flow of blood and water provides further confirmation that

[26] Matt. 27:65.   [27] Mark 15:44.   [28] John 19:33–34.

Jesus was dead. Presumably, fluid had filled the pericardium, the sac around Jesus' heart. In all likelihood, the spear pierced both the pericardium and the heart itself, thus producing the flow of blood and water.[29] After reviewing the available evidence, the *Journal of the American Medical Society* concludes: 'Interpretations based on the assumption that Jesus did not die on the cross appear to be at odds with modern medical knowledge.'[30] In addition to all the evidence for Jesus' death, there is this question to consider: If Jesus did not actually die, then why did his friends bury him?

But suppose that Jesus did not die on the cross after all, but only fell into a coma, later to be revived. This hypothesis raises a host of unanswerable questions:

> Are we then seriously to believe that Jesus was all the time only in a swoon? That after the rigours and pains of trial, mockery, flogging and crucifixion he could survive thirty-six hours in a stone sepulchre with neither warmth nor food nor medical care? That he could then rally sufficiently to perform the superhuman feat of shifting the boulder which secured the mouth of the tomb, and this without disturbing the Roman guard? That then, weak and sickly and hungry, he could appear to the disciples in such a way as to give them the impression that he had vanquished death? That he could go on to claim that he had died and risen, could send them into all the world and promise to be with them unto the end of time? That he could live somewhere in hiding for forty days, making occasional surprise appearances, and then finally disappear without any explanation? Such credulity is ... incredible.[31]

If Jesus had merely been in a coma, the disciples might have given him medical care, but they never would have worshipped him as their resurrected and glorified Lord.

More evidence that demands a verdict

The best explanation for the empty tomb is the one that Paul gave the Jews in Pisidian Antioch: God raised Jesus from the dead. This explains what happened to his body. It accounts for the empty tomb. And it explains why the disciples were willing to preach and to die for their faith: they had met the risen Saviour.

One of the striking things about the alternatives to the resurrection

[29] For further details, consult Davis, 'The crucifixion of Jesus: The passion of Christ from a medical point of view', pp. 183–187.
[30] W. D. Edwards, 'On the physical death of Jesus Christ', pp. 1455–1463 (1463).
[31] Stott, *Basic Christianity*, p. 49.

is that none of them is supported by any positive evidence. There is nothing to support either the claim that the disciples stole Jesus' body or the conjecture that he swooned on the cross. Nor do these theories account for all the known historical facts. This is in sharp contrast to the biblical claim that Jesus rose from the dead, which not only accounts for all the facts, but is also based on an abundance of eye-witness testimony.

Paul based his case for the resurrection on the testimony of those who knew Jesus best: *'For many days* [Jesus] *was seen by those who had travelled with him from Galilee to Jerusalem. They are now his witnesses to our people'* (Acts 13:31). There was Mary Magdalene – the first to see the risen Christ. Her testimony is significant, not only because she was the first, but also because she was a woman. If the disciples had fabricated the resurrection, it would have been folly for them to base their story on the word of a woman. No-one would have believed them, because a woman's testimony was inadmissable in a Jewish court of law.[32] Yet the Bible does nothing to hide what many would have considered an awkward fact. It makes Mary the first witness because she was, in fact, the first to see Jesus after he was raised from the dead.

Then there was John, who believed in the resurrection even before he saw the risen Christ. When he arrived at the tomb, John discovered that it was not quite empty: 'He saw the strips of linen lying there, as well as the burial cloth that had been around Jesus' head. The cloth was folded up by itself, separate from the linen.'[33] Apparently, what John saw were the burial wrappings, left undisturbed. The grave-clothes had not been unrolled by grave-robbers, or by Jesus himself. The bandages were still in the shape of a human body. The turban-like wrapping that had been twirled around Jesus' head was still intact. When John saw this, he understood that Jesus was risen. As the Scripture says, 'He saw and believed.'[34] How could a corpse, which had been tightly wrapped in the Oriental style, be removed without disturbing the burial shroud? The only possible explanation was that somehow Jesus, in a glorious new body, had simply passed through his grave-clothes.

Besides Mary and John, there were many other eyewitnesses to the resurrection. The Bible records at least a dozen post-resurrection appearances in all. There was Peter, who denied Jesus three times, yet met the risen Christ and preached him as boldly as any apostle.[35] There were the rest of the disciples, including Thomas, who met with Jesus in a private home.[36] There was the couple who broke bread with Jesus in Emmaus.[37] There was James, the brother of Jesus, who did not believe that Jesus

[32] 'Rosh Ha-Shanah' 1:8, *The Mishnah*, trans. by Herbert Danby (London: Oxford, 1933), p. 189.
[33] John 20:6b–7.   [34] John 20:8.
[35] Matt. 26:69–75; Luke 24:34; John 21; Acts 2:14–41.   [36] John 20:24–29.
[37] Luke 24:13–32.

was the Christ before he died, but came to trust him after he rose again.[38] There were more than five hundred others who saw Jesus on a single occasion.[39] And there was Paul himself, who met the risen Christ on the Damascus road (Acts 9:1–6).

There is no doubt that all these men and women believed that Jesus appeared to them in his resurrection body. Even scholars who deny the bodily resurrection admit that the first Christians had some kind of personal experience which led them to believe that God raised Jesus from the dead. Gerd Lüdemann, who contends that the corpse of Jesus rotted away in his tomb, nevertheless admits, 'It is historically certain that Peter and the other disciples had experiences after Jesus' death in which Jesus appeared to them as the risen Christ.'[40]

How can these experiences be explained? Were they visions? Were they hallucinations, produced by wishful thinking? Any psychological explanation becomes thoroughly implausible when it is remembered that Jesus did not appear once but many times, to groups as well as to individuals, at various times and in various circumstances. No merely psychological explanation can account for the numerous post-resurrection appearances of Christ. All these witnesses knew Jesus well, so they were well qualified to attest to his resurrection. They all doubted at first because they were unable to conceive how Jesus could have returned from the dead. Thus they were able to give the strong testimony of sceptics who had become believers. Furthermore, they saw Jesus with their own eyes. They were credible witnesses of his bodily resurrection. Some of them even ate meals with him, and had the opportunity to touch him. As Peter told Cornelius, 'He was not seen by all the people, but by witnesses whom God had already chosen – by us who ate and drank with him after he rose from the dead' (Acts 10:41).

Many sceptics have set out to disprove the resurrection. But those who have examined the evidence most honestly have surprised themselves by reaching the conclusion that God raised Jesus from the dead. Some of these sceptics have been journalists, like Frank Morison, who wrote *Who Moved the Stone?*,[41] or Lee Strobel, who wrote *The Case for Christ: A Journalist's Personal Investigation of the Evidence for Jesus.*[42] Others have been lawyers, like Gilbert West or Sir Edward Clarke. All of them would agree with Charles Hodge, who wrote:

> As the resurrection of Christ is an historical fact, it is to be proved by historical evidence. The apostle therefore appeals to the testimony of competent witnesses … To render such testimony irresistible it is

[38] 1 Cor. 15:7; cf. John 3:5.   [39] 1 Cor. 15:6.

[40] Lüdemann, quoted by William Lane Craig in a public lecture at the University of Iowa, c. 1995.

[41] First published by Faber in 1930; 2nd ed. 1944.

[42] Published by Zondervan in 1998.

necessary: (1) That the fact to be proved should be of a nature to admit of being certainly known. (2) That adequate opportunity be afforded to the witnesses to ascertain its nature, and to be satisfied of its verity. (3) That the witnesses be of sound mind and discretion. (4) That they be men of integrity. If these conditions be fulfilled, human testimony establishes the truth of a fact beyond reasonable doubt. If, however, in addition to these grounds of confidence, the witnesses give their testimony at the expense of great personal sacrifice, or confirm it with their blood ... then it is insanity and wickedness to doubt it. All these considerations concur in proof of the resurrection of Christ, and render it the best authenticated event in the history of the world.[43]

According to the Scriptures

The apostle Paul was not content merely to claim the resurrection as a historical fact; he also wanted to proclaim it as a biblical fulfilment. God raised Jesus from the dead on the third day in order to complete the Old Testament promise of salvation. The good news about Jesus is not simply that he rose again, but that by being raised from the dead, he was proven to be the promised Saviour. As the apostle later wrote to the Corinthians, Jesus 'was raised on the third day according to the Scriptures'.[44] His resurrection was the proof of God's promise.

The Old Testament contains many prophecies concerning the coming of Christ. There are at least fifty specific promises that pertain to such matters as the place of his birth and the unusual circumstances surrounding his death. But what of his resurrection? It is sometimes said that there is no doctrine of the resurrection in the Old Testament. In one sense this is true: no-one could fully understand the resurrection until Jesus was raised from the dead. The resurrection is a good example of the gradual progression of God's revelation. What is only latent in the Old Testament becomes patent in the New Testament. Yet the Jews had always hoped for eternal life in the body. Consider Job's stirring confession of faith:

> I know that my Redeemer lives,
>   and that in the end he will stand upon the earth.
> And after my skin has been destroyed,
>   yet in my flesh I will see God;
> I myself will see him
>   with my own eyes – I, and not another.
> How my heart yearns within me![45]

[43] Hodge, *A Commentary on the First Epistle to the Corinthians*, p. 314.
[44] 1 Cor. 15:4.   [45] Job 19:25–27.

From the earliest days, God's people longed for the resurrection of the body, believing that one day a risen humanity would see God face to face.

In his sermon at Pisidian Antioch, Paul mentioned three Old Testament prophecies that had a direct bearing on the resurrection. He had already called attention to the fact that Jesus is a direct descendant of King David (Acts 13:22–23). He went on to mention what the Bible had promised about the resurrection of David's Christ:

'We tell you the good news: What God promised our fathers he has fulfilled for us, their children, by raising up Jesus. As it is written in the second Psalm:

> *'"You are my Son;*
> *today I have become your Father."*

The fact that God raised him from the dead, never to decay, is stated in these words:

> *'"I will give you the holy and sure blessings promised to David."*

So it is stated elsewhere:

> *'"You will not let your Holy One see decay."*

'For when David had served God's purpose in his own generation, he fell asleep; he was buried with his fathers and his body decayed. But the one whom God raised from the dead did not see decay' (13:32–37).

The first quotation comes from Psalm 2, which promises the victory of God's chosen ruler over all his enemies. The psalm starts with a rebellion: 'The kings of the earth take their stand and the rulers gather together against the LORD and against his Anointed One.'[46] Yet the uprising is defeated. Although he is rejected by angry men, the ruler is anointed as God's King and appointed as God's Son.[47] In the end he triumphs, ruling over the whole earth with his fierce justice.[48]

It would seem that Psalm 2 must refer to David, or to one of the other kings of Israel, since the 'Anointed One' is enthroned as king on Mount Zion.[49] But the first Christians understood this psalm to refer also to the Christ, for everything in it perfectly describes his person and work. Jesus was anointed by his Father to be the King. He was opposed by the nations, by Jews and Gentiles alike (Acts 4:25–27). Yet God identified him as the unique Son of God. When Jesus was baptized, the Father said, 'You are my Son',[50] which was practically a direct quotation from Psalm 2:7. Now Jesus is the kingly Son who reigns from God's

---

[46] Ps. 2:2.   [47] Ps. 2:6–7.   [48] Ps. 2:8–12.   [49] Ps. 2:6.
[50] Luke 3:22; cf. Heb. 1:5; 5:5.

supreme throne, ruling the nations by his fierce justice. The point is that whatever promises God made to David find their ultimate fulfilment in Jesus Christ.

What did God promise to David? The answer is given in Paul's second quotation, which comes from the book of Isaiah: 'I will make an everlasting covenant with you, my faithful love promised to David.'[51] God gave his people this promise while they were still in exile to remind them that his covenant would last for ever. The reason it would last for ever was that he had made them unbreakable love-promises through his servant David. His promise to David concerned the kingdom of Israel: 'Your house and your kingdom will endure for ever before me; your throne will be established for ever.'[52]

God had also made a more specific promise to David, and this brings us to Paul's third quotation: *'You will not let your Holy One see decay'* (13:35). This prophecy comes from Psalm 16, in which David wrote,

> Therefore my heart is glad and my tongue rejoices;
>> my body also will rest secure,
> because you will not abandon me to the grave,
>> nor will you let your Holy One see decay.[53]

There is an obvious problem with this promise: David died, and thus he *did* see decay. The apostle Paul was well aware of this difficulty, for he called attention to it in his sermon: *'When David had served God's purpose in his own generation, he fell asleep; he was buried with his fathers and his body decayed'* (13:36). So here is the puzzle: God had made a promise to David which seemed to be false. By his everlasting covenant, he had promised to give David an incorruptible throne, yet David was dead and buried, and his body had returned to the dust.

The answer to this conundrum is Jesus Christ. What God had been planning all along was that someone even greater than David would come to save his people. The way God made good on his promise was by sending Jesus. How do we know that Jesus really is the promised Saviour? Because God never allowed his body to decay, but raised him from the dead on the third day. Paul's biblical argument comes to its climactic conclusion in verse 37: *'The one whom God raised from the dead did not see decay.'* The apostle Peter made the identical argument in his sermon on the Day of Pentecost. He even based it on the same psalm, preaching that David 'knew that God had promised him on oath that he would place one of his descendants on his throne. Seeing what was ahead, he spoke of the resurrection of Christ, that he was not abandoned to the grave, nor did his body see decay. God has raised this Jesus to life, and we are all witnesses of this fact' (Acts 2:30–32). The

[51] Is. 55:3b.   [52] 2 Sam 7:16.   [53] Ps. 16:9–10.

prophecies of the Old Testament find their ultimate fulfilment in Jesus Christ. Jesus is God's appointed Son and anointed King. The historical fact of his bodily resurrection is proof positive for the biblical fulfilment of God's promise to David.

Good news!

Paul presented his resurrection as both a historical fact and a biblical fulfilment. Jesus rose from the dead on the third day, according to the Scriptures. But the apostle's preaching about the resurrection was not merely historical and biblical; it was also practical. His sermon thus closed with this application: *'Therefore, my brothers, I want you to know that through Jesus the forgiveness of sins is proclaimed to you'* (13:38). The reason it matters whether Jesus rose from the dead or not is that salvation depends on it. The resurrection is a historical fact and a biblical fulfilment with a soteriological (saving) function.

We are now in a position to understand why Paul called his sermon in Pisidian Antioch 'the message of salvation' (13:26). He also called it 'the gospel', which is a synonym for 'the message of salvation'. In some versions the word 'gospel' is translated as 'good news': *'We tell you the good news: What God promised our fathers he has fulfilled for us, their children, by raising up Jesus'* (13:32–33a). In Greek the word is *euangelion*, from which we get English words like 'evangel' and 'evangelism'. The ancient Greeks used the term to announce an imperial triumph, like a great military victory or the birth of a new emperor. The same word was used by Greek-speaking Jews to refer to mighty acts of divine deliverance in the Old Testament, such as the exodus from Egypt. Whether it is called 'the good news', 'the gospel' or 'the message of salvation', the meaning is the same. The good news of the gospel is the message that God has saved his people.

The proof that God saves is the resurrection of Jesus Christ. Imagine for a moment that Jesus died on the cross without ever rising from the grave. In that case, how could we be certain that Jesus really had dealt with our sin and all its terrible consequences: guilt, alienation, suffering and death? At most we could say, 'Perhaps God has accepted the cross of Christ as the atonement for my sin, but I cannot know for certain.' We would have no receipt to show that the price of our redemption had been paid in full. We would have no token of affection to show that we had been reconciled to God. Nor would we have any reason to believe in the resurrection of our own bodies. If God did not raise Jesus, how could he be expected to raise anyone else?

That is precisely why Paul calls his sermon 'the message of salvation'. He has already made his case for the resurrection as both a historical fact and a biblical fulfilment. God *has* raised Jesus from the dead. By doing so, God showed that Jesus did not die in vain, that his sacrifice was accepted. The crucifixion, which was the verdict of sinful men, was overturned on appeal. God rendered his verdict on Jesus Christ in the resurrection, which is God's seal of approval on the crucifixion, the proof that his justice is satisfied. By raising Jesus from the dead, God has attested that Jesus is the Saviour 'who through the Spirit of holiness was declared with power to be the Son of God by his resurrection from the dead: Jesus Christ our Lord'.[54]

Now all the blessings of salvation are ours in Christ – deliverance, redemption, expiation, propitiation and reconciliation. A dead Jesus could never communicate such blessings; only a living Christ. Therefore, the resurrection is the proof that we are delivered from our sins. It proves that the price Jesus paid was high enough to redeem us, that our guilt is covered, that God's wrath has been turned aside, and that we are now the friends of God. Paul does not list all these benefits individually; he simply says, *'Therefore, my brothers, I want you to know that through Jesus the forgiveness of sins is proclaimed to you'* (13:38). The resurrection guarantees that we are saved from sin. It also assures us that one day we ourselves will be raised from the dead: 'Because of his great love for us, God, who is rich in mercy, made us alive with Christ even when we were dead in transgressions – it is by grace you have been saved. And God raised us up with Christ'.[55] We have a 'once and future' resurrection: spiritually speaking, we were raised with Christ when he was raised from the dead; one day soon we will also be raised bodily in the final resurrection of the dead.

This message of salvation is good news, but to be saved we must believe it. The message requires everyone to make a personal commitment. Only those who believe are saved. It is through Jesus that forgiveness is promised; therefore, it is only by believing in Jesus that forgiveness can be received: *'Through him everyone who believes is justified from everything you could not be justified from by the law of Moses'* (13:39). Paul thus ended his sermon in Pisidian Antioch by exhorting the congregation to believe the gospel: *'Take care that what the prophets have said does not happen to you: "Look, you scoffers, wonder and perish"'* (13:40–41a).

Sadly, that is exactly what happened to some of Paul's listeners. They perished. Some of the Jews were filled with jealousy and heaped abuse on the apostle (13:45). They stirred up so much persecution that eventually he was driven out of the region altogether (13:50). The reason they did these things was that they did not believe the resurrection, which everyone must believe to be saved. As Paul said on another occasion, 'If you confess with your mouth, "Jesus is Lord," and believe in your heart that God raised him from the dead, you will be saved.'[56] The implication is that anyone who does not believe in the

---

[54] Rom 1:4.   [55] Eph. 2:4–6a.   [56] Rom. 10:9.

bodily resurrection of Jesus Christ is not saved. Such a person is like the people who rejected Paul's message, and thereby proved that they were *not ... worthy of eternal life* (13:46).

Happily, there were many people in the synagogue that day who *were* counted worthy of eternal life. They believed and were saved. The next Sabbath almost the whole city crowded into the synagogue to hear the message of salvation – both Jews and Gentiles. *All who were appointed for eternal life believed. The word of the Lord spread through the whole region* (13:48b–49). This is what happens whenever the message of salvation is preached. Those who are *appointed for eternal life* – that is, who are predestined to glory – accept the bodily resurrection of Jesus Christ as a historical fact and a biblical fulfilment. They believe in the empty tomb, accepting the resurrection as the proof that God has saved them from their sins by his grace.

PART 3: SAVED THROUGH FAITH

'We have gained access by faith into this grace'

(Romans 5:2)

10. Born again
Regeneration: John 3:1–18

The message of salvation is about what God has done by his grace to save us from our sin. What God chiefly has done is to send his Son to be our Saviour. Salvation is based on what Jesus Christ has done in human history. By dying on the cross and being raised from the tomb, he has rescued us, redeemed us and reconciled us to God.

Christianity is all about what Christ has done for the Christian. Therefore the message of salvation does not call attention to our own spiritual experience, primarily, but to God's supreme expression of divine love in Christ. However, in salvation the benefits of Christ are actually transferred to the Christian. Salvation is not simply a past event; it is also a present reality. Somehow the redemption accomplished by Christ must be applied to the Christian.[1] What is his must become ours. As we shall discover, the application of redemption is the work of God's Spirit, who enables us to believe the message of salvation, and thereby to receive grace through faith.

The saving work of God's Spirit begins with the new birth. In the previous chapter, we learned how God raised Jesus from the dead to a whole new form of existence. Something similar happens at the outset of the Christian life. Peter wrote: 'In his great mercy he [God] has given us new birth into a living hope through the resurrection of Jesus Christ from the dead.'[2] This is the doctrine of regeneration, that God grants new life to sinners through the risen Christ. The source of all true life – spiritually as well as physically – is the resurrection of Jesus Christ. The same Spirit who raised Christ from the dead also raises the Christian to new spiritual life. By the power of the Holy Spirit, resurrection produces regeneration.

Nicodemus and the new birth

Perhaps the first person ever to hear Jesus teach about the new birth was

---

[1] This is the structure of John Murray's wonderful book, *Redemption: Accomplished and Applied.*
[2] 1 Pet. 1:3.

a man named Nicodemus. *Now there was a man of the Pharisees named Nicodemus, a member of the Jewish ruling council* (John 3:1). In other words, he was a member of the Sanhedrin, the group of seventy religious leaders who governed God's people from Jerusalem. Nicodemus was a great man – a scholar and teacher. Since he was a Pharisee, he was a theological and cultural conservative.

Nicodemus was curious about Jesus of Nazareth. It was becoming more and more obvious that Jesus was a man from God. He taught such magnificent truths and performed such stupendous miracles that Nicodemus wondered who he was and what he had come to do. *He came to Jesus at night and said, 'Rabbi, we know you are a teacher who has come from God. For no-one could perform the miraculous signs you are doing if God were not with him'* (3:2). This is phrased as a statement, but really it was more of a question. Nicodemus wondered about Jesus' true identity. He was asking if Jesus was the Messiah whom God had promised to send. The question on his mind – the question he could not quite bring himself to ask – was this: 'Is Jesus the Saviour?' Though it was only implied, this was the first of three questions Nicodemus posed to Jesus (3:2, 4, 9). In his answers Jesus taught three fundamental truths about regeneration, explaining the *necessity* (3:3), the *possibility* (3:5–8) and the *availability* of the new birth (3:10–15).

In his first answer Jesus taught Nicodemus that the new birth was necessary for salvation. *In reply Jesus declared, 'I tell you the truth, no-one can see the kingdom of God unless he is born again'* (3:3). The kingdom of God was the central theme of Jesus' teaching. From the very beginning of his ministry, he came 'preaching the good news of the kingdom'.[3] God's kingdom is simply God's rule, the establishment of his kingly authority in heaven and earth. When Jesus spoke to Nicodemus about seeing the kingdom of God, he was looking to the future. In one sense, of course, Nicodemus was in the presence of the kingdom right then and there, although he did not realize it. Since Jesus is the King, whenever and wherever he comes, the kingdom comes. But Jesus was looking forward to his eternal kingdom, when he would come in all his kingly glory. Thus he was speaking to Nicodemus about eternal life, the resurrection life of the age to come, which no-one can enter without being spiritually reborn. It takes a new birth to see the new world, and Jesus was warning Nicodemus that he had to be born again to be saved.

This was hardly the answer Nicodemus expected. He was there to examine Jesus, not to be examined *by* him. It is true that Nicodemus treated Jesus with respect. He recognized him as a teacher, praising him for his miracles and acknowledging that he was doing God's work. He even called him *Rabbi*. But Nicodemus still wanted to retain the

---

[3] Matt. 4:23.

right to judge Jesus for himself, to evaluate his ministry by his own criteria. Jesus responded by turning the tables on Nicodemus. Rather than submitting himself to the judgment of a mere human being, he confronted the Pharisee with God's requirements for salvation. The real question was not whether Jesus was the Saviour (obviously, he was) but whether Nicodemus was saved. This is a reminder that there is more to salvation than recognizing Jesus as a good teacher and a miracle-worker. Jesus demands more than our respect; he demands our total spiritual transformation. No-one can see the kingdom of God unless he or she is born again.

This was a remarkable thing to say to a man like Nicodemus, who thought he had every assurance of salvation. Nicodemus was a Jew, a member of God's covenant people. He was a Pharisee, a man who kept God's law down to the smallest detail. He was also *Israel's teacher* (3:10), one of the leading biblical scholars of his day. Yet Nicodemus had not gone far enough! With one short sentence Jesus dismissed every one of his religious credentials and warned him that he still lacked the only thing God requires for entrance to his eternal kingdom: the new birth. Nicodemus must have been amazed at this teaching. D. A. Carson imagines his consternation: 'Doubtless he himself had for years taught others the conditions of entrance to the kingdom of God, conditions cast in terms of obedience to God's commands, devotion to God, happy submission to his will; but here he is facing a condition he has never heard expressed, the absolute requirement of birth from above.'[4] This stands as a warning to every religious person. It does not matter what family we come from, what church we attend, what doctrinal position we hold, how clever we are, or how much of the Bible we know, we *must* be born again. As John announced at the beginning of his Gospel, God's true children are 'born not of natural descent, nor of human decision or a husband's will, but born of God' (1:13).

The necessity of the new birth

What does it mean to be born again? The word Jesus used for 'born' is the passive of the verb *gennaō*, which is the origin of the English word 'genesis'. It can refer either to the action of the father ('to beget') or to the action of the mother ('to give birth'). In either case, it refers to the generation of a new life. Jesus used the term in a spiritual sense, telling Nicodemus that he needed the new life that is imparted by God's Spirit. He still needed to experience the radical transformation from spiritual death to spiritual life that is fundamental to knowing God.

It is important to emphasize that the new birth is not simply a new beginning; it is a whole new life. In his first epistle, the apostle John lists

[4] Carson, *The Gospel according to John*, p. 198.

some of the spiritual changes regeneration brings. A lifetime of observing born-again believers had taught him that those who are born again 'do what is right'.[5] They do not continue in unrepentant sin, transgressing God's law with gleeful abandon.[6] Born-again Christians love other Christians with a selfless love.[7] They never fall away from the faith,[8] and in the end they will overcome the world.[9] John's list of changes is impressive. As we noticed in our study of reconciliation, 'If anyone is in Christ, he is a new creation'.[10]

Like the word 'born', the word often translated as 'again' has two meanings. The Greek term *anōthen* often refers to something repeated; it provides the basis for the English word 'another'. To be 'born again', therefore, would mean to be 'reborn' or 'born anew'. Obviously, this is what Nicodemus understood Jesus to be saying, for his objection was that a man *cannot enter a second time into his mother's womb* (3:4). This is where the theological term 'regeneration' comes from. If *gennaō* means 'generation' and *anōthen* means 'again', then Jesus was telling Nicodemus that he needed a 're-generation', another genesis. There is another way to translate *anōthen*, however, and that is 'from above'. This would give Jesus' statement a rather different emphasis: 'no-one can see the kingdom of God unless he is born *from above*' (3:3). This fits the context well, because Jesus goes on to explain that regeneration is the work of God the Holy Spirit, and thus it comes from heaven. So which of these two meanings did Jesus have in mind? Was he telling Nicodemus he had to be born again or born from above? Probably both. When Nicodemus spoke of a second birth, Jesus did not correct him because regeneration requires a new spiritual birth. Yet this new birth comes 'from above' (this translation fits John's usage elsewhere in his Gospel; see 3:31; 19:11). Thus the ambiguity was probably deliberate. What Jesus said to Nicodemus had a double meaning: no-one can see the kingdom of God without being reborn from above.

This new birth is essential for salvation. Jesus said it three times: *'I tell you the truth, no-one can see the kingdom of God unless he is born again'* (John 3:3); *'I tell you the truth, no-one can enter the kingdom of God unless he is born of water and the Spirit'* (3:5); *'You must be born again'* (3:7). In the last of these verses, the word 'you' occurs in the plural so as to emphasize the universal necessity of the new birth. Jesus could hardly have made it any plainer. There is no spiritual life without supernatural rebirth. Either you are a born-again Christian, or you are not a Christian at all!

To see why the new birth is so necessary, it helps to remember the problem of humanity. As we have seen from the outset of this book, the problem with humanity is depravity. Nicodemus epitomizes our lost

---

[5] 1 John 2:29. [6] 1 John 3:9. [7] 1 John 4:7; cf. 1 Pet. 1:22–23.
[8] 1 John 5:18. [9] 1 John 5:4. [10] 2 Cor. 5:17; cf. Gal. 6:15.

and sinful condition. There may be spiritual significance in the fact that he came to Jesus *at night* (3:2; cf. 19:39). This is partly a historical fact: Jesus and Nicodemus met sometime in the evening. It also suggests that Nicodemus wanted to keep their meeting a secret, as if he were afraid what the other religious leaders might think. But John – who loved the symbolism of light and darkness (e.g. 1:5) – mentions the night because it provides a clue about the man's spiritual condition. Nicodemus was the kind of man described at the end of the passage: 'Light has come into the world, but men loved darkness instead of light because their deeds were evil. Everyone who does evil hates the light, and will not come into the light for fear that his deeds will be exposed' (3:19–20). The night was blacker than Nicodemus knew. He was lost in the darkness, for he had not yet seen the light.

The reason Nicodemus could not perceive the kingdom of God was that he was unregenerate. He had not yet been born again. He was still the kind of man Jesus had in mind when he said, *'Flesh gives birth to flesh'* (3:6). 'Flesh' refers to fallen humanity in all its frailty. Jesus was talking about natural, physical childbirth. The only thing one sinful human being can give birth to is another sinful human being. The problem with sinful human beings is that our minds are blind, our wills are bound, and our hearts our bad. As long as we remain unregenerate, we cannot see (3:3), cannot enter (3:5), and cannot believe (3:12) the kingdom of God. Unregenerate we are, and unregenerate we will remain until we are born again.

What we require is nothing less than a whole new spiritual life, a total transformation from our total depravity. Somewhere the great Puritan theologian Stephen Charnock (1628–80) wrote, 'Regeneration is a universal change of the whole man ... it is as large in renewing as sin was in defacing.' Thomas Boston compared this universal change to the work of a skilled doctor: 'Man is, in respect of his spiritual state, altogether disjointed by the fall; every faculty of the soul is, as it were, dislocated: in regeneration, the Lord loosens every joint, and sets it right again.'[11] The way the new birth sets everything right is by creating a whole new person. In regeneration, God makes a new spiritual person who is able to think, will, act, believe, feel and live for his glory.

The possibility of the new birth: water and the Spirit

Regeneration may be necessary, but is it even possible? This was the second question Nicodemus had for Jesus: *'How can a man be born again when he is old? ... Surely he cannot enter a second time into his mother's womb to be born!'* (3:4). The Pharisee obviously did not understand what Jesus was saying. This may have been because he was

[11] Boston, *The Complete Works of the Late Rev. Thomas Boston of Ettrick*, vol. 8, p. 141.

thinking too literally. When Nicodemus heard the words 'born again', he assumed that Jesus was talking about natural childbirth. But how could a man possibly be born a second time?! To show how absurd the idea was, he imagined an old man climbing back into his mother's womb to start life all over again! Yet for all his sarcasm, Nicodemus was clever enough to realize that Jesus was speaking not literally, but spiritually. Very likely, he could tell that Jesus was using childbirth to illustrate a spiritual truth. But even so, it still sounded impossible. Nicodemus doubted the possibility of the new birth. How can anyone be born again?

The answer is, 'With man this is impossible, but with God all things are possible.'[12] This is the answer salvation always gives. What is impossible for humanity in our depravity is possible for God in his grace. In regeneration, as in every other aspect of salvation we have discussed to this point, God works solo. Jesus emphasized this by describing the new birth in the passive voice. He told Nicodemus, *'You must be born'* (3:7). The new birth is not something anyone can do for himself; it is something that must be done for him. That is simply the way birth operates. Children never bring themselves into the world. They are always borne by their mothers. In the same way, unregenerate sinners cannot regenerate themselves. We cannot even decide to be reborn. We are as dependent on the Holy Spirit for spiritual rebirth as we were on our parents for physical birth. No matter how much we go into labour – reading self-improvement books, keeping religious rituals, following moral codes – there is no way we can deliver ourselves into new spiritual life.

New spiritual life can come only from God's Holy Spirit. When Nicodemus doubted the possibility of the new birth, Jesus answered by saying, *'I tell you the truth, no-one can enter the kingdom of God unless he is born of water and the Spirit. Flesh gives birth to flesh, but the Spirit gives birth to spirit'* (3:5–6). Regeneration is possible because it is the work of the Holy Spirit, a gift of God's saving grace. It is God's Spirit who brings God's children into God's family by spiritual rebirth. They are 'born not of natural descent, nor of human decision or a husband's will, but born of God' (1:13).

What did Jesus mean when he said, *'born of water and the Spirit'* (3:5)? This is a difficult phrase, and many different interpretations have been offered. Some say the water refers in some way to natural birth, to the bodily fluids present either in sexual intercourse or childbirth. If so, then Jesus was speaking about two different births: a natural birth by water and a spiritual rebirth by the Spirit, *both* of which are necessary for salvation. Although this interpretation fits the context well, it has a number of problems. One is linguistic: neither the Bible nor the Greek

---

[12] Matt. 19:26.

language generally uses the word 'water' to refer to any of the bodily fluids related to childbirth. Another problem is grammatical: 'Water' and 'spirit' are not intended to be taken separately, but together. Jesus did not say, 'born *of* water and *of* the Spirit'; he said, 'born of water and spirit'. Rather than describing two different births, the water and the spirit seem to describe one and the same birth.

A different way to interpret the water in this verse is to take it as a reference to baptism, either of John or of Jesus. This interpretation makes good sense to Christians, but it is doubtful whether it would have made much sense to Nicodemus, since it was not until *after* the resurrection that baptism marked entrance into God's family. Besides, although the Bible sometimes associates baptism with regeneration, it never makes baptism the cause of the new birth. Some theologians have taught that Christians are born again by baptism. Thomas Aquinas (1224–74), for example, taught that 'baptism opens the gates of the heavenly kingdom to the baptized'.[13] Similarly, Martin Luther defined baptism as 'a new birth by which we are ... loosed from sin, death, and hell, and because children of life, heirs of all the gifts of God, God's own children, and brethren of Christ'.[14] This is more than the Bible teaches. Baptism is a sign of salvation,[15] but not the basis for the salvation it signifies.

A third interpretation is that the water refers to God's Word.[16] If so, then Jesus meant that the new birth always comes in response to the gospel. This is certainly a biblical truth. The apostle Peter wrote, 'For you have been born again, not of perishable seed, but of imperishable, through the living and enduring word of God.'[17] Or consider the words of the apostle James: 'He chose to give us birth through the word of truth, that we might be a kind of firstfruits of all he created.'[18] Both apostles taught that new spiritual life is conceived by the dissemination of God's Word. Although regeneration is the direct and immediate work of God's Spirit, the first manifestations of new spiritual life come in response to God's Word as it is read and preached.

It is possible that water refers to God's Word, but a fourth interpretation is the most likely of all. Perhaps we should think of the water and the spirit as a conceptual unity. If so, then they are not two different things, but two words that together describe the spiritual purification of a sinner. What Jesus said might be translated like this: 'Unless one is born of water, even the Spirit, he cannot enter God's kingdom.'[19] This was an especially appropriate thing to say to a Pharisee, because the Pharisees carefully followed all the biblical regulations

[13] Aquinas, *Summa Theologiae* (III.69.7), quoted in Demarest, *The Cross and Salvation*, p. 282.

[14] Luther, *Luther's Works*, vol. 53, p. 103.   [15] Cf. Rom. 6:3–4.   [16] Cf. Eph. 5:26.

[17] 1 Pet. 1:23.   [18] Jas. 1:18.

[19] Wuest, *Wuest's Word Studies from the Greek New Testament*, 3.iii.55–57.

for purification. What Nicodemus really needed was the inward cleansing of God's life-giving Spirit, without which no-one can see the kingdom of God. A similar connection between water and spirit is made in Paul's letter to Titus: 'But when the kindness and love of God our Saviour appeared, he saved us ... through the washing of rebirth and renewal by the Holy Spirit, whom he poured out on us generously through Jesus Christ our Saviour'.[20] As one of Israel's teachers (3:10), the Rev. Dr Nicodemus should have known that he was a polluted sinner who needed to be purified from the inside out. In the words of Jesus, he should have heard an echo from the prophet Ezekiel: 'I will sprinkle clean water on you, and you will be clean; I will cleanse you from all your impurities and from all your idols. I will give you a new heart and put a new spirit in you.'[21] Jesus was offering the fulfilment of Ezekiel's promise: the gift of a clean new spiritual heart.

The possibility of the new birth: some examples

Whatever Jesus specifically had in mind when he told Nicodemus that he had to be *'born of water and spirit'*, he meant that the power of the new birth comes from above. Only God can change a sinner's heart. Therefore, every Christian testimony is a story of being reborn from above.

Consider several examples. The first comes from the Bible, and occurred during Paul's first missionary journey to Philippi. One Sabbath Paul went to speak to a group of women who had gathered by the river to pray. 'One of those listening was a woman named Lydia, a dealer in purple cloth from the city of Thyatira, who was a worshipper of God. The Lord opened her heart to respond to Paul's message.'[22] Lydia became a believer in the Lord Jesus Christ, and what enabled her to believe was the regenerating work of God's Spirit: 'The Lord opened her heart'. As she listened to the message of salvation, there came an instant when she was born again, transformed from within by the Holy Spirit. Lydia's example shows that while conversion may be a gradual process, regeneration itself is an instantaneous change. The Bible generally describes the new birth with an aorist, the Greek tense used to denote an event that transpired at a single time in the past. There is no 'second regeneration'; the new birth is once and for all.

Another example of spiritual rebirth comes from church history. It is the story of Martin Luther. Like Lydia, Luther received the new birth while he was studying the Scriptures. He had been trying to figure out what the Bible meant when it said, 'the righteous will live by faith'.[23] Luther was frightened by this because he knew that he was unrighteous. Then, in a sudden flash of spiritual insight, he realized that God offered

[20] Titus 3:4–6.   [21] Ezek. 36:25–26a.   [22] Acts 16:14.   [23] Rom. 1:17; Hab. 2:4.

his righteousness as a gift for sinners to receive by faith. Luther described his spiritual transformation in these words: 'Now I felt as though I had been immediately born anew and had entered Paradise itself. From that moment the face of Scripture as a whole became clear to me. My mind ran through the sacred books, as far as I was able to recollect them, seeking ... the strength, the salvation, the glory of God.'[24]

The new birth is not just for the women of the New Testament and the men of church history; it is for every believer, right up to modern times. Consider the testimony of Charles Colson, who was convicted and imprisoned for his role in Watergate, the American political scandal that destroyed the presidency of Richard Nixon in the 1970s. Colson was a hard man. In the words of *Time* magazine, few men in Washington were 'tougher, wilier, or nastier'. On one occasion he boasted that he 'would walk over [his] grandmother if necessary' to achieve his political ambitions. Yet as his involvement in the national scandal was uncovered, Colson realized that his life was spiritually empty. A friend began to confront him with his need for a personal relationship with Jesus Christ. Eventually Colson became convinced that 'For Christ to have talked as He talked, lived as He lived, died as He died, He was either God or a raving lunatic ... The words – both exciting and disturbing – pounded at me: Jesus Christ – lunatic or God?' Later that evening he made his commitment: 'I knew the time had come for me: I could not sidestep the central question ... placed squarely before me. Was I to accept without reservations Jesus Christ as Lord of my life? It was like a gate before me. There was no way to walk around it. I would step through, or I would remain outside.' Colson stepped through the open gate to eternal life. When he later wrote his autobiography, he called it *Born Again*.[25]

Those who have experienced this new birth testify that it is the most wonderful thing that ever happened to them. What it brings is nothing less than life after spiritual death. It enables blind eyes to see and broken hearts to believe, freeing the will from its bondage to sin.

The availability of the new birth

The new birth is necessary – because no-one can receive eternal life without it. The new birth is possible – because God is able to do impossible things like save sinners beyond hope of salvation. But how can this new birth be obtained? Having questioned its necessity and its possibility, Nicodemus asked Jesus about its availability: *'How can this be?'* (3:9).

---

[24] Luther, quoted in Reardon, *Religious Thought in the Reformation*, p. 52.
[25] Charles W. Colson, *Born Again* (Old Tappan, NJ: Chosen, 1976).

This was Nicodemus' third question, and what brought it to mind was the comparison Jesus made between the Holy Spirit and the wind. Jesus used this analogy to show the mystery of God's sovereignty in regeneration. He said, *'The wind blows wherever it pleases. You hear its sound, but you cannot tell where it comes from or where it is going. So it is with everyone born of the Spirit'* (3:8). What makes this illustration especially effective is the fact that in the Greek language 'wind', 'breath' and 'spirit' are all expressed by the same word (*pneuma*). The Holy Spirit is the breath of God whose influence is as mysterious as the wind. No-one can control or even see the wind, but its effects are obvious wherever it blows. So it is with the Holy Spirit, the supernatural origin of all spiritual life. No-one can control his gracious influences, or see when he first slips into a sinner's heart, but the effects soon become obvious. The sinner is born again by the power of the Spirit.

If all that is true, then how does someone become a born-again Christian? It seems as if everything is up to God. If the Spirit blows wherever he pleases, then how can I get him to breathe new life into me? As Nicodemus put it, *'How can this be?'* He was saying something like this: 'I *must* be born again, but how can I, since I cannot give birth to myself?' The one thing necessary is the very thing that is beyond our power to perform. What we must do is something we cannot do, which is to give ourselves new spiritual life.

Nicodemus was struggling with God's sovereignty in salvation. From beginning to end, salvation is a matter of divine grace. Regeneration is no different in this respect from election, redemption or reconciliation. God alone determines whom he will save. For Jesus, God's sovereignty in salvation was such a basic truth that he simply mentioned it in passing. But whenever Jesus did happen to mention it, it often aroused questions and objections (e.g. 6:60), as it did in the mind of Nicodemus.

According to Jesus, a man like Nicodemus should have known better than to question God's sovereignty. He should have understood from the Scriptures that salvation does not come by human effort, but only by divine grace: *'You are Israel's teacher,'* said Jesus, *'and do you not understand these things? I tell you the truth, we speak of what we know, and we testify to what we have seen, but still you people do not accept our testimony. I have spoken to you of earthly things and you do not believe; how then will you believe if I speak of heavenly things?'* (3:10–12). Nicodemus' problem was very simple: the reason he could not understand what Jesus was saying to him was that he lacked faith. Nicodemus believed neither Jesus nor his word. He refused to trust his testimony (3:11). He would not even believe what Jesus told him about earthly things (3:12) – elementary things (like regeneration, perhaps) that pertained to God's work on earth. Thus he could never understand the things that pertain to God's kingdom in heaven. Those who refuse to receive Jesus on biblical terms cannot understand the message of salvation. As Jesus later warned Nicodemus, *'God did not send his Son into the world to condemn the world, but to save the world through him. Whoever believes in him is not condemned, but whoever does not believe stands condemned already because he has not believed in the name of God's one and only Son'* (3:17–18).

Faith in Jesus Christ, therefore, is a matter of spiritual life and death. If Nicodemus wanted to understand what Jesus was saying about the new birth – more than that, if he wanted to experience the new birth for himself – he had to put his whole trust in Jesus. Salvation comes by grace *through faith*. The only way to receive new spiritual life is by trusting in Jesus Christ. That is why, at the end of their conversation, Jesus called Nicodemus to trust in him for salvation: *'No-one has ever gone into heaven except the one who came from heaven – the Son of Man. Just as Moses lifted up the snake in the desert, so the Son of Man must be lifted up, that everyone who believes in him may have eternal life'* (3:13–15).

Jesus was speaking about the cross where he would be lifted up to die for sinners. He described his crucifixion in terms Nicodemus could understand, using an illustration from the Old Testament. After the children of Israel were delivered from Egypt, they travelled around Edom. Along the way they grew impatient with their travels and complained against God: 'Why have you brought us up out of Egypt to die in the desert?'[26] While they were grumbling, God sent poisonous snakes among them, and many people died. The people realized that they had sinned, so they asked how they could be saved. When Moses prayed for their salvation, God said, 'Make a snake and put it up on a pole; anyone who is bitten can look at it and live.'[27] Moses did as God commanded: 'Moses made a bronze snake and put it up on a pole. Then when anyone was bitten by a snake and looked at the bronze snake, he lived.'[28]

The story of the bronze serpent was about salvation from sin and its deadly consequence. Jesus used it to explain to Nicodemus the message of salvation. Like the children of Israel, we are liable to die for our sins, but Jesus has come to save us. First he had to be 'lifted up', which is a phrase John uses (cf. 8:28; 12:32, 34) to refer to the Roman gibbet where Christ was crucified (and perhaps also to his ultimate exaltation). Now everyone who looks to Jesus and to his cross will live. Christ crucified is like the bronze serpent in the wilderness: to look to him in faith is to live.

This was the answer to the last question Nicodemus asked Jesus. Remember that his question concerned the availability of the new birth: If regeneration is a work of God's sovereign grace, then how can I be born again? Rather than giving the man a five-step plan for

[26] Num. 21:5.   [27] Num. 21:8.   [28] Num. 21:9.

spiritual rebirth, Jesus told Nicodemus to trust in him for his salvation. Everyone who believes in the crucified Christ will receive eternal life (3:15; cf. 6:47; 20:31). God does not call sinners to believe the doctrine of regeneration, in the first instance; he calls us to faith in Jesus Christ. We do not preach the new birth, therefore, but Christ crucified. To be sure, God tells us about the new birth so that we will see our need for regeneration and understand what his Spirit is doing to transform us, but what he calls us to do is to trust in Jesus Christ. 'You must be born again' is a statement of fact, not a command to obey. What God commands sinners to do is to believe the message of salvation, and as they look to Christ for their salvation, they are born again by God's Spirit.

What about Nicodemus? Was he ever born again? There is good reason to think that he was regenerated, reborn from above by God's Spirit. We next catch a glimpse of him at the end of John 7. The Jewish leaders were plotting to trap Jesus, but Nicodemus tried desperately to stand up for him: 'Nicodemus, who had gone to Jesus earlier and who was one of their own number, asked, "Does our law condemn a man without first hearing him to find out what he is doing?" They replied, "Are you from Galilee, too? Look into it, and you will find that a prophet does not come out of Galilee"' (7:50–51). Nicodemus did look into it, and eventually he came to believe that Jesus was a true prophet from God. The last time we see Nicodemus he is at the cross, where the Son of Man was lifted up to die. At great risk to his career, and perhaps even his life, he came with Joseph of Arimathea to take Jesus' body down from the cross and to bury it in the tomb (19:38–42). The best explanation for his courageous actions is that he was born again by God's Spirit. Once a man is born again, he begins to live a whole new spiritual life. Remember that the apostle John, after a lifetime of reflecting on the results of regeneration, concluded that anyone who is born again 'does what is right'.[29] This was true of Nicodemus. By caring for the dead body of Jesus, he did what was right, giving solid evidence that he had looked to Christ and lived.

The way to become a born-again Christian, and thus to receive eternal life, is to look to Christ and his cross. One snowy Sunday morning a young man was on his way to church. He trudged down a side street and came to a little chapel. He went in and saw a preacher mounting the pulpit. It turned out that the preacher was not actually a minister, but a common labourer. Nevertheless,

> Though his grammar and diction left much to be desired, he spoke earnestly and directly to his audience of twelve. Finally the preacher looked at the young man, who was sitting under the gallery, and

[29] 1 John 2:9.

said, 'Young man, you look very miserable … and you will always be miserable if you don't obey my text. Look to Jesus Christ! You have nothin' to do but to look and live!' [30]

At those words the young man – whose name was Charles Spurgeon (1834–92), and who later became London's most famous preacher – was born again. He looked to Christ in faith and he received eternal life. *For God so loved the world that he gave his one and only Son, that whoever believes in him shall not perish but have eternal life* (3:16).

---

[30] Hoekema, *Saved by Grace*, p. 113.

11. Blind man, beggar man, thief
Faith and repentance: Luke 18:35 – 19:10

Regeneration is only the beginning. A sinner who has been born from above by God's Spirit does not remain an infant, but grows towards spiritual maturity. There is a whole new life that follows the new birth. The Christian begins this new life by looking to Christ and turning away from sin. To use the proper biblical terminology, the Christian life begins with faith and repentance, which are both the result of regeneration. First, God's Spirit generates new spiritual life in the mind, the heart and the will of a sinner. Then this regeneration, in turn, enables the sinner to confess his sins (repentance) and trust in Christ (faith).

Which comes first?

Sometimes regeneration, repentance and faith occur simultaneously. Logically and causally, however, the new birth always must come first. It is certain that no-one is able to look to Christ or turn away from sin without being born again.[1] God's gracious gift precedes our penitent response. Yet when it comes to faith and repentance, theologians sometimes wonder which has the priority. Which comes first, repenting or believing?

Sometimes the Bible describes coming to salvation as repentance. On the Day of Pentecost, when the Jews who crucified Jesus asked what they should do about their sins, Peter said, 'Repent and be baptised, every one of you, in the name of Jesus Christ for the forgiveness of your sins.'[2] On other occasions salvation is described as a matter of faith. When the Philippian jailer asked Paul and Silas what he had to do to be saved, 'They replied, "Believe in the Lord Jesus, and you will be saved – you and your household."'[3] Then there are instances where faith and repentance appear together. According to the Gospel of Mark, Jesus began his public ministry with these words: 'The time has come. The kingdom of God is near. Repent and believe the good news!'[4] Similarly,

---

[1] See 1 John 5:1.   [2] Acts 2:38a.   [3] Acts 16:31.   [4] Mark 1:15.

Paul 'declared to both Jews and Greeks that they must turn to God in repentance and have faith in our Lord Jesus'.[5]

From these and other passages in the Bible, it is clear that faith and repentance are so closely intertwined that they cannot be separated. More than that, they are interdependent, like two sides of a single coin. It is impossible to repent without believing, or to believe without repenting. Faith without repentance is licence; repentance without faith is legalism. Therefore, wherever true faith is found, it is always accompanied by genuine repentance, and vice versa. Repentance means turning away from sin, and the only way to turn away from sin is to turn towards God, which is an act of faith. As Professor John Murray (1898–1975) explained,

> The faith that is unto salvation is a penitent faith and the repentance that is unto life is a believing repentance … The interdependence of faith and repentance can be readily seen when we remember that faith is faith in Christ for salvation from sin. But if faith is directed to salvation from sin, there must be hatred of sin and the desire to be saved from it. Such hatred of sin involves repentance which essentially consists in turning from sin unto God. Again, if we remember that repentance is turning from sin unto God, the turning to God implies faith in the mercy of God as revealed in Christ. It is impossible to disentangle faith and repentance. Saving faith is permeated with repentance and repentance is permeated with faith.[6]

The meaning of faith unto salvation and repentance unto life can be illustrated from two episodes in the life of Jesus. The first is a story about faith. It concerns a blind man – a beggar man – who looked to Christ for his salvation. The second is a story about repentance. It concerns a thief who turned away from his sins. But faith and repentance always go together. Thus the blind man's faith included an element of repentance; and as for the thief, he never would have repented unless he had also believed. Placed side by side in the Gospel of Luke, these two stories show that faith and repentance belong together. If we are to be saved, we must confess our sins and receive God's grace through faith in Jesus Christ.

The blind man

Jesus met both the blind man and the thief while he was walking along the Jericho road. The first encounter took place on his way into the city: *As Jesus approached Jericho, a blind man was sitting by the roadside*

---

[5] Acts 20:21.
[6] Murray, *Redemption: Accomplished and Applied*, p. 113.

begging. When he heard the crowd going by, he asked what was happening. They told him, 'Jesus of Nazareth is passing by' (Luke 18:35–37).

The blind man could not see Jesus, of course, but there were several things he could see. The first was his need. He needed sight. Through his eyes he could see only darkness. When Jesus asked him what he needed, his answer was very simple: *'Lord, I want to see'* (18:41). As a result of his blindness, the man also needed money. He was in extreme poverty. Day after day he sat by the side of the road, begging. What else could he do? He had no way to earn a steady income, for he was a blind man living in a culture that made no special provisions for the disabled. He was destitute!

Out of the misery of his desperate need, the blind man cried for salvation: *He called out, 'Jesus, Son of David, have mercy on me!'* (18:38). The word 'mercy' suggests that he could see his spiritual need as clearly as his physical needs. Mercy is the love of God for sinners, the grace by which he rescues us from our lost and sorry condition. It is what David asked for when he prayed:

> Have mercy on me, O God,
>   according to your unfailing love;
> according to your great compassion
>   blot out my transgressions.[7]

When the blind man asked for mercy he was asking for something more than his sight; he was begging for his salvation. If salvation is God's answer to the problem of humanity, then the first step is to admit that we are part of the problem. The blind man who sat by the side of the road saw his need for a Saviour.

The second thing the blind man saw was who Jesus was. He called him *'Jesus, Son of David'* (18:38–39). This title does not appear often in the Gospels, but it would have been familiar to any Jew who knew the Old Testament. It meant that Jesus was the Messiah, the Saviour whom God had always promised to send. In those days the traditional Jewish synagogue prayers, which were called the Eighteen Benedictions, included a petition asking God to have mercy 'on the kingdom of the house of David, of the Messiah of thy righteousness'.[8] By calling Jesus the 'Son of David', the blind man was acknowledging him as the Saviour. Perhaps he had heard of his miracles, and knew that Jesus was descended from the line of David (2:4). But Jesus was more than one of David's sons; he was also David's heir, Israel's rightful king, and therefore God's promised Saviour.

The blind man not only recognized Jesus as the Saviour, but he also received him as his Lord. When Jesus asked him what he wanted, he

---

[7] Ps. 51:1.   [8] *TDNT*, vol. VIII, p. 481.

addressed Jesus as *Lord* (18:41). This was a sign of respect, but it also seems to have been a confession of faith. By calling Jesus 'Lord', the blind man was getting into a right relationship with God. There is no way to separate salvation in Christ from the lordship of Christ. Jesus is both Saviour and Lord; to receive him as one is to receive him as the other, for the only Saviour is the Lord Jesus Christ. Therefore, when the blind man called Jesus 'Lord', he was putting himself in a position to worship and obey the Saviour.

The blind man could see better than most people, including many people in the crowds that followed Jesus around Jericho! His spiritual acuity was nearly 20:20. Someone once asked Helen Keller (1880–1968), the famous blind social reformer, 'Isn't it terrible to be blind?' She responded by saying, 'Better to be blind and see with your heart, than to have two good eyes and see nothing.'[9] Keller's words are an apt description of the beggar man by the side of the road who, for all his physical blindness, had penetrating spiritual insight.

Sight for the blind

The last thing the blind man saw was Jesus himself. Or perhaps we should say that Jesus was the *first* thing he saw, for by his miraculous power, Jesus made the blind man to see. The Scripture says that 'Everyone who calls on the name of the Lord will be saved.'[10] The blind man experienced this for himself. Jesus heard his cry and opened his eyes, delivering him from blindness and beggary. And as soon as his eyes were opened, the first person the blind man saw was Jesus, his Lord and his Saviour.

The restoration of the blind man's sight is a reminder that salvation is for the body as well as the soul. In biblical times, the line between physical and spiritual well-being was not sharply drawn. S. R. Driver notes that the Old Testament terms for salvation 'seldom, if ever, express a spiritual state exclusively: their common theological sense in Hebrew is that of a material deliverance attended by spiritual blessings'.[11] Similarly, the New Testament verb 'to save' (*sōzō*) can encompass physical as well as spiritual health. Salvation is the sum of divine blessing. It brings relief from every form of human distress, including but not limited to deliverance from the coming judgment. Depending on the context, the term 'salvation' may refer to 'healing, delivering, rescuing, keeping safe, [or] preserving someone'.[12]

[9] Keller, quoted in R. Kent Hughes, *Luke: That You May Know the Truth*, Preaching the Word (Wheaton, IL: Crossway, 1998), vol. 2, p. 215.

[10] Rom. 10:13; cf. Joel 2:32.

[11] Driver, *Notes on the Hebrew Text and Topography of the Books of Samuel*, 2nd ed. (Oxford: Oxford University Press, 1913), p. 119.

[12] Witherington, 'Salvation and health in Christian antiquity', pp. 145–166 (164).

All of these meanings can be illustrated from the writings of Luke, who was particularly concerned to show that in Jesus, God has provided total salvation for the whole person, within the community of God's new humanity. Salvation is a central theme in Luke's Gospel, and also in the book of Acts.[13] The salvation Jesus brings is thoroughly revolutionary, affecting the body as well as the soul, not only for the individual, but also for society. For Luke, 'Salvation is neither ethereal nor merely future, but embraces life in the present, restoring the integrity of human life, revitalizing human communities, setting the cosmos in order, and commissioning the community of God's people to put God's grace into practice among themselves and toward ever-widening circles of others.'[14]

Salvation in this comprehensive sense is announced early in Luke's Gospel, when Mary sings:

> 'My soul glorifies the Lord
>   and my spirit rejoices in God my Saviour ...
> He has brought down rulers from their thrones
>   but has lifted up the humble.
> He has filled the hungry with good things
>   but has sent the rich away empty.'
>
> (1:46–47, 52–53)

Mary expected the saving work of God's Son to bring social transformation by exalting the poor and destroying the proud. Zechariah had the same expectation:

> 'Praise be to the Lord, the God of Israel,
>   because he has come and has redeemed his people.
> He has raised up a horn of salvation for us
>   in the house of his servant David ...
> salvation from our enemies
>   and from the hand of all who hate us –
> to rescue us from the hand of our enemies,
>   and to enable us to serve him without fear.'
>
> (1:68–69, 71, 74)

Like the exodus from Egypt, and like the return from the exile in Babylon, salvation in Christ would be a history-shaping event. It would address the full range of human need, including deliverance from oppression, which Luke describes in social as well as in spiritual terms.

---

[13] Many of the articles in Marshall and Peterson (eds.), *Witness to the Gospel: The Theology of Acts*, address the theme of salvation in Luke as well as Acts.

[14] Green, *The Gospel of Luke*, pp. 24–25.

This salvation, as comprehensive as it was, would come not through some social or political institution, but in the person and work of Jesus. When Jesus was presented at the temple, Simeon said, 'My eyes have seen your salvation, which you have prepared in the sight of all people' (2:30–31; cf. 3:6). Simeon did not see rulers brought down from their thrones, or Israel rescued from her enemies. But he did see Jesus, and by faith he understood that God's salvation was to be found in him. Jesus understood the same thing, of course, which is why he began his public ministry by proclaiming:

> 'The Spirit of the Lord is on me,
>   because he has anointed me
>   to preach good news to the poor.
> He has sent me to proclaim freedom for the prisoners
>   and recovery of sight for the blind,
> to release the oppressed,
>   to proclaim the year of the Lord's favour.'
>
> (4:18–19)[15]

With these words, Jesus identified himself as the transforming agent of salvation. He was quoting from the prophet Isaiah, who in turn was drawing on the Law of Jubilee, which required rest for the land, forgiveness for debtors, and freedom for slaves.[16] The liberation that Jesus promised was not narrowly individualistic, but broadly social; it was not exclusively spiritual, but also held the promise of tangible blessings.

The story of the blind man must be understood against the broad background of everything Luke has already said about salvation. By performing this miraculous healing, Jesus proved himself to be the Saviour, fulfilling his claim that he had come to recover sight for the blind (4:18). Thus the healing itself was part of the man's salvation. When Jesus described what he had done for the man, he said, *Your faith has healed [sesōken] you* (18:42); or, more literally, 'Your faith has saved you.' While the blind man's salvation included much more than the recovery of his sight, his sight was not to be overlooked! Jesus saved the man from his physical distress with a view to his eternal destiny. Ultimately, God promises to provide physical as well as spiritual well-being. He will save us from every last consequence of sin, including sickness, disability, disease and death.

These considerations will enable us to avoid the danger of over-spiritualizing the message of salvation. The New Testament describes salvation in concrete terms, and it is careful not to neglect the implications of faith in Christ for the present age. However, some interpreters have gone to the opposite extreme, and have emphasized

---

[15] Cf. Is. 61:1–2a.   [16] See Lev. 25.

the temporal and material dimensions of salvation to the detriment of its eternal and spiritual aspects. This is true of liberation theology, which views salvation primarily as deliverance from economic exploitation, as well as destruction of the evil social structures that perpetuate exploitation. Liberationists have sensed the revolutionary and subversive nature of biblical salvation. They have also recognized that the gospel has far-reaching socio-political implications. Nevertheless, while a concern for the deprivations of material poverty is not absent from the biblical teaching about salvation, that concern is not primary.[17] What comes first is the sinner's restoration to a right relationship with God and relocation into God's new community. This restoration and relocation, in turn, produce the material blessings that often accompany salvation.

Another temporal aspect of salvation that is commonly overemphasized is physical health. In some charismatic circles, especially, there is the expectation that through miraculous healing, salvation in Christ holds the promise of freedom from disability and disease. One thinks of the American faith-healer who asked, shortly after his conversion, 'When are you going to do the stuff?', by which he meant the kinds of miracles that Jesus performed in the Gospels. There are a number of dangers in expecting a miracle, not least the biblical warning that 'the work of Satan' is 'displayed in all kinds of counterfeit miracles, signs and wonders'.[18] But a more fundamental difficulty is the expectation itself – the expectation that faith in Christ guarantees physical health (and also, in many cases, material wealth). The primary purpose of Jesus' miracles was *not* to demonstrate that total physical well-being would be normative for believers in the present age, but to prove that he was the Saviour God had promised to send. Thus his miracles should not mislead us to expect full salvation right away. We err if we assume that physical healing will be the immediate result of saving faith. Yet God has not promised to save us from suffering in this fallen world. On the contrary, as we shall see in chapter 17, he promises to save us through suffering into glory. The healing miracles hold the promise of a glorious salvation that is still to come. It is only at the end of the age, when Christ returns in all his glory, that God finally will make us whole, right human beings with 'no more death or mourning or crying or pain'.[19]

The beggar man by the Jericho road caught a glimpse of this full and final salvation when Jesus made his blind eyes to see. But his deepest need was for God to remove his most serious blindness of all. This was the blindness we discussed back in chapter 3, the spiritual blindness

---

[17] For a more thorough critique of liberation theology, see Nash (ed.), *Liberation Theology*.
[18] 2 Thess. 2:9.   [19] Rev. 21:4.

that renders a person unable to repent of sin and believe in Christ. For all his emphasis on the temporal and material aspects of salvation, Luke understood that what is most important of all is getting right with God. Or as Zechariah put it in his song of salvation, God's desire is 'to give his people the knowledge of salvation through the forgiveness of their sins' (Luke 1:77).

To illustrate the priority of the eternal dimension of salvation, consider the true story of a young African man named John, as recounted in a prayer letter from Ted Barnett, the US Director of Africa Inland Mission:

[John] and his family live in an island village in the country of Uganda. It is estimated that 95% of the population of this island is infected with AIDS. John is one of the 95%. One day AIM missionaries, Steve and Debbie Wolcott, came to John's village and showed the *Jesus* video. John was irate. How could these people come with only a video? They should be bringing something that would really make a difference. They should have brought medicine to heal this dread disease.

Steve shared the love of Jesus with John once again and reminded him that even if there was a pill that could completely heal his infected body of the AIDS virus, that would only last for this life. What about eternity?

After a few days, John came to Steve and told him he wanted to accept Jesus Christ as his Savior. John is a changed man. Although his physical condition remains essentially the same, he now has hope. He openly shares his faith in Jesus with his family and friends. He wants them to have the same hope he has has found.

This young African man found the same hope that the blind man found in Luke's Gospel, the hope of deliverance from sin, together with the promise of eternal life.

Believing is seeing

The way that the blind man received his sight was by grace through faith. Because he always knew what was in a person,[20] Jesus could tell that this blind man not only confessed with his mouth, but also believed in his heart.[21] So he said to him, *'Receive your sight; your faith has healed you'* (Luke 18:42). It was the blind man's faith that made him well. Properly speaking, of course, it was Jesus who healed him. But the man had received Jesus by faith, and thus faith was the channel by which he received his salvation. B. B. Warfield is right when he says, 'It

[20] See John 2:25.   [21] See Rom. 10:9–10.

167

is not, strictly speaking, even faith in Christ that saves, but Christ that saves through faith. The saving power resides exclusively, not in the act of faith or the attitude of faith or the nature of faith, but in the object of faith ... Christ himself.'[22]

The blind man's belief had all the qualities of saving faith. It was a *persistent* faith. He did not simply call out to Jesus, but kept crying for mercy until Jesus stopped and healed him. Since he could not see his way to Jesus, how else could he get the salvation he so desperately needed? He continued to beg for mercy even after the rest of the crowd told him to shut up: *'Those who led the way rebuked him and told him to be quiet, but he shouted all the more'* (18:39). The man may have been blind, but he was not dumb, in the sense of being unable to speak. The more people tried to quieten him down, the louder he shouted, until his cry became almost a shriek. The blind man's persistence was rewarded: *'Jesus stopped and ordered the man to be brought to him. When he came near, Jesus asked him, "What do you want me to do for you?"'* (18:41). The lesson is easy to apply. There will always be some friends and family members who try to discourage us from turning to Jesus in faith. But we must keep crying out for salvation, the way the blind man did, until we receive it. Jesus will not pass us by. He will stop in the middle of the road and save us completely.

Unless the blind man's faith had been persistent, he never would have had the chance to ask Jesus for what he needed. Unless his faith had been *personal*, he never would have asked Jesus in the way that he did: *'Lord, I want to see'* (18:41). The man called directly on Jesus for his salvation. He personally entrusted himself to Christ for the healing of his own body. Every sinner who does this is saved, for faith in Christ is saving faith. God calls everyone to trust personally in his Son Jesus. If we call out to Christ he will come and be our personal Saviour.

Knowing, believing, and trusting

Protestant theologians have long taught that personal saving faith contains three elements: knowledge (*notitia*), belief (*assensus*) and trust (*fiducia*). The blind man (the beggar man) seems to have had all three.

First there is *knowledge*, the intellectual dimension of faith, which comes from the regenerated mind. It is impossible to have faith in Jesus Christ without knowing who he is and what he has done. Faith is not simply a subjective feeling of ultimate dependence; it has objective, propositional content. In the case of the blind man, faith meant knowing that Jesus was the Son of David, with the power to save. For the Christian, faith means knowing that Jesus is who the Bible says he

[22] Warfield, 'Faith', in *Biblical and Theological Studies*, p. 425.

is and that he has done what the Bible says he has done. Jesus is God the Son – God incarnate – who lived a perfect life, died an atoning death, and was raised to victorious life. Faith means knowing that Jesus Christ is the crucified and risen Saviour who offers redemption from sin and reconciliation to God. Since faith requires knowledge, often the first step to becoming a Christian is to have someone simply explain what Christianity teaches.

Although faith begins in the mind, that is not where it ends. Calvin said that 'the Word of God is not received by faith if it flits about in the top of the brain, but when it takes root in the depth of the heart'.[23] This brings us to the second essential element of personal saving faith, which is *assent* or belief. This is the emotional dimension of faith, which comes from the regenerated heart. It means accepting the message of salvation – not just knowing what the Bible says about Jesus, but believing that it is really true. After all, even the demons believe there is a God;[24] their trouble is that they will not accept him. But the blind man did accept Jesus. He cried out to the Saviour and called him Lord. He had saving faith, in which the mind becomes convinced of the truth of Jesus Christ and the heart adores him as Saviour.

The third element in personal saving faith is *trust*. This is the volitional dimension of faith, in which the regenerated will offers unconditional surrender to Jesus Christ. As Martin Luther explained, there is a difference between 'faith which believes what is said of God is true' and 'faith which throws itself on God'.[25] The trusting aspect of faith was graphically illustrated for a well-known missionary:

Many years ago now, when John G. Paton first went out as a pioneer missionary to the New Hebrides islands, he found that the natives among whom he began to work had no way of writing their language. He began to learn it and in time began to work on a translation of the Bible for them. Soon he discovered that they had no word for 'faith'. This was serious, of course, for a person can hardly translate the Bible without it. One day he went on a hunt with one of the natives. They shot a large deer in the course of the hunt, and tying its legs together and supporting it on a pole, laboriously trekked back down the mountain path to Paton's home near the seashore. As they reached the veranda both men threw the deer down, and the native immediately flopped into one of the deck chairs that stood on the porch exclaiming, 'My, it is good to stretch yourself out here and rest.' Paton immediately jumped to his feet and recorded the phrase. In his final translation of the New

[23] Calvin, *Institutes of the Christian Religion*, III.ii.36.
[24] Jas. 2:19.
[25] Luther, quoted in Bloesch, *Essentials of Evangelical Theology*, vol. 1, p. 224.

Testament this was the word used to convey the idea of trust, faith, and belief.[26]

The best-known definition of faith comes from the letter to the Hebrews: 'Now faith is being sure of what we hope for and certain of what we do not see.'[27] There is no better example of this definition than the blind man by the Jericho road, who was certain of what he did not see! What is significant about this definition of faith is its emphasis on assurance. Faith means being certain of salvation. Calvin thus defined it as 'a firm and certain knowledge of God's benevolence towards us, founded upon the truth of the freely given promise in Christ, both revealed to our minds and sealed upon our hearts through the Holy Spirit'.[28] Genuine biblical faith always includes a measure of assurance. This does not mean that Christians never have their doubts. As we learn from the Gospels, there are times when disciples have little faith,[29] and need to ask God to increase it.[30] What the assurance of faith does mean, however, is that true believers never completely lose their trust in the saving work of Christ. Thankfully, salvation does not depend on the strength of our faith. It depends rather on God's faithfulness, and he has promised that, by the abiding presence of his Spirit, we will never abandon our confidence in Jesus to save.

Personal saving faith includes knowledge, belief and trust. The *Heidelberg Catechism* brings all three elements together when it defines true faith as 'not only a certain knowledge, whereby I hold for truth all that God has revealed to us in his word, but also an assured confidence, which the Holy Ghost works by the gospel in my heart; that not only to others, but to me also, remission of sin, everlasting righteousness, and salvation, are freely given by God, merely of grace, only for the sake of Christ's merits' (A. 21).

The last thing to be said about the blind man's faith is that it was *productive*: *Immediately he received his sight and followed Jesus, praising God* (18:43). As soon as the blind man could see, he became a true disciple, a follower of Jesus Christ. Having been saved by faith, he started to live by faith, for saving faith always leads to obedience. This is what the Bible means when it speaks of 'the obedience of faith'.[31] Faith without works is dead,[32] but this man was alive. He had a working faith, a faith that worked. Once the blind man was saved, he started to fulfil the purpose for which he was made, which was to glorify God. He was saved for God's glory.

The story of the blind man by the side of the road calls us to saving faith. It invites us to have a persistent, personal, productive faith in

[26] The story is recounted in Boice, *The Gospel of John*, p. 195.
[27] Heb. 11:1.   [28] Calvin, *Institutes*, III.ii.7.   [29] Matt. 6:30; Luke 12:28.
[30] Mark 9:24; Luke 17:5.   [31] Rom. 1:5.   [32] Jas. 2:17, 26.

Jesus Christ. To exercise faith in Jesus Christ is to accept him and embrace him. Convinced of the truth of his gospel, and relying on his cross for our salvation, we commit ourselves to Christ and to his service. Henry Wadsworth Longfellow (1807–82) once wrote a poem based on the healing of the blind man, a poem which ends with this call to faith in Christ:

> Ye that have eyes, yet cannot see,
> In darkness and in misery,
> Recall those mighty Voices Three,
> 'Jesus, have mercy now on me!
> Fear not, arise, and go in peace!
> Thy faith from blindness gives release!'[33]

The wee little man

There was another man who found salvation on the Jericho road and, like the blind man, he wanted to see Jesus. He was a 'wee little man' named Zacchaeus: *Jesus entered Jericho and was passing through. A man was there by the name of Zacchaeus; he was a chief tax collector and was wealthy. He wanted to see who Jesus was, but being a short man he could not, because of the crowd. So he ran ahead and climbed a sycamore-fig tree to see him, since Jesus was coming that way* (Luke 19:1–4).

Zacchaeus is well known for being 'vertically challenged', but his biggest problem was that he was short on godliness. Most tax collectors were sinners in those days, but Zacchaeus was a bigger sinner than most. Jericho was one of three major centres for collecting Israel's taxes. It was a wealthy city on a major trade route. Not surprisingly, collecting taxes had made Zacchaeus filthy rich. He did not even have to do the collecting himself. As 'chief tax collector' he was the ultimate middleman, skimming the proceeds off the customs revenue on its way to Rome. No wonder Zacchaeus was wealthy – he was the kingpin of the Jericho tax cartel![34]

As a general rule, tax collectors were swindlers and cheats, traitors to their own people. That explains why Zacchaeus was so unpopular, and perhaps also why no-one gave him enough room to see Jesus. It also explains why later, when Jesus invited himself over for dinner, *All the people saw this and began to mutter, 'He has gone to be the guest of a "sinner"'* (19:7). The reason people were so offended was because the

---

[33] Longfellow, 'Blind Bartimaeus', in *Chapters into Verse: Poetry in English Inspired by the Bible*, ed. by Robert Atwan and Laurance Wieder (New York: Oxford University Press, 1993), vol. 2, pp. 149–150.

[34] R. Kent Hughes, *Luke: That You May Know the Truth* (Wheaton, IL: Crossway, 1998), vol. 2, p. 222.

chief tax collector was Public Enemy Number One. How could Jesus associate with an outcast like Zacchaeus? It was beneath his dignity. In the eyes of some, to eat with a known criminal was to be implicated in his crimes.[35] Hence the grumbling disapproval when Jesus decided to stay at the house of Zacchaeus. What the people did not understand was that the message of salvation is *for* sinners. It is for outsiders and outcasts, swindlers and cheats. Zacchaeus was exactly the kind of man Jesus was looking for: a low-life sinner. *For the Son of Man came to seek and to save what was lost* (19:10). If the Saviour had come to save sinners, then who better to save than Zacchaeus?

The old children's Sunday School song explains what happened next:

> And as the Saviour passed that way,
> He looked into the tree.
> And said, 'Now Zacchaeus, you come down!
> For I'm coming to your house for tea,
> I'm coming to your house for tea.'

Luke's report is more prosaic: *When Jesus reached the spot, he looked up and said to him, 'Zacchaeus, come down immediately. I must stay at your house today'* (19:5).

It was the ultimate 'divine appointment' – supper with the Saviour! Here again we see God's sovereignty in salvation. Zacchaeus did not stop for Jesus; Jesus stopped for Zacchaeus, even calling him by name. Jesus was on a divine mission; he had come to seek and to save. He was offering Zacchaeus the intimacy of a personal relationship. But what he said to the little man was not so much an invitation as an imperative. He commanded Zacchaeus to come down *at once*, because he *must* visit his house *today*. The reason for Jesus' urgency was that he was calling Zacchaeus to faith and repentance. The theological term for this is 'effectual calling'. In the words of the *Westminster Shorter Catechism*, 'Effectual calling is the work of God's Spirit, whereby, convincing us of our sin and misery, enlightening our minds in the knowledge of Christ, and renewing our wills, he doth persuade and enable us to embrace Jesus Christ, freely offered to us in the gospel' (A. 31). Sooner or later, every true child of God receives this effective call. Through the preaching of the message of salvation,[36] Jesus stops us in the middle of life's busy road and calls us to repent and believe.

Like the salvation of the blind man, the salvation of the 'wee little man' shows that genuine faith is always joined to true repentance, and vice versa. The story of the blind man was a story of faith, but it was a penitent faith. Likewise, although the story of Zacchaeus is primarily a story of repentance, it was a believing repentance. When Jesus called

---

[35] Bock, *Luke*, vol. 2, p. 1521.   [36] Rom. 10:17.

him, Zacchaeus believed in the Saviour and repented of his sins.

The faith of Zacchaeus is evident from the way he received Jesus. When Jesus stopped and called him by name, he practically fell out of the tree. But then he gave Jesus the glad welcome of faith, embracing with him with joyous trust: *He came down at once and welcomed him gladly* (19:6). Zacchaeus' welcome is a reminder that faith is a matter of personal trust, and not merely a matter of propositional belief. He had heard about Jesus before. In all likelihood, the word had been passed around in his circles that the man from Nazareth was a friend of tax collectors and sinners.[37] Zacchaeus wanted to see for himself, to investigate the claims of Christ. But he did not have to look long before he decided to welcome Jesus into his heart. There is a time and a place for sitting up in the tree and looking at Jesus. But there is also a time and a place for getting down from the tree and welcoming him with open arms. There is further evidence of Zacchaeus' faith in the way he addressed Jesus: *'Look, Lord!'* (19:8). Like the blind man, he called Jesus his Lord. This was more than a title of respect; it was also his first confession of faith, a sign that he was coming under the lordship of Jesus Christ.

Payback time

There are several signs that Zacchaeus believed in Jesus almost as soon as he was called. But the real proof of his faith was his repentance: *Zacchaeus stood up and said to the Lord, 'Look, Lord! Here and now I give half of my possessions to the poor, and if I have cheated anybody out of anything, I will pay back four times the amount.' Jesus said to him, 'Today salvation has come to this house, because this man, too, is a son of Abraham'* (19:8–9). By calling him a son of Abraham, Jesus was welcoming Zacchaeus into God's family. All his sins were forgiven. Even though he was a tax collector, he was still a Jew, and now he was restored to God's true Israel by faith and repentance.

We have already seen that there are three essential elements in personal saving faith: knowledge, belief and trust. There are also three essential elements in what the Bible calls 'repentance unto life':[38] confession, contrition and change. It is important to notice that both faith and repentance touch the mind, heart and will of the sinner. In both faith and repentance, the whole person makes a total commitment to a complete Christ. Bruce Demarest writes:

Repentance signifies the sinner's determination to turn from all known sin. It involves an intellectual element – recognition of sin, an emotional element – sorrow for sin, and a voluntary element –

---

[37] See Matt. 11:19.   [38] Acts 11:18.

abandonment of sin. *Faith* connotes the sinner's determination to turn to Christ. It too involves an intellectual element – knowledge of the Gospel, an emotional element – feeling the sufficiency of Christ's grace, and a voluntary element – trusting Christ as Savior and Lord' (emphasis his).[39]

To one degree or another, all three elements of repentance were present in the conversion of Zacchaeus. First there must be *confession*, a full acknowledgment of sin. This is the intellectual dimension of repentance, which comes from the regenerated mind. When Zacchaeus heard everyone muttering that he was a sinner, he realized that they were right. So he stood up in front of Jesus and everyone else to confess his sins against God. There were sins of omission: he had not shared his riches with the poor. There were sins of commission: he had cheated people out of their hard-earned income. Zacchaeus took his stand to confess it all – all the covetousness, selfishness, greed, extortion, theft and fraud. True repentance requires genuine conviction of the sinfulness of one's sins.

Another man who acknowledged all his sins was the Rev. J. W. C. Pennington. After escaping from slavery in Maryland, Pennington was converted while living with the family of a Presbyterian elder in New York. He had been deeply scarred by his experiences as a slave, but he could not be saved until he finally realized that he was not just sinned against, but also a sinner. This is how Pennington described his repentance: 'Day after day, for about two weeks, I found myself more deeply convicted of personal guilt before God … Burning with a recollection of the wrongs men had done me – mourning for the injuries my brethren were still enduring, and deeply convinced of the guilt of my own sins against God.'[40] Anyone who wants to be saved must make the same confession, acknowledging the guilt of his or her own sins against God.

A second element of repentance is *contrition*, or genuine sorrow for sin. This is the emotional dimension of repentance, which comes from the regenerated heart. The Bible teaches that 'godly sorrow brings repentance that leads to salvation and leaves no regret'.[41] Contrition means something more than showing remorse for the consequences of sin. In true repentance, the sinner expresses grief for the shame of the sins themselves, for the offence that they have caused against the holiness of God. We saw a good example of this back in chapter 7, when we visited the publican at prayer, beating his breast. Although we do not see Zacchaeus shed any tears, we do see the glad welcome that

[39] Demarest, *The Cross and Salvation*, p. 249.
[40] J. W. C. Pennington, *The Fugitive Blacksmith*, 2nd ed. (London, 1849), p. 53.
[41] 2 Cor. 7:10.

he gave to his Saviour. Surely the joy of his salvation was partly due to his sorrow for his former sins.

The third element of true repentance is *change*, real spiritual change. This is the volitional dimension of repentance, which comes from the regenerated will. If a man recognizes his sin, and is sorry for it, yet there is no lasting change in his life, it may be doubted whether true repentance has ever taken place. Repentance is not repentance unto life unless it includes turning away from sin. There must be a conscious turning back to God, and away from sin, that manifests itself in a completely new way of thinking, feeling and acting. It is by repentance, writes the *Westminster Confession of Faith*, that 'a sinner, out of the sight and sense ... of the filthiness and odiousness of his sins ... so grieves for, and hates his sins as to turn from them all unto God'.[42]

The biblical terms for 'repentance' all refer to a turning away from sin. The most common word in the Old Testament is *šûb*, which means 'to turn around' or 'to go back in the opposite direction'.[43] At the same time that the sinner turns away from his sins, he turns towards God.[44] The key New Testament terms are *metanoia* ('repentance') and *epistrephō* ('to repent'). There is some overlap between the meanings of these two words, but they both emphasize a spiritual change. *Metanoia* refers more specifically to the inward change that takes place in the mind and heart of the sinner,[45] whereas *epistrephō* stresses the outward change in the sinner's actions.[46]

It was in this outward change that Zacchaeus excelled. It was obvious from what he both said and did that a genuine transformation had taken place in his life, that by the grace of God he had been saved from his sins. It is not certain where he made his speech about giving away his money. He may have spoken these words back at his house, in response to what Jesus said over dinner. But it seems as if he repented on the spot, right under the sycamore-fig tree: *'Look, Lord! Here and now I give half of my possessions to the poor, and if I have cheated anybody out of anything, I will pay back four times the amount'* (19:8). The word 'Look' implies that he started emptying his pockets then and there. He did not delay. In an instant he decided to divest himself of the wealth it had taken him years to accumulate. And from that moment forward, he resolved to turn away from sin.

In making amends to those whom he had defrauded, Zacchaeus intended to go well beyond what the law required. For starters, he would give away half of his possessions. At most, God's people were required to give one fifth of their property to the poor, but Zacchaeus

[42] *The Confession of Faith* (Inverness: Publications Committee of the Free Presbyterian Church of Scotland, 1970), XV.ii.
[43] 1 Kgs. 8:35; Ezek. 33:11. [44] Ps. 51:13; Hos. 14:1; Joel 2:12–13.
[45] Rom. 2:4; 2 Pet. 3:9. [46] 1 Thess. 1:9.

was willing to go up to 50%. The way a man uses his money is one of the best indicators of his spiritual condition, and although Zacchaeus may have been a small man, he had deep pockets. Once he came to Christ in faith and repentance, he reached down to help the poor. His spiritual transformation had social consequences, as it always does. Furthermore, Zacchaeus offered to pay back four times the amount he had stolen through taxation. The law required such fourfold retribution only for the theft of an animal.[47] In effect, Zacchaeus was placing himself in the worst category of thieves, identifying himself as the chief of swindlers. But now he was prepared to replace his vice with virtue. He had discovered that it is more blessed to give than to receive, and thus he was eager to 'prove his repentance by his deeds'.[48]

The gift of repentance

Repentance cost Zacchaeus a fortune, but then that is what it takes to pass through the eye of a needle (see 18:22, 25). One of the things that makes his repentance so remarkable is that he was so rich. Remember that in the previous chapter Luke had recounted the story of the rich ruler who refused to repent. What had kept that man from repenting was his great wealth (18:23). He was not willing to give up one shekel of his fortune to feed the poor. As the man sadly walked away, Jesus said, 'How hard it is for the rich to enter the kingdom of God! Indeed, it is easier for a camel to go through the eye of a needle than for a rich man to enter the kingdom of God' (18:24–25). The disciples were amazed when Jesus said this. They thought that wealth was a sign of God's blessing, and therefore offered assurance of salvation. If the rich cannot enter the kingdom of heaven, they wondered, 'Who then can be saved?' (18:26).

The answer that Jesus gave to his disciples is the answer that salvation always gives: 'What is impossible with men is possible with God' (18:27). The truth of these words was confirmed by the conversion of Zacchaeus, who turned out to be one of those rare camels who makes it through the needle's eye. Zacchaeus never could have found this salvation on his own. Only God could do such an impossible thing as bring a rich little thief to repentance. That is why the Bible describes repentance as a gift: 'God exalted [Jesus] to his own right hand as Prince and Saviour that he might give repentance and forgiveness of sins to Israel.'[49] Both faith and repentance are gifts of God's grace.

Of these two gifts – faith or repentance – which comes first? They are so closely connected that it hardly matters. There is no faith without

[47] Exod. 22:1.   [48] Acts 26:20b; cf. Matt. 3:8.
[49] Acts 5:31; cf. 11:18; 2 Tim. 2:25.

repentance. Believing in Christ means admitting that we need to be saved from our sins. But how can we truly repent for our sins without trusting that God will forgive us? Thus there is no repentance without faith. What matters is that we come to Christ believing and repenting. If we want to see Jesus the way that the blind man did, we must look to him in faith for our salvation. And if we want salvation to come to our house the way that it came to Zacchaeus, we must turn away from our sins. As Jesus said on an earlier occasion, 'Unless you repent, you ... will ... perish' (Luke 13:3).

When a sinner first comes to Christ in faith and repentance it is called conversion. After that, faith and repentance are simply called the Christian life. The Christian must continue to repent of sin and to believe in Christ. When Martin Luther posted his famous Ninety-five Theses in Wittenburg, his first thesis stated, 'Our Lord and Master Jesus Christ ... willed that the whole life of believers should be repentance'.[50] In other words, the Christian life requires a continual turning away from sin. But it also requires constant faith, for the Christian daily looks to Christ for loving care. The penitent believer never stops trusting in the saving power of the crucified and risen Saviour.

[50] Luther, *The Works of Martin Luther*, vol. 1, p. 29.

12. Alive in Christ
Union with Christ: Ephesians 2:1–10

When a born-again sinner comes to saving faith, a remarkable thing happens: the new believer is joined to Jesus Christ in an unbreakable spiritual union. 'In the conversion of a sinner,' wrote the Puritan William Perkins (1558–1602), 'there is a real donation of Christ, and all his benefits unto us: and there is a real union, whereby every believer is made one with Christ.'[1] To be a Christian is to be *in Christ*. As Paul told the Ephesians, 'You also were included in Christ when you heard the word of truth, the gospel of your salvation' (Eph. 1:13a).

The theological expression for the Christian's inclusion in Christ is 'union with Christ'. Many theologians have viewed this doctrine as the key to understanding the message of salvation. John Murray called union with Christ 'the central truth of the whole doctrine of salvation'.[2] John Calvin considered the doctrine to be a matter of spiritual life and death. He wrote: 'We must understand that as long as Christ remains outside of us, and we are separated from him, all that he has suffered and done for the salvation of the human race remains useless and of no value for us ... all that he possesses is nothing to us until we grow into one body with him.'[3]

Dead in sin

To understand why union with Christ is so central to the message of salvation, it helps to remember why we need to be saved in the first place. As we have seen throughout this book, the problem of humanity is sin, along with all its deadly consequences. One of the clearest statements of this problem is in the second chapter of Ephesians, where the apostle Paul explains that outside of Christ, humanity is dead – dominated and doomed by sin.

[1] Perkins, *A Commentary on Galatians*, p. 123.
[2] Murray, *Redemption: Accomplished and Applied*, p. 161.
[3] Calvin, *Institutes of the Christian Religion*, III.i.1.

To begin with, sin means *death*: *As for you, you were dead in your transgressions and sins* (Eph. 2:1). These two words – 'transgressions' and 'sins' – include every form of iniquity. A transgression (*paraptōma*) is a trespass. To transgress is to perform a sin of commission, to do something God has commanded not to be done. It is to cross into forbidden territory by overstepping a moral boundary. A sin (*hamartia*), on the other hand, is a failure to do something God has commanded us to do. To sin in this sense is to miss the mark, to fall short of God's perfect standard. The term thus refers to sins of omission. When they are taken together, these two words include every kind of sin imaginable.

The fact that we are transgressors and sinners shows that, apart from Christ, we are spiritually dead. There are really only three ways to describe the spiritual condition of the human race. Either we are healthy, or we are sick, or we are dead. Some say that human beings are healthy, that we are basically good, and that we are making moral progress all the time. This view is hopelessly unrealistic, as any copy of any newspaper in the world will demonstrate. Many others admit that we are not completely well, but think that somehow we can be nursed back to health. If only we could set up the right schools or pass the right laws, then all would be right with the world. But these strategies for solving humanity's problems are bound to fail because they are based on a fundamental misdiagnosis of the human condition. The Bible teaches that we are 'dead in our transgressions and sins' – not merely sick, or even dying, but actually dead. This is not simply a figure of speech, it is a spiritual reality. Spiritually speaking, as long as we remain outside of Christ, we are dead in our transgressions, and there is no way to educate or legislate us back to health. The place to look for us is not in the infirmary, but in the mortuary. Call for the coroner: God has pronounced us dead in sin!

One might say that the Earth is the planet of the living dead. Until we come to Christ, we are like so many spiritual zombies – physically alive, but spiritually dead. Until we are reborn by God's Spirit, we do not hear God's voice speaking in Scripture and cannot understand spiritual truth. We are unable to repent of our sins or turn to Christ. James Montgomery Boice writes, 'Like a spiritual corpse, a sinner is unable to make a single move toward God, think a single thought about God, or even correctly respond to God – unless God is first present to bring the spiritually dead person to life.'[4] Our total spiritual inability explains why salvation must come by divine grace rather than by human effort. We cannot be resuscitated, but only resurrected.

[4] Boice, *Ephesians*, p. 48.

The way we were

Before coming to Christ in faith and repentance, not only were we dead in our sins, but we were also *dominated* by them. Paul thus describes our former sins as the ones *in which you used to live when you followed the ways of this world and of the ruler of the kingdom of the air, the spirit who is now at work in those who are disobedient. All of us also lived among them at one time, gratifying the cravings of our sinful nature and following its desires and thoughts. Like the rest, we were by nature objects of wrath* (2:2–3). In these verses Paul describes a triple domination, in which sinners are controlled by the world, the devil, and the flesh.

He first describes sin as following *the ways of this world* (2:2a). The 'world' means human existence without God; it is creation disordered by sin. The way of the world is to live for self, seeking pleasure and power. Until a sinner becomes a follower of Jesus Christ, he or she cannot help but pursue the world's godless values. In the original Greek Paul actually speaks of 'walking' in the way of the world. This image suggests that worldliness is a whole way of life, the unbeliever's daily habit. It is this thought that lies behind the warning with which the Psalms begin: 'Blessed is the man who does not walk in the counsel of the wicked'.[5]

Second, we are dominated by the devil, whom Paul describes as *the ruler of the kingdom of the air* (2:2b). The 'kingdom of the air' is the unseen world, the realm where good and evil collide, where angels and demons wage spiritual warfare. The ruler of the demonic kingdom is Satan. He is the malevolent presence behind this godless age, trying to control the minds and hearts of men.

In his struggle for control the devil meets with some success. Paul speaks of *the spirit who is now at work in those who are disobedient* (2:2b). What he means by 'spirit' is not so much the devil himself, but something like 'the spirit of the age'. The point is that Satan works through the attitudes and structures of fallen human society to bring sinners under his evil sway. Whether they realize it or not, those who are outside of Christ are followers of Satan. This is obviously true of people who are demon-possessed or who practise the occult. But it is equally true of those who worship idols – not only primitive idols of stone and wood, but also modern idols such as Work, Sex, Leisure, Self, Art, Sport and the State. Ultimately, these idols represent 'the rulers', 'the authorities', 'the powers of this dark world' and 'the spiritual forces of evil in the heavenly realms' (6:12).

To be outside of Christ is to be dead in sin, dominated by the world, the devil and finally the flesh: *All of us also lived among them at one time, gratifying the cravings of our sinful nature and following its desires and*

[5] Ps. 1:1a.

thoughts (2:3a). Here the Authorized Version speaks of 'the lusts of the flesh'. The flesh is fallen human nature in all its frailty. It includes not only our bodies, but especially our hearts and minds, which is why Paul speaks of 'following its desires and thoughts'. The 'lust of the flesh' refers not only to our sexual sins, therefore, but to all our proud ambitions and unholy desires. There is not one living soul who is not subject to these sinful appetites. The Scripture says that 'all of us' – meaning both Jews and Gentiles – lived this way. This is the totality of our depravity, that apart from Jesus Christ, every human being at every time and in every place has gratified the cravings of the sinful nature.

The point is that as long as we remain outside of Jesus Christ we are dominated by the world, the devil and the flesh. As Paul goes on to say, we are 'separate from Christ … and without God in the world' (2:12). From the outside, we are controlled by the world's general outlook, which is inevitably godless. On the inside, we are held captive by our own desires, which are inherently rebellious. Behind it all stands the evil one, who seeks to keep us enslaved to sin. We are dominated by the world, the flesh and the devil, and yet we have only ourselves to blame, for these oppressive forces are only *at work in those who are disobedient* (2:2b). Thus it is our own disobedience that has brought us under this triple domination.

That is not the worst of it, however. It is bad enough to be dead in sin, dominated both inside and out by Satan, but what is worse still is that humanity is *doomed* to fall under the wrath of God: *Like the rest, we were by nature objects of wrath* (2:3b). The problem of humanity is not only sin, but also its final consequence, which is eternal judgment. Wrath is God's holy hatred of sin and his just determination to punish it. John Stott defines it as 'God's personal, righteous, constant hostility to evil, his settled refusal to compromise with it, and his resolve instead to condemn it'.[6] Wrath in this sense is not so much an emotion, as if somehow God were spiteful, as a decision of his perfect will. It is right and good for God to be utterly opposed to sin, and ultimately to punish it. Therefore the Bible everywhere teaches that 'the wrath of God is being revealed from heaven against all the godlessness and wickedness of men'.[7]

When the Scripture says that we are objects of wrath 'by nature', it means that all people everywhere deserve to be punished for their sins. As we discovered in the opening chapters of this book, we are sinners by nature. This is the doctrine of original sin. Adam's sin has been imputed to us, with the result that we have inherited a sinful nature from him and have become members of a fallen race. This view of fallen humanity – that outside of Christ we are spiritually dead, dominated by sin and doomed to divine judgment – is not pessimistic, but realistic.

[6] Stott, *The Message of Ephesians*, p. 76. [7] Rom. 1:18.

The Bible describes our situation as it actually is in the hope that we will see our desperate need of salvation.

From death to life

'But God.' With these two words, which in the Greek original are the first two words of Ephesians 2:4, we pass from sin to salvation, from death to life. Martyn Lloyd-Jones (1899–1981) claimed that 'these two words, in and of themselves, in a sense contain the whole of the gospel. The gospel tells of what God has done, God's intervention; it is something that comes entirely from outside us and displays to us that wondrous and amazing and astonishing work of God.'[8] 'But *God.*' The phrase confronts us with a radically God-centred view of salvation. If we are to be saved at all, we can be saved only by sovereign grace. But God has done what only he could do, which is to save us from our sins by his divine power.

If we ask *why* God takes this gracious initiative, the answer is that salvation flows from his loving heart. Paul's description of the problem of humanity ends with God's wrath (2:3); his description of the answer to all our problems includes many of God's other perfections. Love, mercy, grace and kindness – God's saving attributes spill out one after the other: *Because of his great love for us* (2:4a); *God, who is rich in mercy* (2:4b); *by grace you have been saved* (2:5b); *expressed in his kindness* (2:7b). It is out of his divine affection (love), tender compassion (mercy), unmerited favour (grace), and gentle care (kindness) that God saves doomed and dying sinners. In salvation the kindness of God's love, mercy and grace triumphs over death and judgment.

If we proceed to ask *how* God saves us, the answer is that he saves us by uniting us to Jesus Christ. In previous chapters we have seen what Jesus did in human history to accomplish our salvation. By his death on the cross he redeemed us from slavery, atoned for our sins, and reconciled us to God. Then, by his resurrection from the grave, Jesus triumphed over death. But if we are to be saved, somehow what Christ did on the cross and through the empty tomb must be transferred to us. The salvation which he objectively accomplished must be subjectively applied. This is why every Christian must be united to Christ, joined to him by faith.

Union with Christ is the connection by which the Christian is joined to Christ for every blessing of salvation. What kind of connection is it? It is a *spiritual* connection, a union established by God the Holy Spirit: 'We know that we live in him and he in us, because he has given us of his Spirit';[9] 'he who unites himself with the Lord is one with

[8] Lloyd-Jones, *God's Way of Reconciliation*, p. 59.
[9] 1 John 4:13; cf. John 14:16–17.

him in Spirit'.[10] Union with Christ is also an *incarnational* connection. One of the reasons it is even possible for us to be united to Christ is that he first became a real human being.[11] Furthermore, our union with Christ is *covenantal* in that it finds its legal basis in God's eternal covenant. As we learned back in chapter 2, God connects us to Jesus Christ by appointing him as our representative: 'For as in Adam all die, so *in Christ* all will be made alive.'[12] The mention of life in Christ shows that our union with him is also *vital*, like the fruitful organic union between a vine and its branches.[13] It is such an *intimate* connection that the Bible compares it to the mysterious sexual union between husband and wife.[14] Finally, it is a *corporate* connection, in which the whole church is joined with Christ. Together we are incorporated into one body – of which Christ is the head,[15] or into one building – of which Christ is the chief cornerstone.[16]

It is out of this intimate, vital, spiritual connection with Jesus Christ that Christians receive all the blessings of salvation. Back in Ephesians 1 Paul explained what God did for Jesus Christ by describing the 'mighty strength' which God 'exerted in Christ when he raised him from the dead and seated him at his right hand in the heavenly realms, far above all rule and authority, power and dominion, and … placed all things under his feet' (1:19b–22a). We confess our faith that God has done these things for Jesus every time we recite the Apostles' Creed: 'The third day he rose again from the dead, He ascended into heaven, And sitteth at the right hand of God the Father Almighty.' Amazingly, when God the Father did all this for Christ his Son – raising him from the dead and seating him on his heavenly throne – he was also doing it for all his people. This is the doctrine of union with Christ, that we are included in whatever Christ has done to save us. Everything Jesus ever did counts for everyone who is joined to him by faith.

Risen, ascended and seated with Christ

Ephesians 2 mentions three specific things God did for us also when he did them for Christ. To explain them, Paul virtually invents three new words by adding the preposition 'with' to three standard Greek verbs: God *made us alive with Christ* (syzōopoieō, 2:5), he *raised us up with Christ* (synegeirō, 2:6), and he *seated us with him* (synkathizō, 2:6). These three new words refer to the resurrection, the ascension and the session (or reign) of Jesus Christ, respectively.[17]

---

[10] 1 Cor. 6:17. [11] Phil. 2:7. [12] 1 Cor. 15:22; cf. Rom. 5:12–21.
[13] John 15:1–17. [14] Eph. 5:31–32; cf. Is. 54:5–8.
[15] 1 Cor. 12:12–27; cf. Eph. 4:15–16. [16] 1 Pet. 2:4–5; cf. Eph. 2:19–22.
[17] Stott, *The Message of Ephesians*, pp. 80–81. Alternatively, *syzōopoieō* denotes our new life in Christ generally, with *synegeirō* and *synkathizō* referring specifically to our resurrection and ascension with Christ.

First, God *made us alive with Christ* (2:5),[18] which refers to the resurrection. This appears to be Paul's emphasis in this passage, for 'made alive' is the main verb of what is really one long sentence in Greek (2:1–10). In chapter 9 we saw how God raised Jesus from the dead, elevating him to a whole new mode of existence. Three days after Jesus was dead and buried, God made him alive again, raising him in a glorious body of immortal splendour. As the Scripture says elsewhere, 'He was put to death in the body but made alive by the Spirit.'[19] Here in Ephesians we discover that we were included in that resurrection! Whatever spiritual life we now have flows from our risen Saviour, for God made us alive together *with Christ*. It is a good thing he did, too, for spiritually speaking, we were once as dead as Christ was, *dead in …* *transgressions and sins* (2:1). *But God* gave us life after spiritual death. From the very moment God brought us to spiritual life, regenerating us by his Spirit, we received a whole new life in Christ: 'Just as Christ was raised from the dead through the glory of the Father, we too may live a new life. If we have been united with him like this in his death, we will certainly also be united with him in his resurrection.'[20] God has brought us back from spiritual death by uniting us with the risen Christ and imparting to us his resurrection life.

Next God *raised us up with Christ* (2:6a).[21] This also could refer to the resurrection, but more likely refers to the ascension. Forty days after Jesus was raised from the dead, he ascended to heaven. His disciples saw him taken up from earth before their very eyes, trailing clouds of glory.[22] God raised Jesus to a place of heavenly beauty and power. Here in Ephesians, we discover that we were included in that ascension. Charles Wesley (1707–88) showed the connection in one of his great Easter hymns:

> Soar we now where Christ hath led,
> Following our exalted Head:
> Made like Him, like Him we rise;
> Ours the cross, the grave, the skies.[23]

We have been raised together with Christ and now we are living in the heavenly realms. Not literally, of course, for God has not yet called us to our eternal home. But there is a real sense in which we already live in the atmosphere of heaven, participating in the joyful worship and loving service of the life to come.

Finally, *God … seated us with him in the heavenly realms in Christ* *Jesus* (2:6b). The proper theological term for this is 'session', which means to sit in a place of authority, as in the expression 'the Court is

---

[18] Cf. Col. 2:13.   [19] 1 Pet. 3:18b.   [20] Rom. 6:4b–5; cf. Col. 2:12–13.
[21] Cf. Col. 3:1.   [22] See Acts 1:9.   [23] From 'Love's redeeming work is done'.

now in session'. Having been raised from the dead, and ascended into heaven, Jesus now sits at the right hand of the Father. To sit down is to rest, and one reason Jesus sits is that he has already completed the work of our salvation. When a king sits down, however, it is not only to rest, but also to rule. Having vanquished all his enemies, Jesus now governs his servants. Therefore, when God placed Jesus on his throne, he 'seated him at his right hand in the heavenly realms, far above all rule and authority, power and dominion, and every title that can be given, not only in the present age but also in the one to come' (1:20b–21). Jesus Christ has finished his work and taken his seat. Now he sits on his throne, reigning over heaven and earth in kingly majesty. And we have taken our seat with him. Again, this is not merely a metaphor, but a spiritual reality. Since we are united to Jesus Christ, we share in the victorious exaltation of his eternal kingdom. 'You have been raised with Christ ... seated at the right hand of God ... and your life is now hidden with Christ in God.'[24]

To be united to Christ, therefore, is to be elevated to the very throne of God. Once we were dead in our sins – dominated by the world, the flesh and the devil, and doomed to hell. Now we are alive in Christ, and destined for glory. By virtue of our union with him we have authority over sin and over Satan. In short, we have a whole new life:

> The movement from then to now is a movement from death to resurrection life, from a lifestyle characterized by trespasses, sins, sensual indulgence, and disobedience to one characterized by good works, from this present world-age to the heavenly realms, and from bondage to the forces which rule this world to victory with Christ above hostile powers. It is a movement from the sphere of selfish autonomy to union with Christ, from domination by the devil to a life controlled from start to finish by God, from what humanity is by nature to what it becomes by grace, and from liability to God's wrath to experience of his mercy, love, kindness, and grace.[25]

All these blessings come from being included with Christ when God raised him from the dead, lifted him to heaven, and seated him on his kingly throne. Notice that in each case – whether he is speaking about resurrection, ascension, or session – Paul uses the perfect tense: You *have been* made alive, *have been* raised, and *have been* seated. To sum it all up he uses the perfect tense again, saying, *you have been saved* (2:5b). The perfect tense is used in Greek, as it is in English, to describe a past event with a present consequence. Something done in the past continues to have a bearing on life in the present. So it is with the resurrection, ascension and session of our Lord. We are united to Jesus

[24] Col. 3:1–3.   [25] Lincoln, *Ephesians*, p. 118.

Christ – Christ risen, Christ ascended, and Christ enthroned. The life we have in solidarity with him is an eternal life of heavenly splendour.

In Christ

In Ephesians 2 Paul mentions three specific ways that we are joined to Jesus Christ. We are united with him in his resurrection, ascension and session (or reign). But that is not all, for to be united with Christ is to be connected to everything he has ever done for our salvation.

It is sometimes said that the most important word in the New Testament is the preposition 'in', especially when it is joined to the name 'Christ'. 'In Christ.' It is such a little phrase that it is easy to read right past it, yet it must be important because it occurs more than two hundred times in the rest of the New Testament (including several times in Ephesians 2). The Bible uses these two words – 'in Christ' – to express the vital spiritual union between Christ and the Christian. Often believers are said to be *in* Christ: 'If anyone is in Christ, he is a new creation'.[26] On other occasions the Bible speaks of Jesus Christ in the believer: 'Christ in you, the hope of glory.'[27] You are in Christ and Christ is in you; sometimes the two sides of this relationship appear together in Scripture. Jesus told his disciples, 'Remain in me, and I will remain in you';[28] 'I am in my Father, and you are in me, and I am in you.'[29] What makes a Christian a Christian is being in Christ.

It is very simple: anyone who is not in Christ is not a Christian. But if we are in Christ – that is to say, if we are united to him – then we have a personal share in everything Christ has ever done. Everything? Yes, everything! Not only his resurrection, his ascension and his session, but everything else besides: 'Praise be to the God and Father of our Lord Jesus Christ, who has blessed us in the heavenly realms with every spiritual blessing in Christ' (Eph. 1:3). Whatever spiritual blessings one may care to mention come through being joined to Jesus Christ. Union with Christ is the source of every true spiritual experience and the basis for every genuine spiritual blessing.

To begin at the beginning, *election* is in union with Christ. This is something we first encountered in our study of Ephesians 1, back in chapter 4: 'He [God] chose us in him [Christ] before the creation of the world' (1:4); 'In him [Christ] we were also chosen, having been predestined according to the plan of him [God] who works out everything in conformity with the purpose of his will' (1:11). This is the electing grace of God. In anticipation of our salvation, God chose us in Christ before the creation of the world. Union with Christ, therefore, goes as far back into eternity as God goes. Being united to Christ is not simply the goal of the Christian life, but also its origin. Even when

---

[26] 2 Cor. 5:17.   [27] Col. 1:27.   [28] John 15:4.   [29] John 14:20.

salvation was only a plan in the mind of God, we were already connected to his Son: 'This grace was given us in Christ Jesus before the beginning of time'.[30]

Election is only the beginning, however, and every subsequent aspect of salvation comes to us by virtue of our union with Christ. This is true of *redemption*: '*In him* we have redemption through his blood, the forgiveness of sins' (1:7). It is true also of *reconciliation*: 'God was reconciling the world to himself *in Christ*, not counting men's sins against them.'[31] Furthermore, we are united with Christ in our *regeneration*, for it is *in Christ* that the Christian becomes a new creation (2:10).[32] It is when the Holy Spirit brings us into vital union with Jesus Christ that we are brought from spiritual death to spiritual life.

We are also united to Christ in our *justification*, which is the judicial act by which God imputes (or credits) the righteousness of Christ to a believing sinner. How does that happen? It happens in Christ: 'God made him [Christ] who had no sin to be sin for us, so that *in him* we might become the righteousness of God';[33] 'You are *in Christ Jesus*, who has become ... our righteousness.'[34] It is *in Christ* that the believer has been declared righteous, which is why the Bible claims that 'there is now no condemnation for those who are *in Christ Jesus*'.[35]

What about *sanctification*, the process by which a Christian becomes ever more like Jesus Christ? Such progress in holiness is the supernatural result of being united to Christ. At the end of our passage, Paul explains what we are saved for by saying that *we are God's workmanship, created in Christ Jesus to do good works, which God prepared in advance for us to do* (2:10). Indeed, 'This is how we know we are in him: Whoever claims to live in him must walk as Jesus did.'[36] Just as we are justified in Christ,[37] so we are also sanctified in Christ.[38]

Not even death brings union with Christ to an end. Once in Christ, always in Christ, for those who have been united to Christ can never be separated from him.[39] Thus the Bible speaks of believers as those who 'die in the Lord',[40] or who are 'dead in Christ'.[41] Truly, for the Christian, union with Christ is a matter of life *and* death, for we are united to Christ for ever: 'If we live, we live to the Lord; and if we die, we die to the Lord. So, whether we live or die, we belong to the Lord.'[42] If we are joined to Christ in death, then we must be joined to him for life after death. This brings us back to Ephesians 2, where God declares that we have been raised to heaven with Christ. One day we will finally be *glorified* in union with Christ. Glorification, which is the splendid and instantaneous transformation of the Christian into the glorious image

[30] 2 Tim. 1:9b.   [31] 2 Cor. 5:19a.   [32] Cf. 2 Cor. 5:17.   [33] 2 Cor. 5:21.
[34] 1 Cor. 1:30.   [35] Rom. 8:1.   [36] 1 John 2:5b–6.   [37] Gal. 2:17.
[38] 1 Cor. 1:2.   [39] Rom. 8:39.   [40] Rev. 14:13.   [41] 1 Thess. 4:16.
[42] Rom. 14:8.

of Christ, will take place in connection with Jesus Christ: 'When Christ, who is your life, appears, then you also will appear *with him* in glory.'[43] Thus the end of all our ends and the glory of all our glories will take place *in Christ.* This does not mean that Christians will be absorbed into Christ, incorporated into the Godhead, or otherwise deified; it does mean that we will participate in the divine glory. Union with Christ is not only the origin of the Christian life, but also its glorious destiny, and the life to come will be an eternal unfolding of the implications of that unbreakable union.

From everlasting to everlasting we are united to Christ. Election, redemption, reconciliation, regeneration, justification, sanctification, resurrection and glorification – it all takes place in union with Christ. His election was our election, his death was our death, his resurrection was our resurrection, and his exaltation was our exaltation, so that now his life is our life and his glory will become our glory. Union with Christ 'embraces the wide span of salvation from its ultimate source in the eternal election of God to its final fruition in the glorification of the elect'.[44] Without beginning and without end, every aspect of salvation is wrapped up in our personal participation in Jesus Christ.

The reason God has saved us this way – by uniting us to Jesus Christ – is to bring glory to himself. Union with Christ is one grand display of God's saving grace. What could bring more glory to God than this great truth: that salvation is all of Christ? God made us alive with Christ, raised us up with Christ, and seated us with Christ *in order that in the coming ages he might show the incomparable riches of his grace, expressed in his kindness to us in Christ Jesus* (2:7). Salvation by grace is all in Christ, and because it is all in Christ, it is all to the glory of God.

Getting into Christ

The doctrine of union with Christ is of tremendous practical benefit. God has provided everything we need for true spiritual life in Jesus Christ. Calvin wrote:

> If we seek strength, it lies in his dominion; if purity, in his conception; if gentleness, it appears in his birth. For by his birth he was made like us in all respects that he might learn to feel our pain. If we seek redemption, it lies in his passion; if acquittal, in his condemnation; if remission of the curse, in his cross; if satisfaction, in his sacrifice; if purification, in his blood; if reconciliation, in his descent into hell; if mortification of the flesh, in his tomb; if newness of life, in his resurrection; if immortality, in the same; if inheritance of the heavenly kingdom, in his entrance into heaven; if protection,

[43] Col. 3:4; cf. Rom. 8:17.   [44] Murray, *Redemption*, p. 165.

if security, if abundant supply of all blessings, in his Kingdom; if untroubled expectation of judgment, in the power given to him to judge. In short, since rich store of every kind of good abounds in him, let us drink our fill from this fountain, and from no other.[45]

What the Scripture says is true: God has provided 'every spiritual blessing in Christ' (1:3). These blessings are easy to obtain. Anyone who wants the blessings of salvation may obtain them simply by getting 'into Christ'. And, as we began to see in the previous chapter, the only way to get 'into Christ' is by faith. Faith, remember, involves the knowledge of the mind, the assent of the will, and the trust of the heart. To believe in Jesus Christ is to receive him with open arms, trusting him alone for salvation. More than fifty times the New Testament mentions 'trusting in' or 'believing into' Jesus Christ. It is by faith that Christ dwells in our hearts (3:17). The reason we must come to God in faith is that salvation is a gift: *For it is by grace you have been saved, through faith – and this not from yourselves, it is the gift of God* (2:8). Salvation in Christ is not a bargain, or an achievement, or even a reward; it is a gift of God's grace. Thus there is nothing a human being can do to obtain salvation except to receive it by faith.

It was this doctrine of union with Christ by faith that saved the renowned evangelist George Whitefield (1714–70). Whitefield had been reading a wonderful little book by Henry Scougal called *The Life of God in the Soul of Man*. There Whitefield learned that Christianity 'is a vital union with the Son of God, Christ formed in the heart'. He later wrote, 'O what a ray of divine life did then break in upon my poor soul ... from that moment God has been carrying on his blessed work in my soul: and as I am now fifty-five years of age ... I tell you, my brethren ... I am more and more convinced that this [union] is the truth of God, and without it you never can be saved by Jesus Christ.'[46] Whitefield was right. Salvation is so closely connected to Jesus Christ that unless we are joined to him, we can never be saved. Outside of Christ there is only death and doom, but in Christ there is life, both now and for evermore.

---

[45] Calvin, *Institutes*, II.xvi.19.
[46] George Whitefield, quoted in the introduction to Scougal, *The Life of God in the Soul of Man*, p. 15.

13. Declared righteous
Justification: Romans 3:21–28

Picture the scene. An accused criminal stands before an impartial judge to receive his just sentence. The legal proceedings begin with a court official reciting the laws of the kingdom. As he listens, the criminal starts to realize that he is doomed to be condemned, for it turns out that he has violated every single law in the book. Whatever the charge, he is certain to be found guilty. When the judge finally turns to the defendant and asks how he pleads, the man is speechless. He stands before the judge in mute terror, unable to utter anything in his defence.

This scene helps to illustrate the desperate legal predicament that is described in the opening chapters of the letter to the Romans. Humanity stands in the dock. The religious and the irreligious, Jews and Gentiles, believers and atheists – everyone must appear before God's throne for judgment. The standard for justice is God's perfect law. By that standard, everyone deserves to be condemned, 'for all have sinned and fall short of the glory of God' (3:23). 'Jews and Gentiles alike are all under sin. As it is written: "There is no-one righteous, not even one"' (3:9b–10). When the law is read, therefore, every commandment is an accusation. There is nothing we can say in our defence: 'Whatever the law says, it says to those who are under the law, so that every mouth may be silenced and the whole world held accountable to God. Therefore no-one will be declared righteous in his sight by observing the law; rather, through the law we become conscious of sin' (3:19–20).

This reminds us – yet once more – why we need the message of salvation. The problem of humanity is sin. We are guilty sinners who belong to a guilty race, and who deserve nothing except God's wrath and condemnation. Nor is there anything we can do to save ourselves. God's righteous requirements cannot save us; they can only condemn us, because we cannot keep them. Therefore, when we stand before God for judgment, there is not the slightest chance that we can be accepted on the basis of anything that we have done. This is not a trial in which we are innocent until proven guilty; instead, it is a trial in

190

which we have already been proven guilty and must remain guilty until we are declared righteous.

It is only when we recognize how desperate our situation is, from a legal standpoint, that we can begin to understand the biblical doctrine of justification. As James Buchanan wrote in his masterful book on the subject, 'The best preparation for the study of this doctrine is – neither great intellectual ability, nor much scholastic learning, – but a conscience impressed with a sense of our actual condition as sinners in the sight of God.'[1]

The centrality of justification

Having described our predicament in all its miserable detail, the apostle Paul announces that a legal remedy has been made available: *But now a righteousness from God, apart from law, has been made known* (3:21). The words *but now* mark a major transition in Paul's argument. More than that, they introduce the great turning-point in the history of salvation. Up to this point we stand condemned. God's perfect law tells us that we cannot be declared righteous at the bar of God's justice. *But now* a righteousness from God is revealed. This is part of the good news of salvation, that God has provided the way for us to be declared righteous. Or, to put it in the biblical way, he has provided a way for us to be *justified.*

There is more to salvation than justification by faith. As we have seen throughout this book, sin is a complex problem that salvation solves in all its complexity. The message of salvation is that God has provided everything we need in Jesus Christ. Where sin brings bondage, his salvation purchases our redemption. Where sin brings alienation, his salvation reconciles us to God. Where sin brings wrath, his salvation propitiates God's anger. Where sin leads to death, his salvation raises us to eternal life. Now we can add justification to the list as another aspect of the total salvation God has provided in Jesus Christ. Where sin brings us under condemnation, his salvation justifies us before our righteous Judge.

Without exaggerating the importance of justification, it must be said that this doctrine holds a place near the centre of the message of salvation. This is evident from the fact that justification is one of the central themes of Scripture. Earlier we discussed redemption, propitiation and reconciliation. As important as these doctrines are, the Bible rarely mentions them explicitly. The terms 'redemption', 'propitiation' and 'reconciliation' are each mentioned only a handful of times in the New Testament. By contrast, various forms of the word 'justify' (*dikaioō*) appear more than two hundred times.[2] The prevalence of this

[1] Buchanan, *The Doctrine of Justification*, p. 222.
[2] Morris, *The Apostolic Preaching of the Cross*, p. 251.

vocabulary serves as an index to the importance of justification in biblical theology.

The centrality of justification has been recognized by the best theologians. John Calvin called it 'the main hinge on which salvation turns'.[3] The English Reformer Thomas Cranmer (1489–1556) described it as 'the strong rock and foundation of Christian religion'. Cranmer went on to claim that 'whosoever denieth it is not to be counted for a true Christian man ... but for an adversary of Christ'.[4] Most famously of all, Martin Luther said that justification 'begets, nourishes, builds, preserves, and defends the church of God; and without it the church of God cannot exist for one hour'. 'It is the chief article of Christian doctrine', so that 'when the article of justification has fallen, everything has fallen'.[5] Whether we think of justification as the hinge, the foundation or the standing-and-falling article of salvation, the point is that there is no salvation without it.

The meaning of justification

Justification is central to the Christian faith because it answers the most fundamental question of all: How can a sinful human being be righteous before a holy God? The answer lies in the biblical teaching about justification.

'Justification' is a legal word that refers to a person's judicial standing. The biblical terms surrounding justification find their ultimate origin in legal relationships. According to Leon Morris, the Greek verb *dikaioō*, which means 'to justify', is sometimes used 'in connection with matters where there is no formal giving of sentence in a law-court. But that does not alter the facts that the verb is essentially a forensic one, in the Bible as elsewhere, and that it denotes basically a sentence of acquittal.'[6] Whereas redemption comes from the marketplace, and propitiation comes from the temple, justification comes from the court of law. It describes the Christian's total relationship to God from the perspective of law. To justify is to render a favourable verdict, to declare a person to be in the right, to announce forgiveness in legal terms. Justification is vindication. It is a decision of the court stating that someone has a right relationship to God and his law. It is the pronouncement that, as far as the law is concerned, the defendant is not guilty, but innocent.

One way to define justification is to contrast it with its opposite, which is condemnation. To condemn is to declare a person unright-

---

[3] Calvin, *Institutes of the Christian Religion*, III.xi.1.

[4] Cranmer, 'Sermon on salvation', in *First Book of Homilies*, pp. 25, 26.

[5] Luther, *What Luther Says: A Practical In-Home Anthology for the Active Christian*, ed. by Ewald M. Plass (St Louis: Concordia, 1959), pp. 705, 704, 715.

[6] Morris, *Apostolic Preaching*, p. 260.

eous. It is the judicial verdict that, as far as the law is concerned, he is guilty. This act of condemnation is not what makes a criminal guilty, of course. His own actions make him guilty, and he becomes guilty the moment he violates the law. When he is finally condemned, the court simply pronounces him to be what he already is, namely, a guilty sinner.

Justification is the opposite of condemnation. To justify is to pronounce a verdict of innocence. In justification a person is not *made* righteous (as the Latin term *iustificatio* seemed to suggest; from *justus*, 'just', and *facio*, 'to make'), but *declared* righteous. This is one place where historically the Roman Catholic Church has differed from orthodox Protestant theology. In traditional Catholic theology justification is the process by which grace is infused into the sinner to make him righteous. But this is to merge justification (in which the sinner is declared righteous) with sanctification (in which the sinner actually becomes righteous). In Protestant theology, by contrast, justification is not a process but an act. It is not the impartation of righteousness through faith plus works and the sacraments, but the imputation of righteousness by faith alone. Although various attempts have been made to reconcile Catholic and Protestant views on justification, this crucial difference has yet to be resolved.

One problem with the Roman Catholic view of justification is that it often fails to conform to the biblical vocabulary. In general, when referring to the acquittal of a defendant, the biblical terminology for justification means 'legally to declare righteous' and not 'actually to make righteous'.[7] For example, in Deuteronomy 25:1 the Bible teaches that 'when men have a dispute, they are to take it to court and the judges will decide the case, acquitting the innocent and condemning the guilty'. Obviously, a judge does not *make* a person guilty; he simply declares him to be guilty, thereby condemning him to his sentence. By analogy, the word 'acquit' (which is really the Hebrew verb *haṣdîq*, 'to justify') means 'to declare righteous'. Or consider Proverbs 17:15: 'Acquitting the guilty and condemning the innocent – the LORD detests them both.' Here again, the word 'acquit', or 'justify' (*haṣdîq*), obviously refers to a legal declaration. By lamenting the justification of the guilty, God is not trying to stop anyone from turning the guilty into fine, upstanding citizens. If justifying the guilty means to *make* them righteous, surely God would be in favour of it! His objection is rather to declaring the guilty to be innocent, which would be untrue.

When we turn to the New Testament, we find justification used in much the same way. As in the Old Testament, to justify is the opposite of to condemn. This is clear from the contrast Paul later draws between the sin of Adam and the gift of Christ: 'The judgment followed one sin and brought condemnation, but the gift followed many trespasses and

[7] See Morris, ibid., p. 252.

brought justification' (Rom. 5:16). Or to cite another example, Paul asks, 'It is God who justifies. Who is he that condemns?' (8:33b–34a). To justify, then, simply means to declare that a defendant is innocent of a charge. In the context of salvation, it is God's declaration that a person is acceptable in his sight and now stands rightly before him. Gottlob Schrenk summarizes by saying that 'In Paul the legal usage [of *dikaioō*] is plain and indisputable … For Paul the word *dikaioun* does not suggest the infusion of moral qualities … [or] the creation of right conduct. It implies the justification of the ungodly who believe, on the basis of the justifying action of God in the death and resurrection of Christ.'[8] Note that for Paul justification means something more than acquittal. To acquit is to declare a person 'not guilty'. But in justification God does not simply clear a sinner of all charges; he declares a sinner to be positively righteous. Justification is God's legal declaration that, on the basis of the perfect life and the sacrifical death of Jesus Christ, received by faith, a sinner is as righteous as his very own Son.

Some theologians object to forensic justification on the grounds that it places too much emphasis on judicial categories. Although this is an old objection, it has been rejuvenated by the postmodern impulse to view salvation in relational terms to the exclusion of juridical terms. In the words of one critic, the idea that 'the cross was a legal transaction in which an innocent victim was made to pay the penalty for the crimes of others, a propitiation of a stern God, finds no support in Paul. These notions came into Christian theology by way of the legalistic minds of the medieval churchmen; they are not biblical Christianity.' The truth is quite the opposite. Forensic justification is precisely what the Bible teaches, and with good reason. While there are many different ways to describe God's saving grace (deliverance, redemption, reconciliation, etc.), and also many different analogies that characterize God's relationship to his people (Husband, Shepherd, King, etc.), the legal category of justification is fundamental to the biblical message of salvation. Since God is a Judge as well as a Father, our relationship to him must be a *right* relationship. To eliminate the legal basis for this rightness (i.e. justification) is to make it impossible for a sinner to know God in a saving way. Even worse, it is to believe in a God of unjust love.

The source of justification

Righteousness is necessary for justification, but where does it originate? As we have seen, our problem is that we have no righteousness of our own. So what is the source of justifying righteousness? The source of our justification is God's free grace: *We are justified freely by his grace* (3:24). To say that we are justified by grace is to say that justification is

---

[8] Schrenk, '*Dikaioō*', in *TDNT*, vol. II, pp. 211–219 (215).

far more than we deserve. It is an act of God's unmerited favour. As Cranmer wrote in his *Homily on Salvation*, 'no man can, by his own deeds, be justified and made righteous before God: but every man, of necessity, is constrained to seek for another righteousness or justification, to be received at God's own hands'.[9] The message of salvation is that God offers righteousness to sinners as a gift: 'It is God who justifies' (8:33).

This brings us to a significant point of controversy in New Testament studies. The gift of God's justifying righteousness is mentioned twice in Romans 3, both in verse 21 (*But now a righteousness from God, apart from law, has been made known, to which the Law and the Prophets testify*), and in verse 22 (*This righteousness from God*). Technically speaking, however, these verses do not speak of a 'righteousness *from* God', as the New International Version has it, but of a 'righteousness *of* God'. There is more than one way to interpret the phrase 'righteousness of God'. Perhaps the 'of' is what grammarians call a possessive genitive. An example is the phrase 'house of David', where David is the one to whom the house belongs. So perhaps the 'righteousness of God' is simply the righteousness God possesses, which belongs to him and which he displays in salvation: 'The LORD has made his salvation known and revealed his righteousness to the nations.'[10] There is another possibility, however. The words 'of God' may explain where the righteousness comes from. This would be called a genitive of origin. An example is the phrase 'man of Galilee', where the man originates from Galilee. If the 'righteousness of God' contains a genitive of origin, then God is the origin of the righteousness. Obviously, this is the interpretation the NIV favours when it speaks of 'a righteousness *from* God'. God is the source of the righteousness that he bestows on sinners.

Which interpretation is correct? Does the righteousness belong to God or does it come from God as a gift? The answer is both! Certainly, the 'righteousness of God' is a righteousness that he possesses. Indeed, the dramatic conclusion of Paul's argument will be that even when he justifies sinners, God preserves his righteousness (*he did it to demonstrate his justice at the present time, so as to be just and the one who justifies those who have faith in Jesus*, 3:26). Yet the righteousness of God is also, as Thomas Chalmers (1780–1847) put it, 'that righteousness which His righteousness requires Him to require'.[11] The issue at stake in justification is not simply whether God is righteous, but whether *we* can be found righteous. Paul seemed to cast doubt on this in verse 20,

---

[9] Cranmer, quoted in Clowney, 'The biblical doctrine of justification by faith', in *Right with God*, pp. 17–50 (17).
[10] Ps. 98:2.
[11] Chalmers, quoted in Barnhouse, *The Invisible War*, p. 116.

where he reached the alarming conclusion that 'no-one will be declared righteous in his sight'. Now in verse 21 he announces the good news that we *can* be declared righteous before God, not because of our own righteousness, but because of a righteousness that comes from God. This is confirmed by verse 22, which makes it clear that the right-eousness of God is something that *comes ... to all who believe*. It is also confirmed by Romans 5:17, which speaks of 'those who receive God's abundant provision of grace and of the *gift* of righteousness'.

This is the gift-righteousness Paul had in mind when he testified that he wanted to 'be found in [Christ], not having a righteousness of my own that comes from the law, but that which is through faith in Christ – the righteousness that comes from God and is by faith'.[12] It is also what Martin Luther meant when he spoke of an 'alien righteousness'. Since there is no righteousness in us, we can be justified only by a righteousness that comes from somewhere outside us. The right-eousness of God is God's own righteousness, which he grants to us by virtue of our union with Jesus Christ. John Murray defined it as 'the righteousness of the God-man, a righteousness which measures up to the requirements of our sinful and sin-cursed situation, a righteousness which meets all the demands of a complete and irrevocable justifi-cation, and a righteousness fulfilling all these demands because it is a righteousness of divine property and character, a righteousness un-defiled and inviolable'.[13]

If we are declared righteous on the basis of a gift, then the source of our justification must be the grace of God. For that is what grace is: it is God's free gift for utterly undeserving sinners. The fact that the source of justification is the grace of God confirms what we have been saying throughout this book: we are saved by grace. Just as it is God who delivers, redeems, atones and reconciles, so also it is God who justifies.

The basis for justification

On what legal basis does God grant the gift of his righteousness? The Bible teaches that God 'justifies the wicked' (Rom. 4:5). But how can he declare us to be what we are not? And how can he justify the wicked without becoming wicked himself? It would be an outrage for a righteous God simply to overlook or to excuse sin. If he intends to justify sinners, he must have some legitimate judicial basis for doing so.

The answer to this problem is that God justifies sinners on the basis of the perfect life and sacrificial death of Jesus Christ. 'Justification is not a synonym for amnesty,' writes John Stott, 'which strictly is pardon

---

[12] Phil. 3:9; cf. Heb. 11:7.
[13] Murray, *Redemption: Accomplished and Applied*, p. 128.

without principle, a forgiveness which overlooks – even forgets – wrongdoing and declines to bring it to justice. No, justification is an act of justice, of gracious justice. Its synonym is "the righteousness of God" (Rom. 1:17; 3:21), which might for the moment be explained as his "righteous way of righteoussing the unrighteous".' Stott proceeds to explain that 'When God justifies sinners, he is not declaring bad people to be good, or saying that they are not sinners after all. He is pronouncing them legally righteous, free from any liability to the broken law, because he himself in his Son has borne the penalty of their lawbreaking.'[14]

Justification finds its basis in the cross, for we *are justified freely by his grace through the redemption that came by Christ Jesus. God presented him as a sacrifice of atonement, through faith in his blood* (3:24–25a). These verses mention two themes discussed earlier in this book. One is redemption: we are redeemed from our bondage to sin through the cross, where Jesus offered his blood as the payment for our sin. The other is propitiation: the cross makes God propitious to us by turning aside his wrath against our sin. Now we discover that justification also flows from Christ's redeeming, atoning work on the cross.

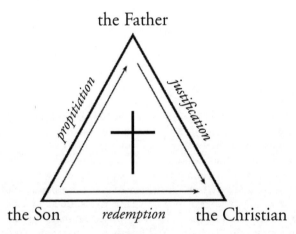

Figure 1

The relationship between redemption, propitiation and justification can be illustrated by a 'salvation triangle' (see figure 1). The top of the triangle represents God the Father, with God the Son in the lower left and the Christian in the lower right. The points of the triangle are connected by arrows. The line connecting the Son to the Christian

[14] Stott, *The Cross of Christ*, p. 190.

represents *redemption*. By paying the price for our sins, Jesus redeemed us from spiritual bondage. Since he is the one who redeems us, the arrow points from Christ to the Christian. The line that connects God the Son to God the Father represents *propitiation*. By offering himself as a perfect sacrifice, the Son reconciled us to the Father; thus the arrow points from the Son to God the Father. Finally, the line connecting God the Father to the Christian represents *justification*. The arrow points from God to us because we cannot justify ourselves; rather, God declares us righteous.

While this diagram has its limitations, it does help to illustrate that in Romans 3, salvation is all of grace. Notice that not one of the arrows points away from the Christian. This is because salvation is something accomplished entirely by God alone: it is God who redeems, God who atones, and God who justifies. Furthermore, God has accomplished all this saving work through the cross, which stands at the centre of the triangle. It was by his blood that Christ purchased our redemption and atoned for our sins. Now we discover that it was also by his blood that he secured our justification: 'We have now been justified by his blood' (5:9). John Stott writes, 'God's saving work was achieved through the bloodshedding, that is, the substitutionary sacrifice of Christ ... The death of Jesus was the atoning sacrifice because of which God averted his wrath from us, the ransom-price by which we have been redeemed, the condemnation of the innocent that the guilty might be justified, and the sinless One being made sin for us.'[15]

The righteousness of justification

When Jesus died on the cross he was treated like a condemned criminal. The Romans reserved crucifixion for the lowest of the low – for traitors and murderers. Jesus was neither a traitor nor a murderer; in fact, he never committed the least sin. Yet God permitted him to be crucified in order to take away our sin. What happened was this: God *imputed* our sin to Christ. We have encountered this term before, both in our explanation of how the sin of Adam came to rest on all his offspring (see chapter 2), and also in our description of the sacrifices that were offered at the mercy seat (chapter 7). To impute is to credit something to someone's account, which is precisely how we became sinners in the first place: Adam's sin was credited to our account (see Rom. 5:12–19). By the imputation of Adam's sin, we are reckoned to be sinners.

Now we are introduced to a second imputation – the imputation of our sin to Jesus Christ. Jesus was perfectly righteous, yet he died a sinner's death. How could God allow such a thing? The answer has to do with imputation. God removed our sin and credited it to Christ's

[15] Stott, ibid., p. 202.

account, just as he had promised through his servant Isaiah: 'My right-eous servant [shall] justify many; for he shall bear their iniquities.'[16] Once our sin was imputed to Christ in this way, so that he was made to bear our iniquity, he was condemned to die – not for his own sin, but for our sin. He was reckoned to be unrighteous on the cross. As the Scripture says, 'God made him who had no sin to be sin for us'.[17] Or again, 'Christ died for sins once for all, the righteous for the unright-eous, to bring you to God.'[18]

But Christ's death is not the end of the story. The Scripture also mentions a third imputation: 'God made him who had no sin to be sin for us, *so that in him we might become the righteousness of God.*'[19] If we are to be justified, it is not enough for our sins to be imputed to Christ; his righteousness must also be imputed to us. Then and only then can God declare that we are righteous. But this is exactly what God has done. The message of salvation offers a righteousness *from* God, a righteousness that flows from God's grace, on the basis of Christ's work imputed to the sinner. This is not merely a 'legal fiction', as some have alleged, because it is based on a real spiritual union. Justification, like every other benefit of salvation, depends on union with Christ. Jesus is our righteousness,[20] and it is by our participation in him that we are considered righteous. As Calvin explained it, 'Justified by faith is he who, excluded from the righteousness of works, grasps the righteous-ness of Christ through faith, and clothed in it, appears in God's sight not as a sinner but as a righteous man.'[21]

Salvation depends, therefore, on a triple imputation: first, by the fall of Adam, sin is imputed to the human race; second, in repentance a believer's sin is imputed to Christ; third, by faith the righteousness of Christ is imputed to the believing sinner. Paul sums this all up in Romans 5, where he writes, 'Just as the result of one trespass was condemnation for all men, so also the result of one act of righteousness was justification that brings life for all men. For just as through the disobedience of the one man the many were made sinners, so also through the obedience of the one man the many will be made right-eous' (5:18–19).

Now we see how salvation solves one of sin's most deeply-rooted problems. The imputation of justifying righteousness restores the righteousness humanity lost through original sin. Marvellous to say, this righteousness is restored without doing any injustice to God's own righteousness. God has dealt justly with our sin by punishing it in the person of the crucified Christ. He has also dealt justly with us by declaring us to be righteous in Christ. God accomplished this redeeming, atoning, justifying work through the cross in order *to*

[16] Is. 53:11, AV.   [17] 2 Cor. 5:21a.   [18] 1 Pet. 3:18a.
[19] 2 Cor. 5:21.   [20] 2 Cor 1:30.   [21] Calvin, *Institutes*, III.xi.2.

demonstrate his justice at the present time, so as to be just and the one who justifies those who have faith in Jesus (3:26). Thus the justification of sinners is also the justification of God. In justification, God proves his justice by dealing justly with sinners through the cross.

There is a simple way to illustrate how imputation works in our justification. The illustration comes from Donald Grey Barnhouse, who first heard it at the age of fifteen from a man who wanted to give him the gospel. Barnhouse writes:

> He took my left hand and drew it out, palm upward, all the while fixing me with an intense gaze. 'This hand represents you,' he said. On that hand he placed a large hymnbook. He then said, 'This book represents your sin. The weight of it is upon you. God hates sin, and His wrath must bear down against sin. His wrath is bearing down upon you, and you have no peace in your heart and life.'
>
> He drew my other hand forward, palm upward, and said, 'This hand represents the Lord Jesus Christ, the Savior. There is no sin upon Him, and the Father must love Him, because He is without spot and blemish. He is the beloved Son in whom the Father is well pleased.' I saw my two hands before me: one covered with the large book, the other empty; I realized that I had the sin, and the Lord Jesus Christ had none.
>
> Then this man put his hand under my left hand, the hand that represented me, the hand upon which the book was lying; with a sweeping gesture he turned my hand over so that the book came down upon the palm of my right hand – the one that represented Christ. My left hand he put back as it had been; I could see that the burden was gone from it entirely. He then said to me, 'This is what happened when the Lord Jesus Christ took your place upon the cross. He was the lamb of God, who was bearing away the sin of the world.'[22]

As Barnhouse finished recounting his story, he said, 'This is the justification that acts upon our sins to take them away from us and to place them upon the Savior.' That is true, but it is only half the story, as Barnhouse came to understand later on. For at the same time that God was imputing our sins to Christ, putting the burden of our unrighteousness upon him, he was also imputing Christ's righteousness to us. This could be illustrated with a second book, perhaps a Bible, resting on the right hand. The second book represents the perfect right-eousness of Jesus Christ, of which we have none at all. But when that righteousness is imputed to us (signified by passing the book from the

[22] Barnhouse, *Let Me Illustrate* (Westwood, NJ: Fleming H. Revell, 1967), pp. 194–195.

right hand to the left), we become as righteous as God's own dear Son. All this is what it means to be justified by his blood. The cross shows that a transaction has taken place: our sin was imputed to Christ, and he was condemned; his righteousness is imputed to us, and we are justified.

For a full understanding of this wonderful exchange, it helps to distinguish between the active and passive righteousness of Jesus Christ. Jesus demonstrated his active righteousness through his life, by perfectly obeying God's law. He demonstrated his passive righteousness through his death, by patiently suffering the agonies of the cross. To put it another way, Christ both obeyed God's law on our behalf (active righteousness) *and* suffered the penalty for our disobedience (passive righteousness). Both forms of righteousness are required for full justification. For us to be declared 'Not guilty', it is necessary for us to receive Christ's passive righteousness through his atoning death. For us to be reckoned positively righteous, however, we need Christ's active righteousness credited (or imputed) to our account.

The means of justification

Earlier we defined justification both legally and biblically. Now we are in a position to summarize the way that we have been defining it theologically. One good definition comes from Anthony Hoekema:

> Justification means a permanent change in our judicial relation to God whereby we are absolved from the charge of guilt, and whereby God forgives all our sins on the basis of the finished work of Jesus Christ. Apart from Christ, our judicial relation to God is one of condemnation – we stand condemned on account of our sins, both original and actual. When we are justified, our judicial relation to God is changed from one of condemnation to one of acquittal.[23]

To this one might wish to add that our judicial relation to God is not simply a legality, but represents our real and total acceptance by God. A more concise definition comes from the *Westminster Shorter Catechism*: 'Justification is an act of God's free grace, wherein he pardoneth all our sins, and accepteth us as righteous in his sight, only for the righteousness of Christ, imputed to us, and received by faith alone' (A. 33).

The last phrase in the catechism's definition is essential because it identifies faith as the only instrument of justification. Faith or believing is mentioned at least six times in Romans 3: *This righteousness from God comes through* faith *in Jesus Christ to all who* believe (3:22); *God presented*

---

[23] Hoekema, *Saved by Grace*, p. 178.

him as a sacrifice of atonement, through faith *in his blood* (3:25). In verse 26 God is described as *the one who justifies those who have* faith *in Jesus.* In verse 27 boasting is excluded on the principle of faith: *For we maintain that a man is justified by* faith *apart from observing the law* (3:28; cf. 5:1). What this passage emphasizes over and over again is essential to the message of salvation: we are justified *by faith.*

People sometimes wonder what they must do to justify themselves before God. The answer, of course, is that there is nothing we can do; only believe. This is where Christianity differs from every other religion, from every merely human attempt to attain righteousness. As much as anything else, it is this difference which is so hard for unbelievers to understand: Isn't there something we can *do* to make ourselves acceptable to God? This is a question the disciples once posed to Jesus: 'What must we do to do the works God requires?' Jesus answered, 'The work of God is this: to believe in the one he has sent.'[24] The Philippian jailor put a similar question to the apostle Paul: 'What must I do to be saved?' And Paul gave a similar answer to the one that Jesus gave: 'Believe in the Lord Jesus, and you will be saved'.[25] In other words, there is nothing that we can do to justify ourselves to God. The only righteousness he accepts comes *apart from law* (3:21). Thus the only thing that we can do is to put our faith in Jesus Christ alone for salvation. If we trust in him, and in his justifying work on the cross, then God will declare us righteous.

When the Bible says that we are justified 'by faith' or 'through faith', what it really means is that we are justified by Christ. Faith is merely the instrument of our justification, the channel by which we receive the righteousness of Jesus Christ. It is often described as the empty hand that reaches out to receive the gift of God's righteousness. The Anglican Bishop J. C. Ryle (1816–1900) once wrote, 'True faith ... is but laying hold of a Saviour's hand, leaning on a husband's arm, and receiving a physician's medicine. It brings with it nothing to Christ but a sinful man's soul. It gives nothing, contributes nothing, pays nothing, performs nothing. It only receives, takes, accepts, grasps, and embraces the glorious gift of justification which Christ bestows.' This means that, properly speaking, it is not faith itself (or even the doctrine of justification by faith) that saves us. Rather, it is Christ who saves us, and faith is simply the way that we appropriate Christ.

Although Romans 3 does not say that justification is 'by faith alone' (at least in so many words), that is what the passage clearly teaches, particularly at its close: *Where, then, is boasting? It is excluded. On what principle? On that of observing the law? No, but on that of faith. For we maintain that a man is justified by faith apart from observing the law* (3:27–28).[26] If we were justified by works, then salvation would be

---

[24] John 6:28–29.   [25] Acts 16:30–31.   [26] Cf. Gal. 2:16.

something to boast about.[27] As it is, however, no-one will be able to boast of making it to heaven on the strength of his or her own merits. We are justified by the perfect life and sacrificial death of Jesus Christ, and there is nothing more that needs to be done.

The goal of justification

It is sometimes thought that this doctrine of justification by faith alone is contradicted by James, who contends that 'a person is justified by what he does and not by faith alone'.[28] What James is really saying, however, is this: 'A person is proved to be justified by his works, and not merely by his faith.' Unlike Paul – who needed to oppose the popular notion that sinners can be saved by good works – James was combating the misconception that believers can dispense with works altogether. To put the difference between them in theological terms, Paul was dealing with people who wanted to make sanctification part of the basis for their justification, whereas James was dealing with people who wanted to be justified without being sanctified. Yet for James, as well as for Paul, 'to justify' means 'to declare righteous'. The difference is that in Paul's case it is God who declares the believer righteous, whereas in James's case it is the believer's works that declare him righteous by proving his faith to be genuine. Both apostles would agree with Calvin that 'it is faith alone which justifies, and yet the faith which justifies is not alone'.[29] Faith does justify and produce good works; but faith and works do not together produce justification. This is a subject to which we will return in chapter 16, where we will discover that sanctification is the inevitable consequence of being justified in Christ. The faith that alone justifies is a faith that works.

As far as justification is concerned, however, Christ's work and our works are mutually exclusive. Our justification thus comes by our trusting rather than by our working. As Paul will later write, 'to the man who does not work but trusts God who justifies the wicked, his faith is credited as righteousness' (4:5). If justification is by faith, then it is not of works. If faith is not of works, then there can be no boasting, because boasting is the bold assertion of personal merit. From the very nature of the case, therefore, if justification is by faith, then it must be by faith *alone*. The doctrine of justification by faith alone thus ensures that all the glory goes to God alone. The goal of justification – like every other aspect of salvation – is the glory of God.

One of the most beautiful affirmations of the biblical doctrine of justification comes from the *Heidelberg Catechism*, which asks, 'How

---

[27] See Eph. 2:9.   [28] Jas. 2:24.
[29] Calvin, 'Antidote to the Canons of the Council of Trent', in *Tracts and Treatises in Defense of the Reformed Faith*, vol. 3, p. 152.

are you righteous before God?' (Q. 60). The answer is:

> Only by true faith in Jesus Christ. In spite of the fact that my conscience accuses me that I have grievously sinned against all the commandments of God, and have not kept any one of them, and that I am still ever prone to all that is evil, nevertheless, God, without any merit of my own, out of pure grace, grants me the benefits of the perfect expiation of Christ, imputing to me his righteousness and holiness as if I had never committed a single sin or had ever been sinful, having fulfilled myself all the obedience which Christ has carried out for me, if only I accept such favour with a trusting heart.

If justification comes through faith, then we must believe in Jesus Christ in order to be justified. Remember how desperate our situation is, legally speaking, and that without Christ we are doomed to be condemned. The Bible warns that 'whoever does not believe stands condemned already because he has not believed in the name of God's one and only Son'.[30] Yet the Bible also promises, in the very same verse, that 'whoever believes in him is not condemned'. For those who believe, God's final verdict – 'righteous for all eternity' – has been brought forward into present experience: *But now a righteousness from God ... has been made known* (Rom. 3:21); 'Therefore, since we *have been justified* through faith, we *have peace* with God through our Lord Jesus Christ' (5:1; cf. 8:30). We are acceptable to God right now and for ever. Our legal standing has already been decided, and we can never be unjustified. Judgment day will only confirm what God has already declared, that 'there is now no condemnation for those who are in Christ Jesus' (8:1).

One man who experienced the joy of justifying faith was the poet William Cowper (1731–1800). Cowper had long suffered from depression, and for a time he lived in an asylum for the insane where conditions were appalling. However, despite all his physical and psychological torments, Cowper's most acute sufferings were spiritual: he considered himself a condemned sinner. Yet the day came when he found his legal remedy in the saving message of justification by faith alone. This is the story he told:

> The happy period which was to shake off my fetters and afford me a clear opening of the free mercy of God in Christ Jesus was now arrived. I flung myself into a chair near the window, and, seeing a Bible there, ventured once more to apply to it for comfort and instruction. The first verses I saw were in the third chapter of

[30] John 3:18.

Romans: 'Being justified freely by his grace through the redemption that is in Christ Jesus, whom God hath set forth to be a propitiation, through faith in his blood, to manifest his righteousness.' Immediately I received strength to believe, and the full beams of the Sun of Righteousness shone on me. I saw the sufficiency of the atonement he had made, my pardon in his blood, and the fullness and completeness of his justification. In a moment I believed and received the gospel.[31]

This salvation is available to everyone who believes and receives the gospel. By his free grace, God offers full and complete justification on the basis of the atoning work of Jesus Christ. Everyone who has faith in Jesus Christ will be declared righteous at the bar of God's justice.

[31] Cowper, quoted in Boice, *Romans*, vol. 2, p. 372.

14. All God's children
Adoption: 2 Samuel 9:1–13

The message of salvation is partly a message of justification. It is the good news that on the basis of the perfect life and the sacrificial death of Jesus Christ, received by faith, God has judged sinners to be once and for ever righteous in his sight. This justification is a legal declaration, a judicial verdict rendered at the bar of God's justice.

Before leaving the courtroom, however, there is one more legal action to be taken. Remember the scene: an accused criminal stands before an impartial judge to receive his just sentence. The man is guilty of all the charges. Yet to his amazement, rather than being condemned, which is what he truly deserves, he is justified. Then, to the man's complete and utter astonishment, he hears the judge legally approve his *adoption*. The declaration of his justification is followed by a decree for his adoption. What is more, the adoptive parent turns out to be the judge himself, who leaves the bench to embrace the guilty sinner as his own dear son!

This scene helps to clarify the place of adoption in the message of salvation. Our deliverance is relational as well as judicial. God does not deal with us simply as our righteous Judge, but also as our loving Father. He is not content to accept us merely as his servants; he wants to adopt us as his sons and daughters, welcoming us into the fellowship of his family as his children and his heirs.

Adoption in Scripture and history

Adoption is essential to the message of salvation by grace through faith. 'If you want to judge how well a person understands Christianity,' writes J. I. Packer, 'find out how much he makes of the thought of being God's child, and having God as his Father. If this is not the thought that prompts and controls his worship and prayers and his whole outlook on life, it means that he does not understand Christianity very well at all … Our understanding of Christianity cannot be better than our grasp of adoption.'[1]

[1] Packer, *Knowing God*, p. 182.

Perhaps the best way to begin grasping the biblical doctrine of adoption is with a simple definition: adoption is the legal act by which God declares a believer to be his own son or daughter. Adoption is closely related to regeneration, the new birth. The two doctrines, however must be kept distinct because they describe sonship in two different ways. Whereas in regeneration God makes us his children, in adoption he recognizes and treats us as his children.[2] Regeneration comes first. It is the supernatural transformation, a creative act of God the Holy Spirit, in which we receive a childlike nature. Adoption comes later, since regeneration is its prerequisite. Adoption is the legal act of God the Father, received through faith in his Son, by which we receive the status of sons and daughters. The differences between regeneration and adoption serve as a reminder that there is no single image or concept that explains the entire message of salvation. Taken together, however, regeneration and adoption show us what it means to be a child of God.

The term 'adoption' (*huiothesia*, or 'adoption as sons') appears only in the writings of Paul, who seems to have developed the concept against the background of the Roman legal system. The imperial practice of adoption served the apostle well, for it illustrated many aspects of the Christian's relationship to God. This is how the Scottish legal scholar Francis Lyall explains Roman adoption and its connection with the message of salvation:

> The adoptee is taken out of his previous state and is placed in a new relationship with his new *paterfamilias*. All his old debts are cancelled, and in effect he starts a new life. From that time the *paterfamilias* owns all the property and acquisitions of the adoptee, controls his personal relationships, and has rights of discipline. On the other hand he is involved in liability by the actions of the adoptee and owes reciprocal duties of support and maintenance. The Christian doctrines of election, justification, and sanctification imply that the believer is taken out of his former state, and is placed in a new relationship with God. He is made part of God's family for ever, with reciprocal duties and rights. All his time, property, and energy should from that time forth be brought under God's control.[3]

While Paul's terminology for adoption may come from the Romans, the idea of sonship begins with the Jews. As far as we know, the Jews did not have a procedure for adoption. The only three examples of adoption in the Old Testament all took place outside Israel.[4] Yet the

---

[2] Girardeau, *Discussions of Theological Questions*, p. 475.
[3] Francis Lyall, 'Roman law in the writings of Paul – Adoption', *JBL* 88.4 (December 1969), pp. 465–466.
[4] See Exod. 2:10; 1 Kgs. 11:20; Est. 2:7, 15.

Old Testament has a great deal to say about what it means to be God's child. The great privilege of the children of Israel was that they were the children of God. Their whole experience as a nation taught them to depend on God's fatherly care: 'When Israel was a child, I loved him, and out of Egypt I called my son.'[5] As Paul later said, concerning the people of his own race, 'Theirs is the adoption as sons'.[6] Thus the distinctively Pauline doctrine of adoption is part of the wider biblical teaching on sonship. Our focus in this chapter is sonship, broadly considered. What does God mean when he says, 'I will be a Father to you, and you will be my sons and daughters'?[7]

A cripple, an orphan and a rebel

One story that illustrates many features of biblical sonship is the story of Mephibosheth. Although the story comes from the Old Testament, and although it does not even use the term 'adoption', nevertheless it shows what it means to be treated as a son of God the great King. The story begins in tragedy, with two great military heroes, Saul and Jonathan, bleeding and dying on a field of battle. Saul was Israel's anointed king; Jonathan was his princely son. Together they fought to defend Israel against the Philistines. Yet God had rejected Saul as king and the two men were slain in battle, with their bodies fastened to the walls of Beth Shan.[8]

The defeat was especially tragic for a little boy named Mephibosheth, who was Jonathan's son, and therefore Saul's grandson. Since he was too small to ride into battle, Mephibosheth was back home when the royal court heard that their king and their prince were dead. In the rush to flee from the Philistines, Mephibosheth fell from his nurse's arms and was crippled for life. The Bible tells his story like this: 'Jonathan son of Saul had a son who was lame in both feet. He was five years old when the news about Saul and Jonathan came from Jezreel. His nurse picked him up and fled, but as she hurried to leave, he fell and became crippled. His name was Mephibosheth' (2 Sam. 4:4).

Mephibosheth had several things going against him. To begin with, he was lame. For the rest of his life he would be defined by his deformity. Whenever he is mentioned in the Bible, reference is always made to his disability, which was severe because it affected both feet. Mephibosheth would never be able to walk, and thus it seemed that he would never be able to earn a steady income. He was also an orphan. When Saul and Jonathan died at the hands of the Philistines, it meant that he had to grow up without a father.

Mephibosheth had another disadvantage, which in a way was the most serious of all. Remember that he was the grandson of King Saul,

---

[5] Hos. 11:1.   [6] Rom. 9:4.   [7] 2 Cor. 6:18.   [8] 1 Sam. 31:1–13.

Israel's first king. That made him a potential rival to David's throne. God anointed David to serve as Saul's successor. But there were some in Israel who thought that one of Saul's sons should remain on the throne. Thus there was war between the house of David and the house of Saul (2 Sam. 2 – 4). Mephibosheth was not only a cripple and an orphan, but, as far as King David was concerned, he was also a rebel. In those days it was customary for kings to put their rivals to death, which is precisely what happened to Mephibosheth's uncle Ish-Bosheth, Saul's oldest surviving son. Ish-Bosheth was assassinated by David's soldiers, who brought his head to David and said, 'Here is the head of Ish-Bosheth son of Saul, your enemy, who tried to take your life. This day the LORD has avenged my lord the king against Saul and his offspring' (4:8). Although the assassination was contrary to David's orders, it nevertheless shows how a king's rivals usually were treated.

Eventually the house of Saul was defeated and David reigned as king over Israel. Mephibosheth, it seems, went into hiding. When the story resumes some years later, he is living in Galilee (*at the house of Makir son of Ammiel in Lo Debar*, 9:4), far from the city of David. After all of Saul's ill will towards David, the last place Mephibosheth wanted to be was in Jerusalem. Yet he found himself unexpectedly summoned to appear before the king. When Mephibosheth arrived at the royal court, he bowed down before David and said, *'What is your servant, that you should notice a dead dog like me?'* (9:8).

Mephibosheth apparently thought that he was a dead man. He knew that as a member of a rebellious house his life was forfeit to the crown. Yet he had nothing to fear, as the king reassured him: *'Don't be afraid,'* David said to him, *'for I will surely show you kindness for the sake of your father Jonathan. I will restore to you all the land that belonged to your grandfather Saul, and you will always eat at my table'* (9:7). Not only did David intend to spare the orphan's life, but he also wanted to treat him like his own dear son. What Mephibosheth received was tantamount to the grace of adoption. First he was granted a royal pardon; but more than that, by being given a place at the king's own table, he practically became a member of the royal family.

Our own situation is not far different. We were born into a rebellious house. As the sons and daughters of Adam, we were born at war with the house of God's Son. The Bible calls us 'God's enemies'.[9] It identifies us as 'children of wrath',[10] even as 'the children of the devil'.[11] In our rebellion, we put Jesus Christ, the Son of David to death, and now our lives are forfeit. The wonder of God's adopting grace is that it turns rebels into princes. Through faith in Christ we have become God's own sons and daughters. In his classic treatment of the subject, John Girardeau (1825–98) thus defined adoption as 'an act of God's free

---

[9] Rom. 5:10.   [10] Eph. 2:3, AV.   [11] 1 John 3:10.

grace, whereby, for the sake of Christ, he formally translates the regenerate from the family of Satan into his own, and legally confirms them in all the rights, immunities and privileges of his children'.[12] The grace of sonship caused Charles Wesley (1707–88) to marvel 'That I, a child of wrath and hell, / I should be called a child of God'.

Covenant sonship

Sonship is a personal relationship between a loving father and a devoted child. The basis for this relationship is the legal act of adoption. In the case of Mephibosheth there was no formal adoption, for this was not the Jewish custom. Nevertheless, Mephibosheth's filial relationship had a proper legal basis because it was based on a covenant between David and Mephibosheth's father Jonathan.

To understand this covenant it helps to know a little family history. David and Jonathan were the best of friends. What made their relationship unusual was the fact that they ought to have been mortal enemies. As the son of King Saul, Jonathan was the reigning prince. However, David had been anointed by God to begin a new dynasty. Therefore, by all rights the two young men ought to have been at war. Indeed, there were many occasions when Jonathan's father tried to take David's life. Yet despite Saul's animosity, Jonathan remained David's most steadfast friend.

David and Jonathan sealed their relationship with a special promise. When it became apparent that it was no longer safe for David to live with Saul at the royal palace, the two men began to plan for David's departure. Jonathan begged David, 'Show me unfailing kindness like that of the LORD as long as I live, so that I may not be killed, and do not ever cut off your kindness from my family'.[13] It was a promise David was willing to make. 'So Jonathan made a covenant with the house of David, saying, "May the LORD call David's enemies to account." And Jonathan made David reaffirm his oath out of love for him, because he loved him as he loved himself.'[14] When the two men made their farewells, it was uncertain whether they would ever see one another alive again. After they had embraced, Jonathan said to David, 'Go in peace, for we have sworn friendship with each other in the name of the LORD, saying, "The LORD is witness between you and me, and between your descendants and my descendants for ever."'[15]

David never forgot his covenant promise, and it was on the basis of the promise that he welcomed Mephibosheth to his palace: *David asked, 'Is there anyone still left of the house of Saul to whom I can show kindness for Jonathan's sake?'* (2 Sam. 9:1). This was covenant sonship.

---

[12] Girardeau, *Discussions of Theological Questions*, p. 486.
[13] 1 Sam. 20:14–15a.   [14] 1 Sam. 20:16–17.   [15] 1 Sam. 20:42.

David had sworn friendship to Jonathan's descendants for ever. By welcoming Jonathan's son into his own home he proved that he was faithful to his covenant. But more than that, David demonstrated that God was faithful to his covenant. Notice how he framed his question: *'Is there no-one still left of the house of Saul to whom I can show* God's *kindness?'* (9:3). By showing Mephibosheth his fatherly care, David was showing God's covenant love. He was treating Mephibosheth like God's own son.

The sonship of Mephibosheth was based on a covenant. Since his story illustrates saving adoption, this raises a question: What is the basis of our adoption in Jesus Christ? Clearly it is a legal adoption, for as we have seen, the Greek term *huiothesia* refers to proper adoption under Roman law.

While the Bible does not explicitly mention the legal basis for our sonship, there are several possibilities. Perhaps adoption is related to creation. In one sense we are all God's offspring,[16] and so some have argued that there is a general sonship shared by all humanity. Yet there is much more to adoption than mere creation. Even if there is such a thing as the universal fatherhood of God, it cannot compare with the special privilege of knowing God personally as Father. It is only by adopting grace that anyone can truly call God Father. Thus the sonship of redemption goes far beyond the sonship of creation. We do not receive the gift of sonship merely by being born, but only by being born again.[17]

Adoption has also been related to the incarnation. Our status as children of God partly depends on the fact that the Son of God has become a man. The sonship of Jesus Christ shows us something of what it means to be a son or a daughter of God. There is, of course, a difference between his Sonship and our sonship. Jesus is God's only-begotten Son, and thus his unique Sonship is exclusive. Whereas he is God's eternal Son by divine nature, we have become God's earthly sons and daughters by grace. Nevertheless, the incarnation bears some relationship to adoption. Jesus entered the family of humanity so that we could enter the family of God. The Son of God became the Son of Man to enable the sinful sons of men to become the sons of God.

Predestination to adoption

So what is the legal basis for our becoming the sons and daughters of God? While adoption may have something to do with creation, and with the incarnation, it finds its ultimate basis in predestination. The Bible teaches that 'in love he [God] predestined us to be adopted as his sons through Jesus Christ'.[18] Adoption goes all the way back before the

---

[16] Acts 17:29.   [17] Packer, *Knowing God*, p. 181.   [18] Eph. 1:5; cf. Rom. 8:29.

beginning of time. Our status as sons and daughters of God is part of the eternal covenant. We were predestined to sonship.

If adoption is part of the eternal covenant, then it must be a demonstration of divine love, for the covenant is God's love-promise. This is precisely what Scripture teaches, that *in love* he predestined us to be adopted'.[19] Adopting grace is the proof of the Father's undying love for dying sinners. In adoption we learn the truth of Jesus' words: 'The Father himself loves you'.[20]

Few things are more precious than a father's love for his adopted children. One woman experienced this love when she and her husband adopted their first child. The couple travelled from America to Korea to arrange the adoption. When they arrived in Seoul they discovered that the little girl they hoped to adopt was in hospital with pneumonia. Anxiously, they went to see her. This is how the prospective mother described their experience:

As we rushed those last few steps toward our little girl, it seemed the world shifted into superslow motion. She was lying in her bed, a fragile little bundle of life just over four pounds, recovering from pneumonia. So beautiful. But so tiny and helpless.

Tim and I both began to cry. And Tim, who had never been comfortable around babies, immediately reached into the crib and swooped up Stephanie. He rocked her ever so gently in his arms.

The two of them bonded in that instant. I kept weeping as I observed an incredible look of love and devotion I had never before seen on my husband's face.[21]

The story of this father's love for his little girl is an illustration of God's adopting love. Our salvation flows from the heart of the Father's affection. God set out to win our love by first loving us, for we were predestined to be adopted. It was this fatherly love that the prophet Zephaniah had in mind when he compared God's people to a little girl in her daddy's arms:

Sing, O Daughter of Zion;
shout aloud, O Israel!
Be glad and rejoice with all your heart,
O Daughter of Jerusalem! ...
The LORD your God is with you,
he is mighty to save.
He will take great delight in you,

[19] Eph. 1:5.   [20] John 16:27.
[21] 'Seoul connection', an excerpt from *Major League Dad*, which appeared in *Focus on the Family* (May 1994), pp. 2–4.

212

> he will quiet you with his love,
> he will rejoice over you with singing.[22]

A place at the table

Adoption's greatest joy is to know a father's love, and thus to rest secure in the identity of sonship. But adopted children also enjoy many other privileges, as Mephibosheth came to appreciate. First, he was given *the status of a son*. Although David did not formally adopt Mephibosheth, he granted him the same status as his own sons. The king signified this by inviting the orphan to eat at his royal table. This high privilege must have been very unusual, for the Bible mentions it no fewer than four times (2 Sam. 9:7–13). Mephibosheth himself could hardly believe it. As he later marvelled, 'All my grandfather's descendants deserved nothing but death from my lord the king, but you gave your servant a place among those who sat at your table' (19:28a). By giving Mephibosheth a place at the table, David was treating him like a family member. The Bible calls attention to this by stating that *Mephibosheth ate at David's table like one of the king's sons* (9:11).

Second, Mephibosheth was granted *a royal inheritance*. *'Don't be afraid,' David said to him, 'for I will surely show you kindness for the sake of your father Jonathan. I will restore to you all the land that belonged to your grandfather'* (9:7). Mephibosheth had no right to claim this land for his own. True, it had originally belonged to his grandfather Saul, but it had become David's property when he ascended the throne. The only way for Mephibosheth to come into possession of the land was to receive it as a legacy from David.

Third, Mephibosheth received *good fatherly care*. A good father is sensitive to the needs of his children. Mephibosheth obviously had special needs, and David was sensitive enough not only to recognize them, but also to meet them: *The king summoned Ziba, Saul's servant, and said to him, 'I have given your master's grandson everything that belonged to Saul and his family. You and your sons and your servants are to farm the land for him and bring in the crops, so that your master's grandson may be provided for'* (9:9–10a). Ziba had fifteen sons and twenty servants of his own, which gives some idea how wealthy Mephibosheth became. He inherited a large farming operation from David, yet without dozens of men to manage it, it would have done him little good. Because of his disability he was unable to farm his land. David anticipated this, and made practical arrangements to meet Mephibosheth's needs, all of which showed genuine fatherly compassion.

[22] Zeph. 3:14, 17.

The full rights of sons

Mephibosheth was granted many of the benefits of adoption: a son's status, a goodly inheritance and fatherly care. His story thus illustrates what the Bible means when it speaks of 'the full rights of sons'. This expression, which comes from Paul's letter to the Galatians, refers to the high privilege of adoption in Christ: 'When the time had fully come, God sent his Son, born of a woman, born under law, to redeem those under law, that we might receive the full rights of sons.'[23] The *Westminster Shorter Catechism* echoes these verses when it defines adoption as 'an act of God's free grace, whereby we are received into the number, and have a right to all the privileges, of the sons of God' (A. 34). The picture is of a slave who has become a son according to the Roman custom. At the time of his adoption, he receives all the privileges of membership in his master's family.

What are the privileges of our spiritual sonship? What are 'the full rights of sons'? First, we receive *the status of sonship*. In adoption we become God's true sons and daughters: 'To all who received him, to those who believed in his name, he gave the right to become children of God'.[24] Saving adoption is not simply a metaphor for salvation; it is a legal reality. Notice that the way to obtain this saving sonship is by trusting in Jesus Christ. The only ones who have the right to become God's children are those who believe in Christ's name. As Jesus said, 'No-one comes to the Father except through me.'[25] Thus adoption is only for those who belong to God through faith in Jesus Christ. Adoption, like all the other benefits of salvation, is only for those who are united to Christ by faith: 'You are all sons of God through faith in Christ Jesus.'[26] Sonship rightfully belongs to those who come to the Father by believing in the Son. Anyone who wants to become a member of God's family by adoption must first come to Jesus Christ in faith.

Once we are adopted by grace through faith, God accepts us as his own beloved children. The story is told of a little girl who felt very unloved. She was born disfigured, and her face was so ugly that even her own parents were repulsed by her appearance. As one might imagine, the little girl had very few friends. The only person who seemed really to care for her was her schoolteacher. One day the teacher said something so wonderful that it changed the rest of the little girl's life. The children were being tested for their hearing. Each child in turn would walk up to the teacher's desk. She would whisper something into the child's ear, and then ask the child to repeat it. When the ugly little girl stood by the teacher's desk, she heard her whisper, very quietly, 'I wish you were my little girl!'

What God whispers into the believer's ear is even more wonderful.

[23] Gal. 4:4–5.   [24] John 1:12.   [25] John 14:6b.   [26] Gal. 3:26.

He says, 'You *are* my little girl!' 'You *are* my beloved son!' God's desire to make us his children is not an idle wish; it is a legal fact. In his heavenly court he has decreed that we are his sons and daughters through faith in Jesus Christ. In keeping with our new status, we have been given a new name, as adopted children usually are. Now we are called the children of God: 'Behold what manner of love the Father hath bestowed upon us, that we should be called children of God.'[27] 'And that is what we are!'[28] That *is* what we are, and it is the highest status we will ever attain. We are princes and princesses, for our Father is the great King.

Heirs of God

Since our Father is the great King, we can expect to receive *a royal inheritance*. This promised inheritance – which is the second benefit of our sonship – is often mentioned when the New Testament speaks of adoption: 'Now if we are children, then we are heirs – heirs of God and co-heirs with Christ'; [29] 'So you are no longer a slave, but a son; and since you are a son, God has made you also an heir.'[30] 'He who overcomes will inherit all this, and I will be his God and he will be my son.'[31] This emphasis on inheritance accurately reflects standard Roman practice, in which adoption was primarily intended to carry on the family name. The advantage of divine adoption, as opposed to merely human adoption, is that we inherit our Father's legacy without ever having to grieve our Father's loss, for God will never die.

The guarantee of an inheritance may explain why the New Testament speaks of adoption in terms of sonship. Believers are generally called 'sons of God' rather than 'daughters of God', even though God's promise of adoption is for both men and women. Why is this? Under Roman law, a father's legacy could be bequeathed only to a son, but God wants us to know that every one of his children will inherit his kingdom. When the Bible says 'You are all sons of God', it means that all of us – men and women alike – will receive a full share of God's eternal blessings in Jesus Christ.

The Bible gives a clue as to what our inheritance might include when it calls us 'co-heirs with Christ'. This is a way of saying that we will inherit nearly everything that Christ inherited. He is our elder brother, and we are to share in his inheritance. We will inherit God's entire estate, with all its riches. We will inherit his heavenly kingdom, with all its splendours. We will inherit new resurrection bodies, in all their glory. After all, 'We are children of God, and … we know that when he [Jesus] appears, we shall be like him, for we shall see him as he is.'[32]

---

[27] 1 John 3:1a, ASV.   [28] 1 John 3:1b, NIV.   [29] Rom. 8:17a.
[30] Gal. 4:7; cf. 3:29.   [31] Rev. 21:7.   [32] 1 John 3:2.

The fact that we are still waiting for our inheritance means that we are still longing to enjoy the full benefits of our adoption. Paul expressed this sense of anticipation when he confessed that 'we ourselves, who have the firstfruits of the Spirit, groan inwardly as we wait eagerly for our adoption as sons, the redemption of our bodies'.[33] We are waiting to receive the full benefits of our adoption, which we will receive only when we are raised in glory. God has promised to bring 'many sons to glory'.[34] Thus we have a 'once and future' adoption, a sonship that spans eternity. We were adopted in Christ before the beginning of time, and we will remain God's sons and daughters for ever. When we go to our Father's house, we will receive a marvellous inheritance, fabulous beyond compare.

The mention of our Father's wealth brings us to a third privilege. In addition to the status of sonship and a royal inheritance, we can expect to receive *good fatherly care*. God is the best of fathers, and he proves his love for his children by lavishing on us the gifts of his providence. Even earthly fathers, as sinful as they are, know how to give good gifts to their children. How much more does our Father in heaven know how to take care of all our needs.[35] He knows what we need even before we ask! He gives us bread for each day, forgiveness for our debts, and deliverance from the evil one. He gives us everything we need when we pray to him as our Father.[36] On occasion, he even affords us the ultimate proof of legitimate sonship, which is fatherly discipline. Beloved children always receive correction, especially if they are under royal training. Thus 'the LORD disciplines those he loves, as a father the son he delights in'.[37]

One of the best summaries of the full rights of sonship comes from the *Westminster Confession of Faith*:

> All those that are justified, God vouchsafeth, in and for His only Son Jesus Christ, to make partakers of the grace of adoption: by which they are taken into the number, and enjoy the liberties and privileges of the children of God; have His name put upon them, receive the Spirit of adoption; have access to the throne of grace with boldness; are enabled to cry, Abba, Father; are pitied, protected, provided for, and chastened by Him, as by a father; yet never cast off, but sealed to the day of redemption, and inherit the promises, as heirs of everlasting salvation (XII).

To say that we have received the 'full rights of sons' is to say that we now have a right to all these privileges – even as we wait for their consummation – because we have received the grace of adoption.

---

[33] Rom. 8:23.   [34] Heb. 2:10.   [35] Luke 11:11–13.   [36] Matt. 6:8–13.
[37] Prov. 3:12; cf. Heb. 12:5–11.

The responsibilities of sons

Adopted sons and daughters have many rights, but they also have many responsibilities. Their main responsibility is simply this: to respond to their father with loving obedience.

Mephibosheth seems to have done this. At the end of our passage we encounter one small but very important detail: *Mephibosheth lived in Jerusalem, because he always ate at the king's table, and he was crippled in both feet* (2 Sam. 9:13). The fact that Mephibosheth always ate at the king's table means that he took David up on his offer. He accepted his status as a son, claimed his royal inheritance, and received David's fatherly care. Mephibosheth gave further proof of his devotion when David faced an uprising led by his son Absalom. Recognizing that his place at the table had earned him a post in the army, Mephibosheth intended to fight for the king. But in the event he was double-crossed by his servant Ziba, who took advantage of his disability by stealing his mount and prevented him from going into battle (see 16:1–4; 19:24–30). Unable to ride to David's defence, Mephibosheth nevertheless showed his loyalty to the king by going into mourning until his safe return. His dishevelled appearance upon David's return was proof of his absolute devotion (19:24).

What God wants from his children is the same kind of devoted love. He wants us to know him and trust him as our Father. He wants us to depend upon his fatherly care. He wants us to maintain our family honour by living for his glory, for we are adopted 'to the praise of his glorious grace'.[38] Our Father wants us to promote our family welfare by loving our brothers and sisters in Christ. He wants us to live up to our family name by behaving as the children of God: 'Be perfect, therefore, as your heavenly Father is perfect.'[39] He wants us to display our family likeness by becoming more and more like his Son Jesus. 'For those God foreknew he also predestined to be conformed to the likeness of his Son, that he might be the firstborn among many brothers.'[40]

Sonship is one of the secrets to the life of daily Christian obedience: 'Those who are led by the Spirit of God are sons of God.'[41] Since we are God's sons, we do not serve him in slavish fear, hoping somehow to earn our way into his favour. 'For you did not receive a spirit that makes you a slave again to fear, but you received the Spirit of sonship.'[42] We are not slaves, but sons and daughters. Since God is the perfect Father, we know that we will never be disinherited. This makes us free to serve him with the joyful obedience of children who are eager to please their Father. And the more we please him, the more we take on our family resemblance.

[38] Eph. 1:6a; cf. Matt. 5:16.   [39] Matt. 5:48.   [40] Rom. 8:29.
[41] Rom. 8:14.   [42] Rom. 8:15; cf. Gal. 4:1–7.

God also wants us to recognize our status as his sons and daughters by calling him Father. He is waiting to hear us say the word that every father longs to hear from the lips of his children: 'Father'. And to help us address him properly, he has given us the gift of his Holy Spirit: 'Because you are sons, God sent the Spirit of his Son into our hearts, the Spirit who calls out, "*Abba*, Father."'[43] It is the Spirit of the Son who enables us to call out to God as our Father.

To understand the importance of calling God Father, consider the story of a little orphan boy who was rescued from the streets of Brazil by a missionary family. When the boy turned ten the family decided to adopt him. Once they had explained that the judge had granted him a new birth certificate with a new name, the boy couldn't wait to tell his friends. 'Uncle,' he said, 'when do I get to tell my friends you are my dad?' 'As soon as you want,' his father replied. 'But how will they believe you if you don't stop calling me Uncle?'

To enter into the joy of our new spiritual family we must learn to call God 'Father'. It is the Holy Spirit who enables us to do this by convincing us that we are not orphans, but dearly loved children. The Spirit whispers to our hearts that we are the sons and daughters of God, assuring us of our sonship by enabling us to cry out to God as our Father. This is one of the secrets to the life of prayer. Jesus taught us to pray, 'Our Father in heaven …'[44] We learn to follow Jesus' example by praying in the Spirit, by whom 'we cry, "*Abba*, Father." The Spirit himself testifies with our spirit that we are God's children.'[45] Now in every joy and trial of life we are able to say, 'I must speak with Father about this.' The more we call him Father, the more deeply we experience the intimacy of true spiritual sonship.

A friend once gave me a copy of the final Adoption Decree that secured his daughter's adoption. The decree was issued by the Court of Common Pleas of Montgomery County, Pennsylvania, Orphan's Court Division. It began with the name of the child. Then it listed the findings of the court: that the court has jurisdiction, that 'the needs and welfare of the adoptee will be promoted by adoption', that 'it is in the adoptee's best interests that the Court approve the adoption', and so on. Once it had made these findings, the Court ordered and decreed the following: '1. That request for adoption is hereby approved … 2. Said ADOPTEE shall have all rights of a child and heir of the adopting parents and shall be subject to duties of such child. 3. Said ADOPTEE shall hereafter be known as …' and then the girl's new name was given.

The terms of my friend's Adoption Decree are nearly identical to the terms of divine sonship. God offers the grace of saving adoption on the basis of his eternal covenant. He proposes to give a new status and a new family name. He is ready to grant all the rights and demand all the

---

[43] Gal. 4:6; cf. Rom. 8:15–16. [44] Matt. 6:9–13. [45] Rom. 8:16.

responsibilities of sons and daughters, with the promise of a royal inheritance. All the papers are in order; the adoption is waiting to be approved. All we need to do is tell God that we want to become his own dear children.

PART 4: SAVED FOR GOD'S GLORY
'All mankind will see God's salvation' (Luke 3:6)

15. God's new people
The communion of saints: Acts 2:42–47

The southern approach to the temple in Jerusalem is dominated by a series of magnificent steps made of white limestone and running the whole width of the Temple Mount. During the major Jewish festivals these steps thronged with pilgrims, who would have paused for ceremonial washings at the bottom, proceeded up to the top, and then poured through giant archways into the temple's outer courts.

'Save yourselves!'

In all likelihood, it was from these steps that Peter preached his famous sermon on the day of Pentecost. Jews from all over the world had gathered to celebrate the Feast of Weeks. They had been amazed to hear the disciples of Jesus 'declaring the wonders of God' in their own languages (Acts 2:11). When they demanded an explanation, Peter offered them the message of salvation, pointing them to the Saviour and promising that 'everyone who calls on the name of the Lord will be saved' (2:21).[1]

Peter's saving message was the same message that we have been exploring throughout this book. It was a message of salvation from sin, especially the sin many of them had committed by crucifying the Saviour of the world. It was a message of salvation by grace, the grace God gives through Jesus Christ. Peter summarized this gospel of grace by saying, 'Men of Israel, listen to this: Jesus …' (2:22a). He went on to preach the perfect, powerful life of Jesus (2:22b); the suffering, bleeding death of Jesus (2:23); the liberating, invigorating resurrection of Jesus (2:24–32); and the glorious, victorious exaltation of Jesus (2:33–36). The message of salvation was all about Jesus. Peter thus ended it by declaring, 'Therefore let all Israel be assured of this: God has made this Jesus, whom you crucified, both Lord and Christ' (2:36). Jesus is the Saviour because he is the crucified, risen and exalted Lord.

As the people heard this message of salvation they realized that they

---

[1] Cf. Joel. 2:32.

were sinners who needed God's saving grace: 'They were cut to the heart and said to Peter and the other apostles, "Brothers, what shall we do?"' (2:37). The answer Peter gave was the answer salvation always gives: there is nothing you can do except believe, because salvation comes only through faith in Jesus Christ. 'Peter replied, "Repent and be baptized, every one of you, in the name of Jesus Christ for the forgiveness of your sins ..."' With many other words he warned them; and he pleaded with them, "Save yourselves from this corrupt generation"' (2:38a, 40).

Many of the people did save themselves. They were rescued from the coming judgment by believing in Jesus Christ. Peter's sermon turned out to be the speech that saved 3,000 souls, for 'those who accepted his message were baptised, and about three thousand were added to their number that day' (2:41). Peter's preaching confronted them with their need for a Saviour, as the message of salvation always does. They turned to Christ, and in turning to him, they were turning away from their sins. By believing and repenting in this way, they were saved by grace through faith.

Everything in common

That is not the end of the story, however, which may come as a surprise to anyone who thinks that salvation begins and ends with making an individual decision for Christ. A decision for Christ must be made, of course, because salvation comes through faith. But there is much more to salvation than praying 'the Sinner's Prayer' or 'going forward' at an evangelistic rally.

Believing the message of salvation is not an end in itself; it is only the beginning. We are not merely saved *from* something (namely, sin), but also *for* something. We are saved for God's glory. The end of Acts 2 shows what happens once people receive salvation in Christ:

They devoted themselves to the apostles' teaching and to the fellowship, to the breaking of bread and to prayer. Everyone was filled with awe, and many wonders and miraculous signs were done by the apostles. All the believers were together and had everything in common. Selling their possessions and goods, they gave to anyone as he had need. Every day they continued to meet together in the temple courts. They broke bread in their homes and ate together with glad and sincere hearts, praising God and enjoying the favour of all the people. And the Lord added to their number daily those who were being saved (2:42–47).

The key statement comes in verse 44: *All the believers were together and had everything in common.* The outstanding characteristic of God's new people was that, rather than leading separate lives, they were all

221

together. They understood that being saved means being saved into a new spiritual community. God's sons and daughters are all adopted into one family of God. This is why the Puritans who wrote the *Westminster Confession of Faith* claimed that outside the church 'there is no ordinary possibility of salvation' (XXV.2). Christianity is not a life alone – it is a life together.

The experience of the apostolic church shows that there is no such thing as private Christianity. Somehow it has become popular in the West to think of religion as a private matter. One thinks of Thomas Jefferson (1743–1826), who said, 'I am a sect to myself.' Or one thinks of the countless postmodern men and women who claim the right to make up their religion as they go along. Christians are prone to think this way, too. Some churchgoers do not want to get too involved. They prefer to slip in and out of the worship service unnoticed. Others claim that they can get all the church they need in the privacy of their own homes through an electronic broadcast. But if you say, 'My religion is private', then whatever else your religion may be, it is not true Christianity.

Christianity is always personal, of course, because it entails a personal relationship with Jesus Christ, but it is never private. True faith in Jesus Christ must be professed publicly and expressed communally. Although we never lose our personal identity, we will always be individuals in community. As we confess whenever we recite the Apostles' Creed, we believe in the communion of saints. James Bannerman writes,

> According to the arrangement of God, the Christian is more of a Christian in society than alone, and more in the enjoyment of privileges of a spiritual kind when he shares them with others, than when he possesses them apart ... The Christian Church was established in the world, to realize the superior advantages of a social over an individual Christianity, and to set up and maintain the communion of the saints.[2]

What did the first Christians share in common? Everything! At least, everything that mattered. For all their ethnic and cultural differences, and for all the variety in their personal circumstances, their dearest treasures were community property. Together they comprised one body, animated by one Spirit, and called to one hope. They had 'one Lord, one faith, one baptism; one God and Father of all, who is over all and through all and in all'.[3] They also had one salvation, for the plan of salvation was never intended for isolated individuals. Whenever the

[2] Bannerman, *The Church of Christ*, vol. 1, p. 91–92.
[3] Eph. 3:4–5.

Bible speaks of God's saving plan, it always uses the plural, because God has always planned to save a *people* for himself. The message of salvation is not so much about personal salvation as about a salvation that all believers share in common. To be included in Christ is to be incorporated into the communion of the saints.

Consider the doctrines of salvation we have considered thus far. Each of them – every aspect of salvation – is for all God's people to share in common. We all have the same need for salvation because we are all sinners. Together we share in Adam's sin, and all of us commit sins of our very own. Thus we are all guilty of sin, both original and actual. Because we are dead in our transgressions and sins, we all have the same inability to save ourselves. We have all been saved by grace. Together we have been delivered from the power of death. Together we have been chosen from the foundation of the world to be redeemed from our bondage to sin. Together we have been reconciled to God, for 'God was reconciling the world to himself in Christ'.[4] Together we have been adopted into his family. When Christ died on the cross, he died for all of us – atoning for all our sins, propitiating God's wrath against every one of us, and justifying us all by his righteousness. When Christ rose from the tomb, he rose for all of us – gaining eternal life and winning our entrance into heaven. Like the first Christians, we have everything in common because everything God has ever done to save any of us he has done to save all of us.

Since the apostolic church in Jerusalem shared all these things in common, it is not surprising that they did nearly everything together. They studied together, worshipped together, prayed together, celebrated the sacraments together, and ate meals together. Together they performed acts of mercy, sacrificing their own goods for the benefit of others. The glimpse we are given of their life together, brief though it is, reveals all the marks of a healthy church. They shared a common foundation in the Word of God. They enjoyed a common fellowship with one another. They found a common purpose in glorifying God. They shared a common passion to care for the needy. They engaged in a common mission to spread the gospel. As they shared these things in common, they became a learning, caring, worshipping community that was growing by the power of God's Holy Spirit.

A learning community

The first mark of God's new people is that together they form a learning community. The first Christians *devoted themselves to the apostles' teaching* (Acts 2:42). It is not surprising that learning should be mentioned first, for everything else depends on the faithful ministry of

[4] 2 Cor. 5:19a.

God's Word. The way we learn how to care for one another, how to worship God, and how to share our faith is by studying the Bible.

If Peter's sermon is any indication, what the apostles taught the people was the message of salvation, as it had been promised in the Old Testament and fulfilled in Jesus Christ. As eyewitnesses of the risen Christ, they were able to testify to his life, his teachings, his death, and especially his resurrection. The first Christians *devoted themselves* to this message. Their dedication was keen, for the word translated 'devoted' (*proskarterountes*) suggests almost a preoccupation with hearing and studying apostolic doctrine.

What may seem surprising about the commitment of the Jerusalem church to learn from the apostles is that all its members were filled with the Holy Spirit. Acts 2 begins with the powerful coming of God's Spirit upon the entire Christian community. One might have expected this Pentecostal blessing to eliminate the need for teaching God's Word. After all, the first Christians were filled with the Holy Spirit! If they had the Spirit, then why did they need someone to teach them God's Word? One way to answer this question is to remember that God's Word is the Spirit's Word. The Holy Spirit is the one who inspired Holy Scripture, the one who breathed the mind of God into the pages of the Bible.[5] His desire is for us to listen to his voice speaking in Scripture. So, rather than eliminating the need for good teaching, the Spirit's coming actually intensifies our desire to receive biblical instruction. The reason the first Christians were so devoted to God's Word was that they were so full of God's Spirit. We ourselves are most spiritual when we are most devoted to God's Word. A Spirit-filled church is a Bible-teaching church.

The church's need to learn from the apostles did not disappear with the death of the apostles themselves. In every generation the church must submit to the authority of the apostolic gospel. The church has always been strong when the Christian community has devoted itself to apostolic teaching, and it has always been weak when that teaching is neglected. The greatest single cause for the failure of the medieval church in Europe was not its bloated bureaucracy, its immoral clergy or even its faulty doctrine of salvation. Rather, the church was in decline because the Bible was on the shelf. By contrast, for all the advances won by the Reformers – theologically, liturgically and spiritually – the greatest single cause of the Reformation was the recovery of God's Word. Luther's Reformation was made possible in part by Gutenberg's printing press. To take another example, consider the accelerating spiritual decline of the mainline Protestant denominations in the West during the twentieth century. In part, this decline was brought about by theological liberalism and political pragmatism. But more than

---

[5] 2 Tim. 3:16.

anything else, the decline was caused by a failure to submit to the Bible's authority as the inerrant, infallible Word of God.

To apply these lessons from church history, the twenty-first century church will only be as strong as its devotion to the teaching of the apostles. Being devoted to their teaching means believing in the authority of Scripture, accepting the Bible as the very Word of God, the only rule of faith and practice. It means believing in the sufficiency of Scripture, trusting that the Bible has all the answers we need for the work of the church and the problems of daily life.

Being devoted to the apostles' teaching is not simply a matter of having the right doctrine of Scripture, however; it also requires personal Bible study. We need to read the Bible every day, both the Old and the New Testament. We need to read the Bible book by book, chapter by chapter, and verse by verse – over breakfast, during lunch break or before bedtime. It is helpful to follow a systematic programme for reading the Bible in a year, using a daily devotional guide, consulting the notes in a study Bible, or reading a biblical commentary. But by all means, let's read and study the Bible!

Reading the Bible includes reading it in public worship. Scripture-reading is disappearing from many churches, perhaps because it is considered too boring for a multimedia age; but being devoted to the apostles' teaching requires a return to the public reading of God's Word. We do well to follow the example of Ezra, who read the Law of Moses from dawn until noon, and had the scribes explain it to the people.[6] We also do well to follow the example of the Puritans, who, in addition to the sermon, enjoyed a long Bible reading (with commentary) during their worship services.

Finally, being devoted to the apostles' teaching requires a return to Bible exposition as the norm for preaching. Often this will mean preaching consecutively through entire books of the Bible, explaining them verse by verse. Yet expository preaching is not so much a method as a mindset. In expository preaching the content of the sermon is governed and directed by the content of the Bible, so that each doctrine and its applications are derived from Holy Scripture. The divine authority of preaching rests on this connection between God's Word and the preacher's words. One of the best twentieth-century models for expositional preaching was William Still (1911–97), who laboured for more than fifty years at Gilcomston South Church in Aberdeen. A visitor once accosted Mr Still at the conclusion of a service, saying, 'But you don't preach!' Upon further questioning, the man explained what he meant: 'You just take a passage from the Bible and explain what it means.' To which Mr Still replied, 'Brother, that is preaching!'[7] Since

---

[6] Neh. 8.

[7] Alistair Begg, *Preaching for God's Glory* (Wheaton, IL: Crossway, 1999), p. 27.

the time of the apostles, the church has flourished best when ministers have been most careful simply to teach the Bible.[8]

A caring community

Koinōnia

Not only was the church in Jerusalem a learning community, it was also a caring community. The first Christians devoted themselves 'to the fellowship'. The Greek word for 'fellowship' is *koinōnia*. In its most basic sense *koinōnia* means 'sharing' or 'participating'. For example, the writer to the Hebrews reminds us 'do not forget to do good and to share with others'; literally 'the doing good and the sharing [*koinōnias*]'.[9] Often the word is used in an explicitly financial sense. With heartfelt appreciation Paul told the Philippians, 'Not one church shared (*ekoinōnēsen*) with me in the matter of giving and receiving, except you only'.[10] When the apostle later explained how much their charity cost them, he again used the word *koinōnia*: 'Out of the most severe trial, their overflowing joy and their extreme poverty welled up in rich generosity. For I testify that they gave as much as they were able, and even beyond their ability. Entirely on their own, they urgently pleaded with us for the privilege of sharing (*koinōnia*) in this service to the saints.'[11]

The contemporary church seems to have forgotten the costliness of *koinōnia*. In the West, for example, fellowship means chatting for a few minutes before a worship service, playing ball games at a church picnic, or having coffee and biscuits after church. All of these things may encourage fellowship, but they are only the beginning. Fellowship is not a superficial friendship, but a deep personal commitment made possible only by the saving work of the Holy Spirit. True *koinōnia* comes with a price tag. It requires a personal investment in the spiritual and material welfare of our brothers and sisters in Christ. Because we are members of the same spiritual family, we must be willing to be burdened with their burdens, acknowledging that they have a legitimate claim on our charity.

When the Bible speaks of '*the* fellowship', it may be referring to services of public worship held at the temple. If so, then it would include both of the things mentioned next: prayer and the breaking of bread (more on these in a moment). Ordinarily, however, *koinōnia* refers to tangible gifts of material support – what the Puritans sometimes called 'relief in outward things'. A related word occurs in Acts 2:44: *All the believers were together and had everything in common*

---

[8] The history of expository preaching is traced in Old, *The Reading and Preaching of the Scriptures in the Worship of the Christian Church*.
[9] Heb. 13:16.   [10] Phil. 4:15.   [11] 2 Cor. 8:2–4.

(*koina*). The Scripture goes on to explain exactly what it was that they held in common: *Selling their possessions and goods, they gave to anyone as he had need* (2:45). Because the first Christians shared a common salvation, they not only worshipped together, but they also shared with one another. They sold their valuables and their land and property to provide for one another's needs. They ate meals together, opening their hearts and homes to one another (2:46b).

The fellowship that Christians share with one another is based on their union with Christ. It is as we are united to Christ that we are united to one another. We are members of one body, the body of Christ; we are siblings in one family, adopted into the same family as Christ our elder brother.[12] Thus our *koinōnia* is first of all with the triune God himself: 'Our fellowship is with the Father and with his Son, Jesus Christ',[13] and also with the Holy Spirit.[14] Our communion with God, in turn, spills over into communion with all his saints. To summarize, fellowship is the living communion of all true believers, who are united to one another in love by their union with Christ, and who share together in corporate worship and mutual assistance.

The fact that Christians share a common life does not mean that Christianity is a form of socialism. The church in Jerusalem was not a commune, and its members did not have to liquidate their property as a prerequisite for church membership. Instead, many of them continued to own private property. One indication of this lies in the grammar of verse 45, where the verbs for 'selling' and 'giving' occur in the imperfect tense, indicating occasional rather than perpetual action. From time to time, as the need arose, the first Christians sold their possessions and gave their money to the poor. Another clue comes in verse 46, where the Scripture says that *they broke bread in their homes*. Some of them, at least, were homeowners.

Two stories from later in the book of Acts confirm that the first Christians owned property. One is the story of Barnabas, who 'sold a field he owned and brought the money and put it at the apostles' feet' (4:37); the other is the tragic story of Ananias and Sapphira in Acts 5. That miserable couple sold a piece of property, kept part of the proceeds for themselves, and then brought the rest to the apostles. They claimed that their gift represented the whole price of the sale, which was a lie. 'Then Peter said, "Ananias, how is it that Satan has so filled your heart that you have lied to the Holy Spirit and have kept for yourself some of the money you received for the land? Didn't it belong to you before it was sold? And after it was sold, wasn't the money at your disposal?"' (5:3–4a). We can infer from what Peter says that the first Christians continued to own private property, and that the giving of their money to the church was strictly voluntary.

[12] Heb. 2:11–12.   [13] 1 John 1:3.   [14] 2 Cor. 13:14.

But give their money to the church they did! Cheerfully and willingly, with little concern for their own welfare, the Jerusalem church gave generously to meet the needs of the poor, especially the Christian poor. The Dutch preacher, politician and social reformer Abraham Kuyper (1837–1920) explained that Jesus, 'through an organized *ministry of* charity, which in the name of the Lord, as being the single owner of all goods, demanded the community of goods to this extent, that in the circle of believers no man or woman was to be permitted to suffer want or to be without the necessary apparel'.[15] The first Christians met their Lord's demand, for at the end of Acts 4 we are given a fuller description of the kind of *koinōnia* Christians practised in those days: 'All the believers were one in heart and mind. No-one claimed that any of his possessions was his own, but they shared everything they had ... There were no needy persons among them. For from time to time those who owned lands or houses sold them, brought the money from the sales and put it at the apostles' feet, and it was distributed to anyone as he had need' (4:32, 34–35).

Christianity is not coercive communism, in which members of the church are forced to give up their goods against their will. Nor is it consumptive capitalism, in which Christians pursue selfish gain. Rather, it is compassionate *koinōnia*, in which each member freely dedicates everything he has to the service of God and to the benefit of his neighbour. In this way, the wider social implications of salvation – which, as we noted in chapter 11, Luke was especially concerned to emphasize – begin to be realized. To a superlative degree, the first Christians entered into the joy of selfless fellowship. They understood that their personal salvation had profound social consequences. All of their possessions belonged to their heavenly Father, and if they belonged to the Father, then they were to be shared with the rest of his children, their own brothers and sisters. Thus they made a radical commitment to Christian community – a community so remarkably caring that 'there were no needy persons among them' (4:34).[16]

Charity

Whenever the church has understood what it means to be saved by grace through faith, it has always become a caring community. This was true in Jerusalem, where the believers 'were one in heart and mind' (4:32), distributing food to needy Christians on a daily basis (6:1). It was true in the cosmopolitan city of Antioch, where Christians reached across divisive racial and cultural boundaries to become a multi-ethnic community (13:1). It was true in Asia, where Gentile Christians raised money to relieve Jewish Christians back in Jerusalem who were

[15] Kuyper, *Christianity and the Class Struggle*, p. 30.
[16] Cf. Deut. 15:4.

suffering from famine. This was something they wanted to do because of the *koinōnia* they shared in Christ: 'For if the Gentiles have shared in the Jews' spiritual blessings, they owe it to the Jews to share with them their material blessings.'[17]

The church was a caring community in the fourth century, when the Emperor Maximinus issued an imperial decree driving Christians from their homes. In his history of the church, Eusebius of Caesarea (c. 265–c. 339) describes the intense suffering Christians endured in those days. Not long afterwards, there was a severe famine throughout the empire, with pestilence in the villages and death in the cities. Eusebius describes wealthy women begging for bread, and grown men falling down to die in the streets. Their bodies were stacked in piles, and no-one cared – except, that is, for the church. Eusebius writes:

> The heathen everywhere beheld a striking proof of the piety and universal benevolence of the Christians. Amidst calamities so numerous and so severe, they alone exhibited in substantial deeds, the offices of mercy and humanity. They daily employed themselves, partly in protecting and burying the bodies of the dead (for innumerable multitudes, of whom no person took care, died every day), and partly in distributing provisions to all the indigent in the whole city that were pining for hunger, whom they collected for that purpose. The consequence was, that this was extensively talked of and divulged, and all men highly extolled the God of the Christians, and confessed that they alone had approved themselves in deed and in truth the sincere worshippers of God.[18]

The church was a caring community in the Middle Ages, when Christians set up inns for travellers and hospitals for the sick. The same was true in Geneva during the Reformation: the hungry were fed, the ignorant were educated, and the sick were nursed back to health. As he laboured in that needy city, John Calvin made it his particular goal to 'raise in each member of the Christian Community the spiritual problem of his material life, of his goods, of his time, and of his capabilities, in view of freely putting them at the service of God and neighbour'.

Christianity has a history of charity. At every time and in every place, to be devoted to 'the fellowship' means to 'share with God's people who are in need'.[19] It means adopting the girl left behind at the orphanage. It means sitting at the bedside of the man dying from AIDS. It means feeding and clothing the homeless. It means sharing table fellowship

---

[17] Rom. 15:27.

[18] Eusebius, *Historia Ecclesiastica*, IX.8, quoted in Witsius, *Sacred Dissertations on the Apostles' Creed*, vol. 2, p. 383.

[19] Rom. 12:13.

with Christians of all races and classes. It means giving 'proper recognition to those widows who are really in need'.[20] It means caring for the elderly rather than forgetting about them. In these postmodern times, when the globe has become a village, being devoted to the fellowship also means extending our *koinōnia* around the world. It means praying for our brothers in prison, redeeming our sisters from slavery, and sending generous relief to God's children in famine or earthquake. This is basic Christianity. 'If anyone has material possessions and sees his brother in need but has no pity on him, how can the love of God be in him?'[21] The answer is that God's love cannot be in him, because true Christians are devoted to the fellowship.

A worshipping community

The third mark of vital Christian community is worship. In addition to devoting themselves to apostolic teaching and costly fellowship, the first Christians *devoted themselves ... to the breaking of bread and to prayer* (2:42). Breaking bread and praying are two different elements of public worship. 'Breaking the bread' was a Jewish expression for opening a meal with prayer and the distribution of bread. When the first Christians broke bread together, however, they were sharing more than a meal. Acts 2:42 speaks of '*the* breaking of bread', meaning the sacrament of the Lord's Supper.[22] It also speaks (translated literally) of '*the* prayers', the standard Jewish expression for the prayers of God's people. To say that they were devoted to 'the prayers', then, means that they regularly participated in public worship.

The sacraments

The celebration of the sacraments was central to worship in the early church. A sacrament is a tangible sign of salvation which represents and applies the benefits of Christ to the believer. Jesus instituted two sacraments for the church: *baptism* and *communion*. Baptism we have already mentioned, for those who believed Peter's message of salvation were baptized. They and their children received the promise of the Holy Spirit. Whether we speak of infant baptism or adult baptism, baptism is a sign that someone belongs to God's family. It is the sacrament that marks one's union with Christ and entrance into the Christian community, 'for we were all baptised by one Spirit into one body'.[23] We were baptized into the communion of the saints, and now we belong to the community of the baptized.

The Lord's Supper communicates many deep mysteries of the gospel. It is partly the undoing of our fall into sin. Humanity first tasted

[20] 1 Tim. 5:3.   [21] 1 John 3:17.   [22] See Luke 24:30.
[23] 1 Cor. 12:13; cf. Gal. 3:26–28.

sin when the serpent said, in effect, 'Take and eat.'[24] Now God's new people taste salvation every time they hear Jesus say, 'Take and eat; this is my body.'[25] The sacrament is partly a remembrance of Christ's death, a reminder that his body was given and his blood was shed for our salvation. It is partly a source of nourishment. Christ is present in the sacrament by his Spirit, who enables us to feed upon Christ and his benefits in a spiritual way. The Lord's Supper also holds the promise of eternity. By partaking of the bread and the cup we proclaim the Lord's death until he comes again. All these things are true, but none of them is what Acts 2 primarily has in mind. What is emphasized here is that the Lord's Supper is a community dinner.

The Lord's Supper is a communal sacrament, which is one of the reasons it is often called 'communion'. Whereas baptism is the sacrament for entrance into the church, communion is the sacrament for continuance in the church. Whether the Lord's Supper was celebrated at the temple or in house churches, as verse 46 might seem to suggest, the important thing is that the first Christians celebrated it together. Sharing in the sacramental meal expressed their spiritual communion with one another. As Paul later asked the Corinthians, 'Is not the cup of thanksgiving for which we give thanks a participation in the blood of Christ? And is not the bread that we break a participation in the body of Christ? Because there is one loaf, we, who are many, are one body, for we all partake of the one loaf.'[26] The Lord's Supper is a sign of our communion with one another as well as of our union and communion with Christ. We eat from one loaf because we are one body, one new people in Christ.

The sacraments helped break down the many social, ethnic and economic barriers that divided the early church. The message of salvation proclaimed that there was only one new people of God: 'You are all sons of God through faith in Christ Jesus, for all of you who were baptised into Christ have clothed yourselves with Christ. There is neither Jew nor Greek, slave nor free, male nor female, for you are all one in Christ Jesus.'[27] Being in Christ brings unity out of diversity, and there are reminders of this unity throughout Acts 2. The people who received Peter's message of salvation came 'from every nation under heaven' (2:5). God poured out his Spirit on women as well as men (2:17). He called children as well as their parents, Gentiles as well as Jews (2:39). These people were all baptized into one Christ, and one way they expressed their true spiritual union was by sharing in one sacrament of the Lord's Supper.

One Christian who understood communion as a community meal was the Swiss Reformer Ulrich Zwingli (1484–1531). Zwingli served as a chaplain in the Swiss army. He had often watched his soldiers swear

[24] Gen. 3:5–6.   [25] Matt. 26:26.   [26] 1 Cor. 10:16–17.   [27] Gal. 3:26–28.

their allegiance to Switzerland and to one another before going into battle, with the red cross on their uniforms serving as the badge of their solidarity. Zwingli suggested that the Lord's Supper has the same function for soldiers in the Lord's Army. The cross is the badge of our union with Christ and communion with one another. This is reflected in the Latin word *sacramentum*, which means 'an oath of allegiance'. When we receive the bread and the cup we are swearing our allegiance to our Lord and to his church.

Public worship

We ought to have the same sense of solidarity when we pray. The first Christians devoted themselves to prayer. This was the secret of their spiritual power. Whenever they had a crisis – after Jesus ascended to heaven, for example, or when Peter was put in prison – we always find them at prayer. This was also their daily habit: *Every day they continued to meet together in the temple courts* (2:46a). They did not go there to offer sacrifices, of course, because Jesus had offered himself as a once-and-for-all atonement. But they did go to the temple to pray; in other words, to worship.

The first Christians worshipped both at home and at the temple. This suggests a balance between formal and informal worship, between large services and small groups. Every day they gathered within the precincts of the temple to pray, probably somewhere in the Court of the Gentiles, which could accommodate as many as 200,000 worshippers. On other occasions they met in people's homes; these were the first house churches. The location was not important. The important thing was meeting together regularly to learn the Scriptures, to celebrate the sacraments and to pray. Whenever and wherever the first Christians met, they worshipped *with glad and sincere hearts* (2:46). This wonderful phrase captures the essence of true worship. Gladness is exultation, an exuberant joy in the being and blessings of God. But their joy was not irreverent. In fact, it was dignified and sincere. They did not try to work themselves into a particular mood; they simply praised God with 'unaffected joy' (NEB), glorifying him with equal parts reverence and rejoicing.

Worship is one form of fellowship. Whenever we worship, we share in the joyful work of glorifying God. As we read Scripture, we join our minds to share in God's Word. As we sing hymns and songs, we join our voices to share in God's praise. As we pray, we join our hearts to share in God's friendship. As we offer our gifts and tithes, we join our wealth to share in God's work. Worship is a corporate enterprise. We are called to worship together, so that 'some assembly is required'. Fellowship is not something that takes place after the worship service. Our worship itself expresses our spiritual union and communion with one another. Whenever we worship together we declare God's worth, offering him the praise and honour he alone deserves. This is what we were made to do. At the beginning of this book we stated that the purpose of human existence is to glorify God. Now we discover that glorifying God is a corporate enterprise. We were saved to worship God *together*. To quote again from the *Westminster Confession of Faith*, we are 'bound to maintain an holy fellowship and communion in the worship of God' (XXVI.2).

Everything we have said thus far about the Word, the work and the worship of the Christian community was observed already in the second century by Justin Martyr (c. AD 100–165). Born a pagan, Justin was led to Christ through a conversation with an old man by the sea. In his writings he describes the typical worship service of his day:

> On the day called Sunday there is a meeting in one place of those who live in cities or the country, and the memoirs of the apostles or the writings of the prophets are read as long as time permits. When the reader has finished, the president in a discourse urges and invites [us] to the imitation of these noble things. Then we all stand up together and offer prayers. And, as said before, when we have finished the prayer, bread is brought, and wine and water, and the president similarly sends up prayers and thanksgivings to the best of his ability, and the congregation assents, saying the Amen; the distribution, and reception of the consecrated [elements] by each one, takes place and they are sent to the absent by the deacons. Those who prosper, and who so wish, contribute, each one as much as he chooses to. What is collected is deposited with the president, and he takes care of orphans and widows, and those who are in want on account of sickness or any other cause, and those who are in bonds, and the strangers who are sojourners among [us], and, briefly, he is the protector of all those in need. We all hold this common gathering on Sunday, since it is the first day, on which God transforming darkness and matter made the universe, and Jesus Christ our Saviour rose from the dead on the same day.[28]

The Christians of Justin's day may have lived in the second century, but they were first-century Christians. Like the Christians in Jerusalem, *They devoted themselves to the apostles' teaching and to the fellowship, to the breaking of bread and to prayer … Selling their possessions and goods, they gave to anyone as he had need* (2:42, 45).

A growing community

An authentic spiritual community always grows. First the message of

---

[28] Justin Martyr, *The First Apology of Justin, the Martyr*, p. 287.

salvation creates community among those who are being saved. God's new people are saved for God's glory, and as they begin to glorify God in their work and their worship, other people want to join them. They, in turn, then receive the message of salvation and begin to glorify God. Thus a learning, caring and worshipping church is always a growing community.

The Bible does not say that the first Christians devoted themselves to evangelism, although we may infer that they shared the message of salvation as often as they could. What it does say is that they devoted themselves to the Word, to one another and to worship. The more they did these things, the more people started to take notice. The first Christians became a worshipping church before a watching world. As a result, *The Lord added to their number daily those who were being saved* (2:47b). It was the Lord who kept adding to their numbers, of course, because it is only God who can save a sinner, and only by his grace. But God ordinarily accomplishes his saving work through a learning, loving, worshipping church. Here we see the biblical method of church growth. The church does not grow by evangelistic crusades or advertising campaigns. Those things may have their place, and they may even boost attendance for a time, but they are incidental to the real work of the church. The way the church wins the lost is simply by being the church. True Christian community confirms the truth of salvation's message in the mind and heart of the unbeliever. Whenever Christians establish a community in which they love one another the way they ought to love one another, and care for one another the way they ought to care for one another, then outsiders want to become part of it.

Outsiders certainly wanted to belong to God's new people in the days of the apostles. The Bible records two responses that non-Christians had to the Jerusalem church. One was amazement: *Everyone was filled with awe, and many wonders and miraculous signs were done by the apostles* (2:43). Certainly the Christians themselves were filled with awe at what God's Spirit was doing among them. But the word 'everyone' suggests that there were also unbelievers who recognized that something awesome was happening in the Christian community. One thing that amazed them was the power of the apostles to perform miracles. But there was something else that impressed them, too, and that was the amazing love that Christians had for one another. The Jerusalem church was exactly the kind of caring community that the world is always looking for. Thus its members *enjoyed the favour of all the people* (2:47).

People who are favourably inclined toward the church often become favourably inclined to Christ. Genuine conversions are the inevitable by-product of vital, healthy, authentic spiritual community. Roland Allen has described this phenomenon as 'the spontaneous expansion of the church'. By 'spontaneous' Allen means 'the expansion which follows the unexhorted and unorganized activity of individual members of the Church explaining to others the Gospel which they have found for themselves; ... the expansion which follows the irresistible attraction of the Christian Church for men who see its ordered life, and are drawn to it by desire to discover the secret of a life which they instinctively desire to share'.[29] This is precisely the kind of spontaneous expansion that the church enjoyed during the age of the apostles, when sinners were saved every day. The first Christians were not occasional evangelists. Witness was part of their daily worship and work. Nor was evangelism a special project for Christians with specialized gifts; rather, it was a product of the common life of the whole Christian church. God's new people were devoted to God and to one another, with the inevitable result that their learning, caring, worshipping community was also a growing community.

The phrase *added to their number* suggests that salvation ordinarily results in church membership. The apostles knew who belonged to the church because new converts joined the Christian community in some formalized way. In modern parlance, they became 'church members'. In those days, writes John Stott, the Spirit 'did not add them to the church without saving them (no nominal Christianity at the beginning), nor did he save them without adding them to the church (no solitary Christianity either). Salvation and church membership belonged together; they still do.'[30]

God has saved us into a learning, caring, worshipping community that grows through the power of the Holy Spirit. Stott summarizes by stating that our life together is marked by 'biblical teaching, loving fellowship, living worship, and an ongoing, outgoing evangelism.'[31] And all these activities require relationships:

Looking back over these marks of the first Spirit-filled community, it is evident that they all concerned the church's relationships. First, they were related to the apostles (in submission). They were eager to receive the apostles' instruction. A Spirit-filled church is an apostolic church, a New Testament church, anxious to believe and obey what Jesus and his apostles taught. Secondly, they were related to each other (in love). They persevered in the fellowship, supporting each other and relieving the needs of the poor. A Spirit-filled church is a loving, caring, sharing church. Thirdly, they were related to God (in worship). They worshipped him in the temple and in the home, in the Lord's Supper and in the prayers, with joy and with reverence. A Spirit-filled church is a worshipping church. Fourthly, they were

---

[29] Allen, *The Spontaneous Expansion of the Church and the Causes which Hinder It*, p. 7.
[30] Stott, *The Message of Acts*, p. 87.
[31] Ibid.

related to the world (in outreach). They were engaged in continuous evangelism. No self-centred, self-contained church (absorbed in its own parochial affairs) can claim to be filled with the Spirit. The Holy Spirit is a missionary Spirit. So a Spirit-filled church is a missionary church.[32]

If all these relationships are necessary to maintain vibrant Christian community, it is important to ask if they are present in our own churches. At a very minimum, every Christian church should have sound teaching, intimate fellowship and reverent worship, with the proper administration of the sacraments. Is our teaching biblical and practical? Is our fellowship caring and affectionate? Is our worship joyous and reverent? Do we celebrate baptism and the Lord's Supper in the biblical way? Are our churches growing steadily and spontaneously? Is the general spiritual atmosphere healthy enough to draw people to faith in Christ?

These questions are important because being a Christian is not a private matter. To be a Christian is to belong to God's new people. Christianity is never an individual event; it is always a team sport. We cannot live alone and apart. We must learn, care, worship and grow with others, which is what it means to confess that we believe in the communion of saints. We believe that we are saved to glorify God together.

[32] Ibid.

16. Saved to sin no more
Sanctification: Romans 6:1–14

To sin or not to sin? That is the question the apostle Paul raises at the beginning of Romans 6. He has just finished explaining how God provided justifying righteousness through the death and resurrection of Jesus Christ. God has answered the problem of our sin with the gift of his salvation, and the more we realize how sinful we are, the more reason we have to praise God for his grace: 'Where sin increased, grace increased all the more' (Rom. 5:20b–21). But if our sin is such a wonderful opportunity for God to show his grace, then perhaps we should sin as much as we can. Hence the question: *Shall we go on sinning so that grace may increase?* (6:1).

Paul's question is not hard to answer, of course, but it is worth pausing to notice what the question itself tells us about the message of salvation. It tells us that we are saved by grace. If we were saved by works of our own righteousness, then it would never occur to ask whether or not we should continue in sin. Of course not, because in that case our salvation would depend on *not* sinning. But the message of salvation is that we are saved by God's amazing, abounding grace, a grace that saves us in spite of our sin. This salvation is so wonderful that it is almost tempting to ask whether we should try to sin all the more to experience even more of God's grace.

Doing such a thing would be unthinkable, of course. God forbid that anyone who has been saved by grace would want to do anything except glorify God! Shall we keep on sinning? *By no means!* says Paul. The very idea is abhorrent: *We died to sin; how can we live in it any longer?* (6:2). If God's grace were to lead us deeper into sin, then the message of salvation would be practically immoral. But in fact God's grace does exactly the opposite. We have not been saved *for* sin, but *from* sin – not only from its guilt and punishment, but also from sin itself. Jesus came to 'save his people from their sins'.[1] Thus the purpose of God's saving plan is to deliver us from the tyranny of sin and to bring us into the dominion of his grace. We have been saved to sin no more.

[1] Matt. 1:21.

What is sanctification?

Everyone who is saved by grace senses the need for personal holiness. We know that we are set apart to be holy, or 'sanctified', as the Bible calls it. And we know that God wants us to become more and more holy all the time: 'Be holy because I, the LORD your God, am holy';[2] 'It is God's will that you should be sanctified ... For God did not call us to be impure, but to live a holy life.'[3] Jesus went so far as to say, 'Be perfect, therefore, as your heavenly Father is perfect.'[4] The Bible calls us 'saints', which means 'holy ones', because God has separated us from sin and consecrated us for his service.

What Christians often have difficulty agreeing about is how holiness happens. How do we grow spiritually? How do we gain victory over sin? What is the gospel method of sanctification? These may sound like simple questions, but there is widespread disagreement about how to answer them. Some teach that sanctification is a matter of moral effort. Human beings were created good and have the capacity for unhindered moral progress. Hence the naïve optimism of the Enlightenment philosopher Marquis de Condorcet: 'The total mass of the human species, through alternating periods of calm and agitation, good and evil, forever marches, albeit at a slow pace, towards a greater perfection.'[5] Others teach that we are made holy primarily by the sacraments, which impart sanctifying grace. Still others maintain that there are two kinds of Christians, carnal Christians and spiritual Christians. One first becomes a Christian by trusting in Jesus Christ as Saviour; however, Christians remain carnally sinful until they also decide to trust Jesus as Lord. Finally, there are those who insist that it is possible to live without committing any known sin. Entire sanctification comes after conversion through a second blessing of the Holy Spirit, and the goal of the Christian life is to achieve perfection on this side of eternity.

It happens to make a great deal of practical difference which view is right. Do I still have a sinful nature, or not? Do I grow in grace by receiving the sacraments, by keeping the Ten Commandments, or by some other method? Is God already working to make me holy, or do I need some special new experience of the Holy Spirit? Confusion about sanctification often leads to spiritual frustration. 'If God wants me to be perfect, then why am I so imperfect?' some Christians wonder. 'I keep committing the same sins over and over again. I know I'm not living the victorious Christian life; maybe I'm not really a Christian after all.'

Unfortunately, the variety of interpretations of Romans 6 tends to add to the confusion. Here Paul asks a rhetorical question: *We died to*

---

[2] Lev. 19:2.   [3] 1 Thess. 4:3a, 7.   [4] Matt. 5:48.
[5] Marquis de Condorcet, quoted in 'Forget Y2K!', *Smithsonian* (February 1999), p. 46.

sin; how can we live in it any longer? (6:2). For the perfectionist, this is proof that Christians do not sin – or, at least, that we do not commit any known sins. We are dead to sin, which means that we are so insensible and unresponsive to its temptations that we no longer succumb to it. Others admit that we do sin, but maintain that it is up to us to put sin to death. Sanctification, they say, is a matter of dying to sin day by day.

Crucified, buried and raised with Christ

The way to resolve this confusion is to see what the Bible actually teaches. When properly understood, Romans 6:2 contains the first key to unlocking the mysteries of sanctification: *We died to sin.* Each word is important. The word *we* shows that death to sin is something that all Christians experience. Like every other aspect of our salvation, sanctification is something for God's new people to share. The word *died* occurs in the past tense, thereby showing that in some way this has *already* occurred. And the words *to sin* show that somehow this death has dealt with the problem of our sin. But when, exactly, did we die to sin?

The Bible gives several clues. One is that the word *died* occurs in the aorist tense, which indicates an event that happened at some definite time in the past. Another clue is that the phrase *died to sin* appears again in verse 10, where it refers to Jesus Christ: *The death he died, he died to sin once for all.* Obviously, the Bible is speaking about the death Christ died on the cross, when 'while we were still sinners, Christ died for us' (5:8b). On the basis of these clues, we may deduce that we died to sin when Christ died to sin, on the very day of his crucifixion.

On that day at least four things were nailed to Calvary's cross. One was a sign announcing that Jesus of Nazareth was the King of the Jews. Another was Jesus himself, who was fixed to the cross with hammer and nails. The third thing was the debt of our sin, which God cancelled by nailing it to the cross.[6] The last thing that was nailed to the cross with Christ was every Christian: *For we know that our old self was crucified with him* (6:6). Or as Paul testified to the Galatians, 'I have been crucified with Christ and I no longer live'.[7] The Puritan William Perkins explained this verse by saying, 'We are in mind and meditation to consider Christ crucified: and first, we are to believe that he was crucified for us. This being done, we must go yet further, and as it were spread ourselves on the cross of Christ, believing and withall beholding ourselves crucified with him.'[8]

Take this one step further: not only were we crucified with Christ, but we were also buried with him. *Or don't you know that all of us who*

---

[6] Col. 2:13–14.   [7] Gal. 2:20a.
[8] Perkins, *A Commentary on Galatians*, p. 124.

were baptised into Christ Jesus were baptised into his death? We were therefore buried with him through baptism into death (6:3–4a).[9] To be baptized into Christ is to be personally identified with him in every way, including his burial. Water baptism thus signifies the termination of the old life (with the inauguration of the new). As it was for Christ, so it is for the Christian. We not only died with Christ, but we were also buried with him.

To understand why the Bible speaks this way it helps to remember the doctrine of union with Christ. The Christian is joined to Christ in a vital, unbreakable, spiritual union. Back in chapter 12 we identified this union as the source of every blessing of salvation. Union with Christ means that we are connected to Christ in the closest possible way. And because we are connected to Christ, we are also connected to everything he ever did for our salvation, including his death. To say that we died to sin is to say that *we died with Christ* (6:8), or that *we have been united with him in his death* (6:5a). Whenever we confess our faith using the words of the Apostles' Creed, we testify that Jesus 'was crucified, dead, and buried'. Sanctification begins with understanding that when Jesus was crucified, dead and buried, we were crucified, dead and buried with him.

But death is not the end, either for Christ or for us, so Paul goes on to say that Christ was raised from the dead, and that we were raised with him. He says it three times. The first is at the end of verse 4: *just as Christ was raised from the dead through the glory of the Father, we too may live a new life.* He says it again at the end of verse 5: *we will certainly also be united with him in his resurrection.* He says it yet once more in verse 8: *Now if we died with Christ, we believe that we will also live with him.* From the time of our conversion, when we are reborn by God's Spirit, we are united to Christ in both his crucifixion and his resurrection. He is the living Christ, and to be united to him is to receive the power of his life as well as the benefit of his death.

Dead to sin, alive in Christ

This is where sanctification starts, with the finished work of Christ – his death on the cross, his burial in the tomb, and his resurrection from the dead. Since these are the basic facts of the gospel,[10] it only makes sense that when we start to live by the gospel, we should start with the same basic facts. Spiritual growth is not based on something we think, feel or even do; it begins with something that Christ did for us on a rough piece of wood, in an empty stone tomb, and in the heavenly realms of glory.

The sanctification of the Christian thus follows the pattern of

---

[9] See Col. 2:12.   [10] 1 Cor. 15:3–4.

salvation in Christ. The historical must become experiential. First comes death. Once we were dead *in* sin. Now we have died *to* sin, just as Christ died to sin. This phrase is often misunderstood to mean that Christ died *for* our sins. That is true, of course, and our salvation depends on it, but that does not seem to be what is taught here. Instead, Romans 6:10 says, *The death he died, he died to sin once for all.* The verse says what it means and means what it says: Christ died *to* sin. In other words, the crucifixion ended his relationship to sin once and for all. While he was dying on the cross, Jesus was carrying all the sins of all his people: 'God made him who had no sin to be sin for us'.[11] In a way, at least during the time that he was on the cross, sin had a kind of power over him. It was for this reason that Jesus had to die, 'for the wages of sin is death' (6:23). But as soon as Jesus died he was done with sin for ever. From that time on, sin had no claim upon him, and thus had no power to hold him.

Something similar has happened to the Christian: *We died to sin* (6:2). Before we were saved by grace through faith, we were alive to sin, with all its perilous possibilities. We were so attached to our sins that we were unable to escape. Paul describes that former sinful life as *our old self* (6:6). In this case, the old self is not the sinful nature that continues to trouble us even after we come to Christ. Rather, it is the sinful life that we lived before we received the message of salvation; it is the whole person enslaved by sin. The only way to be free from 'the man we once were' (NEB) was to die to sin altogether. In the death of Christ we made a decisive, definitive, once-for-all break with the life of sin: *For we know that our old self was crucified with him* (6:6a).

The reason our old self was crucified was *that the body of sin might be done away with* (6:6b). The phrase *the body of sin* does not mean that the body is contaminated by sin, while the soul somehow remains pure. This is the ancient error of gnosticism, which denigrates the human body. The truth is that our bodies are beautiful, made in the image of God, and that sin comes from the deceit of our hearts. However, we are whole persons – body and soul – and sin has a way of gaining mastery over our bodies, using them to commit unrighteous deeds. The 'body of sin' is the unregenerate person 'conditioned and controlled by sin'.[12] The only way for us to be free from our slavery to sin is for our whole old self – body and soul – to be put to death. And not just put to death, but actually buried! The body of sin must be 'done away with', and what better way to remove a dead body permanently than to bury it in the ground? We were buried with Christ in order to entomb the corpse of our old sinful self.

The happy result of our death and burial is that we have been delivered from sin. Sin no longer exercises a controlling or dominating

[11] 2 Cor. 5:21a.
[12] Murray, *The Epistle to the Romans*, vol. 1, p. 220.

influence over us. *For we know that our old self was crucified with him so that the body of sin might be done away with, that we should no longer be slaves to sin – because anyone who has died has been freed from sin* (6:6–7; cf. 6:18). To translate the verse more literally, anyone who has died has been 'justified' from sin. The general principle here is that dead men cannot be slaves; the term of their enslavement ends at death. If we have died to sin, therefore, we can no longer live as if we are under its bondage. Our death and burial with Christ mean the end of our servitude to sin. God has joined us to Christ in his death and burial so that sin will no longer exercise its controlling power over us. We still struggle with sinful desires and inclinations, but from this point on they will not dominate us.

After the death and burial of the old self comes a whole new life of obedience to God. This new life comes from being united to Christ by faith: *Just as Christ was raised from the dead through the glory of the Father, we too may live a new life* (6:4); *Now if we died with Christ, we believe that we will also live with him* (6:8).[13] Union with Christ establishes a logical connection between life and death. Since there is only one Christ, anyone who is united to him in his crucifixion must also be united to him in his resurrection. Christ is the risen Saviour, and the new life we receive from him is resurrection life. It is a life that will never end, a life that we live unto God both now and for ever. *For we know that since Christ was raised from the dead, he cannot die again; death no longer has mastery over him … the life he lives, he lives to God* (6:9, 10b). We are now what Christ is: dead to sin and alive to God. Therefore, sanctification is a matter of death and life – death to sin and eternal life – *in Christ.* Jesus himself is our sanctification;[14] we are 'sanctified in Christ Jesus and called to be holy'.[15]

By virtue of being united to Christ in his death and resurrection, we have a new identity. We have been brought from the old life of sin into a new life of righteousness. John Stott compares the Christian's life, both old and new, to a two-volume biography:

> Our biography is written in two volumes. Volume one is the story of the old man, the old self, of me before my conversion. Volume two is the story of the new man, the new self, of me after I was made a new creation in Christ. Volume one of my biography ended with the judicial death of the old self. I was a sinner. I deserved to die. I did die. I received my deserts in my Substitute with whom I have become one. Volume two of my biography opened with my resurrection. My old life having finished, a new life to God has begun.[16]

---

[13] Cf. Eph. 2:4–5.   [14] 1 Cor. 1:30.   [15] 1 Cor. 1:2.
[16] Stott, *Men Made New*, p. 49.

Sanctification by faith

To this point, not one word has yet been said about anything we do. Sanctification has all been about Christ, and being united to him in his death and resurrection. Romans 6 does not tell us what to do; it tells us what we already know, which is why the word 'know' is repeated so often: *Don't you know?* (6:3); *For we know* (6:6, 9). Spiritual growth begins with knowing the message of salvation by grace, that God has delivered us from our bondage to sin by taking us out of Adam and joining us to Jesus Christ.

If that is the key to living the Christian life, then many Christians seem to have lost it. In our struggle to grow in godliness we try one method after another. We read books. We start ambitious programmes for personal devotions. We fast and pray, vowing never to commit the same old sins again. Yet nothing seems to work, and we end up feeling spiritually defeated. Often, the problem is not what we are doing so much as where we are starting. Sanctification based on human effort is bound to fail. Real progress in holiness starts with *knowing* that we are united to Christ in his death, burial and resurrection. The way we conquer sin is first by believing in what God did for us when he joined us to Christ in our conversion. Here is another way to say it: we are sanctified by faith. We do not become sanctified by trying a little harder to live a little better; we first become sanctified by believing the message of salvation. There is a hint of our need for faith in Romans 6:8: *we believe that we will also live with him.* There is an even clearer statement of it in the commission Jesus gave to Paul. Jesus said, 'I am sending you to them to open their eyes … so that they may receive … a place among those who are sanctified by faith in me.'[17] Sanctification comes by faith in the finished work of Jesus Christ.

We are not sanctified by faith alone, however. This is one of the great differences between justification and sanctification. As we have seen, justification *is* by faith alone. Our standing before God depends on the righteousness of Christ, imputed to us by faith, and thus has nothing to do with our own good works. Sanctification differs from justification in that it deals with *imparted* rather than imputed righteousness. When it comes to imparted righteousness – to actual progress in holiness, worked into us by God's Spirit – God has work for us to do. Thus sanctification demands works as well as faith. We are not saved *by* good works, but we are saved *for* them. 'For we are God's workmanship, created in Christ Jesus to do good works, which God prepared in advance for us to do.'[18]

Many of the biblical texts on sanctification teach that holiness is hard work. God's grace may be free, but it does not come cheap,

---

[17] Acts 26:17b–18.   [18] Eph. 2:10.

inasmuch as it demands costly discipleship. Remember Paul's words to the Philippians: 'Continue to work out your salvation with fear and trembling, for it is God who works in you to will and to act according to his good purpose.'[19] Or consider his exhortation that the Corinthians purify themselves 'from everything that contaminates body and spirit, perfecting holiness out of reverence for God'.[20] Again, the writer to the Hebrews implores us to 'Make every effort ... to be holy'.[21] Sanctification begins with faith, but faith leads to works. Although these works never provide the basis for our justification, they are always part of our sanctification.

The role that works play in our sanctification proves that there is more to salvation than justification. Justification frees us from the guilt and penalty of sin, but sanctification is required to free us from the power and pollution of sin. In justification, the righteousness of Christ is imputed to us; but in sanctification, it is actually imparted to us. God's justifying grace declares us righteous; but his sanctifying grace actually makes us righteous. Both aspects of salvation are absolutely necessary, and both come to us through union with Christ. As Calvin insisted,

We dream not of a faith which is devoid of good works, nor of a justification which can exist without them: the only difference is, that while we acknowledge that faith and works are necessarily connected, we, however, place justification in faith, not in works ... Because by faith we apprehend the righteousness of Christ, which alone reconciles us to God. This faith, however, you cannot apprehend without at the same time apprehending sanctification ... Christ, therefore, justifies no man without also sanctifying him ... Christ cannot be divided ... Thus it appears how true it is that we are justified not without, and yet not by works, since in the participation of Christ, by which we are justified, is contained not less sanctification than justification.[22]

You can count on it!

When it comes to working out our salvation, Romans 6 gives us plenty of work to do:

In the same way, count yourselves dead to sin but alive to God in Christ Jesus. Therefore do not let sin reign in your mortal body so that you obey its evil desires. Do not offer the parts of your body to sin, as instruments of

[19] Phil. 2:12b–13; cf. Eph. 2:10; Heb. 13:21.   [20] 2 Cor. 7:1.
[21] Heb. 12:14a; cf. 2 Pet. 1:5–7.
[22] Calvin, quoted in Sproul, *Faith Alone*, pp. 159–160.

wickedness, but rather offer yourselves to God, as those who have been brought from death to life; and offer the parts of your body to him as instruments of righteousness (6:11–13).

Significantly, these commands are the first 'do's and don'ts' in the entire book of Romans. After more than five chapters of proclamation, finally, some application. Romans 1 to 5 announced the good news of salvation from sin, by grace, through faith. Nearly all the verbs in those chapters were indicatives stating what is true about salvation in Christ. Romans 6 contains the book's first imperatives – that is to say, its first commands.

The striking thing about the very first imperative is that it takes us right back to all the indicatives: *Count yourselves dead to sin but alive to God in Christ* (6:11). Dead to sin but alive in Christ – this is precisely what Paul has been emphasizing since the beginning of the chapter. He has said it about six different times, in half a dozen different ways: having died to sin, we are alive in Christ. Now, when Paul finally tells us what to do, he tells us to count on what God has done! Therefore, even when we begin living for God's glory, we continue to depend on what God has done to save us by his grace.

The word *count* comes from the counting-house. The Greek term for it is *logizomai*, from which we derive English words like 'logarithm' and 'logistics'. It means 'to keep a log' the way an accountant does, to make a careful computation of all known assets. One of the basic principles of accounting is that a bookkeeper is allowed to count only the assets that are actually on account. The same principle holds true for our sanctification: we must consider ourselves to be what we actually are. And the one thing we know we can count on is this: that because we died to sin, we have a new life in Christ. Nothing can change the fact that 'we have been made holy through the sacrifice of the body of Jesus Christ once for all'.[23] This does not mean that we are immune to temptation, or that it is impossible for us to sin. It does mean, however, that we are dead to the old life and cannot go back to it. We are truly new if not yet totally transformed. The way to holiness begins with remembering who we are in Christ and pondering the great events of our salvation – reflecting on them, holding them before our minds, and in every way counting on them.

The Authorized Version translates the Greek word *logizomai* as 'to reckon' instead of 'to count'. This calls to mind the term 'dead reckoning' and suggests a helpful way to illustrate the gospel method of sanctification. The illustration comes from the days when the great ships sailed on the high seas. Under ideal conditions, a sailing vessel would establish its position by means of the sun and the stars. When

---

[23] Heb. 10:10; cf. 1 Cor. 6:11.

the weather was stormy, however, a ship might sail for days or even weeks without being able to get its bearings by direct observation. On these occasions the captain would sail by 'dead reckoning'. He would take out his ship's log, the detailed record of its voyage up that point, and he would continue to chart the ship's progress by keeping track of its speed and direction, with the help of his compass.

There are times when we must rely on 'dead reckoning' to chart our progress towards holiness. On occasion, we are uncertain of our spiritual progress, lost in the fog of sin or tossed by the high seas of doubt. The way to get our bearings is to go back to our ship's log, the gospel message of salvation, where it is plainly recorded that we died and rose with Christ. Even if we are not sure whether we are making any spiritual progress, and even if we cannot get our bearings by direct observation of our own godliness, we know where we have been. We have been with Christ on the cross, in the tomb and on to glory. By that reckoning, we are dead to sin and alive to God. There is no need to doubt our sanctification, still less our salvation. We can count on where we have been, and all we need to do now is to point ourselves to Jesus Christ, the true north of the soul, and continue our voyage.

The war within

Some theologians use the term 'definitive sanctification' to describe the once-for-all break with the old life of sin that takes place at conversion.[24] In principle, we become holy the moment we are united to the life-giving Christ by faith, and from that moment forward there will be progress – however unsteady – toward holiness. Thus there are two aspects of sanctification: definitive and progressive. The writer to the Hebrews brings both aspects together when he contends that 'by one sacrifice he [Christ] has made perfect for ever those who are being made holy'.[25] As far as definitive sanctification is concerned, we have been 'made perfect for ever'. Yet we are also 'being made holy', in practice as well as in principle. This does not happen all at once, of course; hence the term 'progressive sanctification'. The *Westminster Shorter Catechism* describes this process well when it defines sanctification as 'the work of God's free grace, whereby we are renewed in the whole man after the image of God, and are enabled more and more to die unto sin, and live unto righteousness' (A. 35).

In order to help us make 'more and more' progress in our sanctification, there are two more things we must do, one negative and the other positive. This is typical of the biblical teaching on sanctification,

---

[24] See especially Murray, 'Definitive sanctification' and 'The agency in definitive sanctification', in *Collected Writings of John Murray*, vol. 2, pp. 277–293, and also White, *The Fight*, pp. 182–188.

[25] Heb. 10:14; cf. 1 John 3:3.

which often pairs the positive with the negative. Sometimes the Bible speaks in terms of old and new creation: 'If anyone is in Christ, he is a new creation; the old has gone, the new has come!'[26] On other occasions it speaks of old and new selves: 'You were taught, with regard to your former way of life, to put off your old self, which is being corrupted by its deceitful desires; to be made new in the attitude of your minds; and to put on the new self, created to be like God in true righteousness and holiness.'[27]

Here in Romans 6, progressive sanctification is described in terms of not offering ourselves to sin, but offering ourselves to God. Negatively, we must resist the tyranny of sin with everything we have, refusing to put ourselves in its service: *Therefore do not let sin reign in your mortal body so that you obey its evil desires. Do not offer the parts of your body to sin, as instruments of wickedness … For sin shall not be your master* (6:12–13a, 14a). Since the word *instruments* is a word for weaponry, the picture comes from the military. Like an evil commandant, sin wants to deploy us in its war against God. Our 'mortal bodies' are mentioned specifically because sin has a way of getting hold of our physical person. There are some sins we feel almost physically compelled to commit. But we must resist. In effect, Paul is saying, 'Don't become the devil's tool. Do not let sinful desire lead you to use your body parts to commit unrighteous acts. If you belong to Jesus Christ, sin is not your commanding officer … so don't let it order you around.'

The fact that evil desires must be resisted implies that sanctification will always be a struggle. The reason God tells us not to let sin reign is that it is always trying to do so! We are dead to sin, and alive to God, but that does not mean that we find it easy to be holy. Many passages of Scripture speak of the Christian's perpetual warfare with the sinful nature. There is a good example in the very next chapter: 'When I want to do good, evil is right there with me. For in my inner being I delight in God's law; but I see another law at work in the members of my body, waging war against the law of my mind' (7:21b–23a).[28] Paul's words to the Galatians were to the same effect: 'For the sinful nature desires what is contrary to the Spirit, and the Spirit what is contrary to the sinful nature. They are in conflict with each other, so that you do not do what you want.'[29] Peter also warns us, 'Abstain from sinful desires, which war against your soul.'[30] The old self is dead and buried, but the sinful nature is still fighting for life. We should not be surprised, therefore, to find ourselves battling against sin. We may be God's new people, but we are still fighting our old natures. We are caught up in what the

[26] 2 Cor. 5:17.   [27] Eph. 4:22–24; cf. Col. 3:9–10.
[28] Not all commentators agree that Romans 7 describes the ongoing struggle with sin in the life of the believer. For a helpful summary of alternative interpretations, together with a defence of the view taken here, see Boice, *Romans*, vol. 2, pp. 755–762.
[29] Gal. 5:17.   [30] 1 Pet. 2:11b.

Westminster Confession of Faith calls 'a continual and irreconcilable war' (XIII.ii), and we will not be made perfect until we get to glory. In the meantime, we must rebel against sin's tyranny with everything we have.

The war the Christian wages against the sinful nature is mortal combat. Another term used to describe the negative aspect of our sanctification is *mortification*, which simply means the putting to death of sin. As we have seen, we ourselves have already died to sin. Yet the Bible also teaches that sin itself must be killed. Paul later exhorts the Romans to 'put to death the misdeeds of the body' (8:13b). Or again, he commands the Colossians: 'Put to death, therefore, whatever belongs to your earthly nature: sexual immorality, impurity, lust, evil desires and greed, which is idolatry.'[31] We died to sin in the death of Christ. Now we must put sin to death as we live for Christ. The Puritans called this 'the wasting away of sin'.[32] What it means is that we must keep our sin fixed to the cross until it expires.

Our ongoing struggle against indwelling sin does not mean that we are not yet saved, or that we have not yet died to sin. Quite the opposite. It is just because we are free from sin that we must fight so fiercely against it. Our battle for holiness is actually a sign that sin's dominion has ended and that God is beginning to reign. John Murray writes,

> There is a total difference between surviving sin and reigning sin, the regenerate in conflict with sin and the unregenerate complacent to sin. It is one thing for sin to live in us: it is another for us to live in sin. It is one thing for the enemy to occupy the capital; it is another for his defeated hosts to harass the garrisons of the kingdom. It is of paramount concern for the Christian and for the interests of his sanctification that he should know that sin does not have the dominion over him, that the forces of redeeming, regenerative, and sanctifying grace have been brought to bear upon him.[33]

The more intense the struggle, the greater the progress in holiness. To quote again from Murray:

> If there is still sin to any degree in one who is indwelt by the Holy Spirit, then there is tension, yes, contradiction, within the heart of that person. Indeed, the more sanctified the person is, the more conformed he is to the image of his Saviour, the more he must recoil against every lack of conformity to the holiness of God. The deeper

[31] Col. 3:5.
[32] Ames, *The Marrow of Theology*, XXIX.18 (p. 170).
[33] Murray, *Redemption: Accomplished and Applied*, pp. 145–146.

his apprehension of the majesty of God, the greater the intensity of his love to God, the more persistent his yearning for the attainment of the prize of the high calling of God in Christ Jesus, the more conscious will he be of the gravity of the sin which remains and the more poignant will be his detestation of it.[34]

A whole self offered to God

There is a positive as well as a negative side to our sanctification: *Do not offer the parts of your body to sin, as instruments of wickedness, but rather offer yourselves to God, as those who have been brought from death to life; and offer the parts of your body to him as instruments of righteousness* (6:13b). We offer ourselves not to sin, but to God. We have something better to do with our bodies than to volunteer them for Satan's service. We are alive from the dead because God has given himself to us in Christ. Now we can offer ourselves back to God in real gospel holiness.

What we offer to God is nothing less than our whole selves, including every part of the very same bodies that once were buried with Christ. We must offer God renewed minds, which are ready to think his thoughts after him. We must offer him willing hands that are ready to do his work. We must offer him gentle tongues that have been tamed to say what is good and true. We must offer him eyes that do not wander, and feet that are willing to travel in his right path. We must offer him passionate hearts that beat with his love. In short, we must offer our whole selves to God, and not to sin. As Paul will later say in Romans: 'Therefore, I urge you, brothers, in view of God's mercy, to offer your bodies as living sacrifices, holy and pleasing to God – this is your spiritual act of worship' (12:1).

The positive side of our sanctification – in which we offer our whole selves to God – is sometimes called *vivification*, which simply means coming to spiritual life. At the same time that the sinful nature is being put to death, the regenerate nature is being brought to life. This life-giving process is the work of the triune God – Father, Son and Holy Spirit. The ultimate author of this revivifying work is God the Father: 'May God himself, the God of peace, sanctify you through and through.'[35] Therefore, to live the sanctified life is to be infused with the holiness of God. The active agent of this revivifying work is the Holy Spirit, for 'God chose you to be saved through the sanctifying work of the Spirit'.[36] Therefore, to live the sanctified life is to be animated by God's Spirit. The perfect pattern for this revivifying work is Jesus Christ, for 'we ... are being transformed into his likeness with ever-increasing glory, which comes from the Lord, who is the Spirit.'[37]

[34] Murray, *Redemption*, p. 145.   [35] 1 Thess. 5:23.
[36] 2 Thess. 2:13b; cf. 1 Pet. 1:2.   [37] 2 Cor. 3:18b; cf. Rom. 8:29.

Therefore, to live the sanctified life is to live like Christ, and thereby to recover the divine image defaced by humanity's fall into sin. Finally, the gracious means of this revivifying work are prayer, the sacraments, and the ministry of God's Word. To live the sanctified life is to be made holy by God's true Word.[38] As we study the Bible (especially God's law, which instructs us in righteousness), receive the sacrament of communion and meet with God in prayer, the Spirit produces spiritual growth leading towards spiritual maturity.

This is why God saved us: to glorify him with ever-increasing holiness. It is also why Jesus died for us: 'He himself bore our sins in his body on the tree, so that we might die to sins and live for righteousness'.[39] It is unthinkable for anyone who has received such a great salvation to want to continue in sin:

> And shall we then go on to sin,
>   that grace may more abound?
> Great God, forbid that such a thought
>   should in our breast be found!
>
> With Christ the Lord we dy'd to sin;
>   with him to life we rise,
> To life, which now begun on earth,
>   is perfect in the skies.
>
> Too long enthrall'd to Satan's sway,
>   we now are slaves no more;
> For Christ hath vanquish'd death and sin,
>   our freedom to restore.

God has restored our freedom by giving us the best possible motivation for godliness. We obey God not in order to be saved, but because we have been saved already, brought from death to life by the grace of God.

One young woman who died to sin in order to live for Christ was Cassie Bernall. On 20 April 1999, Cassie was killed in the library of Columbine High School in Colorado. Some consider her a martyr. Two of her classmates had gone on a violent rampage, setting off bombs and shooting machine guns. When they came to Cassie, who was lying face down under a table, they asked her if she believed in God. 'Yes,' she said, according to most accounts, and then they shot her. Miss Bernall was an unlikely martyr. During her early teenage years she had begun to dabble in witchcraft. Yet she continued to attend church, and it was on a church youth retreat that she first believed the message of

---

[38] John 17:17, 19.   [39] 1 Pet. 2:24a; cf. Titus 2:14.

salvation. From that time forward she counted herself dead to sin and alive to God in Christ. As she later wrote in her diary:

> Now I have given up on everything else – I found it to be the only way to know Christ and to experience the mighty power that brought Him to life again, and to find out what it really means to suffer and to die with Him. So, whatever it takes, I will be one who lives in the fresh newness of life of those who are alive from the dead.[40]

---

[40] Cassie Bernall, quoted in the tract 'She said Yes' (Wheaton, IL: Good News, 1999).

17. Suffering a little while
Perseverance: 1 Peter 1:1–9

Nothing raises more questions about God than human suffering. C. S. Lewis (1898–1963) called this 'the problem of pain', and defined it as follows: 'If God were good, he would wish to make his creatures perfectly happy, and if God were almighty he would be able to do what he wished. But the creatures are not happy. Therefore, God lacks either the goodness, or the power, or both. This is the problem of pain, in its simplest form.'[1]

The problem of suffering becomes especially acute in an age of technological advance. We live in a world of wonders, yet it remains a world of woe. For the unbeliever, this raises doubts about God's existence and nature. Malcolm Muggeridge observed that for the non-Christian,

> suffering is … an inflamed nerve which, touched, gives rise to howls of rage and anguish, especially today. Surely, when we can go to the moon, and ride through space faster than light; when our very genes are counted, and our organs replaceable; when we can arrange to eat without growing fat, to copulate without procreation, to flash a gleaming smile without being happy – surely suffering should be banished from our lives. That *we* should have to go on suffering, and watch others suffering, is an outrage; and a deity who, having the power to stop it, still allowed it to continue, would be a monster, not a loving God.[2]

For the Christian, the problem of suffering is slightly different. Even if we are unable to explain the origin of evil, we know that God is not a monster. He is the God of all grace, who saves us in his love. We also know that much of our pain is self-induced, the product of human sin (see chapter 2), and therefore that God is not to blame.

[1] Lewis, *The Problem of Pain*, p. 14.
[2] Malcolm Muggeridge, *Something Beautiful for God* (London: Collins, 1971), p. 131.

But we still have questions that challenge our faith, and one of the most difficult is this: if we are saved by grace, then why do we still suffer?

Saved, yet suffering

The question 'Why do we still suffer?' is a question the first Christians posed to the apostles. They had been delivered from sin and death through the crucifixion and resurrection of Jesus Christ. They were God's new people, a community established to spread God's love throughout the world. Yet they were persecuted and oppressed, battered and beaten, imprisoned and even crucified. There were times when they wondered if it was all worth it. What is the point of being saved, if not to be saved from suffering?

The apostle Peter wrote his first letter to address the problem of pain. 'Dear friends,' he wrote, 'do not be surprised at the painful trial you are suffering, as though something strange were happening to you' (1 Pet. 4:12). Apparently, the early church *was* surprised. It seemed strange to them that they had to endure so many painful trials. There are times when we are surprised, too, when it seems strange to have to suffer. At such times we need to remember that suffering is not unexpected. Indeed, it is part of our salvation, for God does not save us from suffering, but through suffering into glory.

From the very beginning of 1 Peter, suffering is placed in the context of salvation. Peter opens by saying, *Grace ... be yours in abundance* (1:2b). The kind of grace he has in mind is God's saving grace for sinners. With a deep sense of joy, he reminds us that salvation is ours in Jesus Christ. Salvation begins with sovereign election; we have been *chosen according to the foreknowledge of God the Father.* It includes sanctification; we are saved *through the sanctifying work of the Spirit, for obedience to Jesus Christ.* This sanctifying work is based on the atonement, the *sprinkling by his blood* (1:2a). These are the great doctrines of salvation by grace: election by the Father, redemption by the Son, and sanctification by the Spirit.

Peter goes on to explain that God has made this salvation ours through regeneration: *In his great mercy he has given us new birth into a living hope* (1:3; cf. 1:23). Our newborn life is generated *through the resurrection of Jesus Christ from the dead,* and it holds the promise of eternity: *an inheritance that can never perish, spoil or fade – kept in heaven* (1:3b–4). This glorious and indestructible inheritance is as secure as the promises of God, who has promised to keep it safe for us in heaven. It will become our possession at *the coming of the salvation that is ready to be revealed in the last time* (1:5), but the way to receive it right now is by trusting in Jesus Christ: 'Through him you believe in God, who raised him from the dead and glorified him, and so your faith and hope are in God' (1:21). In short, what Peter wrote to the church was the same message he preached at Pentecost in Acts 2, and which we have been studying throughout this book: the message of salvation by grace through faith.

This saving message brings joy to everyone who receives it. Peter exclaims, *Praise be to the God and Father of our Lord Jesus Christ!* (1:3a); *In this you greatly rejoice* (1:6). What Peter means by *this* is the coming of salvation. The Christian's great joy is to know that salvation is ready, and that when it comes, it will bring full and final deliverance from God's wrath against sin.

The painful presence of suffering

In the meantime, however, there will be suffering: *now for a little while you may have had to suffer grief in all kinds of trials* (1:6). Christians sometimes expect salvation to be the end of all their troubles. One day it will be, but in the meantime, suffering is a painful presence in the Christian life. Indeed, the pain of our existence partly explains the joy of our salvation: we rejoice because we can hardly wait for our troubles to be over. When Peter said, *In this you greatly rejoice*, he meant that our joy comes from knowing that when our salvation is fully revealed, we will never suffer again. *In the last time* (1:5) – *the* time, the time of greatest tribulation – Christ will come to save us.

The Bible is honest about the painful reality of suffering, even for Christians. Jesus said to his disciples, 'In this world you will have trouble.'[3] Eventually Peter learned from his own experience that when Jesus said 'trouble', he meant all kinds of trouble. He does not mention any specifics here, but when Peter speaks of suffering *grief in all kinds of trials* (1:6), he obviously intends to include every kind of suffering there is. His point is not so much how often we suffer, but how many different ways we suffer.

Our sufferings are manifold. We suffer all the little disappointments of life – the minor inconveniences and the short-term setbacks. Young or old, man or woman, married or single, black or white – there is not one person who does not suffer. We suffer hunger and home-lessness. We suffer unfulfilled dreams and unsatisfied desires. Whether it is painful abuse or debilitating disease, lonely isolation or hateful prejudice, personal failure or tedious boredom, we all experience the futility of life on a fallen planet. Some of our sufferings are undeserved, as Peter recognized (2:19). The world is so shattered by sin that suffering is the background music of our existence. The Bible says that creation itself is groaning under the weight of suffering, frustrated by its bondage to decay.[4] Homes are destroyed by fire and flood. Towns are

---

[3] John 16:33.   [4] Rom. 8:19–22.

struck by tornados and mud-slides. Islands are flooded by hurricanes. Cities are shaken by earthquakes and covered with volcanic ash. Entire nations are blasted by warfare and choked by famine. Everywhere in the world people suffer loss, injury and death.

Christians are not exempt from these sufferings. As we mentioned back in chapter 11, believers in Jesus Christ should not expect miraculous deliverance from common problems. And in addition to the trials everyone must endure, Christians also suffer persecution. Peter called this 'suffering as a Christian' (4:16). He had been warned about it by Jesus himself, who said, 'You will be handed over to be persecuted and put to death, and you will be hated by all nations because of me'.[5] This prophecy has been proven true over and over again: 'Everyone who wants to live a godly life in Christ Jesus will be persecuted'.[6] From the very first days of the church, God's new people have been oppressed, beaten, imprisoned, tortured and put to death. Peter was writing from Rome to Christians who were burned by flames and devoured by lions under the imperial tyranny of Nero. As history draws ever closer to its destiny, our sufferings seem to be getting worse. More Christians were killed for their faith in Christ during the twentieth century than in all previous centuries combined.

Given our history, it is not surprising that the biblical word for 'witness' is also the term for 'martyr'. Anyone who lives for Christ must be prepared to die for him. Perhaps death is what Peter especially had in mind when he spoke of *grief in all kinds of trials*. Grief is the heaviness of spirit that accompanies any loss, but which we associate primarily with loss through death, our 'last enemy'.[7]

When the Bible speaks of suffering *grief in all kinds of trials*, it includes everything we suffer as we live for Christ. It recognizes that these trials, with all the pain and distress they bring, are a present reality. Now, for a little while, we have to suffer grief in all kinds of trials. Peter knew this to be true from his own experience, for he had many troubles of his own. He witnessed the unhappy events leading up to Jesus' crucifixion. Under duress, he denied Christ three times. He was seized and imprisoned for preaching the gospel. Although he was delivered by angels, he knew – because Jesus had told him – that one day he would stretch out his hands to die.[8] Christian tradition maintains that Peter indeed was crucified at Rome. Given his experiences, it is not at all surprising that he wrote a letter telling the church not to be surprised by suffering.

The christological pattern of suffering

One man who suffered grief in all kinds of trials was the German Carl

---

[5] Matt. 24:9.　[6] 2 Tim. 3:12.　[7] 1 Cor. 15:26.　[8] John 21:18–19.

Goerdeler, who was imprisoned and executed for his involvement in the conspiracy to assassinate Adolf Hitler. Goerdeler's prison diary shows that he spent his final days struggling to understand the horrors he had witnessed:

> In sleepless nights I have often asked myself whether a God exists who shares in the personal fate of men. It is becoming hard to believe this. For this God must for years have allowed rivers of blood and suffering, and mountains of horror and despair for mankind to take place ... He must have allowed millions of decent men to die and suffer without lifting a finger. Is this meant to be a judgment? ... Like the Psalmist, I am angry with God, because I cannot under-stand him ... And yet through Christ I am still looking for the merciful God.[9]

Goerdeler was looking in the right place, for when we look to Christ we see that our suffering is fashioned after his suffering. As we learned from Dorothy L. Sayers back in chapter 1, the answer to the question, 'What is the meaning of all this suffering?' is 'Christ crucified'.[10] For the Christian, suffering follows a christological pattern. Peter mentions this pattern in 1:11, where he refers to 'the sufferings of Christ and the glories that would follow'.[11] The humiliation and the exaltation of Christ set the pattern for the Christian: through suffering into glory.

Jesus suffered throughout his whole life. As the Bible says, he was 'a man of sorrows, and familiar with suffering'.[12] It started with his birth, for even to be born was to suffer. In his divine being the Son had lived in glory from eternity past. But when he became a human being, he had to suffer all the weakness and weariness of life in a human body. He was hungry, tired and thirsty. Homeless, he wandered on earth. He was despised and rejected. People plotted against him and tried to stone him. Then, finally, as Peter himself had witnessed, they stripped him, beat him and crucified him. From birth to death, 'Christ suffered in his body' (4:1).

If that is what happened to Christ, then what do you suppose will happen to the Christian? We are united to Christ by faith, and the Christ to whom we have been united was a suffering, bleeding man. The obvious implication is that we, too, will suffer. 'If they persecuted me,' Jesus said, 'they will persecute you also.'[13] Therefore, to be united to Christ is to be united to him in his sufferings. Later Peter will call this 'participating in the sufferings of Christ' (4:13). The apostle Paul

---

[9] Carl Goerdeler, quoted in McGrath, *Luther's Theology of the Cross*, p. 180.
[10] Dorothy L. Sayers, quoted in Janice Brown, *The Seven Deadly Sins in the Work of Dorothy L. Sayers* (Kent, OH: Kent State University Press, 1998), p.1.
[11] Cf. Luke 24:26.   [12] Is. 53:3.   [13] John 15:20.

described it as 'the fellowship of sharing in his sufferings',[14] and described how 'the sufferings of Christ flow over into our lives'.[15] The point is that the Christian life is patterned after the life of Christ, suffering and all. We do not suffer in spite of our salvation, but precisely because of it. Christian theology is a theology of the cross, and the Christian life is a life lived under the cross. As Martin Luther said in his *Heidelberg Disputation*, 'God can be found only in suffering and the cross.'[16]

Suffering is one of the high privileges of the Christian life. Paul went so far as to consider it a divine gift: 'For it has been granted to you on behalf of Christ not only to believe on him, but also to suffer for him'.[17] What gives meaning to our suffering is our self-conscious connection with the sufferings of Christ. We suffer in solidarity with the one who took our sufferings upon himself. The British medical doctor Helen Roseveare has given eloquent testimony to the sense of privilege she experienced as she suffered for Christ. Dr Roseveare worked for many years as a medical missionary in Zaire. During the revolution of the 1960s, she often faced brutal beatings and other forms of physical torture. On one occasion, when she was on the verge of being executed, she momentarily feared that God had forsaken her. Yet in that moment she sensed that the Holy Spirit was reminding her of her calling as a Christian: 'Twenty years ago you asked Me for the privilege of being a missionary, the privilege of being identified with Me. This is it. Don't you want it? This is what it means. These are not your sufferings; they are My sufferings. All I ask of you is the loan of your body.' As a result of this reminder, Dr Roseveare was overwhelmed with the privilege of serving Christ through her sufferings. After she was delivered, she wrote: 'He didn't stop the sufferings. He didn't stop the wickedness, the cruelties, the humiliation or anything. It was all there. The pain was just as bad. The fear was just as bad. But it was altogether different. It was in Jesus, for Him, with Him.'[18]

As we share in the sufferings of Christ, we may be sure that God understands what it is like for us to suffer. Edward Shillito has written:

> The other gods were strong; but thou wast weak;
> They rode, but thou didst stumble to a throne;
> But to our wounds only God's wounds can speak,
> And not a god has wounds, but thou alone.[19]

[14] Phil. 3:10; cf. Rom. 8:17.   [15] 2 Cor. 1:5.
[16] Martin Luther, *Heidelberg Disputation*, quoted in *Modern Reformation* (March/April 1999), p. 15.
[17] Phil. 1:29.
[18] Helen Roseveare, recounted in Boice, *The Gospel of John*, pp. 1212–1213.
[19] Edward Shillito, 'Jesus of the scars', quoted in Stott, *The Cross of Christ*, p. 337.

This is what is meant by compassion, which literally means 'a suffering with'. To say that God is the 'Father of compassion'[20] is to say that he suffers with us, not in his eternal being (which is a common error of postmodern theology), but through Jesus Christ, the God-man. Alister McGrath writes:

> God suffered in Christ. He *knows* what it is like to experience pain. He has travelled down the road of pain, abandonment, suffering and death ... God is not like some alleged hero ... who demands that others suffer, while remaining aloof from the world of pain himself. He has passed through the shadow of suffering himself. The God in whom Christians believe and hope is a God who himself suffered.[21]

If Christ is our pattern, then there is much to learn from his sufferings: 'Christ suffered for you, leaving you an example, that you should follow in his steps' (1 Pet. 2:21). Consider Jesus' response to suffering at the tomb of his dear friend Lazarus. After a brief illness, Lazarus had suddenly died. To the dismay of the deceased man's family and friends, Jesus arrived too late to heal him, and the community was already in mourning. When Jesus saw them weeping, he himself wept. The Bible states that 'he was deeply moved in spirit and troubled'.[22] When Jesus was confronted with human suffering in the face of death, he experienced two powerful emotions: sorrow and anger. The Greek word used to describe his emotions (*embrimaomai*) speaks of righteous indignation. To put it literally, Jesus groaned with fury over the painful realities of death and suffering.

When we think of Jesus at the tomb of Lazarus, weeping and raging at death, we begin to understand that he struggled with suffering as much as we do. As he pondered this episode from Jesus' life, the Christian apologist Francis Schaeffer wrote,

> To me, what Jesus did at the tomb of Lazarus sets the world on fire ... Jesus came to the tomb of Lazarus. The One who claims to be God stood before the tomb, and the Greek language makes it very clear he had two emotions. The first was tears for Lazarus, but the second emotion was anger. He was furious; and he could be furious at the abnormality of death without being furious with Himself as God. This is tremendous ... When I look at evil – the cruelty which is abnormal to that which God made – my reaction should be the same. I am able not only to cry over the evil, but I can be angry at the evil ... I have a basis to fight the thing which is abnormal to what God originally made.[23]

[20] 2 Cor. 1:3.   [21] McGrath, *Bridge-Building*, p. 144.   [22] John 11:33.
[23] Schaeffer, *Escape from Reason*, in *The Complete Works of Francis A. Schaeffer*, vol. 1, pp. 301–302.

It is not surprising if suffering produces sorrow and anger. It ought to! Jesus experienced the same emotions himself, and we are sharing in his sufferings. Nor is it wrong to ask questions about the problem of pain. This is another thing to learn from our Lord's example. Even Jesus had a question or two about suffering. Remember his agonizing question from the cross: 'My God, my God, why have you forsaken me?'[24] It is the same question we ask when we cannot comprehend our suffering: Why, God? We may never understand what it meant for the Son to be forsaken by the Father. But at least we know that Jesus faced up to all the hard questions about human suffering. He not only raged against the sufferings of a dying humanity, and shed sympathetic tears over them, but he actually experienced them in such an intense way that it made him ask for an explanation from the cross.

The redemptive purpose of suffering

If suffering is the question, then what is the answer? Do our troubles accomplish anything? What is the explanation for our tribulation? Is there any solution to the problem of pain? These questions are hard for anyone to answer, but they are much harder to answer without Jesus Christ. In Christ, God has entered into the sufferings of humanity. But without Christ, what answer can we give to the problem of pain? For the unbeliever, suffering has no ultimate purpose. One thinks of the anguished cry of the French poet, Charles Baudelaire (1821–67), who cried out, 'Behave, O my pain!' Baudelaire's problem was that his pain refused to behave. Pain never does behave, and the unbeliever is faced with the absurdity of senseless suffering.

Christians struggle with suffering, too, but we know that suffering is part of God's saving plan for us, which makes all the difference. Throughout his letter Peter explains the various purposes of suffering in the Christian life. Suffering is a *tether*; it ties us more closely to Christ. Suffering is a *testimony*; it affords us the opportunity to display God's grace in time of trial. Suffering is a *teacher*; it instructs us in humility and righteousness. As the psalmist wrote, 'Before I was afflicted I went astray, but now I obey your word.'[25] Suffering is a *trainer*; it prepares us for glory. Nor is Peter's list complete. According to Hebrews, suffering is the way God disciplines his true sons and daughters.[26] As Jesus said, 'Those whom I love I rebuke and discipline.'[27] This chastisement is neither punitive nor destructive, but redemptive. 'God disciplines us for our good, that we may share in his holiness.'[28]

Suffering has many salutary purposes in the Christian life. In one way or another, it always displays the glory of God. One day we will be

---

[24] Matt. 27:46. [25] Ps. 119:67. [26] Heb. 12:5–11. [27] Rev. 3:19.
[28] Heb. 12:10b.

glorified through suffering, just as Jesus was.[29] 'In bringing many sons to glory, it was fitting that God, for whom and through whom everything exists, should make the author of their salvation perfect through suffering.'[30] The English preacher and poet John Donne (1573–1631) once wrote, 'No man hath affliction enough that is not matured and ripened by it, and made fit for God by that affliction.' Indeed, it is hard to identify any experience that is a greater stimulus to spiritual growth than the experience of suffering. The flowers of holiness are watered by the tears of affliction.

Suffering has so many purposes that it is not always possible to tell what God is trying to accomplish in any particular trial. But there is one thing suffering almost always does for believers, and that is to prove the genuineness of our faith. Peter introduces this theme at the beginning of his letter. Referring to the grief that we suffer 'in all kinds of trials', he explains that *these have come so that your faith – of greater worth than gold, which perishes even though refined by fire – may be proved genuine and may result in praise, glory and honour when Jesus Christ is revealed* (1:7; cf. 4:12).

The basis for Peter's comparison is that both gold and faith are purified by fire. According to the standard practice of metallurgy, golden ore is refined by burning away its impurities until nothing is left but pure gold. In the divine alchemy, our faith is purified in much the same way. It takes 'the furnace of affliction'[31] to burn away our self-reliance, so that nothing remains except absolute trust in God.

The reason a miner takes so much trouble to refine gold is that it is so valuable. Pure gold is among the most precious of metals. Yet as precious as it is, it will not last for ever. One day it will be lost or stolen, which is why Jesus warned us not to make a foolish investment: 'Do not store up for yourselves treasures on earth, where moth and rust destroy, and where thieves break in and steal.'[32] Even if we could gather an enormous pile of gold, and hoard it until the end of our lives, we would have to leave it all behind when we die. Faith is infinitely more precious than gold because it will never perish. It is by faith that we store up 'treasures in heaven, where moth and rust do not destroy, and where thieves do not break in and steal'.[33] Thus it is by faith that we make the best investment, laying hold of glory, with all its splendours. An ounce of pure faith is worth more than all the gold in the world.

If faith is so much more precious than gold, then one would expect it to go through an even more intense process of refinement. And so it does. This is the point of Peter's comparison. Our faith must pass through many burning and fiery trials before we are ready for glory. Suffering is the crucible of faith. If our faith is false, it will be consumed

---

[29] Heb. 5:8–9.   [30] Heb. 2:10.   [31] Is. 48:10, AV.   [32] Matt. 6:19.
[33] Matt. 6:20.

by the fire. But if it is genuine, it will come out shining like pure gold. In the words of a hymn by Margaret Clarkson:

> O Father, You are sovereign,
> The Lord of human pain,
> Transmuting earthly sorrows
> To gold of heavenly gain.[34]

The purpose of suffering, then, is to verify our faith. Suffering is the touchstone God uses to prove that our faith is golden. We are tested not to see if our faith will fail, but to prove that by God's grace it cannot fail. When we find that we are still holding on to Christ, in spite of our many sufferings, we may be sure of our salvation, which will *result in praise, glory and honour when Jesus Christ is revealed* (1:7). Suffering looks forward to glory, not only for Christ, but also for us.

Persevering through suffering

It is not easy to hold on to Christ, especially when life is hard and suffering seems more than we can bear. The Christian life is difficult, and we can expect to suffer grief in all kinds of trials. But by the grace of God we must persevere, because that is what Jesus did. He did not leave a question mark hanging over his cross. There were times when suffering brought Jesus to tears, or aroused his anger, or even raised a question, but he persevered to the very end in order to finish the work of our salvation. With his dying words, he committed his spirit to his Father.[35] For the glory set before him, he 'endured the cross'.[36] If Jesus endured, then we must endure, even when our suffering seems unjust (see 2:19). Perseverance is part of what it means to follow the christological pattern of suffering. In *Cry, the Beloved Country*, Alan Paton's novel about life in South Africa, Kumalo learns this profound lesson from his friend Msimangu, who said, 'I have never thought that a Christian would be free of suffering. For our Lord suffered. And I come to believe that he suffered, not to save us from suffering, but to teach us how to bear suffering. For he knew that there is no life without suffering.'[37]

We must and we will persevere! Peter tells us that through faith we *are shielded by God's power until the coming of the salvation that is ready to be revealed in the last time* (1:5). The picture is of a city under siege, surrounded and attacked by enemies. Yet the city is preserved and protected by a garrison of mighty soldiers. In times of suffering, the

---

[34] Margaret Clarkson, quoted in Stott, *The Cross of Christ*, p. 324.
[35] Luke 23:46.   [36] Heb. 12:2.
[37] Alan Paton, *Cry, the Beloved Country* (New York: Macmillan, 1987), p. 227.

Christian is like a city under siege, attacked by fear and doubt. But faith is the believer's garrison, and no matter how desperate the situation becomes, a faith that has been proved genuine will not fail. Such a faith *cannot* fail, because it holds on to Jesus Christ, and *he* cannot fail. True believers never finally fall away; they always persevere to the end because Christ always preserves them.

What Peter says about faith and perseverance captures both sides of the biblical doctrine of the perseverance of the saints. By the preserving power of God's grace, the Christian will persevere through suffering into glory. Ultimately, it is God who perseveres, preserving us and protecting us to the very end. As Peter puts it, we are *shielded by God's power until the coming of salvation* (1:5). God has placed us in his protective custody. We are 'kept by Jesus Christ'.[38] Thus our eternal security does not depend primarily on our holding on to God, but on his holding on to us. Nevertheless, we must hold on, which is why Peter says that we are shielded *through faith* (1:5). We must persevere, for as Jesus said, 'he who stands firm to the end will be saved'.[39] And like everything else in the Christian life, perseverance is by faith. We are kept by God through faith unto salvation.

The doctrine of perseverance is a great comfort because it guarantees that a true believer will never fully or permanently fall away. In the words of the *Westminster Confession of Faith*, 'They whom God hath accepted in his Beloved, effectually called and sanctified by his Spirit, can neither totally nor finally fall away from the state of grace; but shall certainly persevere therein to the end, and be eternally saved' (XVII.1). True, many people who claim to be Christians will fall away. But not all professing Christians are believing Christians, and when suffering comes, those who were never truly saved by grace cannot endure the fiery trial. By contrast, it is impossible for those who have been saved by grace through faith to lose their salvation. Jesus promised that he would lose none of his elect people,[40] that no-one could snatch us out of his Father's hand.[41] No-one knew this better than Peter, for he himself had fallen away. Three times he denied the Christ. Yet Christ had prayed for him that his faith would not fail,[42] and in the end Peter repented for his sins and was restored.

A little while longer

Perhaps the best news of all is that although we must persevere to the very end, we will not have to persevere for very long. The Christian life is difficult, and we can expect to suffer grief in all kinds of trouble. But we will not have to suffer much more or hold on much longer, for we

[38] Jude 1.   [39] Mark 13:13; cf. Heb. 10:36.   [40] John 6:39–40.
[41] John 10:28–29.   [42] Luke 22:32.

walk this vale of tears only 'for a little while' (1:6). Peter uses this phrase not to minimize our suffering, but to put it into perspective. Although suffering is real, it is not ultimate; although it is painful, it is not permanent. We are being saved through suffering into a glory that is soon to be revealed.

It is significant that Peter addresses Christians as *strangers in the world* (1:1). A better translation would be 'sojourner', for the word refers to a traveller or a visitor, a temporary resident in a foreign land. In the Greek translation of the Old Testament, called the Septuagint, the word is applied to Abraham, that pilgrim among the patriarchs.[43] After the exile it was used to describe the Jews who were scattered among the nations. The first Christians used the term because they, too, were scattered among the nations. In the words of *The Epistle to Diognetus*, which was written as early as the second century, Christians 'live in their own countries, but only as aliens; they participate in everything as citizens, and endure everything as foreigners'.[44] Since we are 'strangers' on earth, the term also applies to us. In the words of the old gospel song, 'This world is not my home, I'm just a-passing through.' We will not suffer here for ever. Our ultimate citizenship is in heaven,[45] which makes us resident aliens, living here on temporary visas. We should travel light, looking forward to the day when we will all go home.

As if to emphasize the brevity of our adversity, Peter moves immediately from our present sufferings (1:6–7) to our future glory in Christ: *Though you have not seen him, you love him; and even though you do not see him now, you believe in him and are filled with an inexpressible and glorious joy, for you are receiving the goal of your faith, the salvation of your souls* (1:8–9). These verses gain added lustre when we remember that as an eyewitness of the resurrection, Peter *had* seen Christ in all his glory. He also loved Jesus, as he insisted three times by the Sea of Galilee.[46] But Peter was writing to people like us, who are still waiting to see the glorious Christ, and he wanted to assure us that by believing we are receiving our salvation already. Even while we suffer, we are holding on to glory through faith in 'the Unseen Christ'.[47]

Our present grasp of our future glory means that our salvation spans eternity. We have been saved by grace – that is something God has already done for us through Jesus Christ. We are also saved for God's glory, which means that one day we will praise God in the revelation of Jesus Christ. In the meantime, we are living by faith. The faith that enables us to endure all kinds of trials looks back to the cross and the

---

[43] Gen. 23:4.
[44] *The Epistle to Diognetus*, Lightfoot and Harmer, in *The Apostolic Fathers*, pp. 291–306 (299).
[45] Phil. 3:20; cf. Heb. 13:14.   [46] John 21:15–17.
[47] See Vincent, *The True Christian's Love to the Unseen Christ*.

empty tomb, and also forward to our glorious inheritance in Christ. Thus our salvation embraces the past, the present and the future: we have been saved, we are being saved, and we will be saved. And this is all because we are united to Jesus Christ, the eternal Son of God. 'Our hope is anchored in the past: Jesus rose! Our hope remains in the present: Jesus lives! Our hope is completed in the future: Jesus is coming!'[48]

It is this future hope that enables us to *greatly rejoice* in our present sufferings (1:6).[49] We do not rejoice in the sufferings themselves, of course, but when we suffer, we do rejoice. The apostle Paul made the same point: 'We rejoice in the hope of the glory of God. Not only so, but we also rejoice in our sufferings, because we know that suffering produces perseverance; perseverance, character; and character, hope.'[50] The hope of glory fills us with what Peter called *an inexpressible and glorious joy*. What makes our joy inexpressible is the fact that we experience it right now, while we are still afflicted with sorrow. This is ineffable, something we cannot find the words to explain.

Our suffering lasts only a little while, but our glorious life in Christ will last for ever. I once read the story of a little boy who had a terminal illness. His parents, who were Christians, did not try to hide the severity of his condition. They frankly told their son that he would have to suffer, and that in the end – barring a miracle – he would die. They also spoke with him about the joys of heaven, for the boy believed the message of salvation. Together they tried to imagine what heaven would be like. The more his condition worsened, and the more his suffering intensified, the more joyful and expectant the boy became. His parents would comfort him by saying, 'It will not be long now; soon you will go to be with Jesus.' Finally it was time. The day came when the boy passed from this suffering, sinful world into eternal glory. As he gasped for his last few breaths, a remarkable peace descended upon his hospital room. The boy's face was radiant, and it seemed to those standing there that he could no longer see them, that he was already stepping through the gates of paradise. They saw him smile, and although they could hear no voice, he seemed to be listening to a whisper from heaven. His dying words were not addressed to them, but spoken to an unseen angel, as if to answer a question: 'Yes,' the boy said, 'I'm ready!'

The little boy's experience contains the essence of the Christian's path through suffering into glory. It will not be long now. No, it will not be long. 'And the God of all grace, who called you to his eternal glory in Christ, after you have suffered a little while, will himself restore you and make you strong, firm and steadfast. To him be the power for ever and ever. Amen' (5:10–11).

---

[48] Clowney, *The Message of 1 Peter*, p. 46.
[49] Cf. Ps. 13:5.   [50] Rom. 5:3.

18. Glory! Glory!
Glorification: Revelation 7:9–17

Who are these people? And where did they come from? These questions came to John in a vision. He had been taken up into heaven, where God revealed the secrets of glory. There John saw an enormous crowd of people, vast beyond human comprehension, gathered from the four corners of the earth. The people were dressed all in white and standing around heaven's throne, waving palm branches and praising God. But who were they? Someone asked John, *'These in white robes – who are they, and where did they come from?'* (Rev. 7:14). John simply answered, *'Sir, you know.'* It was a polite way of saying that he was not sure who they were, or where they had come from.

The salvation people

If John had been thinking clearly, he might have been able to identify this heavenly host. Certainly he was given plenty of clues. First, there was the sheer number of them to consider: *After this I looked and there before me was a great multitude that no-one could count* (7:9a). John had never seen so many people before in his life. From his perspective, they were innumerable. Another way to identify the great multitude was by their ethnicity. Where were they from? Literally everywhere – *from every nation, tribe, people and language* (7:9b). Yet another clue was what they were doing. John saw them *standing before the throne and in front of the Lamb. They were wearing white robes and were holding palm branches in their hands* (7:9c). Since palm branches were a sign of royal triumph, apparently they were celebrating some kind of victory. And they cried out in a loud voice: 'Salvation belongs to our God, who sits on the throne, and to the Lamb' (7:10; cf. 12:10).

On the basis of these clues, John should have been able to deduce that he was looking at God's new people, glorified. They could not be counted because God had always promised that his people would be as countless as the stars in the heavens.[1] They came from everywhere

[1] Gen. 15:5.

because the message of salvation is for everyone. This multi-national, multi-cultural, multi-ethnic and multi-linguistic multitude was gathered around God's throne because they had ascended into glory. What John saw was all God's people – ransomed, redeemed and resurrected.

Scholars are divided as to whether or not the great multitude in verse 9 should be identified with the people described in verses 4–8, the ones called '144,000 from all the tribes of Israel' (7:4). Because of the reference to Israel, some think that the 144,000 were all Jews, either from the old covenant or from the Christian church. This interpretation is possible. However, the 144,000 are first identified as 'the servants of our God' (7:3), which is true of all God's people. It seems more likely, therefore, that the 144,000 also represents the whole people of God. The New Testament church – including both Jews and Gentiles – is the true new Israel.[2] The number 144,000 is not a statistic, but a symbol. It is twelve times twelve thousand, a number of completion and perfection representing God's whole new humanity. It shows that God knows each and every last one of his servants. Thus the 144,000 and the great multitude are one and the same. There is no contradiction between verse 4, which assigns a number to them, and verse 9, which says that they could not be counted. What John saw was more people than anyone could count because, from the human perspective, God's new people are innumerable. What John heard, however, was an angel saying that there were 144,000 of them. This is because, from God's perspective, all were present and accounted for.

In a word, the people John saw were Christians. They were the salvation people, the people *saved from sin*. The victory they celebrated was deliverance from the wrath and curse of God (see Rev. 6). Secondly, they were the people *saved by grace*. As they themselves claimed, their salvation belonged exclusively to God (7:10), and not to themselves. The grace they had received was sovereign grace, grace that flowed from God's royal throne through Jesus Christ, the Lamb who takes away the sin of the world. Thirdly, they were the people *saved through faith*. They praised God as *their* God, the gracious God whom they had received personally by faith. Finally, they were the people *saved for God's glory*, who worshipped with angels and princes: *All the angels were standing round the throne and around the elders and the four living creatures. They fell down on their faces before the throne and worshipped God, saying: 'Amen! Praise and glory and wisdom and thanks and honour and power and strength be to our God for ever and ever. Amen!'* (7:11–12; cf. 5:12).

It is perhaps significant that John saw *all* the angels in his vision, for this provides further confirmation that what he saw was the final destiny of all God's servants. When the angels spoke, they began with the word 'Amen!' to announce their agreement with the praise of the

[2] See Gal. 6:16.

great multitude. The voices of men and women were joined by the voices of cherubim and seraphim. Together they returned all praise, glory, wisdom, thanksgiving, honour, power and strength back to God, so that all the glory of salvation would redound to his praise, for ever.

Who are these people? *We* are these people, if we receive the message of salvation. Here is a surprising way to think of it: when John saw heaven opened, and beheld the great multitude standing around God's throne, he saw *us* standing there! Everything said of these people is true of everyone who is united to Christ. Jews and Gentiles, Asians and Africans, Europeans and Americans – we come from everywhere. One day we will gather around God's throne to praise him for the victory of his salvation. Together we will glorify God for his saving grace, which we receive by faith in Jesus Christ. 'Therefore,' as it says in *The Book of Common Prayer*, 'with Angels and Archangels, and with all the company of heaven, we laud and magnify thy glorious Name, evermore praising thee, and saying: Holy, holy, holy, Lord God of hosts, heaven and earth are full of thy glory: Glory be to thee, O Lord most High. Amen.'

The tribulation people

Perhaps John could have figured out who these people were, and where they had come from, but when he seemed to hesitate, his questioner decided to help him: *And he said, 'These are they who have come out of the great tribulation; they have washed their robes and made them white in the blood of the Lamb'* (7:14).

Again we are reminded that these people were saved by grace, especially the grace that flows from Christ's death on the cross. The Lamb, of course, is Jesus Christ, whom John had already described as 'the Lamb who was slain' (5:6, 12). The blood of the Lamb is the blood that Christ shed at Calvary. It was the blood of redemption that paid the price for our salvation. It was the blood of propitiation that turned aside God's wrath. It was the blood of reconciliation that brought us back to God. It was the blood of expiation that covered all our guilt. God's glorified humanity is saved by the grace of Christ's atoning work. He is 'the Lamb of God, who takes away the sin of the world!'[3]

The great multitude was saved by grace, but they were not saved from suffering. Instead, they had entered glory *through* suffering. They had *come out of the great tribulation*. Scholars have offered various interpretations of the tribulation people. Some think they were martyrs. This seems unlikely because there is nothing in the passage to indicate specifically that the people in white robes were martyrs. Ordinarily, when John refers to martyrs, he explains that they were put to death because of their faith (e.g. 6:9). Thus we may conclude that the

[3] John 1:29.

triumph these people celebrate has to do not with their own deaths, but with the death of Christ. Others think that the tribulation refers to a special period of persecution in the end times, what John elsewhere calls 'the hour of trial that is going to come upon the whole world' (3:10). This interpretation has much to commend it, for the sufferings of these saints are described as *the* tribulation, the *great* tribulation. This suggests an intense period of persecution – a tribulation to end all tribulations – that will come immediately prior to the return of Christ.

The main difficulty with this interpretation is that everything said about the people in white robes is true of every Christian. We have all been saved by God's sovereign grace, we have all been cleansed by Christ's atoning sacrifice, we must all enter glory through suffering, and so forth. It seems best, therefore, to understand Revelation 7 as a description of God's whole new humanity. Even if these verses refer more specifically to the martyrs, or to the church of the last days, they apply to all Christians generally because one day we will all stand before the throne of God's glory. The great multitude is the church triumphant, the entire people of God gathered and glorified.

Everyone who believes the message of salvation will take his or her place among them. Glory is our destiny. One day we will stand before the throne and in front of the Lamb, wearing the robe and waving the palm. Yet before getting swept up into the glories of heaven, the Bible takes one last, backwards glance at the trials of earth. Everyone who stands in that great and glorious multitude must persevere during the great tribulation. Remember that the pattern of salvation is through suffering into glory. As it was for Christ, so it is for the Christian: tribulation before glorification, the cross before the crown. If we wish to enjoy the ecstasies of heaven, we must endure the agonies of earth: loss, grief, persecution and finally death. As the apostle Paul said, 'We must go through many hardships [literally, "tribulations"] to enter the kingdom of God.'[4]

This is meant not to discourage us, but to give us hope and comfort. When we 'suffer grief in all kinds of trials',[5] as we surely must, it helps to know that there is no way to enter glory except by way of suffering. If, while we go through great tribulation, we are able to hold on to Christ as he holds on to us, then our present suffering becomes the proof of our future glory. This is why the Scripture tells us: 'Rejoice that you participate in the sufferings of Christ, so that you may be overjoyed when his glory is revealed.'[6] The tribulation is only for a little while, but the joy is for ever, and we do well to 'consider that our present sufferings are not worth comparing with the glory that will be revealed in us.'[7] Whatever difficulties we face, they are only 'light and momentary

---

[4] Acts 14:22.   [5] 1 Pet. 1:6.   [6] 1 Pet. 4:13; cf. 5:10.   [7] Rom. 8:18.

troubles' that are 'achieving for us an eternal glory that far outweighs them all.'[8]

The biblical doctrine of glorification

In our present condition, it is not easy to believe that one day we will be glorious, and yet this is what the Bible plainly teaches. The proper theological term for it is *glorification*. Glorification means that one day everyone who is united to the risen Christ will become as glorious as Christ himself. To be glorified is to be raised with all God's people in a perfect, immortal, eternal and imperishable body of dazzling splendour.[9] John Murray thus defined glorification as 'the complete and final redemption of the whole person when in the integrity of body and spirit the people of God will be conformed to the image of the risen, exalted, and glorified Redeemer, when the very body of their humiliation will be conformed to the body of Christ's glory.'[10]

This glory will be revealed in us at the second coming, 'the glorious appearing of our great God and Saviour, Jesus Christ'.[11] Salvation in Christ is not only a past event, and a present reality, but also a future hope. As the Bible has promised, Jesus 'will appear a second time, not to bear sin, but to bring salvation to those who are waiting for him'.[12] On that 'great and glorious day', when 'everyone who calls on the name the Lord will be saved',[13] everyone who is united to the risen Christ by faith will become as glorious as Christ himself: 'When Christ, who is your life, appears, then you also will appear with him in glory.'[14] The Bible thus describes the second coming as 'the day [Jesus] comes to be glorified in his holy people'.[15]

As we noted in chapter 9, it was in the resurrection that God 'glorified his servant Jesus'.[16] To this day, the glorious body of the risen Christ – the very body that was buried in the tomb – reigns in all its dazzling brightness and radiant splendour. In the famous words of John 'Rabbi' Duncan (1796–1870), 'The dust of the earth is on the Throne of the universe.'[17] One day we will 'share in the glory of our Lord Jesus Christ'.[18] Just as God glorified Jesus in his resurrection, so also he will make us glorious in our resurrection. What Christ is by virtue of his resurrection, we will become at our resurrection; just as his resurrection is his glorification, so also our resurrection will be our glorification.[19] By

---

[8] 2 Cor. 4:17.　　[9] 1 Cor. 15:50–54.
[10] John Murray, *Redemption: Accomplished and Applied*, p. 175.
[11] Titus 2:13.　　[12] Heb. 9:28.　　[13] Acts 2:20–21.　　[14] Col. 3:4.
[15] 2 Thess. 1:10.　　[16] Acts 3:13.
[17] John Duncan, quoted in Derek Prime, 'The man in glory', *Evangelicals Now* (May 1999), p. 14.
[18] 2 Thess. 2:14.
[19] Gaffin, *The Centrality of the Resurrection*, p. 126.

virtue of our vital union with Jesus Christ, we will be 'raised in glory'.[20] This is the work of the Holy Spirit, for 'if the Spirit of him who raised Jesus from the dead is living in you, he who raised Christ from the dead will also give life to your mortal bodies through his Spirit, who lives in you'.[21] By the power of the Holy Spirit, our bodies and our souls will be completely, permanently and instantaneously transformed into the glorious image of the risen Christ. The *Westminster Larger Catechism* summarizes the biblical teaching as follows: 'The bodies of the just, by the Spirit of Christ, and by virtue of his resurrection as their head, shall be raised in power, spiritual, and incorruptible, and made like to his glorious body' (A. 87).

Everyone who believes the message of salvation is destined for glory. Glorification is the climactic event in salvation, the last link in the golden chain that stretches from election to eternity: 'For those God foreknew he also predestined to be conformed to the likeness of his Son, that he might be the firstborn among many brothers. And those he predestined, he also called; those he called, he also justified; those he justified, he also glorified.'[22] Thus glorification is joined to every preceding act of salvation. As the Puritan Thomas Watson once observed, 'It is absurd to imagine that God should justify a people and not sanctify them, that He should justify a people whom He could not glorify.'[23] Glorification is the proof of our predestination and the perfection of our sanctification.

In one sense, our glorification has already begun. We are now in Christ, just as Christ is now in us, and thus we are beginning to reflect his glory. The image of God, which was defaced in the fall (see chapter 2), is being restored by the transforming work of the Holy Spirit: 'We, who with unveiled faces all reflect the Lord's glory, are being transformed into his likeness with ever-increasing glory, which comes from the Lord, who is the Spirit.'[24] The more sanctified we are, the better we are able to glorify God, and the more glorious we become. In another sense, however, our glorification will not actually take place until the second coming, when we will be glorified all the way through. Properly speaking, glorification is the total physical and spiritual transformation that will take place only at 'the glorious appearing of our great God and Saviour, Jesus Christ'.[25] 'When Christ, who is your life, appears, *then* you also will appear with him in glory.'[26] The inward process of spiritual renewal has already begun, but it must come to outward expression in the body of every believer. And so 'We eagerly await … the Lord Jesus Christ, who, by the power that enables him to bring everything under his control, will transform our lowly bodies so that they will be like his glorious body.'[27]

---

[20] 1 Cor. 15:43.   [21] Rom. 8:11.   [22] Rom. 8:29–30.
[23] Thomas Watson, quoted in Demarest, *The Cross and Salvation*, p. 408.
[24] 2 Cor. 3:18.   [25] Titus 2:13.   [26] Col. 3:4.   [27] Phil. 3:20b–21.

Then face to face

Remarkably, this glorious transformation will be brought about by seeing Jesus face to face. Jesus himself prayed that one day we would be
able to see him in all his glory. 'Father,' he said, 'I want those you have
given me to be with me where I am, and to see my glory, the glory you
have given me because you loved me before the creation of the world.'[28]
Here is how Thomas Boston imagined it:

> [The saints] shall see Jesus Christ, God and man, with their bodily
> eyes, as He will never lay aside the human nature. They will behold
> that glorious blessed body, which is personally united to the divine
> nature, and exalted above principalities and powers and every name
> that is named. There we shall see, with our eyes, that very body
> which was born of Mary at Bethlehem, and crucified at Jerusalem
> between two thieves: the blessed head that was crowned with thorns;
> the face that was spit upon; the hands and feet that were nailed to
> the cross; all shining with inconceivable glory. The glory of the man
> Christ will attract the eyes of all the saints.[29]

The effect of this beatific vision will be to make every Christian as
glorious as Christ himself. The magnificence of the divine majesty will
be made to shine in God's new humanity.[30] In glorification, seeing is becoming. To see the unseen Christ *as* he is means to become *what* he is:
'What we will be has not yet been made known. But we know that when
he appears, we shall be like him, for we shall see him as he is.'[31] It is by
seeing Jesus that humanity will achieve its destiny. Our intimacy with
God will be restored, and we will once again have the kind of relationship that Adam and Eve shared with God in the Garden of Eden. By
seeing Jesus face to face, we will become what God has always intended
us to be: men and women fashioned in the glorious image of his glorious
Son. This is not simply a return to Eden, but an advancement to glory,
for the grace of salvation is greater than the goodness of creation.
'Perhaps the most wonderful thing of all is this,' writes Sinclair Ferguson:

> God lifts us not only from what we are by nature to what Adam
> was in the Garden of Eden, but to what Adam was to become in
> the presence of God, and would have been had he persevered
> in obedience. The gospel does not make us like Adam in his inno-
> cence – it makes us like Christ, in all the perfection of his reflection
> of God. This is the essence of the salvation Christ provides.[32]

[28] John 17:24; cf. Matt. 5:8; John 17:5.
[29] Boston, *Human Nature in its Fourfold State*, pp. 452–453.
[30] Witsius, *The Economy of the Covenants between God and Man*, vol. 2, p. 81.
[31] 1 John 3:2; cf. 1 Cor. 13:12; Rev. 22:4.   [32] Ferguson, *The Christian Life*, p. 16.

Since glorification will not finally take place until we see Christ return, it is the only aspect of our salvation that will happen to all of us all at once. Glorification is a corporate event. The bodies of many believers are still resting their graves. They are in what theologians sometimes call 'the intermediate state'. Only their souls are with Christ in glory;[33] their bodies – though still united to Christ – remain in their graves. As the *Westminster Larger Catechism* explains:

> The communion in glory with Christ, which the members of the invisible church enjoy immediately after death, is, in that their souls are then made perfect in holiness, and received into the highest heavens, where they behold the face of God in light and glory, waiting for the full redemption of their bodies, which even in death continue united to Christ, and rest in their graves as in their beds, till at the last day they be again united to their souls (A. 86).

On the last day, Jesus will come 'to be glorified in his holy people and to be marvelled at among all those who have believed'.[34] When that glorious, marvellous day arrives, the dead will be raised to meet the living in the air, and all God's people will be glorified, body and soul, instantaneously and simultaneously. Ferguson exclaims:

> What a tremendously exciting prospect this is! Here we are, at such different stages of Christian experience: some who have been Christians for many years, others converted recently; some highly gifted, others weak in both grace and gifts. Moreover, how many thousands and millions of God's children have passed out of this world before us? But on that day we shall all together share in the glorification of Jesus, and our glorification with him.[35]

Not only that, but the whole creation will share the glory with us, for 'the creation itself will be liberated from its bondage to decay and brought into the glorious freedom of the children of God'.[36] We are not saved out of our bodies, but our bodies themselves are redeemed and glorified. Just so, we will not be saved out of the world, but the world itself will display God's infinite glory. The goal of glorification is 'a new soul in a new body in a new universe, each in perfect harmony with the others, and man able at last to live out his full potential to the glory of God'.[37]

---

[33] 2 Cor. 5:8.   [34] 2 Thess. 1:10a.
[35] Ferguson, *The Christian Life*, p. 194.
[36] Rom. 8:21.
[37] Macleod, *A Faith to Live By*, p. 290.

Our beautiful adornment

Revelation 7 mentions three features of our glorious life in heaven: our beautiful adornment, our blessed employment, and our endless enjoyment. To begin with our adornment, when we all get to heaven we will all wear long white robes. This must be theologically significant because it is mentioned twice in our passage (7:9, 14), and again in 19:8, where the Bible says that we will wear 'fine linen, bright and clean'. Another reason for thinking that the white robes are significant is that what we wear always says something about who we are. In fact, the history of salvation may be described as a series of fashion statements.

Start with Adam and Eve in their state of innocence: The first man and the first woman 'were both naked, and they felt no shame'.[38] The Bible tells us that they felt no shame because it is something that we ourselves have never experienced. We *are* ashamed of our nakedness. But unlike us, Adam and Eve had never sinned. Thus they were able to eat and sleep, work and play in the nude. What they were wearing – or not wearing – was directly related to their spiritual condition. In their innocence they had nothing to hide, either from God or from one another.

Then Adam and Eve sinned, and the fashions changed. No sooner had they eaten the forbidden fruit than they decided that it was time for a change of clothes: 'Then the eyes of both of them were opened, and they realised that they were naked; so they sewed fig leaves together and made coverings for themselves.'[39] What they were making was not as much a theological statement as a fashion statement. They were admitting that they had become guilty sinners. Unfortunately, as our first parents soon discovered, fig leaves are not much use when it comes to covering up sin. Nevertheless, human beings have been trying ever since to make their own clothes, spiritually speaking. Every false religion tries to dress people up so they will be good enough for God. The trouble with trying to wear your own good deeds, however, is that they always smell like dirty laundry. The prophet Isaiah lamented, 'All of us have become like one who is unclean, and all our righteous acts are like filthy rags'.[40] Two things are shocking about Isaiah's comment. One is that the word he uses for 'filthy rags' is somewhat crude, as it is associated with a woman's menstrual period. But what is even more shocking is that Isaiah is talking not about our sins, but about our very best deeds: 'All our *righteous* acts are like filthy rags.'

It gets worse, because heaven has a dress code. In order to stand before God's throne, it is absolutely necessary to come suitably dressed. Jesus once told a parable about a wedding reception in a banquet hall filled with guests: 'When the king came in to see the guests, he noticed

---

[38] Gen. 2:25. [39] Gen. 3:7. [40] Is. 64:6a; cf. Zech. 3:1, 3.

a man there who was not wearing wedding clothes. "Friend," he asked, "how did you get in here without wedding clothes?" The man was speechless. Then the king told the attendants, "Tie him hand and foot, and throw him outside, into the darkness, where there will be weeping and gnashing of teeth."[41] The day will come when every bad dresser will be banished from God's presence for ever. So the question becomes, What will I wear to heaven? We cannot 'come as we are', and nothing in our own wardrobes is at all suitable. Even our very best spiritual clothes are morally filthy, and if we try to wear any of them, we will be denied entrance.

What every sinner needs is a brand new set of clothes. There is only one way to get them, and that is by washing them in the blood of the Lamb (7:14). Although this metaphor is familiar to most Christians, it is a highly unusual one. What a strange cleansing agent! Blood is an organic fluid that leaves an indelible stain. How could a robe dipped in blood come out pure white? The answer is that this is no ordinary blood. It is the blood of the Lamb, and the Lamb is Jesus Christ, 'who takes away the sin of the world!'[42] His blood is the blood that he shed at Calvary, when he died on the cross for our sins. Jesus was nailed bleeding and dying to the cross. The Bible teaches that the blood he shed is the blood of redemption that paid the price for our salvation. It is the blood of atonement that covers all our sin. It is the blood of reconciliation that brings us back to God. Through some mysterious, miraculous act of divine chemistry, this crimson tide makes us clean and spotless. By washing our robes in the blood of Christ – in other words, by going to the cross and asking Jesus to apply his perfect sacrifice to our filthy sins – we are justified in the sight of God. The spotless Son of God took our stains upon himself, and in return he clothes us with his purity.

If we do not ask Jesus – personally and directly – to make us clean, then it is doubtful whether we have anything suitable to wear for the rest of eternity. But if we go to Christ for cleansing, we will find that God's promise is true:

> 'Though your sins are like scarlet,
>   they shall be as white as snow;
> though they are red as crimson,
>   they shall be like wool.'[43]

The poet and hymnwriter William Cowper (1731–1800) described how this miraculous cleansing takes place:

[41] Matt. 22:11–13.   [42] John 1:29; cf. Heb. 9:14.
[43] Is. 1:18.

> There is a fountain filled with blood
> Drawn from Immanuel's veins;
> And sinners plunged beneath that flood
> Lose all their guilty stains.

When we emerge from that cleansing fountain, we come out as spotless as the Lamb himself. It makes for quite a fashion statement! We exchange our filthy rags for the pristine robes of Jesus Christ, becoming clothed in his very righteousness. J. Gresham Machen writes:

> We deserved eternal death, in accordance with the curse of God's law; but the Lord Jesus, because He loved us, took upon Himself the guilt of our sins and died instead of us on Calvary. And faith consists simply in our acceptance of that wondrous gift. When we accept the gift, we are clothed, entirely without merit of our own, by the righteousness of Christ; when God looks upon us, He sees not our impurity but the spotless purity of Christ, and accepts us 'as righteous in His sight, only for the righteousness of Christ imputed to us, and received by faith alone'.[44]

Having received his perfect righteousness, we glorify God, saying:

> I delight greatly in the LORD;
> my soul rejoices in my God.
> For he has clothed me with garments of salvation
> and arrayed me in a robe of righteousness.[45]

Our blessed employment

Thomas Boston once wrote an essay on the history and theology of fashion. In it he explained that there were five times in the ancient world when people wore spotless white robes.[46] One was when Roman bondservants were freed from slavery: the white robe was a symbol of their emancipation. A second was a bride on her wedding day, who wore white to symbolize the joy of sexual purity. Third, white robes were worn by champions from battle to show that they were the victors: the warriors would be crowned with laurels, and then paraded around the city in their victory robes. Again, people going to religious festivals often wore white robes as a sign of celebration. Finally, Jewish priests wore white robes in the temple to show that they were set apart for God's holy service.

---

[44] Machen, *What is Faith?*, pp. 143–144.
[45] Is. 61:10a.
[46] Boston, *The Complete Works of the Late Rev. Thomas Boston of Ettrick*, vol. 8, pp. 319–324.

We will wear glorious robes in heaven for the same reasons. We will wear white for liberty: like freed slaves we have been delivered from our bondage to sin (Rev. 1:5b). We will wear white for chastity: like a virgin bride on her wedding day we will preserve our passion for Jesus (19:7–8). We will wear white for victory: like conquering heroes we will win the victory over death through Jesus Christ (15:2). We will wear white for the party: life in heaven will be an endless celebration (1:6). And we will wear white for purity: like temple priests we will be set apart to serve the Lord (5:10).

The mention of the temple priests brings us to our blessed employment. There will be more for us to do in heaven than simply to admire the latest fashions. We were made to serve God, so there will be work for us to do. We will be employed in the serious, joyous business of heaven, which is to glorify God. We will stand *before the throne of God and serve him day and night in his temple* (7:15a). The idea of praising God day and night comes from the Levites in the Old Testament: 'Those who were musicians, heads of Levite families, stayed in the rooms of the temple and were exempt from other duties because they were responsible for the work day and night.'[47] The God of unending grace deserves unceasing praise, so the Levitical musicians praised him all day and all night. Their worship thus anticipated the glories of heaven. Strictly speaking, of course, there is no temple in heaven. John would later write, 'I did not see a temple in the city, because the Lord God Almighty and the Lamb are its temple' (21:22). A temple is a place where God is present, and since God is present throughout heaven, all of heaven is his temple. And if all of heaven is a temple, then all of us will be priests praising God with endless song (cf. 1:6; 5:10). Perhaps this explains why Revelation contains so many pages from heaven's hymnal!

Notice the reason for our unending worship: *'These are they who have come out of the great tribulation; they have washed their robes and made them white in the blood of the Lamb. Therefore, they are before the throne of God and serve him day and night in his temple'* (7:15a). The word 'therefore' establishes a connection between grace and glory, between *soteriology* (the message of salvation) and *doxology* (the praise of God). The reason we will give God the glory is that we have been saved by grace. Notice also the object of our worship, which is God himself, who sits at the centre of the whole heavenly scene. The great multitude stands before his throne, all the angels surround him, and the elders and the four living creatures bow down at his feet. Thus the glorious vocation of heaven is God-centred worship. When we all get to glory we will stand before God's throne, singing praise to God and to the Lamb.

[47] 1 Chr. 9:33.

We are starting to praise God already here on earth. We get a taste of eternity every time we go to church and worship God. Our problem is that we soon tire of worship. About the most we can manage is one hour of praise at a time. In fact, many of us secretly doubt whether we will want to worship God all the time, even in heaven. But it will be different once we are glorified: then we will have the capacity to worship God without growing weary. Perhaps we will spend all our time in heaven singing. It seems more likely to me that we will continue to do many of the things we do on earth, flourishing in every area of human endeavour: creating works of art, conducting experiments of science, playing games of sport – all to the glory of God. In the words of the great English hymnwriter Isaac Watts (1674–1748), 'every power' will 'find sweet employ, in that eternal world of joy'.[48]

There will be this difference, however, that our work and our play will be unstained by sin. At present, we are striving to become more and more holy, and making some progress, however slow. But we will not become completely and perfectly holy until we are glorified. The sanctifying work initiated in this life will not be consummated until the next; glorification is the perfection of sanctification. Only in heaven will we finally be free from sin for ever, living as 'sinless creatures in deathless bodies'.[49] On the basis of the saving work of Jesus Christ, God will present us 'holy in his sight, without blemish and free from accusation'.[50] Augustine taught that God made the first man 'able to sin' (in his phrase, *posse peccare*). Having fallen from innocence to experience, in our unregenerate condition we are 'not able not to sin' (*non posse non peccare*). By God's saving grace, however, we are now 'able not to sin' (*posse non peccare*), at least on occasion. But we still long for glory, when we will be 'unable to sin' (*non posse peccare*).[51] Then God will glorify us so that we can glorify him all day and all night for all eternity.

Our endless enjoyment

Glorifying God is the hope of all our dreams and the aim of all our aspirations. As Jonathan Edwards said, 'The great end of God's works, which is so variously expressed in Scripture, is indeed but ONE; and this *one* end is most properly and comprehensively called THE GLORY OF GOD.'[52] We were made not only to glorify God, but also to enjoy him

---

[48] Isaac Watts, from 'Sweet is the work', quoted in Helm, *The Last Things*, p. 94.

[49] Packer, *Concise Theology*, p. 256.

[50] Col. 1:22.

[51] See Philip Graham Ryken, *Thomas Boston as Preacher of the Fourfold State*, Rutherford Studies in Historical Theology (Carlisle: Paternoster, 1999), pp. 67–76.

[52] Edwards, 'A dissertation concerning the end for which God created the world', in *The Works of Jonathan Edwards*, vol. 1, p. 119.

for ever. Thus Revelation 7 ends with the promise of our endless enjoyment:

> *He who sits on the throne will spread his tent*
>   *over them.*
> *Never again will they hunger;*
>   *never again will they thirst.*
> *The sun will not beat upon them*
>   *nor any scorching heat.*
> *For the Lamb at the centre of the throne will be*
>   *their shepherd;*
> *he will lead them to springs of living water.*
> *And God will wipe away every tear from*
>   *their eyes* (7:15b–17).

These verses, which largely consist of quotations from the Old Testament, contain some of God's most precious promises. One is that we will find shelter in his glorious presence. The promise that God will 'spread his tent' over us goes all the way back to the exodus from Egypt. It is a reference to the Shekinah – the visible, hovering presence of God's glory in the tabernacle. Isaiah prophesied of the day when God would draw all his people into the shelter of that glory: 'Then the LORD will create over all of Mount Zion and over those who assemble there a cloud of smoke by day and a glow of flaming fire by night; over all the glory will be a canopy. It will be shelter and shade from the heat of the day, and a refuge and hiding-place from the storm and rain.'[53]

God's protective presence will keep us safe from every evil thing. We will not suffer illness or injury. There will be no hunger in heaven, and no thirst. This, too, was part of Isaiah's prophecy:

> They will neither hunger nor thirst,
>   nor will the desert heat or the sun beat upon them.
> He who has compassion on them will guide them
>   and lead them beside springs of water.[54]

This is exactly what John saw: God's glory spread like a canopy over God's people, caring for every need and keeping them safe from every evil thing. His vision provides hope and comfort for everyone who still walks in the hungry, thirsty wilderness. Do not be discouraged. God will bring his people safely to the promised land, where every need will be met and every desire will be satisfied. Remember what Jesus promised: 'Blessed are those who hunger and thirst for righteousness, for they will be filled.'[55]

[53] Is. 4:5–6.   [54] Is. 49:10; cf. Ps. 121:5–6.   [55] Matt. 5:6.

The best promise of all is that in heaven we will live in the very presence of the Lamb. That is to say, we will be with Jesus, enjoying direct access to our saving God: *The Lamb at the centre of the throne will be their shepherd* (7:17a). The reason we will neither hunger nor thirst is that the Lamb is there, and he is our shepherd. It may seem strange for a flock to be shepherded by a lamb, but it is a great comfort to the sheep! Their shepherd knows exactly what they need because he knows what it is like to be a sheep. Jesus knows what we need because he himself has a human body and a human nature. He will lead us to *springs of living water* (7:17), where our souls will be satisfied in the full enjoyment of God for all eternity. Then we will know, to an infinite measure, what David meant when he said, 'The LORD is my shepherd; I shall not want.'[56]

All the promises of heaven's joy are meant for people who still suffer earth's sorrow. That is why they end with the promise that God will wipe every tear from our eyes (9:17b; cf. 21:4). In heaven there will be no reason to weep, because there will be no more sin, pain, death or sorrow. But we are still passing through the tribulation, and tribulation always has its tears. When we go through suffering into glory, it seems that we will arrive with our eyes still wet from crying. But our Father will be there to touch our cheek with his hand and wipe away every last one of our tears. The message of salvation is that in the end we will be saved from sin, with all its sorrows. Isaiah promised, 'The Sovereign LORD will wipe away the tears from all faces'.[57] Once our tears are wiped away, we will give God the glory, saying,

> 'Surely this is our God;
>> we trusted in him, and he saved us.
> This is the LORD, we trusted in him;
>> let us rejoice and be glad in his salvation.'[58]

---

[56] Ps. 23:1, AV.   [57] Is. 25:8a.   [58] Is. 25:9.

19. Getting the message out
Mission: Matthew 28:18–20

The previous chapter ended in glory, with countless Christians offering ceaseless praise for God's unchanging grace. We were transported to heaven itself, where we saw a vast multitude, from every tribe and nation, wearing white robes and standing before God's throne. There, with all the angels, we gave God all the glory and honour for our salvation by grace through faith.

This might seem like the perfect place to end our studies in the message of salvation – with our destiny in glory. Once we pass from tribulation to triumph, where God wipes away the last tears of our sorrow, there is nothing left to do except to glorify God and to enjoy him for ever. Glorification is the goal of our salvation, and once we are glorified, God's saving work is done.

But the end has not yet come. While many millions have been saved already, millions more are waiting to hear the message of salvation. God still has people he intends to save by grace, through faith, for his glory. He has not finished gathering the great multitude that one day will worship at his throne. Jesus prophesied that the message of salvation 'will be preached in the whole world as a testimony to all nations, and *then* the end will come' (Matt. 24:14). Since the end has not yet come, the message of salvation must still be preached ... and it is up to us to preach it.

The Great Commission

The last thing Jesus told his disciples before he ascended to heaven was to spread his saving message all over the world. The disciples had gone to meet Jesus at the top of a Galilean mountain.

Then Jesus came to them and said, 'All authority in heaven and on earth has been given to me. Therefore go and make disciples of all nations, baptising them in the name of the Father and of the Son and of the Holy Spirit, and teaching them to obey everything I have commanded you. And surely I am with you always, to the very end of the age' (Matt. 28:18–20).

280

These famous words are often called the Great Commission. God's mission is to save a new people for his glory. Our co-mission – the mission we share with God himself – is to take the message of salvation into all the world.

One significant feature of the Great Commission is the fourfold repetition of the word 'all'. Jesus claims to have *all authority*. His disciples will come from *all nations*, and they will be taught to obey 'all things', or *everything*. Finally, Jesus promises to be with us 'all the days', or *always*. By taking this structural clue, we discover that salvation's message is sent by a *universal authority*, intended for a *universal audience*, demands a *universal obedience*, and comes with the promise of God's *universal presence*.

Having all authority

First, the message of salvation is sent by a *universal authority*. Jesus said, *'All authority in heaven and on earth has been given to me'* (28:18). Authority is power plus the right to use it, and Jesus has both. He has the power because he is divine. He is very God of very God; therefore, he is omnipotent. He has the right to use this absolute power because he has received it from his Father. This is why Jesus described his universal authority as something that had been *given* to him. By his resurrection from the dead, including his ascension into heaven and his exaltation to God's throne, he was 'declared with power to be the Son of God'.[1]

Jesus has all authority in heaven. This is one of his strongest claims to deity. Who has authority in heaven, except God alone? Yet Jesus claims to have divine authority over all the angels and all the saints in glory. The Bible teaches that God 'raised him from the dead and seated him at his right hand in the heavenly realms, far above all rule and authority, power and dominion, and every title that can be given, not only in the present age but also in the one to come'.[2] To have this heavenly authority, both now and for ever, Jesus must be God himself. Jesus also has all authority on earth. He is not like the pagan deities, whose power was thought to be limited by their geography. Instead, he is the Lord of all nations, for 'the LORD does whatever pleases him, in the heavens and on the earth'.[3] The unlimited authority of Jesus Christ stretches from pole to pole and spreads from sea to sea.

It is this universal authority that gives the church its global commission. Jesus has sent the message of salvation into all the world because he has all the authority in the world. The reason Christianity is a world religion is that Jesus has the right to command all people everywhere to follow him. John Stott summarizes by saying,

[1] Rom. 1:4.   [2] Eph. 1:20–21.   [3] Ps. 135:6.

The fundamental basis of all Christian missionary enterprise is the universal authority of Jesus Christ, 'in heaven and on earth'. If the authority of Jesus were circumscribed on earth, if he were but one of many religious teachers, one of many Jewish prophets, one of many divine incarnations, we would have no mandate to present him to the nations as the Lord and Savior of the world. If the authority of Jesus were limited in heaven, if he had not decisively overthrown the principalities and powers, we might still proclaim him to the nations, but we would never be able to 'turn them from darkness to the light, and from the power of Satan unto God' (Acts 26:18). Only because all authority on earth belongs to Christ dare we go to all nations. And only because all authority in heaven as well is his have we any hope of success.[4]

The fact that Jesus has all authority does not mean that he rules the world by force. The way he exercises his authority is simply by sending a message, the message of salvation. Therefore Christianity must never become an excuse for tyranny. The gospel advances by persuasion rather than by coercion. The early Christian work known as *The Epistle to Diognetus* asks,

Now, did [God] send [Jesus], as a human mind might assume, to rule by tyranny, fear, and terror? Far from it! He sent him out of kindness and gentleness, like a king sending his son who is himself a king. He sent him as God; he sent him as man to men. He willed to save man by persuasion, not by compulsion, for compulsion is not God's way of working.[5]

Discipling all nations

On the basis of Christ's universal authority, the message of salvation is intended for a *universal audience*: *'Therefore go and make disciples of all nations, baptising them in the name of the Father and of the Son and of the Holy Spirit'* (28:19). This is the second of the four 'alls' in the Great Commission: *all nations*.

For thousands of years, the God of Israel had been saving the Jews. Beginning with Abraham, he had called one family to be his special people. He turned that one family into a great nation, delivering them from captivity, establishing them as a kingdom, and then rescuing them from exile. Yet for all the favour God showed to Israel, it had always

---

[4] John R. W. Stott, 'The Great Commission', in *One Race, One Gospel, One Task: World Congress on Evangelism, Berlin 1966*, ed. by Carl F. H. Henry and W. Stanley Mooneyham (Minneapolis: World Wide Publications, 1966), vol. 1, p. 46.

[5] 'The so-called Letter to Diognetus', trans. by Eugene R. Fairweather, in *Early Christian Fathers*, LCC 1 (Philadelphia: Westminster, 1953), p. 219.

been his mission to save the world, to 'bring my salvation to the ends of the earth'.[6] As he promised Abraham at the very beginning, 'all peoples on earth will be blessed through you'.[7] God's saving plan was for the whole human race. Even as the Old Testament people of God sang praises for their own salvation, they longed for the day when they would 'declare his glory among the nations, his marvellous deeds among all peoples'.[8] Finally God sent Jesus Christ to be the Saviour of the world. By his death and resurrection Jesus did everything necessary to save the nations by grace, and now all that remains is for the nations to receive salvation through faith.

The way God intends to complete this cosmic mission is through the church. One might have expected Jesus to tell us what *he* intended to do with his universal authority; instead, he tells us what he wants *us* to do with it. On the basis of his authority, he authorizes us to take the message of salvation to the ends of the earth. Our Great Commission is the extension of Christ's own global mission to save the nations for his glory. 'The goal of missions', writes John Piper, 'is the gladness of the peoples in the greatness of God.'[9]

What we are supposed to do with the nations is to disciple them. Of the four primary verbs in the Great Commission, one is an imperative (a command), and the other three are participles. The central imperative is to 'make disciples', and the other three verbs – going, baptizing and teaching – are all related to discipleship. The church's prime directive is to make disciples. Notice what Jesus did not tell his disciples to do. He did not tell them to preach the gospel. He did not tell them to win converts. He did not tell them to hold crusades, go knocking on doors, or follow some other method for evangelism. He did not even tell them to share the message of salvation. That is because these things, by themselves, do not fulfil the Great Commission. We are called not to record decisions, but to *make disciples*. There is more to salvation than coming to Christ; there is a whole new life to be lived in obedience to Christ. What Jesus wants is followers, not merely converts, and thus he commissioned us to make disciples.

The cost of discipleship

The word 'disciple' is associated with learning; it means 'pupil' or 'student'. In ancient times students learnt by spending time with their teachers. Thus the word 'disciple' is closely related to the idea of following. A disciple is simply a follower of Christ, a person who is determined to live like Jesus. The best place to learn how to follow Christ is in the Gospels, which are manuals for Christian discipleship. The first disciples became disciples by following Jesus, which is what he

[6] Is. 49:6. [7] Gen. 12:3b. [8] Ps. 96:3; cf. 67:2.
[9] Piper, *Let the Nations Be Glad!*, p. 222 (Baker ed., p. 219).

called them to do from the very beginning. Their discipleship began with election; Jesus 'called his disciples to him and chose twelve of them, whom he designated apostles'.[10] Peter and Andrew were called while they were mending their fishing nets, Matthew was called while he was sitting in his toll booth, and so forth. Jesus simply said, 'Come, follow me',[11] and from that time on they were his disciples.

Jesus' principal strategy for training his disciples was for them to spend time with him. The disciples talked with Jesus; they travelled with Jesus; they studied Scripture with Jesus; they ate with Jesus and prayed with Jesus. They were always *with Jesus*; and they even went fishing together. Robert Coleman calls all of this 'the master plan of evangelism'. He writes:

> Having called his men, Jesus made a practice of being with them. This was the essence of his training program – just letting his disciples follow him. When one stops to think of it, this was an incredibly simple way of doing it. Jesus had no formal school, no seminaries, no outlined course of study, no periodic membership classes in which he enrolled his followers. None of these highly organized procedures considered so necessary today entered into his ministry. Amazing as it may seem, all Jesus did to teach these men his way was to draw them close to himself. He was his own school and curriculum.[12]

In Christ's school of discipleship, the most basic lesson is that following Jesus will cost you everything. Jesus is Lord as well as Saviour, so becoming his disciple means surrendering your whole life in absolute submission to his sovereignty. Discipleship means leaving everything else behind to follow Jesus, which is what Peter and Andrew did when Jesus called them by the Sea of Galilee: 'They pulled their boats up on shore, left everything and followed him.'[13] Disciples are sometimes tempted to turn back, so Jesus repeated this lesson many times. 'If anyone would come after me,' he said, 'he must deny himself and take up his cross daily and follow me.'[14] It was this demand that led the German theologian Dietrich Bonhoeffer (1906–45) to observe, 'The cross is not the terrible end to an otherwise God-fearing and happy life, but it meets us at the beginning of our communion with Christ. When Christ calls a man, he bids him come and die.'[15] Unless we are willing to follow Jesus to the death, we *cannot* be his disciples. Jesus said it again and again: 'Anyone who does not carry his cross and follow me

[10] Luke 6:13.   [11] Mark 1:16–17; cf. 2:14.
[12] Coleman, *The Master Plan of Evangelism*, p. 41.
[13] Luke 5:11.   [14] Luke 9:23.
[15] Bonhoeffer, *The Cost of Discipleship*, p. 99.

cannot be my disciple';[16] 'Any of you who does not give up everything he has cannot be my disciple.'[17]

This is hard teaching, so it is not surprising that when Jesus started counting the cost of discipleship, 'many of his disciples turned back and no longer followed him'.[18] What *is* surprising is that when they started to turn away, Jesus did not go running after them. But it was never his intention to meet people half-way. With Jesus, it is all or nothing, and receiving his saving grace means leaving everything else behind. Salvation is free, but it does not come cheap, for it demands the high price of discipleship. In his famous book *The Cost of Discipleship*, Bonhoeffer warned against the danger of what he called 'cheap grace'. He had observed many Christians who were unprepared to live for Christ, let alone to die for him. As a result, they were setting their salvation at a discount. 'Cheap grace', wrote Bonhoeffer, 'is the preaching of forgiveness without requiring repentance, baptism without church discipline, communion without confession, absolution without personal confession. Cheap grace is grace without discipleship, grace without the cross, grace without Jesus Christ living and incarnate.'[19] But of course there is no saving grace without discipleship, without the cross, or without Jesus Christ. Anyone who is saved by grace must live for God, following Christ through suffering into glory.

The method of discipleship

In addition to teaching us how to *become* disciples, the Gospels also teach us how to *make* disciples. Almost without realizing it, the whole time that Jesus' disciples were learning how to follow Jesus, they were also learning how to help others follow him, too. Gradually Jesus began to let them share in his work, sending them out by twos on short mission trips to preach and to heal.[20] After all the on-the-job training they had received, when Jesus finally told them to go and make disciples, they knew exactly what to do. As they shared the message of salvation, they would invest their lives in the kind of close personal relationships that Jesus had established with them. The difference was that instead of training people to follow themselves, as most ancient teachers did, they would train people to follow Jesus. They would teach their followers to become what they were themselves – followers of Christ. This is the method the apostle Paul was adopting when he said, 'Follow my example, as I follow the example of Christ.'[21] The crucial thing is to follow Christ.

God's plan for getting the message out has not changed. The Great Commission calls for Christians to reproduce themselves by the power

[16] Luke 14:27.   [17] Luke 14:33.   [18] John 6:66.
[19] Bonhoeffer, *The Cost of Discipleship*, p. 47.
[20] See Matt. 10.   [21] 1 Cor. 11:1.

285

of the Holy Spirit. One Christian is to help one sinner learn how to follow Christ through prayer and Bible study, and also by answering practical questions about the Christian life. That new Christian, in turn, is to help another sinner learn how to follow Christ, until finally the whole world is reached for Jesus Christ. The entire plan depends on multiplication. At first it may seem surprising to realize how few disciples Jesus himself reached. But as Coleman explains,

> His whole evangelistic strategy – indeed, the fulfilment of his very purpose in coming into the world, dying on the cross, and rising from the grave – depended on the faithfulness of his chosen disciples to this task. It did not matter how small the group was to start with so long as they reproduced and taught their disciples to reproduce. This was the way his church was to win – through the dedicated lives of those who knew the Savior so well that his Spirit and method constrained them to tell others. As simple as it may seem, this was the way the gospel would conquer. He had no other plan.[22]

Jesus calls us to be disciple-making disciples who reach the world one disciple at a time. This kind of loving personal discipleship takes time, which perhaps explains why it is so rarely practised in the church. To quote again from Coleman:

> Building men and women ... requires constant personal attention ... The example of Jesus would teach us that it can be done only by persons staying close to those whom they seek to lead. The church obviously has failed at this point, and failed tragically. There is a lot of talk in the church about evangelism and Christian nurture, but little concern for personal association when it becomes evident that such work involves the sacrifice of personal indulgence ... new Christians ... are left entirely on their own to find the solutions to innumerable practical problems confronting their lives, any one of which could mean disaster to their new faith. With such haphazard follow-up of believers, it is no wonder that about half of those who make professions and join the church eventually fall away ... There is simply no substitute for getting with people, and it is ridiculous to imagine that anything less, short of a miracle, can develop strong Christian leadership.

Coleman closes by asking this question: 'If Jesus, the Son of God, found it necessary to stay almost constantly with his few disciples for three years, and even one of them was lost, how can a church expect to

---

[22] Coleman, *The Master Plan of Evangelism*, p. 99.

do this job on an assembly line basis a few days out of the year?'[23]

This does not mean that discipleship always requires exclusive friendships. In some Christian circles the term 'discipleship' has come to mean a special kind of relationship in which an older Christian serves as a mentor or 'spiritual director' for a more recent convert. In fact, however, any relationship that helps us to follow Christ is part of our discipleship. And while some spiritual relationships prove more valuable than others – especially friendships with more mature Christians – every disciple needs a variety of nurturing influences. No single individual can do for us what Jesus did for his disciples, for he was the very source of their spiritual life.

Furthermore, Jesus himself carried on discipleship at several different levels. He devoted most of his attention to the training of the twelve. Yet even within this group there were three – Peter, James and John – who formed his inner circle. And beyond the twelve there were many others: the seventy he sent out to preach the gospel, the crowds who followed him to hear his preaching, the five hundred who saw him after his resurrection, and so on. All of this suggests that we can learn how to follow Christ in many ways, from many people, in many contexts. Pastors disciple their congregations whenever they teach and preach. Elders and deacons and other church leaders make disciples by giving spiritual care and material assistance. Friends disciple friends when they meet for Bible study and prayer. Husbands and wives disciple one another by praying for one another. Parents disciple their children as they train them in righteousness. In one way or another, discipleship should be part of every true Christian friendship.

Going and baptizing

The Christian's prime directive is to make disciples, but Jesus used three participles to explain precisely how this disciple-making is to happen. Discipleship requires going, baptizing and teaching: *'Go and make disciples of all nations, baptising them in the name of the Father and of the Son and of the Holy Spirit, and teaching them to obey everything I have commanded you'* (28:19–20a).

First, making disciples means *going* to all nations. The word *'Go'* shows that the message of salvation will not spread by itself. It is up to God's new people to get the message out, and that means taking it to the nations. Because the word 'go' appears first in most English translations, it is sometimes thought that the Great Commission is mainly about international missionary work. In fact, as we have seen, Jesus' main emphasis is on making disciples. Nevertheless, due to its proximity to the verb for 'make disciples', the participle 'going' also has the force of an imperative.[24] The church of Jesus Christ is not only

---

[23] Ibid., p. 49.   [24] Carson, 'Matthew', p. 595.

commissioned, but also commanded, to go all over the world with the gospel. On another occasion, Jesus told his disciples, 'The Christ will suffer and rise from the dead on the third day, and repentance and forgiveness of sins will be preached in his name to all nations, beginning at Jerusalem.'[25] The implication was that once salvation was preached in Jerusalem, as Peter preached it on the Day of Pentecost (see chapter 15), it would be preached everywhere else. In the longer ending of the Gospel of Mark, Jesus issued the same commission in slightly different words: 'Go into all the world and preach the good news to all creation.'[26]

If we are to complete our commission to evangelize the world, we cannot wait for the nations to come to us – we must go to them, because they will not come to Christ until we do. We must be like the shepherds who found Jesus lying in the manger, and then spread the word to everyone they met.[27] Or like the servants in the parable of the great banquet: when the invited guests spurned their master's invitation, the servants were told, 'Go out quickly into the streets and alleys of the town and bring in the poor, the crippled, the blind and the lame … Go out to the roads and country lanes and make them come in, so that my house will be full.'[28] We cannot disciple the nations without going to the nations.

The word 'nations' does not refer to nation-states, in the modern sense, but to what missiologists call 'people groups'. The Greek word is *ethnē*, from which we derive English words like 'ethnic' and 'ethnicity'. It refers to cultural and linguistic groupings that establish ethnic identity but may or may not correspond to political or geographic boundaries.[29] The 1982 Lausanne Strategy Working Group carefully defined a 'people group' as 'a significantly large grouping of individuals who perceive themselves to have a common affinity for one another because of their shared language, religion, ethnicity, residence, occupation … the largest group within which the Gospel can spread as a church planting movement without encountering barriers of understanding or acceptance.'[30] What Jesus meant, therefore, is that the message of salvation is for every group of people in the whole wide world. To disciple the nations is to disciple the world's people groups.

In this respect our *missiology* (theology of missions and evangelism) flows from our *eschatology* (doctrine of the last things). Since God has promised to glorify a countless multitude 'from every nation, tribe,

---

[25] Luke 24:46–47.   [26] Mark 16:15.
[27] Luke 2:17.   [28] Luke 14:21, 23.
[29] This point is thoroughly developed in Piper, *Let the Nations be Glad!*, pp. 168–221 (Baker ed., pp. 167–218).
[30] Lausanne Strategy Working Group (1982), quoted in Ralph Winter, 'Unreached peoples: Recent developments in the concept', *Mission Frontiers* (August/September 1989), p. 12.

people and language', we must disciple every nation, tribe, people and language. In the words of John Oxenham (1852–1941),

> In Christ there is no East or West,
> In Him no South or North,
> But one great fellowship of love
> Throughout the whole wide earth.

The principle is not merely geographic, but can be extended to every barrier that divides human society. The message of salvation is for young and old, rich and poor, healthy and sick, deaf and hearing, civilized and uncivilized, black and white, Arab and Asian. The message is for everyone because God's grace is for everyone – everyone made in God's image, marred by sin, and in need of salvation.

One obvious implication of this international commission is that the message of salvation must be taken across boundaries of language and custom. Sharing God's mission to the world requires cross-cultural communication. This does not mean that every Christian is required to be an overseas missionary. It does mean that every Christian must be outreach-minded, prepared to share the message of salvation with those who come from a different culture. It also means that every Christian must be a world Christian, taking an active interest in reaching the unreached peoples of the world.

Christianity has always been a cross-cultural religion. Already on the Day of Pentecost, the message of salvation was preached in many languages to many people from many parts of the world. Indeed, the Bible says that the people who heard salvation's message that day were 'from every nation under heaven'.[31] As soon as they received the message, they started getting it out to the rest of the world. Not many years later, the apostle Paul was able to testify that he had 'fully proclaimed the gospel of Christ' from Jerusalem all the way to Illyricum, now in Albania.[32] By the middle of the next century, there were churches in nearly every Roman province from North Africa to Europe. A second-century tombstone from Hieropolis, Turkey, provides dramatic evidence for the spread of the Christian gospel. As its epitaph explains, the tomb belongs to Avircius Marcellus, who had travelled not only to Rome, where he had met the emperor, but also from the plains of Syria all the way to Nisibis, east of the Euphrates. Wherever he travelled, Avircius Marcellus discovered that the message of salvation had preceded him, so that he could enjoy fellowship with other Christians. Every place he visited, people drew the early Christian symbol of the fish and offered him the bread and wine of the sacrament.[33] In the

---

[31] Acts 2:5.   [32] Rom. 15:19.
[33] Dale T. Irvin, 'The gift of mission', *Christianity Today* (6 December 1999), pp. 58–59.

centuries to follow, missionaries took the message of salvation to Britain, Scandinavia and all the barbarian tribes of Europe. The sixteenth century witnessed the dawn of a new age in missions, with Christians fulfilling their Great Commission in the New World of the Americas. In the eighteenth century the focus shifted to the Far East. By the nineteenth century, even the vast inlands of Africa and China had been penetrated with the gospel. At the dawn of a new millennium, nearly every people group in the world has heard the name of Jesus Christ, and many can read the Scriptures in their own language.

This does not mean that we have fulfilled our Great Commission, however. Jesus commanded us not simply to go to the nations, but also to disciple them, and there is still much work to be done. The important thing is to recognize that wherever we find ourselves in the world, we have been sent to make disciples. The Great Commission is not so much about going as about having been sent. The first disciples understood this. Jesus said to them, 'As the Father has sent me, I am sending you.'[34] Wherever they went – down the street, into prison, across the sea – they preached God's saving message.[35] They said, 'In Christ, we speak before God with sincerity, like men sent from God.'[36] We must understand this, too. Even if we stay right where we are, we are on a mission. Robert Coleman is right when he says:

> Christian disciples are sent men and women – sent out in the same work of world evangelism to which the Lord was sent, and for which he gave his life. Evangelism is not an optional accessory to our life. It is the heartbeat of all that we are called to be and do. It is the commission of the church which gives meaning to all else that is undertaken in the name of Christ.[37]

When Christ calls us to a lifetime of discipleship, he calls us to a lifestyle of disciple-making.

As we go into the world and make disciples, we are also to baptize them. The second participle used to explain how we make disciples is *baptising*. Except in the most unusual circumstances, baptism is essential to our salvation. Jesus said, 'Whoever believes and is baptised will be saved, but whoever does not believe will be condemned.'[38] Baptism is also essential to our discipleship. Making disciples means *baptising them in the name of the Father and of the Son and of the Holy Spirit* (28:19).

This is one of the few places in the New Testament where all three persons in the Trinity are brought together in a single verse. It is highly

[34] John 20:21b.   [35] Acts 8:4.   [36] 2 Cor. 2:17b.
[37] Coleman, *The Master Plan of Evangelism*, pp. 87–88.
[38] Mark 16:16.

significant that the threefold name of God should appear specifically in this verse, in which the church receives its Great Commission. We are called to make disciples in the name of the Father, the Son and the Holy Spirit. Notice that there is only one 'name', with three divine persons to share it. Discipleship thus draws us into fellowship with the Trinity. At the moment we enter the Christian community through baptism, we are identified with the name of the Triune God.

The fact that disciples are to be baptized means that discipleship is a job for the church (which means, incidentally, that church-planting is one the most effective ways to fulfill the Great Commission). Baptism – whether it is practised for infants or adults – is the sacrament of initiation into the covenant family of God's new people. It is a sign of cleansing, renewal and rebirth by God's Spirit. Since it is a holy sacrament, instituted by Jesus Christ, it is properly administered by an ordained minister of the Christian church. Thus discipleship was never intended to take place outside the church. A disciple is someone who comes under the authority of Christ, which includes submitting to the spiritual care of his church. The sign of coming under that spiritual authority is Christian baptism.

Teaching them to obey all things

The third participle that explains our discipleship is *teaching*. Making disciples means going, baptizing, and finally *teaching them to obey everything I have commanded you* (28:20a). This is also the third of the four 'alls' in the Great Commission. What Jesus literally says is 'teaching them to obey all things': the message of salvation demands a *universal obedience*.

It is perhaps significant that the teaching about obedience follows the baptizing. This is part of the logic of infant baptism. Parents are to disciple their children in the faith into which they were baptized. It is also part of the logic of adult baptism. Obviously, some teaching must take place before a believer is baptized. In order to be baptized, a new convert must understand the message of salvation, which requires having at least a basic grasp of the doctrines we have been studying throughout this book. Disciples need to be taught the doctrine of *sin*, that the totality of our depravity makes us liable to God's wrath and curse. They need to be taught the doctrines of *grace*, that we are saved through Christ's redeeming, reconciling work on the cross and in the empty tomb. They need to be taught the doctrine of *faith*, that by turning away from sin and trusting in Jesus Christ we become God's righteous sons and daughters. Before becoming a disciple at all – let alone before being baptized – a convert must be taught that salvation from sin is by grace through faith.

The message of salvation is only the beginning, however. As we saw

291

when we studied sanctification back in chapter 16, Christianity is a whole new way of life. What disciples need to know is not simply the basic gospel message, but everything Christ taught about every aspect of the Christian life. Thus making disciples means teaching them to obey *every* command of Christ. To put it another way, to be a disciple is to live a disciplined life.

This has many practical implications. One is that we need to focus on the life and teaching of Jesus himself. To follow Christ we must learn from Christ, and we must never stop learning. A disciple is a person who receives a lifetime of instruction from Jesus Christ. Such knowledge may fall out of fashion, but it will always be practical, and those who pursue it will never fall out of favour with God. Another implication is that Christians need to study the whole Bible, faithfully and systematically. Jesus never intended Christianity to be reduced to its bare minimum; he expects our unqualified obedience to everything he ever taught. Therefore, we are not at liberty to pick and choose among the commands of Christ, obeying only the instructions that we feel as if we want to obey. Instead, we must submit to what the Bible itself calls 'the obedience that comes from faith'.[39]

One final implication of giving Jesus our unqualified obedience is that we must become disciple-makers ourselves. We are to obey everything that Jesus taught. Obviously, 'everything' includes his last and greatest commission to the church. Methods of evangelism come and go, but the command to make disciples will be ours until Christ returns. There are no alternatives, and there are no shortcuts. The Great Commission itself requires us to fulfil the Great Commission – going, baptizing and teaching. Our own discipleship is not complete until we become disciple-makers.

Staying with us always

Christ's command comes with an abiding promise: *'And surely I am with you always, to the very end of the age'* (28:20b). This great promise is the last of the 'alls' in the Great Commission: all authority, all nations, all things, and always or 'all the days'. This promise of Christ's *universal presence* gives a clear indication that the command to make disciples was not only for the apostles, but also for us. Jesus promised to be with us to the end of the age, a promise that could not be restricted to the apostles because they did not live to see Christ's return. Therefore, both the commission and the promise are for the church in the present day.

The promise is perpetual. What Jesus literally promises is to be with us 'all the days'. Day after day, he will be with us all day long. The promise is also personal. The Christ who saves us, and to whom we are

---

[39] Rom. 1:5b; cf. Acts 6:7.

united by faith, pledges to go with us as we take his saving message to the world. Leon Morris comments:

> The Gospel ends with Jesus' breathtaking promise that he is with his followers *all the days to the end of the age*. He does not say 'I will be with you,' but *'I am with you,'* and his *I* is emphatic, 'no less than I.' … In other words, the disciple is not going to be left to serve God as well as he can in the light of what he has learned from the things Jesus has commanded. The disciple will find that he has a great companion as he goes on his way through life.[40]

The risen Christ has given us the promise of his undying presence. The way he fulfils this promise is by sending us his Spirit: 'You will receive power when the Holy Spirit comes on you; and you will be my witnesses in Jerusalem, and in all Judea and Samaria, and to the ends of the earth.'[41] The message of salvation is that through the Holy Spirit, Jesus Christ is with us from now until for ever. This is our only comfort as we pass through suffering into glory. It is also our only hope of success as we share the message of salvation. The Christ who goes with us into all the world is the very same Christ who has all authority in heaven and earth, and who has promised that the message of salvation will be preached to all nations.

Jesus gives us the promise of his presence so that we will have the confidence to fulfil our Great Commission. The commission is as urgent now as it was the very day that Christ stood on the mountain and sent his disciples into all the world. One man who sensed the urgency of getting the message out was D. L. Moody, one of America's foremost evangelists during the nineteenth century:

> He also preached the Gospel powerfully in London and other cities of Great Britain. Some clergymen, who were jealous of this uneducated Yankee, wanted to know his secret. So they knocked on the door of his hotel room, the story is told, and greeted him by saying, 'Mr. Moody, we would like to have a word with you. You come here to London, you have a sixth-grade education, you speak horrible English, your sermons are simple, and yet thousands of people are converted. We want to know, how do you do it?'
>
> Moody invited his guests into his room and walked over to a window. 'Tell me,' he said, 'what do you see?'
>
> One gentleman looked out and said, 'I see a park and some children playing.'
>
> 'Anything else?' Moody asked.

[40] Morris, *The Gospel according to Matthew*, p. 749.
[41] Acts 1:8.

Another man said, 'I see about the same thing except there is an older couple walking hand in hand, enjoying the evening.'

A third clergyman added that he saw a young couple, and then he asked, 'Mr. Moody, what do you see?'

As Moody stood there staring out the window, tears began to roll down his cheeks onto his gray beard. 'Mr. Moody, what are you looking at?' one of his curious guests asked. 'What do *you* see?'

'When I look out the widow, I see countless thousands of souls that will one day spend eternity in hell if they do not find the Saviour,' Moody said.[42]

Anyone who looks carefully will see what D. L. Moody saw. Every day we meet people who have not yet received the message of salvation, including some who have never even heard it. They do not know that salvation is by grace, the grace that God has given through his one and only Son. They do not know that salvation is through faith in the death and resurrection of Jesus Christ. As a result, they are still lost in sin and doomed to face all its deadly consequences. The only way they will ever find the Saviour is by hearing his saving message. It is the greatest message there is, the best news that anyone has ever heard. How will you share it?

---

[42] Recounted in Lane T. Dennis, 'What do we see?' *Share the Good News* (September/October, 1999), p. 3.

Study guide

The aim of this study guide is to help you get to the heart of what Philip Ryken has written and to challenge you to apply what you learn to your own life. The questions have been designed for use by individuals or by small groups of Christians meeting, perhaps for an hour or two each week, to study, discuss and pray together.

The guide provides material for each of the sections in the book. When used by a group with limited time, the leader should decide beforehand which questions are most appropriate for the group to discuss during the meeting and which should perhaps be left for group members to work through by themselves or in smaller groups during the week.

In order to be able to contribute fully and learn from the group meetings, each member of the group needs to read through the section or sections under discussion, together with the passages of Scripture to which they refer.

It's important not to let these studies become merely academic exercises. Guard against this by making time to think through and discuss how what you discover *works out in practice* for you. Make sure you begin and end each study by focusing on God in praise and prayer. Ask the Holy Spirit to speak to you through your discussion together.

PART 1: SAVED FROM SIN

1. Why we need to be saved
Creation and fall: Genesis 2:15 – 3:6 (pp. 17–30)

'Things are not getting any better. If anything, they are getting worse, for the twentieth century was the bloodiest in human history. One intellectual rightly described it as "the worst century our planet has yet endured – spectacular advancements in science and technology obscured by evil pure and unadorned". The new millennium can only promise more of the same: more people, more greed, more lust and more violence. There is no doubt about it: humanity has a problem. Or, perhaps we should say, humanity is the problem' (p. 17).

---

1 Read Genesis 1:1, 1:26 and 2:7. How do these verses define us as human beings?

2 Given that we are made in the image of God, in what ways (p. 20) can we see what he is like?

3 Philip Ryken describes three ways in which we are made to glorify God. How can we serve him in our work, rest and relationships?

4 Reflect on the statement from the *Westminster Shorter Catechism* (p. 23). To what extent does the reality of our everyday lives match the theory?

5 'Adam lived in covenant with God, standing as representative for the entire human race' (p. 24). What were the wider implications of Adam and Eve failing God's ultimate obedience test?

6 Many theologians speculate on what would have happened if Adam and Eve had never sinned (p. 25). But what one thing is certain?

7 Describe how the couple gave in to temptation, paying particular attention to how Satan challenges God's goodness and contradicts God's truthfulness. Why is it so vital to understand that the entry of sin into the world actually happened during human history (p. 27)?

8 'Eve was not content to reflect God's glory, she wanted to grab the glory for herself' (p. 29).What is at the very heart of our sin?

9 Read Acts 16:30. Why can't we save ourselves?

2. What we need to be saved from
Sin and judgment: Genesis 3: 7–24 (pp. 31–45)

1 Contrast the two different types of guilt: original sin (p. 32) and actual sin (p. 34). How are they similar and how are they different?

2 Explain the theological term 'total depravity' (p. 34). How is the double weight of our sin paid for (p. 35)?

'We cannot dress up for God, spiritually speaking, but God does have a plan for covering our guilt with his grace ... Clothing our first parents was a way of showing that things could never be the same, that fallen human beings cannot go back to naked innocence. But the clothes were also a sign of God's grace. They showed that God can do something for us that we cannot do for ourselves, and that is to cover up our guilt and shame' (p. 35).

---

3 'Adam's children were not sinners simply because they sinned. Rather, they sinned because they were sinners' (p. 33). Why should this be the case?

4 Philip Ryken asserts that: 'God holds us morally responsible for what Adam did, reckoning his sin to be our sin, and condemning us for it. This is not unjust' (p. 33). Why not?

5 According to the author, there are four main consequences of sin, the first of which is guilt. Think of a time when you did something wrong. How did that make you feel?

6 What feeling does the second consequence, alienation from God, produce? How did Adam cope with this feeling (p. 37)?

7 Give some examples of how the third consequence, alienation from each other, shows itself in relationships. To what extent can the message of salvation put an end to these conflicts (p. 40)?

8 How does Satan work to 'drag human beings into sin and despair, and finally down into the pit of hell' (p. 39)? In what way does God deliver us from the evil one, the fourth consequence?

9 In what ways does the penalty for sin (p. 40) reveal itself today?

10 How can being 'outcasts from Eden' (p. 42) also be a demonstration of God's grace?

11 'To deny the reality of hell is to deny the truth and the justice of God.' Describe the two kinds of death we face. What is the ultimate purpose of salvation (p. 43)?

3. Why we cannot save ourselves
Inability: Isaiah 59:1–21 (pp. 46–60)

1 Give two reasons why people do not glorify God (p. 46). How does Isaiah 59:1–2 address the issues raised (p. 47)?

2 In chapter two, Philip Ryken lists four consequences of sin, drawn from Genesis. How does the book of Isaiah go on to confirm these?

'The one problem we cannot solve for ourselves is sin. Not only is this true biblically and historically, but it is also true logically, and therefore universally. The one who is guilty cannot remove his own guilt. The one who is alienated and estranged cannot reconcile himself to God or to his neighbour. The one who is embattled cannot defeat the devil. The one who suffers cannot ease his pain. And even if we could remove all the other consequences of sin, we cannot make ourselves immortal' (p. 51).

---

3 In what ways do people try to save themselves (p. 52)?

4 'Because we are totally depraved, there is not one part of us that wants to live for God' (p. 52). If this is true, then how can we know God?

5 To what extent do we choose to follow God (p. 53)?
6 Think about the doctrine of inability (p. 54). Why is it so central to the Christian faith and why is it so unpopular even in the church?
7 'For a religion to have any credibility at all, it has to explain what is wrong with human beings, and it has to offer some kind of remedy. By this standard, Christianity is the only credible option' (p. 55). Summarize why this is so.
8 Reflect on Isaiah 59:15b–17. Why is salvation described as something for which God needs to fight (p. 57)?
9 Read Ephesians 6:10–17. Explain what it means to put on the armour of God.
10 In what ways does Isaiah indicate the redeemer is both God and man (pp. 58–59)? Why is Jesus Christ the one who was prophesied?
11 'Although God offers the message of salvation to everyone, not everyone is willing to receive it' (p. 59). Why is repentance so important for salvation?

PART 2: SAVED BY GRACE

4. Chosen in Christ
Election: Ephesians 1:3–14 (pp. 61–75)

1 Define the doctrine of the Trinity. In what way does salvation involve every person of the Trinity (pp. 61–62)?
2 Read Ephesians 1:4–12. Explain how the verses contain the whole message of salvation (p. 64).
3 Why is the Holy Spirit called a *seal* and an advance *deposit* in Ephesians 1:13–14?
4 'God is not sovereign; he is a finite being who does not even know the future, but he is open to the possibilities' (pp. 65–66). Give some reasons why, according to Ephesians, this statement is incorrect.

'God knew the solution even before we caused the problem. He developed his plan for salvation before the foundation of the world. Perhaps this helps explain why God permitted humanity to fall into sin. From the beginning, God had planned for us a blessing even greater than mere creation: he had purposed our salvation in his Son' (p. 66).

---

5 What is the doctrine of election (p. 66)? How can you be sure you are among God's elect (p. 68) and why is election best understood in the hindsight of becoming a Christian?

6 'God not only chose his people, but he also chose their Saviour' (p. 70). Why is the theme of God's electing choice significant?

7 Think about the argument that predestination is actually a form of fatalism. How can divine sovereignty allow for human responsibility (p. 71)?

8 If God is just, how can he save some without saving others (p. 71)?

9 'Do we choose God because he first chose us, or does God choose us because he knows in advance that we will choose him' (p. 72)?

10 'What is the point of sharing the message of salvation, if God has already chosen those whom he has elected to save' (p. 72)?

11 Why is election actually the basis for 'genuine spiritual humility' (p. 73)?

5. Out of Egypt
Deliverance: Exodus 15:1–21 (pp. 76–89)

'God did not love the Israelites because they were lovable, but because he was loving. He saved them for no other reason than that he chose them to receive the covenant promise of his salvation' (p. 76).

---

1 Show how the essential meaning of the biblical concept of salvation is deliverance (p. 78). Why has the exodus become synonymous with salvation (p. 79)?

2 'Salvation is always *to* something as well as *from* something' (p. 81). Contrast the salvation from Egypt to the promised land with salvation from sin to glory.

3 In what way is the Lord our salvation?

4 Read Exodus 14:28. Why was it necessary for God to destroy the Egyptians (p. 83)?

5 To what extent was the conflict between Israel and Egypt really a spiritual battle, pitting the God of Abraham, Isaac and Jacob against the gods of the Nile (p. 84)?

6 According to Philip Ryken, why is it wrong to worship other gods (p. 85)?

7 'In many ways, the salvation that Jesus offers is the same kind of salvation that God's people experienced when they came out of Egypt' (p. 85). List some of these ways.

8 'Salvation is what puts the song into the believer's heart' (p. 87).

Meditate on Exodus 15:1–2a. How closely can you identify with these verses?

'God has called us out of the Egypt of our sins, saving us from Satan, wrath, death, and all the rest of our enemies. Now we have something to sing about. It is time to take up the chorus and shake out the tambourine, to put on dancing shoes and give God the glory. The Lord is our strength and our song, and he has become our salvation' (p. 89).

---

6. Paid in full
Redemption: Ruth 4:1–22 (pp. 90–103)

1 According to Philip Ryken, what are the three parts of any redemption (p. 91)? Explain how these three parts fit with Israel's redemption from Egypt.
2 Consider the different types of redemption listed by the author: that of livestock, land and the freeing of slaves (p. 92). How would these experiences lead people to the knowledge that God was their redeemer?
3 Contrast the ways Ruth was in economic, emotional and social bondage (p. 93), with the ways we are in bondage today. Why can't we redeem ourselves?
4 To what extent is the fact that Boaz was related to Naomi significant (p. 95)?
5 Define the connection between Boaz and Jesus (p. 95). Why could our redemption never be carried out by an angel?
6 Read Hebrews 2:11–17. How do these verses show that Jesus is our kinsman-redeemer?
7 Note the similarities between the redemption Boaz provided for Ruth and the redemption God has provided in Jesus Christ (pp. 99–102).

'No other religious faith has ever claimed that the one and only Supreme Deity shed his own blood to save his people. What has Buddha – or Muhammad – ever done to purchase men for God? Yet redemption requires the ultimate sacrifice. Jesus was willing to pay the price because he loves his people. He was able to pay it because he is God the eternal Son, which makes his death of inestimable worth' (p. 100).

---

8 'As costly as it was to redeem Ruth, the price of her redemption is not to be compared with the price of redemption in Jesus Christ' (p. 100). Why not?
9 Reflect on the romance of redemption, pictured by the story of Boaz and Ruth. In what way does receiving the message of salvation mean being 'married to Christ'? How should we respond to God in this love relationship?

7. God, be merciful to me
Expiation and propitiation: Luke 18:9–14
(pp. 104–117)

1 Define atonement (p. 104). Why is atonement so important for contemporary theology?
2 According to Philip Ryken, what was wrong with the Pharisee's prayer (p. 106)? Give the reason why, despite his prayer and good works, he remained unsaved.
3 'Whereas the Pharisee was counting on his own merits, the "publican" was begging for God's mercy' (p. 107). What were the three parts to the tax collector's prayer? Why was it significant that he started with God and ended with himself?

'Who was closer to God – the Pharisee or the publican? The Pharisee was nearer to the altar, but much farther away from God. He was so full of himself that there was hardly any room for God at all. By contrast, although the publican was far from the altar, he was close to the heart of God, for he came in reverent fear' (p. 107).

---

4 Look at Leviticus 16. What was the correct way to come into God's presence and what was the significance of the ritual (p. 109)?
5 'Sprinkling blood on the mercy seat was a way to show that the atoning sacrifice had come between God and his sinful people' (p. 110). Explain the theological terms 'expiation' and 'propitiation'. Define how the sprinkling of blood was both an expiation and propitiation.
6 When the tax collector asked for mercy, what was he really asking for in theological terms (p. 111)?
7 Contrast Jesus' sacrifice with that of the goat on the Day of Atonement (p. 112). Give reasons why his death on the cross expiates our sin and propitiates God's wrath.

8 Why does it matter whether or not Christ's death was a vicarious atonement (p. 115)?
9 'From beginning to end, propitiation is all of God' (p. 115). Consider why God made atonement part of his plan.
10 On what basis are we justified (p. 116)?
11 Explain what salvation means in the light of atonement (p. 116).

8. Together again
Reconciliation: 2 Corinthians 5:14 – 6:2 (pp. 118–129)

1 Explain how 'atonement' actually means 'reconciliation' (p. 118).
2 Define the doctrine of reconciliation (pp. 118–119).

'Why does man feel so bad in the very age when more than any other age he has succeeded in satisfying his needs and making the world over for his own use? We can put people on the moon. We can send rockets into the deepest reaches of space, yet we're no nearer discovering meaning in our world, within its horizons, than we were three thousand years ago' (Walker Percy, quoted on p. 119).

---

3 Think about how much we have in the Western world. Why do these things fail to satisfy? Why do we still feel so empty and alone in the universe (pp. 119–120)?
4 What separates us from God? How does sin bring a double alienation (p. 120)?
5 Outline the two tests which show whether a person is alienated from God (p. 120). To what extent are they effective, and why is our estimation of Jesus Christ so important?
6 What is so remarkable about God being the author of reconciliation (p. 122)?
7 In what way did the crucifixion reconcile us to God (p. 124)?
8 Describe double imputation (p. 125). What impact does this have on our lives?
9 Give some of the practical implications of the doctrine of reconciliation (p. 126).
10 What role do we play as God's ambassadors (p. 127)?
11 Given that every Christian is reconciled to God once and for all through faith in Christ, why do we need to keep on being reconciled?

9. Proof positive
Resurrection: Acts 13:32–48 (pp. 130–146)

1 How does Paul go about preaching the message of salvation in Acts 13 (p. 131)? Why was what he said news to the Jews in Pisidian Antioch (p. 132)?
2 In what way is the crucifixion of Christ a fulfilment of Old Testament promises (pp. 132–133)?

'If all Jesus had done was to die on the cross, we could never be saved. Salvation comes by grace alone in Christ alone, but it does not come through the cross alone. Whenever the New Testament presents the message of salvation, it always preaches the crucifixion plus the resurrection' (p. 133).

---

3 Explain the meaning of resurrection (p. 133).
4 List the physical properties of Jesus' resurrection body (pp. 133–134). Why is it significant that he was raised bodily?
5 According to some sceptics, Jesus didn't rise from the dead. Why do these objections demand an answer (p. 135)?
6 If the resurrection didn't happen, how do you account for the disappearance of Jesus' body (p. 136)? What are the problems associated with these theories (pp. 138–139)?
7 'No merely psychological explanation can account for the numerous post-resurrection appearances of Christ' (p. 140). Consider this statement and give reasons why it is true.
8 In what way is the resurrection of Christ a fulfilment of Old Testament promises (p. 141)?
9 Why did Paul call his sermon in Pisidian Antioch the 'message of salvation' (p. 144)?

PART 3: SAVED THROUGH FAITH

10. Born again
Regeneration: John 3:1–16 (pp. 147–159)

1 How is the redemption accomplished by Christ applied to the Christian (p. 147)?
2 In what way did Jesus answer Nicodemus' question with truths about regeneration? Why was Jesus' way of answering so

remarkable (p. 149)? What warning does the conversation between Nicodemus and Jesus contain for religious people?

3 List the spiritual changes that regeneration brings (pp. 149–150).

4 Explain what it means to be born again. Why is new birth so necessary (p. 150)?

'We cannot even decide to be reborn. We are as dependent on the Holy Spirit for spiritual rebirth as we were on our parents for physical birth. No matter how much we go into labour – reading self-improvement books, keeping religious rituals, following moral codes – there is no way we can deliver ourselves into new spiritual life' (p. 152).

---

5 Read John 3:5–6. In what ways is it possible to interpret the water in this verse (p. 152)?

6 According to Philip Ryken, water and spirit should be thought of as a conceptual unity (p. 153). Define what this means.

7 Reflect on the examples of new birth (pp. 154–155). To what extent can you identify with them?

8 'It seems as if everything is up to God. If the Spirit blows wherever he pleases, then how can I get him to breathe new life into me?' (p. 156). How does someone become a born-again Christian?

9 Imagine Nicodemus' battle of thoughts during his conversation with Jesus. If he ever was born again (p. 158), how do you think he might have come to this state?

11. Blind man, beggar man, thief
Faith and repentance: Luke 18:35 – 19:10 (pp. 160–177))

1 Philip Ryken asserts that new birth must always come first. Which comes next, repenting or believing (p. 160)?

'The meaning of faith unto salvation and repentance unto life can be illustrated from two episodes in the life of Jesus. The first is a story about faith. It concerns a blind man – a beggar man – who looked to Christ for his salvation. The second is a story about repentance. It concerns a thief who turned away from his sins' (p. 161).

---

2 What are the 'several things' the blind man could see (p. 162)? What was the last thing he saw (p. 163)? Reflect on the significance of the restoration of the blind man's sight. What is salvation for?

3 'The primary purpose of Jesus' miracles was *not* to demonstrate that total physical well-being would be normative for believers in the present age' (p. 166). Explain the primary purpose of his miracles.

4 Contrast the blind man's story with that of Steve and John on p. 167. Why wasn't John healed physically and what would have been different if he had?

5 How did the blind man receive his sight (p. 167)?

6 Theologians teach that there are three elements of saving faith (p. 168). List them with their explanations. How was the blind man's faith also productive (p. 170)?

7 Consider the story of Zacchaeus. In what way was Jesus on a divine mission (p. 172)?

8 What was the real proof of Zacchaeus' repentance (p. 173)?

9 Define the three essential elements in 'repentance unto life' (p. 173)?

10 To what extent was Zacchaeus 'one of those rare camels who makes it through the needle's eye' (p. 176)? Why is repentance a gift?

12. Alive in Christ
Union with Christ: Ephesians 2:1–10 (pp. 178–189)

1 Define the meanings of 'transgressions' and 'sins' (p. 179).

'One might say that the Earth is the planet of the living dead. Until we come to Christ, we are like so many spiritual zombies – physically alive, but spiritually dead. Until we are reborn by God's Spirit, we do not hear God's voice speaking in Scripture and cannot understand spiritual truth. We are unable to repent of our sins or turn to Christ' (p. 179).

---

2 In Ephesians 2:2–3 Paul describes a triple domination. Explain how we are controlled by (a) the world, (b) the devil and (c) the flesh (pp. 180–181).

3 'It is bad enough to be dead in sin, dominated both inside and out by Satan, but what is worse still is that humanity is *doomed* to fall under the wrath of God' (p. 181). What is God's wrath?

4 Imagine you only had the two words 'But God' to explain the

gospel. How would you go about doing so (p. 182)?

5 In what six ways are Christians connected with Christ (pp. 182–183)? How do these connections translate into the blessings of salvation?

6 Explain how we are made (a) alive with Christ, (b) raised up with Christ and (c) seated with him in the heavenly realms (pp. 184–185).

7 What are the implications of being 'united with Christ' (p. 185)?

8 Why does Paul use the perfect tense when speaking about resurrection, ascension and session (p. 185)?

9 'It is sometimes said that the most important word in the New Testament is the preposition "in", especially when it is joined to the name "Christ"' (p. 186). Read through to p. 188 and give some reasons why this is the case. Why has God saved us by uniting us to Jesus Christ (p. 189)?

'It is very simple: anyone who is not in Christ is not a Christian. But if we are in Christ – that is to say, if we are united to him – then we have a personal share in everything Christ has ever done' (p. 186).

---

10 How do we get 'into Christ' (p. 189)?

11 What is the doctrine of 'union with Christ by faith' (p. 189)?

13. Declared righteous
Justification: Romans 3:19–28 (pp. 190–205)

'When we stand before God for judgment, there is not the slightest chance that we can be accepted on the basis of anything that we have done. This is not a trial in which we are innocent until proven guilty; instead, it is a trial in which we have already been proven guilty and must remain guilty until we are declared righteous' (pp. 190–191).

---

1 Why is justification so central to the message of salvation (p. 191)?

2 Contrast justification with condemnation (pp. 192–193). What is the problem with the traditional Catholic view of justification (p. 193)?

3 Given that 'righteousness is necessary for justification', what is the source of our justification (p. 194)?

4 Philip Ryken points to controversy in the New Testament about interpretation of the phrase the 'righteousness of God' (p. 195). What are the two interpretations and how may they both be true?

5　What is the significance of righteousness being a gift (p. 196)?
6　Look at figure 1 (p. 197). How does this diagram explain justification's basis in the cross?
7　'But Christ's death is not the end of the story' (p. 199). Why does salvation depend on three imputations?
8　Read the illustration given by Donald Grey Barnhouse (p. 200). Philip Ryken asserts this is only half the story. What is the full story?
9　Define justification in theological terms (p. 201). What is the importance of faith in the definition?
10　Why is James' statement that 'a person is justified by what he does and not by faith alone' not at odds with the doctrine of justification by faith alone (p. 203)?

14. All God's children
Adoption: 2 Samuel 9:1–13 (pp. 206–219)

'Our deliverance is relational as well as judicial. God does not deal with us simply as our righteous Judge, but also as our loving Father. He is not content to accept us merely as his servants; he wants to adopt us as his sons and daughters, welcoming us into the fellowship of his family as his children and his heirs' (p. 206).

1　Summarize the difference between adoption and regeneration (p. 207).
2　In what way is our situation similar to that of Mephibosheth (p. 209)?
3　What is the significance of a legal agreement in sonship (p. 207)?
4　What is the basis of our adoption in Jesus Christ (p. 211)?
5　List the privileges that Mephibosheth enjoyed as an adopted child (p. 213). To what extent do they illustrate the privileges of our spiritual sonship?
6　Why does the Bible refer to 'sons of God', rather than sons and daughters, when addressing the issue of inheritance (p. 215)?
7　How should knowing our identity as sons and daughters of the loving Father affect the way we serve God (p. 217)?

PART 4: SAVED FOR GOD'S GLORY

15. God's new people
The communion of saints: Acts 2:42–47 (pp. 220–236)

'There is much more to salvation than praying "the Sinner's Prayer" or "going forward" at an evangelistic rally. Believing the message of salvation is not an end in itself; it is only the beginning. We are not merely saved from *something (namely, sin), but also* for *something. We are saved for God's glory' (p. 221).*

---

1   In what way is Christianity personal but not private (p. 222)?
2   How do the doctrines studied in previous chapters show that all of God's people have everything in common (p. 223)?
3   'The first mark of God's new people is that together they form a learning community' (p. 223). Why should this be so?
4   To what extent does the filling of the Holy Spirit eliminate, or not eliminate, the need for teaching God's Word (p. 224)?
5   List some instances where the lack of Bible teaching has led to church decline (p. 224). Why is the Bible so important and how can its teaching remain central to the life of the individual Christian and the church?
6   On what basis do Christians have fellowship, and what is its true meaning (p. 227)?
7   Explain why sharing a common life does not necessitate living in a commune (p. 228).
8   'Whenever the church has understood what it means to be saved by grace through faith, it has always become a caring community' (p. 228). Give some examples of how the charity of a caring community has made an impact through history. What does being devoted to 'the fellowship' mean for us today?
9   How does the Lord's Supper 'communicate many deep mysteries of the gospel' (p. 230)? Why is it often called 'communion' (p. 231)?

'The first Christians devoted themselves to prayer. This was the secret of their spiritual power. Whenever they had a crisis – after Jesus ascended to heaven, for example, or when Peter was put in prison – we always find them at prayer' (p. 232).

---

10 What can the first Christians teach us about prayer (p. 232)? How is prayer one form of fellowship?
11 'The church does not grow by evangelistic crusades or advertising campaigns' (p. 234). Study or discuss.
12 Why is it so important for churches to demonstrate the basic biblical characteristics of Christian community (p. 235)?

16. Saved to sin no more
Sanctification: Romans 6:1–14 (pp. 237–251)

1 Why is it misguided to think that we should try and sin all the more to experience more of God's grace (p. 237)?
2 What is the purpose of God's saving plan (p. 237)?

'What Christians often have difficulty agreeing about is how holiness happens. How do we grow spiritually? How do we gain victory over sin? What is the gospel method of sanctification? These may sound like simple questions, but there is widespread disagreement about how to answer them' (p. 238).

---

3 'When properly understood, Romans 6:2 contains the first key to unlocking the mysteries of sanctification' (p. 239). How have we died to sin?
4 In what way is it significant that we have been buried and raised with Christ (p. 240)?
5 Define the pattern of the sanctification of the Christian (pp. 240–241).
6 Reflect on the ways we try and grow in godliness (p. 243). Where does real progress in holiness begin and what is the place of good works or discipleship in sanctification?
7 Explain the link between justification and sanctification (p. 244).
8 'There are times when we must rely on "dead reckoning" to chart our progress towards holiness' (p. 246). Why is the 'dead reckoning' principle so important in our spiritual lives?
9 What are the two aspects to sanctification (pp. 246–247)? How do these aspects affect our struggle with sin and why is our ongoing battle with it not a bad thing?
10 'God has restored our freedom by giving us the best possible motivation for godliness' (p. 250). Describe the positive side to our sanctification.

17. Suffering a little while
Perseverance: 1 Peter 1:1–9 (pp. 252–264)

'Even if we are unable to explain the origin of evil, we know that God is not a monster. He is the God of all grace, who saves us in his love. We also know that much of our pain is self-induced, the product of human sin, and therefore that God is not to blame. But we still have questions that challenge our faith, and one of the most difficult is this: if we are saved by grace, then why do we still suffer?' (pp. 252–253).

1 'We are united to Christ by faith, and the Christ to whom we have been united was a suffering, bleeding man' (p. 256). Why are Christians not exempt from suffering?
2 Give some examples of suffering or an instance from your own experience. What consolation can be found in pain (p. 257)?
3 Describe four purposes of suffering (p. 259). What is its ultimate meaning (p. 261)?
4 Explain why the doctrine of perseverance 'is a great comfort' (p. 262).
5 Read 1 Peter 1:6–7 and Romans 5:3. How do these verses put suffering into perspective (pp. 263–264)?

18. Glory! Glory!
Glorification: Revelation 7:9–17 (pp. 265–279)

'They came from everywhere because the message of salvation is for everyone. This multi-national, multi-cultural, multi-ethnic and multi-linguistic multitude was gathered around God's throne because they had ascended into glory. What John saw was all God's people – ransomed, redeemed and resurrected' (pp. 265–266).

1 What is the significance of the number 144,000 in relation to the great multitude in verse 9 (p. 266)?
2 Describe some of the characteristics of 'the salvation people' (p. 266).
3 What is the great tribulation (pp. 267–268)? Why should suffering give us hope and comfort (p. 268)?
4 Define the term 'glorification' (p. 269)? When will the glory be revealed to us?
5 How is glorification linked to 'every preceding act of salvation' (p. 270)?

6 In what way will seeing Jesus face to face affect us (p. 271)?
7 Explain the goal of glorification (p. 272).
8 Read Revelation 7. What are three features of our life in heaven (p. 273)? Why will we need special clothes and how do we get them (p. 274)?
9 'There will be more for us to do in heaven than simply to admire the latest fashions' (p. 276). Imagine and note/discuss what heaven will be like.

19. Getting the message out
Mission: Matthew 28:18–20 (pp. 280–294)

'Once we pass from tribulation to triumph, where God wipes away the last tears of our sorrow, there is nothing left to do except to glorify God and to enjoy him for ever. Glorification is the goal of our salvation, and once we are glorified, God's saving work is done. But the end has not yet come. While many millions have been saved already, millions more are waiting to hear the message of salvation' (p. 280).

1 On what basis has the church the right to preach globally (p. 281)?
2 Given that Jesus has all authority, in what way does he rule the world (p. 282)?
3 In what way is the church to fulfil the Great Commission (p. 283)? Explain Jesus' strategy for training his disciples (p. 284). What is the cost of discipleship (p. 285)?
4 'Almost without realizing it, the whole time that Jesus' disciples were learning how to follow Jesus, they were also learning how to help others follow him, too' (p. 285). Describe the method of making disciples as taught by the Gospels.
5 Give some instances where discipleship might take place without exclusive friendships (p. 287).
6 What is the correct order of disciple-making (p. 287)? Why do we need to 'go' and not wait?
7 Define the meaning of 'nations' (p. 288). What is the implication of the international commission for every Christian?
8 In what way is baptism essential to our discipleship (pp. 290–291)?
9 What kind of teaching do (a) new converts and (b) older Christians need (p. 291)?
10 Think about the promise of Christ's *universal presence* (p. 292). How does this affect our ability to fulfil the Great Commission?